A CULTURAL HISTORY OF THE SEA

VOLUME 2

A Cultural History of the Sea
General Editor: Margaret Cohen

Volume 1
A Cultural History of the Sea in Antiquity
Edited by Marie-Claire Beaulieu

Volume 2
A Cultural History of the Sea in the Medieval Age
Edited by Elizabeth Lambourn

Volume 3
A Cultural History of the Sea in the Early Modern Age
Edited by Steve Mentz

Volume 4
A Cultural History of the Sea in the Age of Enlightenment
Edited by Jonathan Lamb

Volume 5
A Cultural History of the Sea in the Age of Empire
Edited by Margaret Cohen

Volume 6
A Cultural History of the Sea in the Global Age
Edited by Franziska Torma

A CULTURAL HISTORY OF THE SEA

IN THE MEDIEVAL AGE

VOLUME 2

Edited by Elizabeth Lambourn

BLOOMSBURY ACADEMIC
LONDON • NEW YORK • OXFORD • NEW DELHI • SYDNEY

BLOOMSBURY ACADEMIC

Bloomsbury Publishing Plc, 50 Bedford Square, London, WC1B 3DP, UK
Bloomsbury Publishing Inc, 1359 Broadway, New York, NY 10018, USA
Bloomsbury Publishing Ireland, 29 Earlsfort Terrace, Dublin 2, D02 AY28, Ireland

BLOOMSBURY, BLOOMSBURY ACADEMIC and the Diana logo are
trademarks of Bloomsbury Publishing Plc

First published in Great Britain 2021
This edition published in Great Britain 2024
Reprinted in 2025

Copyright © Bloomsbury Publishing, 2021

Elizabeth Lambourn has asserted her right under the Copyright,
Designs and Patents Act, 1988, to be identified as Editor of this work.

Cover image © *Alexander lowered into the Sea* © The British Library, Royal 15 E VI, f. 20v

All rights reserved. No part of this publication may be: i) reproduced or transmitted in
any form, electronic or mechanical, including photocopying, recording or by means of any
information storage or retrieval system without prior permission in writing from the publishers;
or ii) used or reproduced in any way for the training, development or operation of artificial intelligence
(AI) technologies, including generative AI technologies. The rights holders expressly reserve this
publication from the text and data mining exception as per Article 4(3) of the Digital Single
Market Directive (EU) 2019/790.

Bloomsbury Publishing Plc does not have any control over, or responsibility for,
any third-party websites referred to or in this book. All internet addresses given
in this book were correct at the time of going to press. The author and publisher
regret any inconvenience caused if addresses have changed or sites have
ceased to exist, but can accept no responsibility for any such changes.

Every effort has been made to trace copyright holders and to obtain their
permissions for the use of copyright material. The publisher apologizes for any
errors or omissions and would be grateful if notified of any corrections that
should be incorporated in future reprints or editions of this book.

A catalogue record for this book is available from the British Library.

Library of Congress Cataloging-in-Publication Data

Names: Cohen, Margaret, editor.
Title: A cultural history of the sea / edited by Margaret Cohen.
Description: London ; New York : Bloomsbury, 2021. | Series: The cultural histories series |
Includes bibliographical references and index. |
Contents: V.1. A cultural history of the sea in antiquity / edited by by Marie-Claire
Beaulieu – v.2. A cultural history of the sea in the Medieval Age / edited by Elizabeth
Lambourn – v.3. A cultural history of the sea in the Early Modern Age / edited by
Steven Mentz – v.4. A cultural history of the Sea in the Age of Enlightenment /
edited by Jonathan Lamb – v.5. A cultural history of the sea in the Age of
Empire / edited by Margaret Cohen – v.6. A cultural history of the sea in the
Global Age / edited by Franziska Torma.
Identifiers: LCCN 2020052073 | ISBN 9781474299107 (set ; hardback) |
ISBN 9781474299015 (v. 1 ; hardback) | ISBN 9781474299022 (v. 2 ; hardback) |
ISBN 9781474299039 (v. 3 ; hardback) | ISBN 9781474299046 (v. 4 ; hardback) |
ISBN 9781474299084 (v. 5 ; hardback) | ISBN 9781474299091 (v. 6 ; hardback)
Subjects: LCSH: Ocean and civilization. | Civilization–History. | World history. | Ocean–History.
Classification: LCC CB465 .C85 2021 | DDC 910.4/5–dc23
LC record available at https://lccn.loc.gov/2020052073

ISBN: HB: 978-1-4742-9902-2
Set: 978-1-4742-9910-7
PB: 978-1-3504-5103-2
Set: 978-1-3504-5130-8

Series: The Cultural Histories Series

Typeset by Integra Software Services Pvt. Ltd.
Printed and bound in Great Britain

For product safety related questions contact productsafety@bloomsbury.com.

To find out more about our authors and books visit www.bloomsbury.com
and sign up for our newsletters.

CONTENTS

List of Illustrations — vii

General Editor's Preface — x
Margaret Cohen

Introduction — 1
Elizabeth Lambourn

1 Knowledges — 27
   Eric Staples

2 Practices — 49
   Stephanie Wynne-Jones and Jennifer Harland

3 Networks — 73
   Jonathan Shepard

4 Conflicts — 95
   Elizabeth Lambourn

5 Islands and Shores — 119
   Roxani Margariti

6 Travelers — 141
   Sharon Kinoshita

7 Representations — 161
   Emmanuelle Vagnon

8 Imaginary Worlds *James L. Smith*	195
NOTES	221
BIBLIOGRAPHY	223
NOTES ON CONTRIBUTORS	257
INDEX	260

ILLUSTRATIONS

0.1	Map of the principal sites and regions discussed in this volume	5
0.2	The bodhisattva Suparaga prays and makes libations to the Buddha preventing a ship from sinking	11
0.3	Aerial view of the central temple complex, Angkor Wat, Cambodia	12
0.4	Vishnu Churning the Ocean of Milk	13
0.5	Ritual vessel for holy water	15
0.6	Conch carved with Lakshmi-Narayana and other figures	16
0.7	Routes and dates of Austronesian migrations and Viking explorations and raiding voyages	20–21
0.8	View of the interior of the Anaweka canoe	22
1.1	Map of the Indian Ocean monsoon system	33
1.2	The so-called Carte Pisane, portolan chart of the Mediterranean	37
1.3	Modern reconstruction of a *khashaba*	40
1.4	Two of the four stellar diagrams from Mao Yuanyi's *Wu Bei Zhu*	42
1.5	Illustration from Marco Polo's *Livre des Merveilles*	45
1.6	Arabic stellar compass rose	46

2.1	Scale reconstruction of the Belitung wreck	52
2.2	Archaeologically retrieved fish bones from the medieval North Atlantic	54
2.3	Uzio fish weir at Vanga, Kenya	55
2.4	Fish grilling over coconut shells on the beach at Songo Mnara, Tanzania	59
2.5	Fishing technology from the Islamic layers of Quseir al-Qadim, Red Sea	62
3.1	Map of Central and Eastern Europe showing the river connections between the eastern Mediterranean, Black Sea, and Caspian with the Baltic and North Seas	78
3.2	Silver from the Silverdale hoard, including Abbasid dirhams, in Lancashire, England	79
3.3	Mambrui pillar tomb with inset Far Eastern ceramics	83
3.4	Detail from the Catalan Atlas of 1375	93
4.1	View of Aden's main town and anchorage in the mid-sixteenth century	102
4.2	Relief-carved panel from a Kadamba hero stone showing close combat on a ship, ca. twelfth century	106
4.3	Relief-carved panel from a Kadamba hero stone showing an oared dugout canoe, ca. thirteenth century	108
4.4	Ottoman galleys defend Jedda from Portuguese attack in 1517	113
5.1	The Muslims burning their own fleet from Ioannis Skylitzae, *Synopsis Historion*	121
5.2	Detail of the island of Crete from Cristoforo Buondelmonti's *Liber Insularum Archipelagi*	125
5.3	Fish swimming around a pearl on a Rasulid silver *dirham*	131
5.4	Chimu gold earspool from the Central Andes	132
5.5	The trickster Abu Zayd talking his way onto an ocean-going ship from al-Hariri's *Maqamat*	133
7.1	World map from an English Psalter	167

7.2	Depiction of Noah's Ark, from the Latin Psalter of Saint Louis and Blanche de Castille	169
7.3	Jonah and the Whale, from Rashid al-Din's *Jawāmi' al-tawarīkh*	170
7.4	Double-page world map from al-Idrisi's *Nuzhat al-mushtāq fī ikhtirāq al-āfāq* (Book of Roger)	176
7.5	World map from Paulin de Venise's *Chronologia Magna*	177
7.6	Composite view of the Catalan Atlas	179
7.7	World map by Fra Mauro	181
7.8	Ma Yuan, *Clouds rising from the Green Sea*	185
7.9	Fan painted with *Waters in the Moonlight*	186
7.10	*Ch'onhado* (Map of All Under Heaven)	188
7.11	Yi Hoe and Kwon Kun, *Kangnido* world map	191
7.12	Headings and routes around southern Sumatra, from Mao Yuanyi's *Wu bei zhi* (A Treatise on Armament Technology)	193
8.1	Low-relief carving of a sea turtle, from part of a much larger East Polynesian voyaging canoe	204
8.2	Engraved copy of the so-called "Tuki's map," from David Collins, *An Account of the English Colony in New South Wales*	205
8.3	Handscroll depicting the Immortals' islands of Fanghu, Yingzhou, and Penglai, part of the Isles of the Blessed	207
8.4	Detail of handscroll of the Isles of the Blessed showing one of the seven islands of the human realm with its inhabitants	209
8.5	An eastern island, "Thirty-Ninth Assembly" from the *Maqāmāt* (Assemblies) of al-Hariri	214

GENERAL EDITOR'S PREFACE

MARGARET COHEN

Over the past thirty years, oceanic studies has emerged in the humanities as a leading interdisciplinary field. It owes its importance to its capacity to give an account of globalization spanning millenia that is robustly cross-cultural. As this new field has taken shape, it has both incorporated and revised an earlier generation of scholarship, which attended to maritime transport, naval warfare, and global exploration, often within a framework of national history. Contributions of oceanic studies range across scales: from showing how maritime transport and marine resources join separated lands into water-based regions to resurrecting how a meeting on a beach between societies never before in contact could create intractable structures of domination to revealing the impact of a single photograph from outer space of the earth as a blue planet. Today, oceanic studies aims to tell the stories of all who have traveled the seas: professionals, adventurers, passengers, forced migrants—and animals.

Further, this emerging field recognizes that the seas are a rich realm for the imagination, all the more so given the paradoxical tension between their remoteness for many people and yet their life-sustaining importance. It is telling that a poet, the Nobel prize-winning Derek Walcott, has penned the memorable phrase, "The Sea is History."[1] At the same time, the imagination of the seas is not purely fanciful but rather takes shape in relation to located marine environments and how humans practice them, leading humanists to engage the reality of the physical world. When modern oceanography and marine biology took shape in the nineteenth century, these sciences established the oceans as nonhuman natural realms, despite their prehistory in mixed, practical knowledge conjoining environmental curiosity with the pursuit of power and wealth. Since this disciplinary cleavage, the sea has time and time again shown us the need to recognize its existence for and with humans, as well as in itself.

In the twenty-first century, the importance of the sea in world-defining developments, including second-wave globalization, postcolonial conflict and climate change, has become so evident that its social and cultural reality cannot be ignored. In the words of Franziska Torma, volume editor of *The Global Age*, such developments have "forced us to 'think science and humanities' together, because science provides data and humanities 'translate' them into social and academic interpretation; this opens up historical perspective on the oceans from antiquity to the present" (Franziska Torma, personal communication, May 2020). Whether drawing on nautical archaeology resurrecting sunken cities and shipwrecks, or using scientific research about the impact of climate change on coastal communities, oceanic studies is taking the lead among humanities fields in pursuing this urgent, if vexed, disciplinary crossing.

In editing *A Cultural History of the Sea*, I have been fortunate to work with volume editors who have made major contributions to setting the agenda of oceanic studies in its twenty-first-century form. Taken together, their expertise encompasses the oceans of the globe, notably the Mediterranean, the Indian Ocean, the Atlantic, and the Pacific and includes the history of science and the environment as well. We have launched our project from our institutional homes in transatlantic universities, even as we mark our starting point at once to acknowledge and brush against the grain of Western-oriented perspectives. Further, readers will see that the abstraction Western itself fractures when subjected to the pressure of water-based movement and seafaring practices. Thus, maritime travel creates far-flung contact zones across thousands of kilometers, which cannot be reduced to the orientation of the West, even if Western Europe may have been a point of departure. These contact zones are characterized by extreme social complexity, which modify those whom they involve, and the importance of the physical environment in such contact zones creates yet another set of considerations. The demands of sea-oriented life, moreover, unmoor those who work on ships to the point where they may be a culture unto themselves, unnervingly apart for their societies, due to such factors as the rigors of shipboard living and the multicultural *habitus* even on vessels enforcing the routes of empire.

Our interest in conveying the heterogeneous histories that meet on the sea extends to the themes we have chosen for our series' organization. A unique feature of the Bloomsbury *Cultural History* series is to devise eight chapter headings for each volume that can run from antiquity to the present. These headings address culture understood in its expansive, anthropological sense: as designating the diverse realms of practices organizing the structures of a society. In the case of the seas, important aspects include but are not limited to war, technology, and trade at sea, scientific knowledge, as well as myth and imagination. We defined our themes in a fashion that would enable contributors to present a democratic history. Thus, for example, we framed histories of

"War and Empire," at sea as "Conflicts," to take account of the many scales of violent struggles at sea, including frames of state-supported navies, non-state actors, and the violence of shipboard life, ranging from mutinies to treatment of passengers and transport of the enslaved. Or thus, we reframed the theme "Science and Technology," as "Knowledges," to provide an opportunity to include knowledge beyond the strict boundary of science. Such knowledge ranges from philosophical speculation in classical antiquity to sea knowledge and practice outside Western paradigms.

In organizing the chapters, we have respected conventional Western historical periodization, which has been shaped by events on land. At the same time, readers will find within the volumes chapters that take up the question of whether such periodization stops at shore, due to the previously mentioned pressures of a sea perspective on concepts whose operations are focused toward the land. Thus, the history of Egyptian seafaring and contacts with other cultures of the Mediterranean basin traverses the land-based periodization of this particular culture, traditionally understood in terms of its ruling dynasties, from Greek prehistory through the classical period and into Roman times, roughly the second millennium BCE to the first century CE. Within the modern era, to take the example of a single technology, the years from 1769 to 1989 form one period in the history of navigation, although this epoch runs across three volumes in the series. In 1769, British engineer John Harrison perfected a chronometer that would keep accurate time over a long traverse. With the ability to compare noon during a ship's traverse and noon at an arbitrarily defined starting point—it became the Greenwich Meridian by convention—navigators could finally establish their longitude while a ship was sailing, a development that would vastly improve safety at sea, even if it took decades to expand beyond naval circles. Celestial navigation would remain the best practice for establishing a ship's location until the invention of the global positioning system (GPS) in the third quarter of the twentieth century, which could be dated to 1989, when the US Department of Defense launched a satellite system that would become GPS, replacing with the touch of a few buttons the arduous calculations needed for celestial navigation.

Another dimension to the specificity of sea-based periodization is the timescale of the oceans as a physical environment. For eons marine history moved at a geological pace, but in the age of the Anthropocene we are learning about the human impact on a realm of the planet long considered an inexhaustible resource and a vast power beyond human reach. Such an impact can occur within a person's lifetime, as is the case, for example, with melting ice caps at the poles, which have drastically diminished in satellite visualizations, dating back to 1979 (Starr 2016). This impact in turn is affecting societies, from Indigenous inhabitants of the Arctic to farmers around the world, who depend on weather patterns disrupted by global warming. Yet further entangling human and geological timescales at sea, melting ice caps open up new shipping routes through the Arctic, which present potential for a greater human footprint there.

The global consequences of polar ice melt exemplify how a sea perspective reorients terrestrial units of geographical analysis, which is the case not only for the oceans as an environment but also for the oceans as an arena of human practice. Chapters across the series reveal how state-drawn borders may be less important for cultures at sea than fluid spaces defined by natural features, and how islands or coasts eccentric from the perspective of land-based history may play an outsized, formative role in a nation's oceanic ambitions. Further, sea transport produces states that are at once joined under the same flag yet are also territorially disconnected, with unique and uniquely difficult administrative features. Yet another challenge, at the lexical level, is that when we try to express oceanic phenomena with language from the land, we reach to unsatisfactory imagery that impedes understanding. A good example today is the great "garbage patch" of pollution in the Pacific Ocean. The figure of a "patch" misleadingly limits its reach and does not capture the microscopic pervasion of plastic in sea water.

The seas are vast expanses, whose study drives home the point that any research is necessarily fragmentary and located. Contributors to these volumes include established and emerging voices, who have written chapters that are original research around our central themes rather than summaries of secondary literature. Volume editors have encouraged their contributors to present their insights in whatever way they thought would best bring out the originality of their topic and suit their disciplinary expertise. Some have used the narrative of a survey. Others have taken a single event as their canvas, whether the event is exemplary or tellingly anomalous. Yet others have spun out their questions at the scale of one marine environment.

Such flexibility is also important because "the sea" of our series' title is not one thing. Rather, the saltwater element is culturally constructed and imagined in widely different ways, depending on who is engaging with it and to what ends. This range is evident as well in the rich imagery accompanying the chapters, which is another feature of the *Cultural History* series. Thus, readers will see how in antiquity, the sea was never represented directly but rather suggested metonymically on frescoes and vases, with depictions of fish, ships, or mythological sea creatures. Grand seascapes, exhibiting the ocean as a theatre of awe, in contrast, compelled audiences in Enlightenment and Romantic eras. One constant across centuries are practical charts, which have used a variety of methods, shaped by different epistemes and environments, to find and mark paths across the waters, all nonetheless sharing an aim of safety. To draw a parallel between navigating vast, and in many cases, untracked waters and emergent areas of scholarship: as readers constellate the diverse subjects and approaches collected in this series, I hope they will gain a better understanding of the abiding, pervasive human interface with the seas as well as recognize new and future directions for oceanic studies.

Introduction

Charting a Cultural History of the Sea for the Medieval Age

ELIZABETH LAMBOURN

Scholars are still working out what a cultural history of the sea in the Medieval Age might look like. The idea that seas can have histories, even specifically *cultural* histories, is not as recent as it might first seem, but the cultural history of the sea is nevertheless still a comparatively young field, particularly so for the Middle Ages. The cultural history of the sea has its beginnings in the study of modern—eighteenth- and nineteenth-century—Western cultural products such as the novel, the travel diary, or the seascape painting. Born and first explored among literary and art historians, the field is now at a crux as medievalists and others "try on" this idea in their own fields and geographical areas, and adjust its fit to their own particular sources and disciplinary preoccupations. For our period, the very idea of a cultural history of the sea is, in effect, so underexplored and diffuse that in commissioning this volume Bloomsbury have in fact demanded significantly original thinking from its contributors, in the process sparking and advancing the study of the cultural history of the sea in ways they probably did not originally intend.

As the contributors to *The Sea: Thalassography and Historiography* all underlined, histories of seas have "always been a minority [...] within the historiography" (Miller 2013: 278). More to the point in the context of the present volume, there have been very few histories of the sea and certainly few historiographic reflections on a large scale about the *cultural* history of the sea in the Middle Ages. What exists in this case is not only diffuse but often disconnected too. As volume editor Peter Miller astutely pointed out, historians working in this area have done so mainly in isolation "disconnected from one another and from wider conversations" (17). Conversely, a substantial amount of relevant work has been produced as part of these "wider conversations," but outside the explicit frameworks of cultural history or watery histories: in religious studies, across the many subdisciplines of archaeology, in material culture study, to name but a few.

This volume offers a much-needed opportunity to develop and share this conversation with a wider audience, and it comes at an important moment. As mentioned, the writing of cultural histories of the sea in the Middle Ages has thus far been grounded in the literary criticism of European sources, with the support of European visual iconographies. If literary studies have been able to lead the way in this history it is perhaps because topoi and other literary devices so clearly communicate the fact that seas and oceans were not only highways for the circulation of people, ideas, and things but also important as "spaces of imaginative projection," as noted historian of the Atlantic Kären Wigen expresses it (2007: 16). To repeat a hackneyed phrase, "the sea is good to think with." Yet the cultural history of the sea risks settling into a cozily established and largely literature-driven format that is not only implicitly Eurocentric but also focused on the imaginative projections of a small literate minority who may have had very little experience of the sea and the communities that inhabited it. Those who intellectualized the sea though literary topoi and visual iconographies were not necessarily those who inhabited its shores, or sailed and fished across it. These latter, often illiterate, inhabitants have other cultural histories of the sea and it is through the—perhaps less obviously "readable"—material culture of such communities and societies or indeed their oral history and folklore that we can begin to grasp these other narratives.

It goes without saying that these processes of "imaginative projection" were not uniquely European but common to all human engagement with seas and oceans across the globe. The literary and visual approaches pioneered in the European context are certainly ripe to be tested beyond Europe, and in turn, Europe will undoubtedly benefit from the ideas and new approaches that develop beyond it. However, if the cultural history of the sea is to flourish, it must also consider how to integrate and interpret a far wider range of sources: oral traditions certainly, but also the huge body of nonrepresentational cultural products, the material things made by, and in, the sea. In the European context, material things bring important counterpoints to elite literary projections, but beyond Europe they often supply the principal, sometimes only, sources for writing cultural histories of the sea. This volume does not assume that literary texts or indeed visual representations are the only starting points for cultural histories of the sea. The next wave of cultural history must venture beyond its safe European havens in the North Atlantic and the Mediterranean, but remain acutely aware that this geographical translocation also involves a significant methodological and theoretical shift.

As these first paragraphs already hint, this volume does not pretend to offer a definitive answer, it offers not *"The"* but *"A" Cultural History of the Sea* for the period between 800 and 1450 CE, shaped as much by the parameters of the series itself as by the vision, curiosity, and expertise of its editor and individual contributors. Without wishing to "silo" contributors too tightly, this volume deliberately challenges the literary focus of preceding medieval cultural histories of the sea with only two contributions from literary historians: Sharon Kinoshita is a specialist in medieval French literature and global comparative literature, James L. Smith's work has focused, until the chapter in this volume at least, on European medieval water histories. The chapters here are otherwise authored by historians and archaeologists of various inflections. Jonathan Shepard is a historian specializing in early medieval Russia, the Caucasus, and the Byzantine Empire, the work of Elizabeth Lambourn, Roxani Margariti, and Emmanuelle Vagnon is heavily grounded in material and visual culture history across the Mediterranean and Indian Ocean worlds. Three archaeologists have also written for this volume: Eric Staples is a maritime archaeologist with substantial experience in experimental archaeology; Stephanie Wynne-Jones is an archaeologist of the Swahili coast who focuses on ceramic evidence and domestic material culture; and Jennifer Harland is a zooarchaeologist who specializes in the North Atlantic and the study of fishing and fish consumption through the analysis of excavated fish remains.

The Mediterranean naturally occupies a central place in the existing cultural history of the sea and this is reflected in many chapters in this volume—those on "Travelers" by Sharon Kinoshita, "Islands and Shores" by Roxani Margariti, and "Representations" by Emmanuelle Vagnon, all of whom are Mediterraneanists—however, these and other chapters also push out beyond these waters, combining Mediterranean material with other maritime regions or, indeed, focusing on non-Mediterranean waters around Afro-Eurasia. The chapters on "Knowledges" (Eric Staples) and "Islands and Shores" (Roxani Margariti) combine discussion of the Mediterranean with the wider Indian Ocean world, from eastern Africa to the eastern Chinese coast, Korea, and Japan. The chapter on "Practices" by archaeologists Stephanie Wynne-Jones and Jennifer Harland explicitly compares two key maritime regions of the medieval period: the North Atlantic and the western Indian Ocean. Jonathan Shepard's "Networks" ranges across the North Atlantic and Black Sea with a focus on the riverine networks that connected northern waters to the Eastern Mediterranean. The chapter on "Conflicts" (Elizabeth Lambourn) explores the way that existing bodies of scholarship developed around the topic of violence in European waters (broadly defined) can translate to the Indian

Ocean. Most geographically ambitious of all are the chapters by Emmanuelle Vagnon on "Representations" and by James L. Smith on "Imaginary Worlds," which draw on material from the early North Atlantic to the eastern Chinese coast, Korea, and Japan, and in Smith's case even Maori Aotearoa (New Zealand). Within the word limits for this volume no chapter can hope to provide anything like a comprehensive global coverage of its topic. As the map of sites and regions discussed in this volume shows (see Figure 0.1), for the main part we have focused our efforts on connecting histories across the "Old World" of Afro-Eurasia, leaving the Americas and Oceania to enter the picture in the later volumes in this series. James Smith's chapter on "Imaginary Worlds" is, in this respect, pioneering, dedicating as it does a substantial subsection to Polynesian cultural histories and imaginative projections. As editor I am painfully aware of this shortcoming, and one might justifiably argue that even then, there is still insufficient coverage of West Africa. This focus was dictated not by intellectual laziness but by the sheer challenge involved in connecting, across the already vast expanse of Afro-Eurasia, histories and data sets that are currently "disconnected from one another and from wider conversations," to reprise Peter Miller's assessment (2013: 17). Synthetic overviews and comparative histories are complex to write, and the conception of this volume has necessitated a trade-off between synthesis and coverage. The approach to global coverage chosen for Michel Balard's *The Sea in History: The Medieval World* (2017) is not appropriate here. While his volume achieves a global coverage by including a small number of separate chapters on specific aspects of Caribbean, South American, West African, and Far Eastern maritime history, readers are left to pick and choose which material to engage with and to make their own sense of this non-European material within larger frameworks that remain overwhelmingly centered on Europe and the Mediterranean. This model goes counter to the spirit of the Bloomsbury Cultural History series, which is precisely to synthesize and knit together. Though geographically limited, our chapters actively engage with synthesis and the comparison of widely different material. A large part of the challenge for me as an editor has been to find scholars brave enough to roam so far from home; even within these geographical limits. This has not been an easy volume to commission. We can only hope that scholars of the Americas and Oceania, and West Africa, will join this nascent conversation and contribute in future to a fully global history of the sea in the Middle Ages.

Our use of the terms "Medieval" or "Middle Ages" is, we recognize, also problematic, an application of Eurocentric terms and concepts to a narrative that has just stated its intention to decenter Europe. These are categories set by the publisher, but they also reflect common academic usage. In spite of voluminous scholarly debate, no workable alternatives to the terms "medieval" or "Middle Ages" have yet been found and so we continue to use them here, "warts and

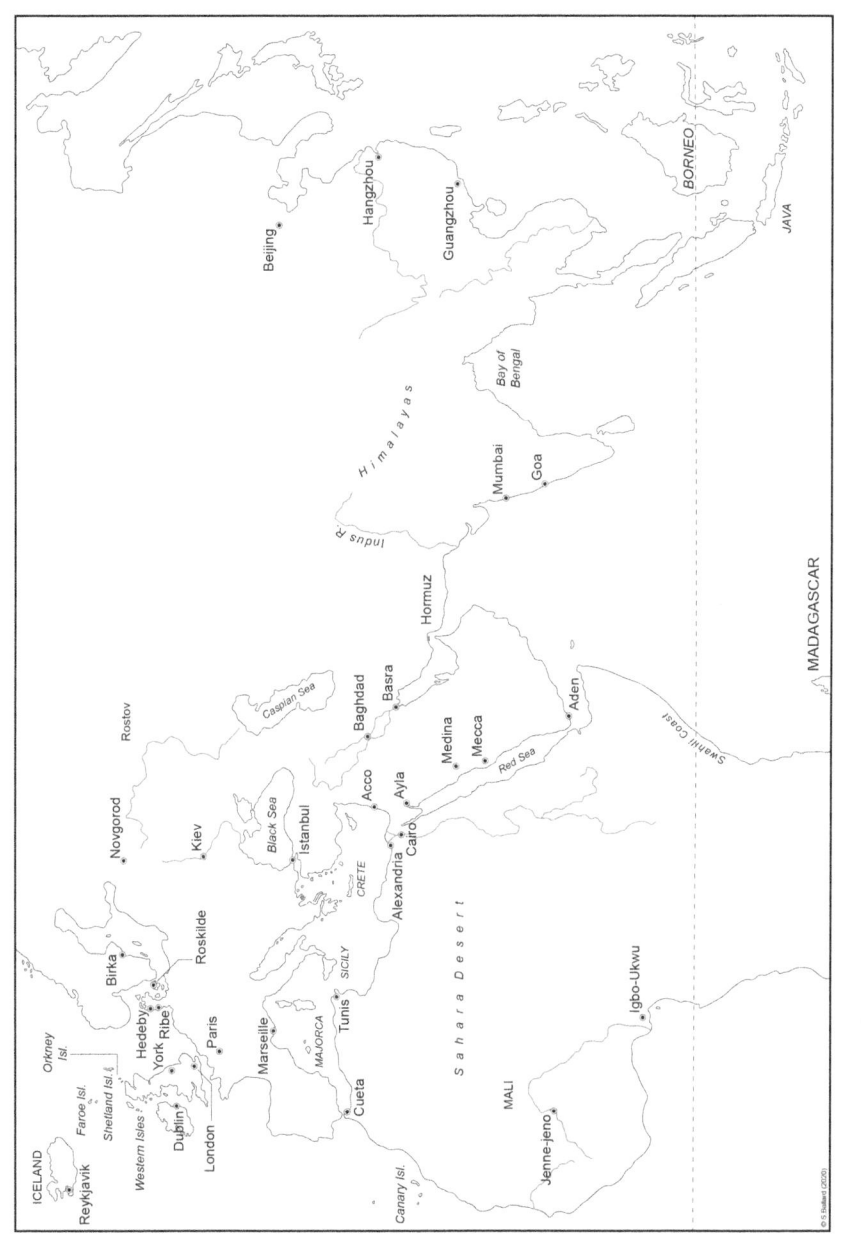

FIGURE 0.1 Map of the principal sites and regions discussed in the volume. © Sebastian Ballard.

all," hoping that their problematic status will not stop readers from engaging with the material and ideas set before them. All the contributors here recognize that expanding the terms medieval and Middle Ages beyond their European home involves, as historians Kathleen Davis and Michael Puett expressed it in an early conversation around the idea of a Global Middle Ages, "pushing against many of the major claims of colonial and nationalist history" (2016: 2). Both terms are heavy with colonial meanings and yet, carefully and self-consciously employed, they can help us to think in terms of the world's "coeval cultures," sparking new conversations, substantially enriching existing ones and offering important alternatives to global histories too easily constructed around processes of connection and encounter. While this volume cannot, and does not, claim consistent global coverage, it joins with, and appeals to, those now writing more global histories of the Middle Ages.

Series such as this typically position themselves as places to go for a methodical introductory overview of existing literature and the broad intellectual currents flowing beneath a particular topic, this volume, by contrast, offers a forum in which to begin connecting disconnected scholarly discourses and engaging with the "wider conversations" of the cultural history of the sea. This is the place to state what we do *not* know, as much as it offers an opportunity to set out what we *do* know, and to flag what we might possibly know with further research, particularly if we translate approaches and questions from better-studied regions and centuries to the far larger mass of raw, uninterpreted medieval sources—textual, visual, and material—in existence. Inevitably, these chapters are oftentimes exploratory and reflective, tentative even, reticent to adopt the confident, certain tone we expect of "overview" series.

Imperfect as they are, we hope that our first attempts at mapping the largely uncharted intellectual space that is the cultural history of the sea in what Bloomsbury term "the Medieval Age"—and the fact that we are willing to state as much so clearly—will stimulate fresh dialogues amongst cultural historians of the sea as much as it will bring new ideas and questions to the greater numbers of readers just now venturing in from other disciplines. The comparative youth of this field is good news in many ways, no need here to jostle for originality when so much is still unclaimed; many of the chapters in this volume represent world firsts in their attempts to write across such a broad seascape and temporal range. As volume editor and on behalf of all the contributors to this Medieval Age volume, I welcome you to this endeavor.

WRITING THE SEA IN EUROPE AND BEYOND

Literary criticism has been a leading driver in the development of cultural histories of the sea during the twentieth century so it should come as no surprise that it is also from within the literary criticism of broadly "European" medieval sources that some of the most focused and dynamic work on the cultural history of the sea in the Middle Ages has taken place, and continues to be generated. I begin with an overview of this European literary material before widening the discussion to non-European literary and material sources, and the rich potential they hold.

Sebastian Sobecki's 2008 monograph *The Sea and Medieval English Literature* exemplifies in many ways the rich opportunities that await scholars of the medieval. Responding to the deafening absence of the sea "from our awareness of pre-modern [English] literature and its horizons," Sobecki offers a pioneering study of the sea "as a culturally charged and changing literary topos in pre-modern England" (2008: 17, 20). In a United Kingdom sundered as never before by the question of its island status, Sobecki's mapping of the manner in which these topoi became "a part of the vernacular discourse of Englishness" (4) could not be more relevant.[1] Yet the fact that this should be considered—in 2008, and thus comparatively late in the history of English literary criticism—a pioneering endeavor, almost totally reliant on primary source material, only underlines how very young our field is. Original studies of different European regions' relationships to the sea continue to be produced from the scantiest of secondary literature but the richest of primary sources. Simone Pinet's *Archipelagoes: Insular Fictions from Chivalric Romance to the Novel* (2011) is an ambitious examination of the representation of the sea and islands across the literature and also the art of the Iberian Peninsula up to the nineteenth century. Once again, at least for the medieval period, it is elaborated almost entirely from raw source materials. Yet in keeping with Europe's rich regional individuality its insights and conclusions are entirely different from Sobecki's. *Archipelagoes* proposes that the medieval period constitutes a critical moment in the Iberian representation of the sea. By the medieval period, argues Pinet, deforestation had so eroded the established trope of the forest as the iconic place of wilderness that it was replaced by a new wilderness, the sea. Once again, cultural histories of the sea yield insights directly into landed histories, this time, however, environmental as much as political.

Fernand Braudel's home country, France, has made major contributions to understandings of the sea as a culturally charged idea across medieval French society. Since at least the mid-1980s French scholars have shown a remarkably sustained and broad-ranging interest in the cultural history of the sea at our period, explored across a series of conference collections and edited volumes, including, to name but a few: *L'eau au Moyen Âge* (1985), *La mer dans la culture médiévale* (1997), *Dans l'eau, sous l'eau: Le monde aquatique au Moyen Âge* (2002), *Mondes marins du Moyen Âge* (2006), and the most recent offering *Le bathyscaphe d'Alexandre: l'homme et la mer au Moyen Age* (2018). This French scholarship has been not only voluminous but also noticeably multidisciplinary too, adding to its literary core, insights from art history and archaeology.

As the titles here suggest the sea is sometimes discussed as part of the larger category of water, considered in all its forms—sweet, salty, contained, boundless, and interconnected—together with the practices associated with these. Of note also is an Italian volume *L'Acqua Non è Mai la Stessa* ("Water is Never the Same" or, perhaps more smoothly translated, "Water is Ever Changing") (2009), which focused on water in Chinese and Japanese culture. This broader framing is now entering English-language writing with James L. Smith's *Water in Medieval Intellectual Culture. Case-Studies from Twelfth-Century Monasticism* (2017) and the online series *New Approaches to Medieval Water Studies* (Smith and Howes 2018). Certainly one question to ask in future is whether this "Water" category—one sometimes also preferred by geographers (Anderson and Peters 2016)—is more appropriate to premodern understandings of watery bodies than the problematic categories of "Sea" or "Ocean" (Miller 2013). Many medieval cultures did not distinguish conceptually between closed water bodies such as lakes and what we now categorize as seas and oceans, any large expanse of water, whether sweet or salty, was "sea." The new energy within the field of water studies certainly raises the question of whether the cultural history of the sea before 1500 might find more purchase as a research topic and garner more interest if it joined this larger scholarly community.

Surprisingly, this vibrant French scholarship has yet to produce a single monographic *A Cultural History of the Sea in the French Middle-Ages*. The only large-scale synthetic account, Philipp Kramer's published PhD dissertation *Das Meer in der altfranzosischen Literatur* (The Sea in Old French Literature) (1919), is over a century old while Simon Leys's *La mer dans la literature française* (The Sea in French Literature) (2003) begins only with Rabelais (1494–1553). For the moment, insights offered by this huge body of scholarship remain highly heterogeneous and resistant to a single narrative. This, as much as the language barrier, may explain why this scholarship has been largely overlooked in Anglophone work on the medieval cultural history of the sea. Distinct, linguistically constituted, bodies of scholarship are nevertheless typical in our field, confirming (if confirmation were needed) Peter Miller's observation of the insularity that prevails. German language studies, for example Carola Fern's pioneering quantitative textual analysis of the sea storm topos *Seesturm im Mittelalter* (Storms at Sea in the Middle Ages) (2012), remain similarly compartmentalized.

Another fracture complicating the writing of a cultural history of the sea even "simply" at the European level is that between scholars of what we might broadly call the Celtic and Viking north, and scholars of later medieval Europe. The 800 to 1450 CE timeframe of the present volume subsumes distinct subperiods with their own distinctive literatures and scholarly traditions of study. Here, at the very fringes of mainland Europe, societies were often fundamentally amphibious and the sea is omnipresent as a place of movement and exchange, possessed of its own distinct imagining. In a rare longue durée consideration of the literary topoi that mixed and mingled across Europe Alain Corbellari characterized the sea as projected in Celtic texts as an "almost infinite space [...] one of the incarnations *par excellence* of adventure and the Otherworld" (2006: 105, my translation).

Little surprise that in the period before 1000, as James L. Smith discusses, the sea features most frequently within the context of narratives of early Christianization and as an underwater mirror of the world on land (Siewers 2009).

The new cultural history of the sea emerging from within broadly speaking "European" and "medieval" literary criticism is hugely exciting and should inspire and provoke scholars near and far. Medieval Europe's literate elites spent a considerable amount of energy thinking and representing the sea—textually and visually—if only as a metaphor for something else. The few examples just mentioned, and the many others cited across the following chapters, should be enough to persuade any scholar working on any literate society with a history of medieval maritime interaction to listen out for the sea in their sources. The insights these sources bring to questions as varied as national identity or environmental history, should leave skeptics in no doubt as to the potential of cultural histories of the sea to contribute to larger historical questions.

European elites were not alone in using the sea as a site of "intellectual projection" and the sea was also a literary subject and sometimes an iconographic subject across North Africa and the Middle East, in South and Southeast Asia, and in the Far East too. The work of European medievalists thus invites transfer to the many other regions or cultures where maritime tropes and representations of the sea, and the cultural histories they build, are only beginning to be heard. Sobecki's overview of the critical void within English literary criticism that spurred his research—one book chapter and less than a handful of articles attempting a comprehensive overview of the subject, a further five more focused studies (Sobecki 2008: 17–20)—might easily sum up the state of the field for the study of the sea "as a culturally charged and changing literary topos" (20) not only elsewhere in Europe but equally in the literatures of the Middle East and North Africa (e.g., 'Atwan 1982; Belhamissi 2005; de Planhol 2000; Montgomery 2001), or again in any number of South Asian (see the Bibliography at the end of this volume) or Far Eastern literary traditions (e.g., Maeda 1971; Park 2012).

PROJECTIONS AND ICONOGRAPHIES IN THE HINDU AND BUDDHIST WORLDS

Lest this be seen as an implicit invitation to European medievalists to colonize premodern water studies, there is already exciting work beyond Europe that is revealing quite distinct intellectual traditions. The literatures and visual cultures of South and Southeast Asia appear to be particularly ripe for participation in a new, less Eurocentric cultural history of the sea in the Middle Ages. Both regions offer large bodies of edited, and often translated, religious and literary texts in which the sea is very obviously a "site of intellection" (Wigen 2007: 16). Additionally, both areas developed abundant and complex visual iconographies that—like the European Noah's ark or the mermaid—offer comparable "readability."

One notion much repeated in literature on the Indian Ocean world is Brahmanical Hinduism's purported ban on high-caste Brahmins traveling by ship due to the pollution imparted by sea travel. This is an idea that has been discussed extensively since the nineteenth century, as the bibliography to one of the latest overviews of this topic illustrates (Bhindra 2002), although too often only within the context of trade and economic history. Reframed within cultural history and an understanding of elite discourses about the sea within Hinduism, this material has not exhausted its potential. However, new work is revealing a much more nuanced picture of ideas about water in South Asia, and intellectual projections onto it. As Srinivas Reddy notes in his recent chapter "Seven Seas and an Ocean of Wisdom: An Indian Episteme for the Indian Ocean," "in India, water, the seas, and the great ocean itself are all symbols of knowledge" (2021: 26) and the study of Hindu water myths holds the potential to provide "productive metaphors for conceptualizing both the creation and circulation of knowledge in India" (26). Reddy sees the fluidity of water as a symbol of human cognition and in particular "the flexibility and openness of Indian epistemologies and ontologies" (27).

Maritime worlds, and boats in particular, also play an important role in Buddhist and Jain narratives and iconographies, although the latter are still often studied principally for technical information about historic shipbuilding, and the former for clues about early trade practices. Sea voyages feature in Buddhist life-histories of the Buddha, the *jātaka*s and *avadāna*s, produced during the late first millennium BCE and the first millennium of our era. Here, the voyage, and particularly the hardships and dangers intrinsic to it, were one of a number of types of travel that functioned as metaphors for life's journey. Douglas Inglis has made the point that "Buddhists capitalized on the excitement, danger, avarice, and courage inherent in maritime folklore, and populated Jātakas and Avadānas with greedy merchants, daring sailors, horrible sea monsters, oceans filled with treasure, islands populated by demons, spirits, and goddesses" (2014: 8). The underlying message was, however, serious. As Sarah Shaw discusses, in these Buddhist narratives the ocean represents the endless cycle of death and rebirth (*samsāra*) and crossing the ocean, with all the dangers and wonders it presented, is a metaphor for the journey toward enlightenment (2012: 133). As Inglis argues, while images of ships from the Buddhist site of Borobodur (see Figure 0.2) in Java are regularly used by maritime archaeologists to reconstruct ship technologies, these representations must also be understood within the narrative cycles to which they belong (2014). Figure 0.2 shows a panel from Borobudur narrating the *Jātaka* story of the Bodhisattva Suparaga (a Bodhisattva is a person on the path to buddhahood) and his intervention to save a group of merchants from being swallowed by the jaws of the ocean at the end of the earth. The story belongs to the well-established, one might say universal, trope of the wondrous aversion of a shipwreck. Suparaga can be seen at the stern pouring libations to the Buddha as passengers behind him pray and his crew climb the rigging to take

FIGURE 0.2 The bodhisattva Suparaga prays and makes libations to the Buddha preventing a ship from being swallowed by the jaws at the end of the ocean. Relief from Borobodur, Indonesia, Level 1, Balustrade, constructed *c*. 778 to 850. © Anandajoti Bhikku (public domain).

down the sail; the jaws of the ocean are represented bottom right as a large openmouthed fish. An abundant body of Jain romances, a good number of which have been translated, sit within our timeframe and offer similarly rich material (e.g., Uddyotanasūri 2008). The potential of a more culturally oriented study of both maritime iconographies and texts from South to Southeast Asia is clear. More recently Andrea Acri has demonstrated the potential of working across faiths and regions, producing an impressive study of the trope of the wondrous aversion of a shipwreck (2019) in texts from the Buddhist and Hindu worlds of South and Southeast Asia. The resonances between the sea-journey as a path toward enlightenment in the Indic religions and the classical literary topos of the *navigatio vitæ* later adopted into medieval European literature (Noacco 2006) is only one of a number of topoi that raise important questions about the universality of human experience and beg transregional dialogue and comparative study.

No less important in terms of regional iconographies is the Hindu creation myth, the story of the Churning of the Ocean of Milk, an episode in which a team of gods and demons led by the god Vishnu churned the ocean to produce the Elixir of immortality (*amrita*) as well as a host of other beings and substances. Mount Meru, the sacred mountain of Hindu cosmology, became the churning stick, the snake Basuki offered his body as the churning rope and teams of demons and asparas pulled vigorously to churn the Ocean of Milk. This episode is known through multiple retellings across South and Southeast Asia, as Reddy shrewdly noted, it is an "unbound narrative, and although it is ostensibly couched within a stable text, that text too is variable and manifold" (2021). The episode is perhaps best known through its abundant representation in miniatures, and later prints, of the sixteenth century onwards, however, this mythic event also structured landscapes and objects across the Hindu world with a unique force. A short but prescient paper by Joanna Williams in 1992 already pointed to the wide currency of the iconography of the Churning of the Ocean of Milk in architecture and waterworks across South and Southeast Asia from the sixth century onwards. Yet while Reddy focuses on the narrative as a key to Indian epistemes, the fact remains that the iconography itself is still poorly studied.

The twelfth century site of Angkor Wat in Cambodia, locus of the former Khmer capital of Yasodharapura, stands as one of the most ambitious materializations of this idea at the scale of an entire temple plan (Figure 0.3). Placed at the center of a large tank, the Angkor temple (originally dedicated to Vishnu) is Mount Meru and the encircling tank its own Primal Ocean.

FIGURE 0.3 Aerial view of the central temple complex, Angkor Wat, Cambodia, founded early twelfth century as a Hindu temple to Vishnu. Situated at the center of a large artificial lake the temple directly references Mount Meru and the encircling Ocean of Milk. © Charles C. Sharp via Wikimedia Commons (public domain).

The temple complex is huge, the external enclosure around the tank seen in Figure 0.3 encloses an area of 208 hectares or 500 acres and has a total perimeter of 5.5 kilometers (3.4 miles). As if to make this iconography perfectly explicit, the wall of the temple's outer south gallery is carved with a low-relief frieze depicting Vishnu's Churning of the Ocean of Milk. Figure 0.4 shows the center of this long frieze with Vishnu dynamically organizing the teams of demons and asparas who pull on Basuki's rope-like body to rotate Mount Meru, the churning stick. This is not a discreet metaphor: this one episode occupies a frieze some 49 meters long. The gallery spaces were used as part of the temple's ritual processions, thus placing participants—and today, tourists— at the very heart of watery creation. Although the cosmological basis of this, and much other, temple architecture had been understood by Western scholars in the nineteenth century, the oceanic or watery dimension of this iconography is only now becoming the object of more focused study. As Veronica Walker Vadillo has shown, the iconography of the Angkor Wat temple is only part of a far larger "nautical iconography" of kingship developed across this huge capital city (2016, 2021).

FIGURE 0.4 Vishnu Churning the Ocean of Milk, bas-relief on the south of the east wall of Angkor Wat's third enclosure. © Olaf Tausch via Wikimedia Commons (public domain).

This was an iconography that permeated objects too. Holy water was especially central to Hindu rituals in Indonesia and water vessels became a prominent category of ritual object. As Nandana Chuttiwongs notes "consecrated water was credited with the same potency as the *amrta* (ambrosia), which sprang out of Mount Meru [...], and was considered fully charged with the power to restore life" (Chutiwongs 2000: 73). Figure 0.5 shows a magnificent East Javanese water vessel of the thirteenth century whose design embodies this principle. In this bronze, shaped like a butter churn with its protruding churning stick and rope, every component of "the ancient Indian myth [is] symbolically represented. The tall, narrow set of parasols with their stylized rock motifs represent Mount Sumeru [Meru], and the ovoid vessel the ocean of the universe. The *nāga* represents Basuki, the giant snake" (Fontein 1990: 278). The ritual water contained in the vessel, in effect the *amrita* it delivered, was poured not through the mouth of the snake as those familiar with traditional ewers might first assume, but from the top of the churning stick. Significantly perhaps, in this and other vessels designed with a similar symbolism, the bodies of the vessels themselves are entirely undecorated. While Chutiwongs suggests that the ovoid body of this and other vessels evokes the mythical Golden Egg containing the nucleus of the universe (2000: 73), in the context of Fontein's more literal interpretation as this as the body of the butter churn one might also read this lack of decoration as a reference to the unformed emptiness of the Primal Ocean from which the elixir of immortality was brought forth.

Related iconographies pervade other objects, often less literally. The Turbinella pyrum seashell, commonly known as chank or *shanka*, was widely used across Asia as both a libation vessel and trumpet, as a still classic study of the shell by James Hornell showed (Hornell 1942; also Ray 2003: 31–4). The *shanka* as battle trumpet is one of the symbols of Vishnu and commonly appears in representations of this god, however, chanks were widely used in rituals across Asia and many elaborately carved examples, often with precious metal additions, survive today (Lerner 1985: 82–5). The *shanka* seen in Figure 0.6, now in the collections of the Metropolitan Museum of Art in New York, illustrates the long and complex landed life of such marine shells. Fished in the waters around the Indian subcontinent this chank was originally relief carved in the eleventh or twelfth century, probably in eastern India under the Pala dynasty and for an obviously Hindu context given its Vaishnavite iconography; the main panel shows Vishnu in the form of Narayana with his favorite consort Lakshmi, the goddess of beauty and fortune, herself rescued from the Ocean of Milk as it was being churned. The openwork carving of some chanks suggests that they were made as libation vessels for holy water since the openwork makes them unsuitable as trumpets; this example, however, seems to have been purpose carved as a ritual trumpet (Lerner 1985: 82). At a later, as yet undetermined date, it was carried far inland to Tibet where its opening was covered with a silver repoussé panel of a dragon, a symbolic protector of the

FIGURE 0.5 Ritual vessel for holy water referencing the Churning of the Ocean of Milk with Mount Meru as the churning stick and Basuki the snake the churning rope. Bronze, Eastern Java, thirteenth century. H: 31 cm. Collection Nationaal Museum van Wereldculturen. Coll. no. RV-1403-2346. © The National Museum of World Cultures, The Netherlands.

FIGURE 0.6 Conch carved with Lakshmi-Narayana and other figures. India (possibly West Bengal) or Bangladesh, Pala period, eleventh or twelfth century. Shell with later silver additions, Tibet or China. H: 20.5 cm; W: 9.5 cm; D: 9.2 cm. Metropolitan Museum of Art, New York 1986.501.6. Gift of Evelyn Kossak, The Kronos Collections, 1986. © Metropolitan Museum of Art (public domain).

Buddha in Tibetan Buddhism (84). In Tibet chanks were commonly adorned with mouthpieces and other additions in precious metals, however, as Michael Lerner's careful analysis of the iconography of this piece has demonstrated, in this case the long edge of the chank had been damaged, whether in India or in Tibet we do not know, and the silverwork here is both repair and adornment (83–4).

The neglected potential of the South and Southeast Asian material underlines just how intermittent and isolated studies of the cultural history of the sea have been thus far, outside as well as inside Europe. These rich regional intellections of the sea have barely dialogued with their coeval European histories—to the impoverishment of both.

WHOSE HISTORY?

Yet however exciting the potential of the material just discussed, a cultural history of the sea written only from elite sources and precious objects such as these has to be severely limited. Not all cultures have textual and visual sources, or have preserved them, in equal measure. With the exception of South America and Meso-America where writing systems did exist, "medieval" Australasia, the Pacific, and North America were prehistoric societies. Here I use the term "prehistoric" as it is used, for example, by archaeologists of Africa, to describe periods antedating the production of written histories, literally "before history." Here cultural histories of the sea must be read from their, perhaps less obviously readable, daily material cultures, their oral histories, and increasingly their genomic histories.

European medievalists have much to learn here from scholars working on other parts of the world and from other data sets. In contrast to the rich corpora of texts and visual iconographies available in Europe, South and Southeast Asia, in the Near East and central Islamic lands we have few maritime iconographies and even fewer images of ships (Agius 2008; Nicolle 1989), although textual sources abound. The Swahili culture of coastal eastern Africa is an extreme example since it has preserved no indigenously composed texts earlier than the fifteenth century, while a few rare graffiti of ships constitute the only surviving visual representations relating to the sea. Yet, the Swahili world was profoundly maritime at least after 1000 (Fleisher at al. 2015). In this context, the interpretation of material culture and archaeological data take on a singular importance. The inclusion of the Swahili, and other societies like them—the coastal dwelling First Peoples of Australia and of many parts of the Americas—in premodern cultural histories of the sea depends upon our integration of other types of source material and the very different methods they bring.

Material culture and the archaeology of animal and plant remains offer important new sources for writing cultural histories of the sea if dialogue between the two areas can be developed and sustained. One volume is, in this respect, pioneering. John R. Gillis's *The Human Shore* (2012) constitutes an important intellectual milestone, the closest any scholar has yet come to writing a cultural history of the sea in deep time, from *homo sapiens*' largely coastal exit from Africa around 75,000 years ago,[2] via its peopling of the furthest ends of the Americas, Oceania, and the Pacific, to our present-day reinhabitation of coasts. In the present context, however, his work stands out particularly for being one of the few cultural histories of the sea to engage meaningfully with anthropology and material culture. Certainly, Gillis's focus is on coasts and his book devotes little time to the kinds of themes dear to modern cultural history such as life at sea or ships as societies. Nevertheless, as he points out, few human societies have ever been truly amphibious, and none entirely aquatic, the shore has always been the most active interface between most societies and the sea. Although Gillis does not raise the questions of sources as an overtly methodological issue, as I have here, in writing his two premodern chapters—"An Alternative to Eden" and "Coasts of the Ancient Mariner"—Gillis attempts to do so, not only in as non-Eurocentric a manner as possible but also by integrating data from anthropology and archaeology alongside a wide variety of textual and visual sources. Indeed, in these two chapters archaeology and anthropology provide Gillis's main datasets. There is no denying that the truly global focus of the first chapter gives way in the second to a narrower Mediterranean and Atlantic focus with a passing nod to the Indian Ocean. The field is furthermore so fast-changing that many sections now require updating. In spite of these shortcomings, Gillis's willingness to read across disciplines to offer the first broad narrative of humans and the sea is both impressive and hugely important for the future of cultural histories of the sea.

The potential of archaeological material for writing cultural histories of the sea has been well demonstrated for medieval England where it predates literary and documentary sources. Research over the last decade and a half has now identified that around 1000 fish-hungry consumers, and the maritime communities able to meet their demands, began to look to the open sea for new sources of fish, and to seas often very far from home. Archaeologists have named the massive expansion in saltwater fishing and the consumption of sea fish that resulted as the "Fish Event Horizon" (FEH) (Barrett and Orton 2016). As Stephanie Wynne-Jones and Jennifer Harland discuss in "Practices," archaeology in this instance offers a far more detailed view and a more refined dating tool than textual sources. Not only is the increased availability of salt cod and preserved herring visible in the archaeological record centuries before the first written sources, the archaeology demonstrates that the FEH substantially changed the food culture of the British Isles and other regions of the North Atlantic in perhaps as little as half a century. Historians and literary scholars are now working to understand, and disagreeing healthily about, what drove this change and what it means for the cultural history of the Middle Ages. If it seems certain that new maritime fishing grounds began to be exploited as more easily fished freshwater fish stocks on land became depleted, the key question is why so much fish was being consumed? Was fish's potential use as a fasting food within Christianity the cause for higher demand, or were these new grounds opened up due to an expansion of demand for what remained an essentially luxury foodstuff (Frantzen 2014: 232–45)? Do fish remains signal a greater religiosity across society, or are they evidence of the democratization of an elite foodstuff?

Whatever the answer, many more questions still remain substantially unexplored, notably, as Wynne-Jones addresses, whether this was a singular European change or part of wider, global trends, and if so, how and why? The archaeology behind the "Fish Event Horizon" underlines how little we still know about fish consumption and historical patterns of saltwater fishing and maritime interactions elsewhere around Afro-Eurasia before the early modern period. The answers will have important consequences for the types of sources and disciplines that will participate in writing future cultural histories of the sea in our period. Even more importantly, they impact on the geographical scope of these future histories and their inclusion, or not, of the many cultures that were still "prehistoric" up until the late fifteenth century. In this respect the archaeology of Central and South America is more than ready to be brought into the discussion, and I am only sorry that this has not proven possible here. Archaeology of the Postclassic Maya period (900–1500) in Central America, its sea trade and salt exploitation, or the varied and vigorous maritime cultures of the Central Andean Pacific coast, is well advanced and has much to contribute in terms of excavation methods and theoretical approaches. The inclusion in Michel Balard's *The Sea in History: The Medieval World* (2017) of three essays by Heather McKillop, Jorge Ortiz-Sotelo, and Emiliano Melgar on different aspects of Central and South American maritime archaeology is highly innovative and offers medievalists of Afro-Eurasia an easily accessible overview and starter bibliography.

Linguistic evidence has long played an important part alongside material evidence in mapping cultural interactions and migrations where no written histories survive. The unique and deep imprint of Austronesian culture and language on Madagascar—in language, music, funerary rites, boat technology, and foodways—was noted in the nineteenth century although the mechanics and chronology of adoption remained largely speculative. Over the last decade, linguistic and archaeological data is fast being outpaced by the potential for ancient DNA (aDNA) analysis of material from human, faunal, and plant remains. New techniques of genomic analysis have now revolutionized the field with new data indicating the arrival in Madagascar by the eighth century of populations and plants from maritime Southeast Asia, specifically southern

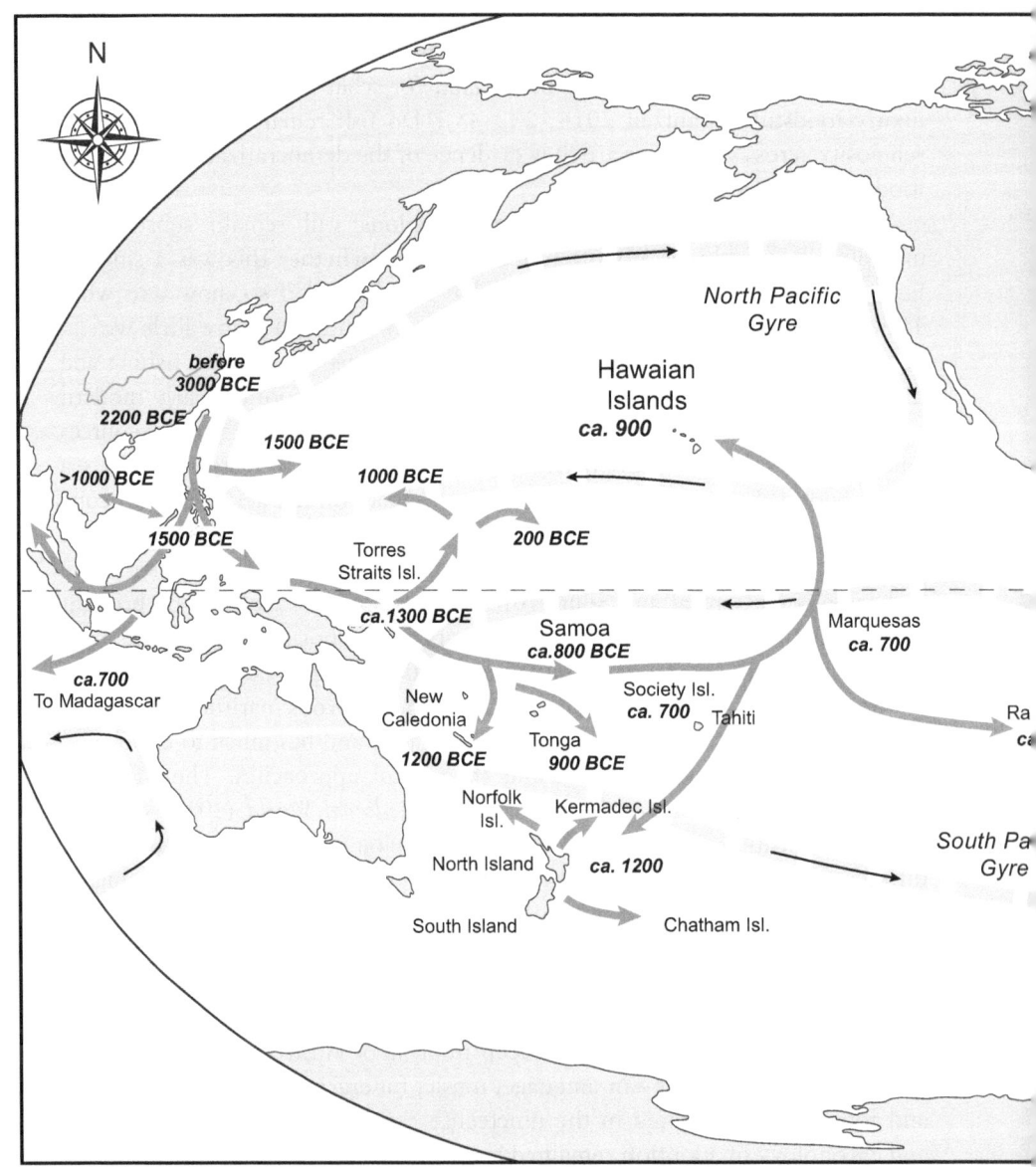

FIGURE 0.7 Routes and dates of Austronesian migrations and Viking explorations and raiding voyages. © Sebastian Ballard.

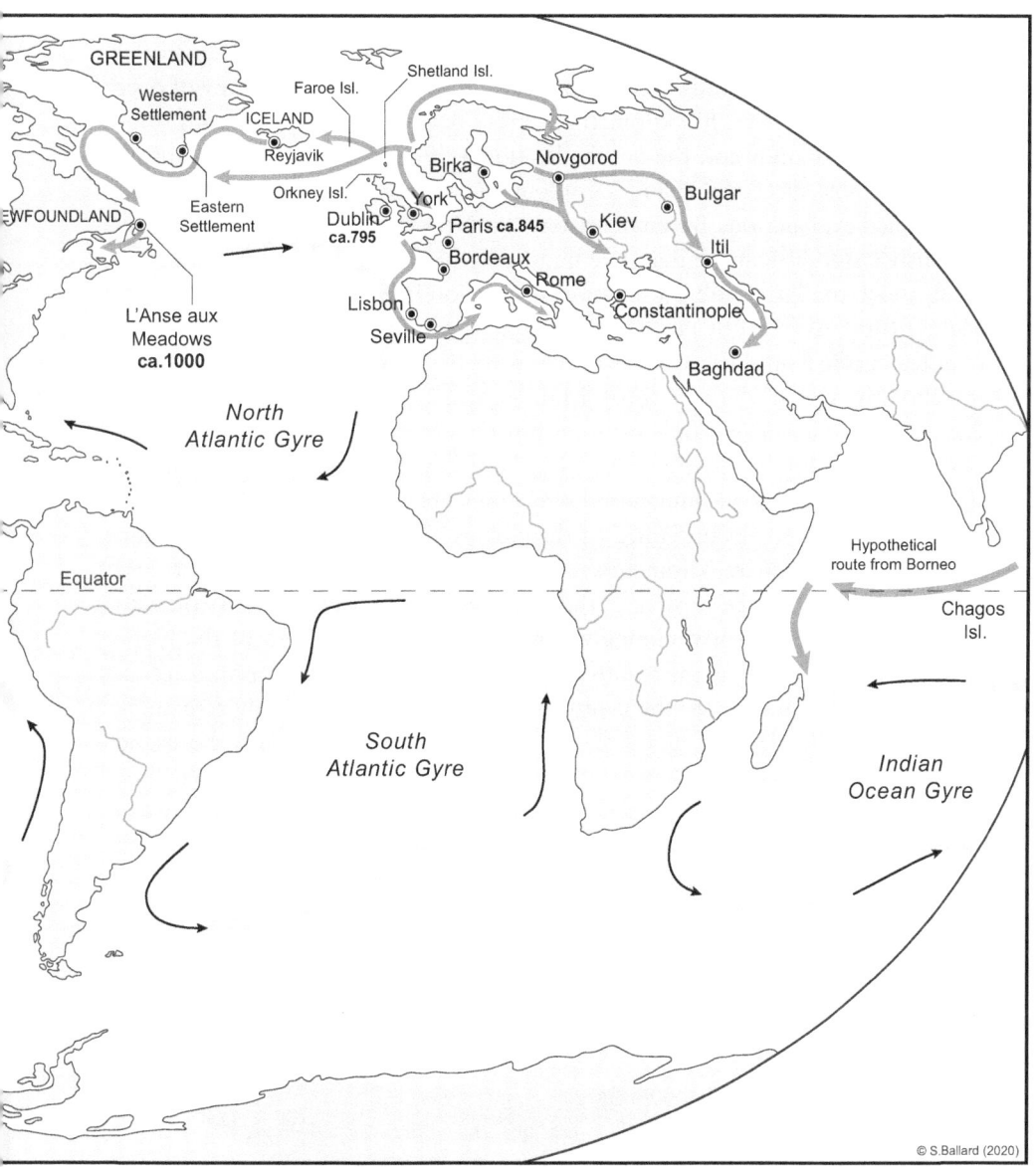

Borneo (Hoogervorst and Boivin 2018). As Tom Hoogervorst and Nicole Boivin underline in their discussion, following the work of other scholars, this phenomenon needs to be understood as part of an active and larger set of Indian Ocean voyages and trade networks coming out of Southeast Asia. This migration is generally accepted to have made use of favorable equatorial currents to sail from islands in Southeast Asia to Madagascar, a journey of over 1,600 nautical miles (3,000 kilometers) across open ocean, perhaps with stops at the Chagos islands and the Seychelles (Figure 0.7). Madagascar is arguably one of the most successful examples of long-distance settlement and integration in the medieval period. By comparison, the Norse settlements in Greenland famously lasted little more than five hundred years.

Although the Pacific finds only passing mention in these chapters, as Roxani Margariti points out, our period also saw the settlement of "some of the most remote oceanic lands in the Pacific [...] in ways that have yet to be incorporated in scholarly views of the Global Middle Ages" this volume, p. 119. The Pacific poses particular problems in terms of historical sources, as Eric Staples discusses regarding navigation, however, here too aDNA is fast rewriting the story and chronology of humankind's relationships to the sea across this huge area. The Pacific covers one-third of the globe's surface, it is our largest ocean at 165,200,000 square kilometers (63,800,000 square miles). Genetic and archaeological evidence now date the final phases of eastwards Austronesian expansion into this overwhelmingly watery "other" hemisphere of the globe to the eleventh through thirteenth centuries (Figure 0.7) (Wilmshurst et al. 2011: 1815–20). These are the centuries in which the world's only remaining unpeopled archipelago of any size, Aotearoa (New Zealand), and the island of Rapa Nui (Easter Island) were first settled though long-distance maritime migrations from eastern Polynesia. The six-meter-long section of the Anaweka canoe (Figures 0.8 and 7.1) was originally part of a much larger east Polynesian voyaging canoe and was excavated on the northwestern coast of Aotearoa's South Island. Radiocarbon dated to around 1400, this ghost of a boat is a powerful but all too rare material reminder of the fully global scale of medieval

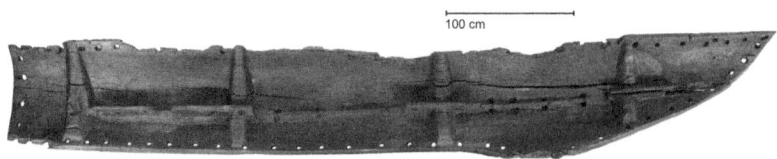

FIGURE 0.8 View of the interior of the Anaweka canoe, a section of an East Polynesian voyaging canoe excavated on the northwest coast of New Zealand's South Island, radiocarbon dated *c.* 1400. Section length 608 cm. © Dilys Johns.

connectivities (Johns, Irwin, and Sung 2014). The Pacific—already present in John Mack's *The Sea: A Cultural History* (2011) for its navigational technologies and in Gillis's *The Human Shore* as a significant theater of human expansion—will undoubtedly occupy a larger place in future cultural histories of the sea as the scale and ambition of Polynesian voyaging and exploration during our period becomes apparent.

Genomics, linguistics, boat technology, and the full array of archaeological specializations should in future be majorly important contributors: the cultural history of the sea is also to be found in plant, animal, and human DNA, in pots and pans and food remains, in votive offerings, in the traces of maritime resources processed and consumed on land, in port and harbor architecture, or in shipwrecks and experimental reconstructions of medieval ships. The problem, at least in many parts of Europe, is that the two fields rarely dialogue, archaeology has not found it necessary or useful to frame its discussions within the discourses of cultural history, while a cultural history still heavily wedded to literary and iconographic sources has often shown itself ill at ease with archaeological materials and technologies. Literary historians of the British Isles, for example, have been more ready to engage with data and models of seafaring developed for the nineteenth century Pacific, than with the very considerable bodies of medieval archaeological evidence available for their own regions (Goldie and Sobecki 2016; Sobecki 2008: 13–15). Conversely, while medieval archaeologists of course include evidence from written sources, as is usual in historical archaeology, this does not mean that they necessarily engage with the same sources as literary historians and art historians, or with the discourses of cultural history. Truly transdisciplinary, trans-regional volumes such as Vicki Szabo's *Monstrous Fishes and the Mead-Dark Sea* (2008), a pioneering attempt to capture the history of whaling in the medieval north Atlantic, are the exception rather than the rule. Szabo's difficult confrontation of literary understandings of whales as symbolic fish, archaeological remains and more ethnographically grounded insights into the practices and cultures of those who actually hunted, or more accurately scavenged, and consumed whales is exactly the kind of exercise that the cultural history of the sea should engage with in future.

Thus, while the following chapters rely heavily on literary studies and visual sources for their content, several bring into the cultural history of the sea evidence from material culture, zooarchaeology, as well as experimental archaeology and ethno-archaeology. In so doing their authors raise important questions about where the stuff of cultural history is to be found, and whose cultural history is being represented and discussed. When the Americas and Oceania join the "Old World" in a truly global cultural history of the sea before 1500, overwhelmingly it will be from archaeological and anthropological sources that it is written.

"THE MOST LAND-BASED PERIOD OF THEM ALL"?

Scholars of seas and oceans will agree with Kären Wigen's observation that "oceans are oddly occluded" on most scholars' mental maps (2007: 1); the deafness to the sea that Sebastian Sobecki lamented will be all too familiar to them. Importantly, several historians of the European Middle Ages have asked whether something more than scholarly deafness is at work here, whether the Judaeo-Christian tradition was in fact particularly disposed against the sea, by implication, more so than other world faiths (Connery 2006; Gillis 2012; Sobecki 2008). Fundamental to this attitude they argue was the establishment of land as "the central player in biblical geography" (Gillis 2012: 10) in the Judaeo-Christian tradition, leaving the sea—non-land—as a strange and fearful void. There are plenty of sources that build on this idea and appear to substantiate it, not least the use of the sea to represent the new Iberian "wild" as identified by Simone Pinet. Nevertheless, study after study, be it of literary sources or material culture, stubbornly suggest that it is more often modern scholars who are deaf to the sea (Rüdiger 2017), than the sources themselves that are silent. The sea is abundantly present across a wide variety of sources and, as Sobecki showed, is a site of intellectual projection for ideas far more varied than that of the sea simply as a terrifying and empty space.

As already mentioned, suggestions of an intrinsic terracentricity have been made in relation to Brahmanical Hinduism but have proven to be more than unfounded. Likewise in studies such as Xavier de Planhol's *L'Islam et la mer: la mosquée et le matelot, viie-xxe siècle* (Islam and the Sea: Mosques and Sailors, Seventh–Twentieth Centuries) (2000), ideas of a fundamental "Islamic" aversion to the sea have been roundly refuted and contradicted by rich bodies of textual and material evidence (Conrad 2001). As Sobecki showed, our sources often speak volubly of other relationships to the sea than fear alone and some have suggested that, more than Judaeo-Christianity per se, it is a Protestant "fear of the sea" that has actively occluded many scholars' mental maps (Delumeau 1989; Hegel 1970). The whole matter of terracentricity within the Judaeo-Christian tradition and its impact on the study of the sea deserves closer scrutiny and a more nuanced evaluation. But the likelihood is that it is the Western academic tradition that is intrinsically terracentric rather than the cultures or faiths that it studies. For the moment, however, there is no doubt that, as medievalist Jan Rüdiger decries, "to present-day Europeans, the Middle Ages are, by and large, the most land-based period of them all" (Rüdiger 2017: 35).

The new evidence for Austronesian migrations in both the Pacific and the Indian Ocean during our period can only help challenge terracentric perceptions of the Middle Ages. Indeed, if we add to these voyages Viking sailing and settlement across the North Atlantic as far as Greenland and Newfoundland as compared in Figure 0.7, the centuries between 800 and 1450 emerge as no less engaged with the oceans than subsequent periods. The ninth through fifteenth centuries saw intense and extreme oceanic voyaging along both Afro-Eurasia's northwestern *and* southeastern shores, to the eastern and western fringes of the Americas. At present the fifteenth century is cast as a key moment in the cultural history of the sea, one of only two "centuries of oceans," to use Peter Miller's terminology (2013: 2–3). During the fifteenth and twentieth centuries, he argues, first through exploration and later naval warfare, oceans became an unavoidable presence in human experience and so assured their place in cultural history. If it is difficult to argue against the newly global nature of human circulation after the later fifteenth century, or the thick and newly three-dimensional inhabitation of the oceans brought about by the invention of large ocean-going ships and submarines, the new archaeological finds and techniques of scientific analysis just discussed usefully wear away at such neat periodizations. How many human beings need to travel, how far do they have to sail to assure their place in the cultural history of the sea? How long before we acknowledge that the Middle Ages were centuries of oceans as much as the fifteenth and twentieth centuries?

CONCLUSIONS

In 2007 Kären Wigen presciently announced that the growing "cultural turn" in maritime history had much to contribute to sea histories. Wigen's point was that cultural history, led by literary studies and anthropology, has a relatively theoretical "culture and traditions," as well as a deep, "cumulative experience in handling inter- and intra-cultural issues" that make it uniquely well suited to maritime spaces. "More traditional practitioners, especially historians," she warned, ignored these opportunities at their peril (2007: 36). The opportunities opened up by literary studies are indeed vast and exciting, but other fields such as archaeology or visual and material culture studies are no less well theorized and increasingly engaged in the exploration of inter- and intra-cultural issues and can also bring much. The fact remains that, a decade on, the cultural history of the sea in the Middle Ages remains a young and still substantially disconnected field as compared to later periods. As this chapter and the volume's consolidated Bibliography illustrate, for the most part, the cultural history of the sea in the Middle Ages has to be hunted down in single articles or chapters contributed to encyclopedias, edited volumes, journals and special issues of larger temporal, or thematic scope, or indeed within other disciplines. Frequently—too frequently—the searcher must also be the interpreter, translating questions and results produced within altogether different disciplinary frameworks, into the frameworks and discourses of cultural history.

It will be all too evident to readers that a volume of this comparatively modest size, with chapters of only eight thousand to ten thousand words, cannot aim to offer comprehensive global coverage. Nevertheless, each chapter aspires to be innovative and path-breaking and at least signals significant developments and sources from around the globe. Even within these imperfectly global parameters, the task facing every contributor here has been daunting, necessitating both broad reading to connect disconnected studies, whilst trying to step back and form some understanding of how all this might be understood within a cultural history of the sea. In simply pointing to material not usually included within medieval cultural histories of the sea we hope to encourage new conversations that will dynamize this field and ensure their future inclusion. The Bibliography generated is inevitably multilingual and constitutes an early reminder of the fact that the future of the cultural history of the sea will depend upon international collaboration. Still very little research is carried out, very little is written, as a direct, explicit contribution to the cultural history of the sea in the Middle Ages. This volume hopes to begin that change.

CHAPTER ONE

Knowledges

From Natural Wayfinding to Instrumentation

ERIC STAPLES

INTRODUCTION: NAVIGATIONAL KNOWLEDGE

The period between 800 and 1450 was one of extraordinary maritime accomplishments. During this time, new technologies and improvements in scientific knowledge combined with a growing understanding of geography and navigation to generate a remarkable period of commercial, political, and cultural interaction. Europeans were only one of many cultures that expanded and refined their knowledge of the sea during the medieval period. While the Scandinavians traversed hitherto uncrossed waters in the North Atlantic to establish, however briefly, colonies in North America, Polynesians sailed back and forth to Hawaii, achieving one of the great feats of premodern navigation in the central Pacific (see Figure 0.7). Arabs, Persians, East Africans, Chinese, Indians, and Malays sailed along previously established routes in the Indian Ocean and western Pacific with greater frequency than ever before—intertwining economies and creating more culturally pluralistic seascapes in the process (Fernández-Armesto 2006). Iberians ventured farther into the central and southern Atlantic, founding colonies along the west coast of Africa; and under Zheng He the Chinese conducted a series of voyages in the Indian Ocean on a scale hitherto unknown. All this activity fundamentally changed and expanded human knowledge of the sea as sailors from diverse cultures shared, and compared, their techniques for navigation, shipbuilding, and seafaring. Interaction between Mediterranean sailors who established regular routes across the Atlantic resulted in the development of the "fully-rigged ship" by the end of the fifteenth century—a design that dominated trade routes for the next half-millennium. Further east, the maritime silk route brought Arab knowledge of star-altitude navigation into the western Pacific, and the Chinese compass into the Indian Ocean.

It would take more than a single book, let alone one chapter, to discuss all aspects of global knowledge related to the sea between 800 and 1450. Therefore, this chapter will present an overview of specific areas of applied knowledge relating to maritime navigation, with a particular focus on those shared navigational practices that transcended individual cultures. There has been a marked tendency within the history of science to view premodern fields of knowledge within a cultural or national context. Thus, libraries are filled with titles related to Islamic science, Chinese science, or Western science. However, scholars for the past several generations have challenged such paradigms and have conceptualized different ways to frame the study of knowledge production, transmission, and adaptation (Elshakry 2010; Raj 2016; Sivasundaram 2010). In some cases, such as knowledge relating to ship construction, regional analyses are appropriate. However, in other cases, a more global and less regional approach is required. Navigational knowledge is a particularly interesting field in this regard, as the degree of cultural fluidity and interaction in long-distance maritime trade engendered a considerable amount of shared knowledge that transcended cultural boundaries. What is apparent is that although there were regional traditions of maritime navigation that developed in relative isolation from one another at the beginning of the medieval period, by the end of the era, the evidence strongly suggests that Afro-Eurasian maritime communities shared navigational knowledge and practices within their own culturally specific contexts. Individual societies participated and contributed to this knowledge, but the knowledge itself was neither rooted in nor inherent to any single society. Rather, it was a shared body of knowledge with regional variations. To demonstrate this, we shall begin our discussion by examining the forms of environmental navigation evident in most maritime cultures at the beginning of the medieval era; then focus on larger, specific examples of shared knowledge, practices, and technologies that took place by the end of the medieval period. These will include the development of a navigational literature, the increased reliance on astral heights, and the incorporation of new navigational instruments such as the compass.

Historians must nevertheless contend with a relative paucity of sources related to that era. Most of the littoral societies they study, such as the Polynesians and the Thule, transmitted knowledge orally and through practice, and such knowledge is also difficult to identify in the archaeological record unless it is in the form of boats and ships. Consequently, much of the written work relating to the sea at this time was written by geographers, or literate travelers, relying on secondhand information. Clearly, it was the actual sailors, fishermen, navigators, and captains who were most responsible for generating the incremental advances in maritime-based knowledge, but it was often a literate elite who later recorded and assessed these developments. It is essential, therefore, that we move away from past "great man" conceptions of history and develop a more nuanced understanding of the networks of production that incorporate the multiplicity of actors who often remain unrecognized in popular narratives. In his work *A People's History of Science* (2005), Clifford Conner discusses this phenomenon, providing examples such as that of Portugal's famous Prince Henry the Navigator. He points out that although Prince Henry sponsored maritime exploration and the accumulation of navigational knowledge, he did so mainly for political purposes. Despite his special distinction as "the Navigator," he was neither a navigator nor a sailor, and possessed little technical knowledge of the sea. In fact, the skills and understanding that enabled the Portuguese to explore the West African coast in the fifteenth century were created, collected, and disseminated by the sailors and navigators who undertook the actual voyages, many of whose names are lost to history. Indeed, it could be argued that the men with practical, working knowledge of the seas and skies contributed more to the medieval world's understanding of celestial bodies and the oceans than the theories of land-bound geographers and astronomers.

Michael of Rhodes (Michalli da Ruodo as he referred to himself) is one example of such a practical seaman. Michael was a Venetian mariner who rose from the ranks of a common oarsman to become an *armiraio*, well versed in seafaring and shipbuilding. His treatise shows that he had a professional understanding of navigational practices in the fifteenth-century Mediterranean, in particular the mathematical approach to navigation known as *marteloio*, as well as knowledge relating to shipbuilding, astrology, and theoretical mathematics (Falchetta 2009: 196–210). Michael was not born a member of the intellectual elite but was rather a practical mariner who had risen through the ranks, accumulating a deep and varied knowledge of the sea and theoretical mathematics in the process. It often appears that practical navigators were providing more detailed and nuanced understandings of the movement of celestial bodies and the seas than the geographers and astronomers sitting in their observatories. Our understanding of knowledge production and transmission for this period, therefore, remains partial even in the better-documented regions.

Although this chapter focuses on the period between 800 and 1450, some chronological flexibility is necessary, for rarely does something as porous and complex as knowledge of the sea fit neatly into such artificially constructed temporal boundaries, particularly in a global context. The historically significant navigational literature of the Indo-Pacific extends slightly beyond both dates, such as the navigational poems of the most famous Arab navigator, Ibn Majid, which were written after 1450. Nevertheless, they constitute essential historical sources for understanding the development of maritime knowledge during the medieval period and are therefore included here (Ibn Majid 1993, 1971; Tibbetts 1981; Zhao Rugua 1966: 9–14).

ENVIRONMENTAL NAVIGATION

Environmental navigation, also known as "natural navigation" or "wayfinding," is perhaps the most regionally specific knowledge related to the sea. Since antiquity, navigators had relied on their understanding of the maritime environment to determine their way at sea, and this method still constituted the vast majority of knowledge that navigators used in the medieval period. All of the available navigational literature from the period refers to the importance of using environmental markers to determine one's location at sea, and descriptions of ideal navigators emphasize this fact. For example, in his depiction of the archetypical "Shipman," Geoffrey Chaucer stresses the importance of distinct types of knowledge.

The specific types of markers that navigators relied on varied widely depending on the marine environment, but almost all navigators were familiar with the distinctive features of the seascapes in which they sailed. For example, Arab and Persian navigators would watch for a specific type of sea snake, the *māraza*, that indicated that they were near the southwest Indian coastline (Ibn Majid 1993: 79; al-Mahri 1970: 164–5). Viking navigators looked for a plethora of whales or seabirds to identify the steep submarine slope south of Iceland (Taylor 1956: 77). Other natural landscape features such as mountains or high hills, and prominent or distinctively shaped rocks were also frequently used. Wayfinding knowledge such as this was rarely written down, let alone illustrated, however, the sea birds visible out to sea as ships approached the Island of Socotra off the Horn of Africa were considered important enough to be mentioned by the Iranian traveler Ibn al-Mujawir and were included as seven circles in the diagrammatic map of the island that illustrates his manuscript (Ibn al-Mujawir 2008: fig. 12). Although published after our time period strictly defined, the *Historia de gentibus septentrionalibus* (Description of the Northern Peoples) written by Oleus Magnus (1490–1557), Bishop of Uppsala, and published in Rome in 1555 includes numerous references and illustrations of such traditional wayfinding points. As oceanic exploration increased during the medieval period, navigators expanded the boundaries of their knowledge of natural navigation. Arabs, Persians, and Africans sailed back and forth across the China Seas, the Chinese voyaged to the western Indian Ocean, Polynesians sailed across vast reaches of the Pacific, and Scandinavians became familiar with the islands of the North Atlantic.

Although we know relatively little about them, Pacific mariners were perhaps the greatest natural navigators of the medieval period. The islands of

Hawaii were settled around the eighth century by seafarers from the area of the Marquesas, over 2,000 nautical miles (3,500 kilometers) to the southeast. Ancestors of the Maoris later sailed, probably around 1200, from southern Polynesia to Aotearoa (New Zealand), settling what was at the time one of the largest remaining uninhabited archipelagos on the planet (Johns, Irwin, and Sung 2014; Wilmshurst et al. 2011). The Pacific is an immense ocean, presenting navigational challenges different from those encountered by mariners in the Atlantic and Indian Oceans. Modern studies of "traditional" South Pacific navigation have noted that their "navigational abilities depend on a profound general knowledge of the sea, the sky, and the wind; on a superb understanding of the principles of boat-building and sailing; and on cognitive devices–all in the head–for recording and processing vast quantities of ever changing information" (Frake 1985: 256). However, our understanding of Pacific long-distance navigation relies so heavily on such ethnographic evidence and oral traditions, as well as descriptions from Europeans in the eighteenth and nineteenth centuries, that it is impossible to discuss in any detail the development of specific navigational knowledge in this time period. What we do know is that in the Pacific Austronesian mariners were able to engage in regular, long-distance voyaging between a network of islands, including Tahiti and Hawaii, a distance of over 3,500 nautical miles, as well as other remarkable feats of nautical navigation during the medieval period (Johns, Irwin, and Sung 2014; Kirch 2000; Lewis 1994; Richards 2008). The Anaweka canoe (see Figures 0.8 and 7.1), already discussed in the "Introduction" bears witness to the success of these voyages and the types of knowledge, such as boat construction, that traveled with them (Johns, Irwin, and Sung 2014). Ethnographic studies show that South Pacific navigators in the twentieth century relied heavily on environmental navigation, as well as star charts, but we should avoid assuming that theirs was a static navigational tradition that changed little over time. Indeed, all that can be said confidently is that Austronesians in the Pacific sailed great distances in the medieval period and that they relied primarily on their knowledge of environmental navigation.

The Vikings were another seafaring culture that emphasized natural wayfinding, but their methods are better documented. The Atlantic is a more daunting body of water to navigate than the more cloistered Mediterranean, with its brutal storms, high seas, bone-chilling northern waters, extreme tidal variations, and strong currents. Nevertheless, it was during the medieval period that the Vikings explored much of the northern Atlantic, and dramatically increased their knowledge of the seas beyond the confines of the Western European seaboard (Figure 0.7). After settling much of Britain, the Vikings ventured westwards across the Atlantic, establishing settlements in Iceland after Ingolf Arnarson's initial voyage in 874, and then Greenland, before reaching North America and building small communities in "Vinland." Artifacts and settlement remains have been found at L'Anse aux Meadows in Newfoundland in modern-day Canada, indicating that a permanent Viking community was established there in the tenth to mid-eleventh century (Jones 1984: 269–311; Paine 2013: 247–54). They also sailed south to the Mediterranean in 859, as well as down the trans-European river corridors such as the Volga. For the vast majority of this remarkable range of maritime exploration, they relied on their knowledge on environmental navigation, supplemented with the sounding lead, to measure depth, and potentially other instrumentation such as the sunstone.

Environmental navigation was also the foundation for navigation in the Indian Ocean, where for millennia sailors had been developing knowledge of the marine environment. One such field of knowledge related to the winds, which in the northern half of the Indian Ocean were based on the seasonal wind patterns known in English as monsoons, from Arabic *mawsim* meaning "season." As shown in Figure 1.1, from November through March the northeast monsoon sends winds down from the Asian landmass toward the southern Indian Ocean. Once the landmass begins to heat, the winds reverse, blowing more strongly from May to September during what is known as the southwest monsoon. The periods in between see fluctuating lighter winds and uncertain weather, interspersed by severe storm events such as cyclones in the Bay of Bengal. Mariners used these winds to their advantage, sailing from one port to another and back, depending on the time of year and direction of the wind. Evidence indicates that mariners had a deep understanding of the monsoonal wind patterns and used these from at least the first millennium BCE, if not earlier. However, it is also apparent that during the medieval period mariners developed a more sophisticated system of regulating these sailing dates, and by the fifteenth century the term *mawsim* came to mean not just season but specific sailing dates based on the Persian solar calendar (Ibn Majid 1971: 309–42; Lunde 2013: 75–82, 119–26; al-Mahri 1970: 111–21; Tibbetts 1981: 225–42).

This knowledge of winds also became culturally contextualized in the medieval period. With the spread of Islam, the Arab mariner's windrose integrated two distinct systems of marking wind, one based on Islamic sacred geography and the other on stellar rhumbs. Many of the winds in the Arabic navigational tradition were named according to the direction of the star they blew from. Thus, *al-Jāhī* was a northern wind, named after the Persian term for Polaris, *al-Jāh*, and *al-Suhaylī* was a southern wind based on the Arab name for Canopus, *Suhayl*. However, this became integrated with the directions of the Islamic windrose, which labeled winds according to their alignment to the Kaʿaba in Mecca (King 1991: 839–40: Tibbetts 1981: 382–4). These examples demonstrate that knowledge of natural phenomena was constantly adopted and modified within culturally specific contexts.

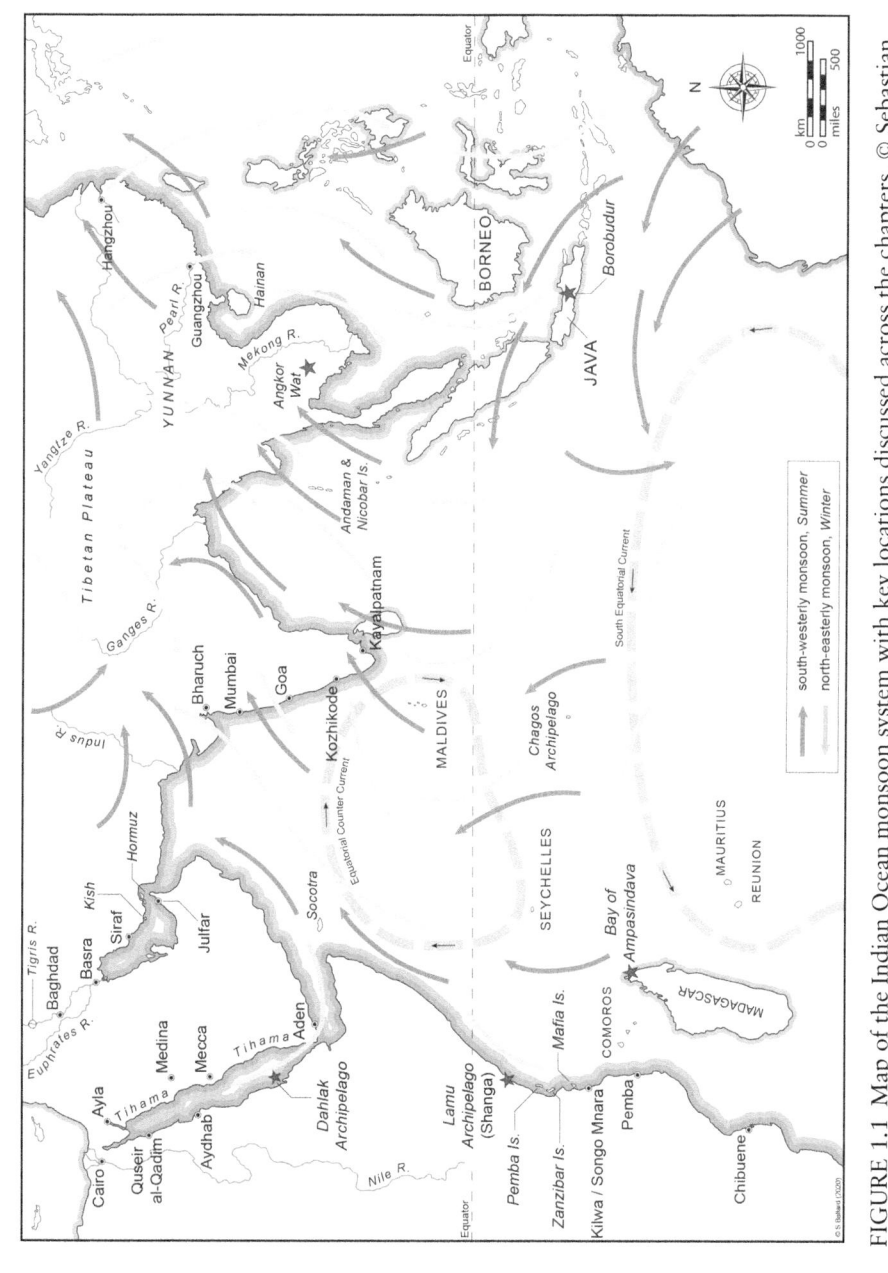

FIGURE 1.1 Map of the Indian Ocean monsoon system with key locations discussed across the chapters. © Sebastian Ballard.

It is clear that the majority of navigation during the medieval period consisted of environmental navigation, sometimes supplemented by a sounding lead to determine water depth. However, within this broader intellectual framework of natural navigation, we see several developments during the medieval period that have a broader significance for the development of navigation as a whole. Three will be discussed in this chapter: (1) the development of a specifically navigational literature, (2) an increased reliance on, and refinement of, the use of astral heights for "latitude sailing," and (3) the creation and widespread use of new instrumentation for nautical navigation such as the mariner's compass. An interesting aspect of these developments is that it is difficult to pinpoint a single "inventor" or "originator" of the technology. Rather, they take place in roughly similar periods amongst different seafaring communities of the China Seas, the Indian Ocean, the Mediterranean, and the Atlantic. Although evidence, for instance, of direct technological transmission is frustratingly scarce, the existence of such developments in multiple locations strongly suggests that navigational knowledge was becoming increasingly integrated between disparate maritime cultures, and that a series of widespread transmissions of knowledge took place. Additionally, each regional development shows active and inventive adaptation of specific concepts or instruments suited to each seafaring tradition's own cultural landscape.

NAVIGATIONAL LITERATURE

Navigational literature existed in antiquity, as literate merchants, geographers, and mariners recorded their knowledge of sea travel. The origins of this genre in oral traditions of environmental navigation are often obvious, but the medieval period saw the development of a much larger corpus of navigational guide literature together with nautical charts in different languages. These sources recorded navigational knowledge for future generations of navigators in a variety of visual and written forms, much of which survives to this day. This literature expands far beyond the initial Graeco-Roman tradition, and includes the portolans and *roteiros* of Europe, the *rahmānij* of the Islamic world, and Chinese navigational manuals, stellar diagrams, and maps. Collectively, these works represent a significant collection of primary source material that provides us with a more detailed and global perspective of the state of maritime knowledge in the medieval period.

In the ninth and tenth centuries, we see the emergence of literature related to sea routes in Islamic and Chinese geographical works. The first source, a Chinese text written by Jia Dan between 785 and 805, describes sailing from Tang China to Abbasid Iraq (Zhao Rugua 1966: 9–14). The nascent Islamic geographical tradition, largely written in Arabic, also records this route in the ninth century, but in the opposite direction, from West Asia to China. The oldest section of the *Akhbār al-sīn wa-l-hind* (Accounts of China and India) (2014), dated to 851, contains a description of the sailing route from the Siraf to Guangzhou. Although not as detailed as later descriptions, between them the accounts mention sailing directions, navigational hazards or wayfinding markers, ports of call, provisioning stops, or the estimated days it would take to sail from one port to the next. The *Kitāb al-masālik wa-l-mamālik* (The Book of Roads and Kingdoms) written by the Abbasid administrator Ibn Khurdadhbih in the second half of the ninth century also includes a description of this route (Ahmad 1989: 3–30). By the tenth century, Arab and Persian geographers were including descriptions of the sea in the more ethnographic sections of their works. The polymath al-Mas'udi (1861–77), for example, who traveled the western Indian Ocean himself and describes seafaring in the tenth century, also includes several chapters on the seas of the world in his *Murūj al-dhahab wa-ma'ādin al-jawhar* (Meadows of Gold and Mines of Gems).

Navigational literature of a more technical nature is also alluded to at this time. The tenth-century geographer al-Muqaddasi makes reference to navigational guides that shipmasters and merchants, people whom he considered "among the most discerning of people about this sea" would "study carefully together and on which they rely completely, proceeding according to what is in them" (al-Muqaddasi 1906: 10; 2001: 9). These observations are supported by references from the fifteenth-century Arab navigator Ahmad b. Majid to navigational works composed prior to his lifetime. Ibn Majid mentions three authors of previous navigational texts, which he refers to as the three "lions" of navigation: Muhammad b. Shadhan, Sahl b. Abban, and Layth b. Kahlan. Although their dates are debated, the general consensus among scholars is that they lived in the eleventh and/or twelfth centuries, strongly suggesting that a navigational literature (in Arabic and/or Persian) had developed, and was in use, by the tenth or eleventh centuries, if not earlier.

Significant navigational documentation also developed in other parts of the world in the eleventh through thirteenth centuries. For example, we have the first evidence of tide tables being written down in this period. The earliest known tide table is from China and dates from some time prior to the eleventh century. It originated near Hangzhou—famed, as Emmanuelle Vagnon discusses in Chapter 7 "Representations," for its tidal bore (see Figure 7.9)—indicating that they understood the lunar impact on tides. In the thirteenth century, monks from St. Albans monastery made the first tide tables in Europe, although Robin Ward (2009) has noted that it appears to be primarily based on a theoretical rather than empirical understanding of tidal variations. However, in the Catalan Atlas of 1375, tides are recorded in a circular diagram for fourteen ports in the North Atlantic (Figure 7.6). The large tidal variations found in northern European waters made tides an important topic and Ward estimates that roughly a third of the material in Atlantic European rutters from the medieval period relates to them. Other navigational literature, such as that pertaining to the Indian Ocean, does not focus on tides to the same degree, primarily because tidal changes are less dramatic in those waters (Aleem 1967: 459–67; Needham, Ling, and Gwei-Djen 1971: 3:483–94; Ronan 1986: 3:178–9; Taylor 1956: 136–9; Ward 2009: 139).

As navigational instructions were increasingly written down and eventually rendered visually we also see the development of navigational manuals and portolan charts in the Mediterranean and Black Sea during the thirteenth century. The oldest surviving portolan text as such is the *Compasso da navigare*, an Italian text dated to the late thirteenth century, which gives detailed sailing instructions for the Mediterranean but is, however, unillustrated. However, an older twelfth-century Latin text, the *Liber de existencia riveriarum*, already describes a marine map of the Mediterranean (Gautier Dalché 1995) suggesting a longer history of visual representation. The term portolan is thus commonly used to describe regionally focused charts, most often drawn on parchment and that represent the coast but only a few inland features. The names of ports are inscribed at ninety degrees to the coastline while specific symbols such as red dots or crosses indicate shoals. These charts are crisscrossed by a network of lines forming stars, known as wind lines or rhumb lines, which are further subdivided into sixteen and then thirty-two secondary directions corresponding to the main directions of a compass. Portolans include a distance scale in miles. The earliest surviving portolan chart is the so-called Carte Pisane of around 1275 illustrated in Figure 1.2, a large chart on untrimmed parchment that takes its name from the Italian city Pisa, from which it was acquired by the Bibliothèque nationale de France in the nineteenth century (Kelly 1979: 33.2; Taylor 1956: 98–114). Although fine examples such as the Carte Pisane were probably not used onboard ships, there is abundant evidence that portolans were carried onboard Mediterranean ships from the late thirteenth century onwards, and alongside some of the first European magnetic compasses. Several texts describe these charts as technical tools to facilitate navigation, in particular helping seafarers to find their way if blown off course.

In the fourteenth century, portolan charts expanded to include the Atlantic, in particular the British Isles, and by the fifteenth century, Portuguese mariners were using them in their navigation along the West African coast (Campbell 1986: 67–9; Diffie and Winius 1977: 135–7). When Portuguese monarchs hired Italian and Majorcan navigators to assist in their maritime expeditions, they applied Mediterranean techniques to Atlantic portolan charts, such as the use of black, green, and red rhumb lines (loxodromes) and crosses to mark inshore submerged rocks (Baldwin 1980: 41). We also see this tradition amongst Muslim mariners in the Mediterranean, such as on an Arabic chart found in the Ambrose Library and dated to 1325, or on Tunuslu Ibrahim Katibi's portolan chart from 1413 (Brice 1977: 55–6). With varying degrees of accuracy, these

FIGURE 1.2 The so-called Carte Pisane, portolan chart of the Mediterranean, late thirteenth century, ink on parchment. © Bibliothèque nationale de France, CPL GE B-1118 (RES).

charts recorded vital geographical and nautical details that improved safety and navigational efficiency.

These documents also illustrate the gradual refinement of navigational knowledge over time. The Carte Pisane is fairly accurate regarding the Mediterranean but is less so for the Atlantic coastline; however, later portolan charts contain much more precise renditions of this area. This increased level of accuracy in the charts reflects the efforts of countless, and mostly un-named, seafarers who corrected previous errors such as the distance estimates for the Atlantic coast, recorded new coastal features, and slowly augmented and refined their knowledge of the waters. The improved reliability of the charts also reflects the increased level of maritime commercial interaction between the Mediterranean and the Atlantic in the late thirteenth and fourteenth centuries, particularly on the part of Genoese and Venetian merchants (Kelly 1979: 19–23). The manuscript of an early-fifteenth-century Venetian mariner, known as *The Book of Michael of Rhodes*, is another interesting source regarding European navigation, which has recently received a fair amount of attention, and illustrates the use of mathematical principles applied to navigation (Long, McGee, and Stahl 2009).

In the North Atlantic, the earliest surviving navigational manuals are from the fifteenth century, although there are sections relating to navigation in earlier literature, such as the passage on navigation found in the Old Norse work *Konungs Skuggsjá* (King's Mirror) from the mid-thirteenth century, as well as references in the Norse sagas and Icelandic law books (*Konungs Skuggsjá* 1917: 156–62). The fifteenth-century navigational sources consist of the *Seebuch*, a pilot guide written in Middle Low German, and a rutter composed in Middle English. Both rely on nautical knowledge from prior centuries, much of it from southern European sources. The *Seebuch* is particularly rich in environmental knowledge, listing tides, compass bearings, ports, soundings, distances, and navigational hazards (discussed in Ward 2009: 152–4). There is little of the astronomical content so distinctive of Ibn Majid's work, suggesting differences in local navigational practices, with almost no attention paid to the altitudes of stars in the North Atlantic. As discussed by Emmanuelle Vagnon in Chapter 7 of this volume, technical navigational literature is more evident in the Indo-Pacific in the fifteenth century, and includes a variety of Chinese navigational manuals, maps, and diagrams.

In the western Indian Ocean, the earliest surviving corpus of detailed technical navigational literature was produced by the Arab navigator Ahmad b. Majid between 1462 and 1492. He wrote over forty works that provide a detailed insight into of the state of Indian Ocean navigation in the fourteenth to mid-fifteenth century (Ferrand 1921–8; Ibn Majid 1993, 1971; Tibbetts 1981). The fact that all but one of his works were poems—written in a simple *rajāz* meter that facilitated easy memorization—is a reminder of the oral dimensions of navigational knowledge across so much of the globe. The vast majority of this information was committed to memory and recited by often illiterate but highly knowledgeable mariners. This oral tradition was a universal practice in this period, and it enabled illiterate mariners to store vast amounts of knowledge through poems and songs. The unique value of this medieval navigational literature is that it has captured in manuscript form a portion of this much larger oral tradition otherwise lost to history.

In one of his final works, Ibn Majid mentions the knowledge that a competent navigator should possess: "The navigator (*sāhib al-dark*) needs to have knowledge of the risings, the settings, horizontal star combinations, and the preparation and taking of star-altitude measurements, as well as the rising and setting points of the stars [for bearings], and their latitude, longitude, declination, and celestial orbit, in order to be a skilled navigator (*mu'allim*)" (Ibn Majid 1971: 28–9; Tibbetts 1981: 77). If one compares this with Chaucer's earlier description cited in this chapter it indicates that, in the Indian Ocean at least, by the fifteenth century environmental navigation had been integrated with astronomical concepts to form a broader, applied body of knowledge. Although these texts are written in Arabic, they in fact represent a diverse range of nautical and astronomical knowledge from different intellectual traditions, weaving within a single text Islamic lunar mansions, Persian solar calendars, Bedouin star lore, and Indian latitude measurements. Much of this material is thought to be derived from the earlier literature of the "three lions" that Ibn Majid mentions, even if the individual sources are almost impossible to disentangle.

Thus, we see the emergence across much of Afro-Eurasia of a shared culture of navigational literature, as navigators increasingly began to preserve their knowledge in ink. However, the forms in which this knowledge were recorded were diverse and culturally varied. Tide tables, charts, stellar diagrams, navigational manuals, and poems were all produced in various languages so that mariners might better understand, and more safely traverse, the seas. Collectively, they represent a larger trend to document and transmit knowledge in written form for the benefit of future generations.

LATITUDE SAILING

Latitude is a geographic coordinate that specifies the position of a point on the earth's surface along an imagined north–south line. The practice of using astral heights to estimate one's approximate latitude was known in antiquity, but mariners in Eurasia and Africa refined this practice during the medieval period, and developed more standardized and sophisticated instrumentation to measure celestial bodies at sea. In the Indian Ocean latitude sailing was especially useful for long open ocean crossings between north Sumatra and Sri Lanka, southern

India and the Arabian coast, and again between the mouth of the Gulf and the coast of western India. P. J. Rivers has questioned the use of the modern term "latitude sailing" in a medieval context, preferring the term *altura*, but for the sake of the modern reader, this discussion uses the term "latitude sailing" while acknowledging that not every mariner using astral heights conceptualized the sea as a geographical space divided into lines of latitude (2012: 88–9). When and where the development of using astral heights at sea to determine one's position relative to north and south first took place is not entirely certain. The earliest reference to astral heights in the Mediterranean is from the first century CE, but it is clear that such measurements were used prior to this (Cunliffe 2001: 82–3; Taylor 1956: 46–7). By the medieval period, mariners were using different instrumentation to measure astral heights, such as the *khashaba*, the quadrant, or the "guiding star stretch–boards" of China. Figure 1.3 shows a modern reconstruction of a *khashaba*, used for navigational experiments on a sailing voyage in 2010 from Muscat to Singapore.

In the North Atlantic, it is apparent that mariners were already using the height of the sun at noon to establish their approximate latitude. In the fourth century BCE, Pytheas in his travels along the North Atlantic coast recorded the variation of the heights of zenith of the sun and these were later translated by Hipparchos into degrees of latitude (Cunliffe 2001: 81, 91). By the medieval

FIGURE 1.3 Modern reconstruction of a *khashaba*, "a piece of wood" used for measuring astral heights on the 2010 voyage of the ninth-century replica Indian Ocean vessel, *Jewel of Muscat*, from Muscat to Singapore. © Alessandro Ghidoni.

period, the Vikings were aware of variations in the height of the sun at its zenith, and there is evidence that they made records of sun altitudes. There are also claims that the Vikings used a sunstone and a sun compass to help them determine their approximate latitude and bearing. However, the evidence regarding these instruments has been disputed, and therefore we cannot be entirely certain that Vikings used these tools in this period to help them sail east to west across the Northern Atlantic (Bernáth et al. 2014: 1–18; Jones 1986: 5–14; Rosedahl 1987: 92; Ward 2009: 130).

In the Indo-Pacific, it is assumed that star altitudes, measured from the horizon, were used to determine approximate latitude well before our period, but concrete evidence for this practice is found only well into the medieval period. Navigators used the height of stars from the horizon—in particular in the Northern Hemisphere, the Pole Star—and measured it in finger heights to determine their latitude. The Pole Star was most useful between the latitude 23° north to latitude 6° north, where it was close enough to the horizon to be measured accurately, and it was the primary star used for navigation according to all the available literature. Just when this form of navigation began in the Indo-Pacific is uncertain. In one of the fantastical sea tales in the tenth-century book, *Kitāb 'ajā'ib al-hind* (The Book of the Wonders of India), a man stranded on an island of man-killing women mentions being so far south that Canopus (*al-Suhayl*) sat directly above the island (al-Ramhurmuzi 1929: 17–21; 1990: 57–9). Aside from this reference to the height of Canopus, however, no concrete evidence exists for the use of stars for latitude sailing until the fifteenth century when it is mentioned in both Arabic and Chinese sources.

In the Chinese context, the so-called Mao K'un Map—in fact a set of navigation charts published in the Ming military treatise *Wubei zhi* of 1628 but believed to reproduce data gathered during the expeditions of the Chinese admiral Zheng He in the early fifteenth century—also includes four surviving stellar diagrams recording astral heights (Figure 1.4). The diagrams include a series of measurements taken in fingers based on the height of Polaris that are associated with specific locations (Ma Huan 1970: 236–302). The four stellar diagrams give specific star heights of a variety of stars given in a directional pattern surrounding the central illustration of the ship, that are used to mark the latitude of specific routes and ports in the Indian Ocean (333–43). Those above the ship are to the north, those below to the south, those on the right are to the east, and those on the left are to the west. The stellar diagram on the left of Figure 1.4 details astral height measurements for the Bay of Bengal crossing from Sri Lanka to Sumatra, the one on the right for sailings from a location on India's west coast to Hormuz in the Gulf. It has been assumed that since all evidence of star altitude measurements in Chinese sources relates to the Indian Ocean voyages in the medieval period, and not to the China Sea, that the Chinese relied on Indian Ocean navigators for this information. While

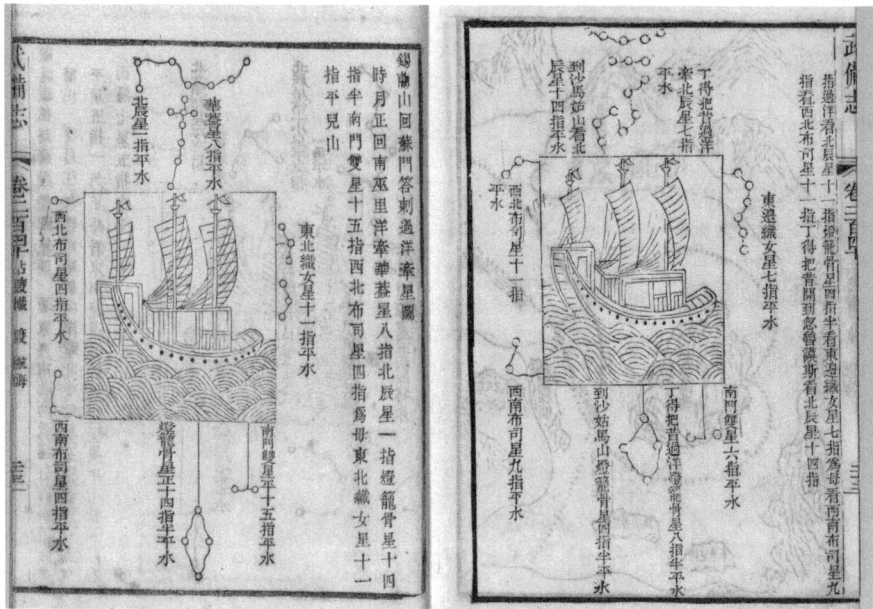

FIGURE 1.4 Two of the four stellar diagrams from the Mao Yuanyi's *Wu bei zhu*. Each of the brief textual passages surrounding the image of the ship mentions specific stars and their heights in fingers in different directions. Woodblock print, after 1644 but believed to reproduce data gathered during Zheng He's voyages in the first half of the fifteenth century. Library of Congress, Geography and Map Division. © Library of Congress (public domain).

this may have been the case, the manner in which the map uses astronomically significant Chinese constellations such as "Bone of the Lantern" and the "Imperial Canopy" as the basis for their star altitude measurements makes these distinctively Chinese representations.

Ibn Majid's writings provide even more detailed information about astral heights, notably four different methods of star altitude measurements, three of them relying on measuring two or more stars simultaneously. He devotes entire poems to specific star-combination measurements, and his final work, *Kitāb al-fawā'id*, lists seventy-three different star combinations that could be used for determining latitude. All of this indicates that Indian Ocean navigators had, by the fifteenth century, developed a sophisticated understanding of navigating by this method (Clark 1993: 360–73; Ibn Majid 1971; Sheriff 2010: 120–7; Staples 2013: 47–60; Tibbetts 1981: 329–54).

Alongside this comes clear evidence for the development of relatively standardized instruments to measure star altitudes. Ibn Majid mentions a device he calls on occasion "a piece of wood" (*khashaba*), at other times a bow (*qaws*; pl. *qiyās*), as well as twelve different instruments of varying sizes used to measure altitudes accurate to within a quarter of a finger (Fatimi 1996: 283–92; Ibn Majid 1971: 27). The existence of similar instrumentation is also recorded in Chinese sources in the early seventeenth century (Needham, Ling, and Gwei-Djen 1971: 574–5; Ronan 1986: 3:175).

Instrumentation specifically related to determining star altitudes also appears in Iberia at roughly the same time as the Indian Ocean, but it is difficult to provide precise dates. After the universal astrolabe was developed in al-Andalus in the eleventh century, such devices were used on land to measure astral heights. In addition, other instruments such as the quadrant and cross-staff emerge in at least the fourteenth century. Strong evidence for their use at sea, however, does not appear until somewhat later, in Portuguese sources. Alvise de Cadamosto is credited with giving the first recorded astral heights at sea in 1455, and Diogo Gomes mentions using a mariner's quadrant off West Africa in 1460. There is also a reference to the use of a simplified astrolabe, known as the mariner's astrolabe in 1481 (Paine 2013: 383; Parry 1981: 145–7; Ward 2009: 147–9). Both astrolabe and quadrant were used to measure the height of celestial bodies to determine latitude, but systematic recording of astral heights does not occur in Europe until the sixteenth century, suggesting that the Portuguese may have been influenced by the Indo-Pacific practices they eventually encountered at the end of the fifteenth century.

Collectively, all of this evidence indicates that the use of astral heights for navigation was becoming increasingly important in Indian Ocean and Atlantic contexts, and that a variety of maritime societies from the Far East, the Islamic World, and Western Europe increasingly relied on this practice by the end of the medieval period. Unfortunately, exact details regarding its development and transmission in these cultural contexts are frustratingly sparse. However, the sources nonetheless illustrate a relatively sophisticated understanding of the system and evidently took considerable time to develop.

NAVIGATIONAL INSTRUMENTATION: THE MARINER'S COMPASS

During the medieval period, seafarers began to rely on increasingly sophisticated instrumentation to refine and augment their navigation and a wide variety of devices was developed for use at sea. These included the sand-glass, the Chinese starboards, the Arabic *khashaba* (mentioned above), as well as the traverse board, and the quadrant in Europe. This process established an age of "instrument-based navigation," also referred to as "indirect navigation," that began sometime in the eleventh and twelfth centuries, and continued into the eighteenth century. This innovative age does not fit neatly into the temporal categories of the series, as it continues well into the early modern era with the development of the mariner's astrolabe in the late fifteenth century, the chip log in the sixteenth century, and the sextant and the chronometer in the eighteenth century. These sophisticated technologies added to earlier, comparatively simple, instruments such as the sounding lead (often pressed with pitch or tallow) that was in use in antiquity to determine the depth and composition of the seafloor (Ward 2009: 133). Despite the length of the process, it is clear that the increased dependence on navigational instruments began during the medieval period. Although there is not space in this chapter to discuss in detail all of the relevant instrumentation, we can look at one important example of a device that emerged in the Indo-Pacific, the Mediterranean, and the Atlantic: the mariner's compass.

The mariner's compass was among the most important nautical instruments to appear during our period because it greatly enhanced sailors' ability to determine direction at sea. The mariner's compass improved the accuracy of sailing over open ocean, thus encouraging the long-distance trading ventures and migrations that took place in this period and the subsequent early modern period. The compass appears to have been developed first in China, before spreading throughout the Indian Ocean, the Mediterranean, and the eastern Atlantic Ocean. Although Chinese texts allude to an earlier invention of the compass, the first clear description of the device dates to the eleventh century (Guangqi 2000: 296; Needham, Ling, and Gwei-Djen 1971: 562–4; Ronan 1986: 3:9–17). The following passage in the 1044 *Wu jing zong yao* (Collection of the Most Important Military Techniques [Compiled by the Imperial Order]) describes a Chinese compass:

> In the fish method a thin leaf of iron is cut into the shape of a fish five centimetres long and a centimetre broad, having a pointed head and tail [...]. To use it a small bowl filled with water is set up in a windless place, and the fish is laid as flat as possible upon the water–surface so that it floats, whereupon its head will point south.
>
> (Ronan 1986: 3:11)

By the late twelfth and early thirteenth centuries, both Islamic and European sources describe compasses and the device features several times in illustrations to Marco Polo's text included in an early fifteenth-century French manuscript (Figure 1.5). The first reference to a compass in the Atlantic is found in the *De Naturis Rerum* (On the Nature of Things) written by the English monk Alexander Neckham in 1180 (Taylor 1956: 95–6; Ward 2009: 144). This slightly precedes the first references to a (fish-shaped) compass in the Islamic world in Sadid al-Din Muhammad b. Muhammad Bukhari's Persian work of 1232–3 the *Jawāmiʿ al-hikāyāt* (Collections of Stories). However, the first explicit mention of a nautical compass is found fifty years later in the 1282 work by Baylak al-Qibjaqi the *Kitāb kanz al-tujjār fī maʿrifāt al-ahjār* (The Book on the Merchants' Treasure of the Knowledge of Stones) (Schmidl 1997–8: 82). By the time of Ibn

FIGURE 1.5 Illustration from an early-fifteenth-century French copy of Marco Polo's *Livre des Merveilles* showing navigation with a compass. Bibliothèque nationale de France, Ms français 2810, fol. 188v. © DEA Picture Library/Getty Images.

Majid, the compass was an essential instrument in any Indian Ocean captain's toolkit, and he also refers to the needle specifically as "*samaka* (a fish)" (Ibn Majid 1971: 194; Tibbetts 1981: 165). Such clear parallels between earlier Chinese and later Muslim descriptions strongly suggest that Muslim navigators adopted the Chinese compass sometime in the eleventh and twelfth centuries. In the fourteenth century, the needle was attached to a compass card indicating the points of the compass—a modification that has been questionably attributed to Flavio Gioia of Amalfi in 1302 (Ward 2009: 145).

The compass is a relevant example of how navigators shared knowledge and technology from the China Seas to the Atlantic, and how each culture then inventively adapted it to suit their own specific cultural practices. For example, Muslim mariners adopted the magnetized fish compass and then modified it to make it compatible with their preexisting cultural conceptualizations of direction, based on their stellar "compass." The Arabic stellar compass relied on thirty-two stellar rhumbs (*akhnān*; sing. *khann*), related to star positions that rose and set within a specific zone of latitude near the equator, to determine direction (Figure 1.6). Thus, southeast was not the literal Arabic translation of "southeast" on the compass rose but rather "the rising point of Antares (*matlā' al-'Aqrab*)" (Ibn Majid 1971: 113–28; Tibbetts 1981: 121–56, 294–8).

FIGURE 1.6 "The Arabic stellar compass rose," from James Prinsep, "A Note on the Nautical Instruments of the Arabs," *Journal of the Asiatic Society of Bengal* (1836): 784. © Out of Copyright (public domain).

This Arab Indian Ocean stellar compass, while inappropriate in the North Atlantic or southern latitudes where the locations of such stars would have been dramatically different, was particularly well suited to the predominant zones of seafaring in the Indian Ocean. Therefore, while the Arabs adopted the Chinese fish-shaped needle and the lodestone, they rejected the Chinese system of direction on the compass—which had twenty-four rhumbs named after different branches of Chinese philosophy—and incorporated them according to their own celestial understanding instead (Saussure [1923] 1928: 3:41). These directional markers, most likely inherited from desert wayfinding practices, had remarkable cultural resilience and were still being used well into the twentieth century on Arabic compasses and in Arabic navigational manuals.

A similar process took place with the mariner's compass in the Mediterranean and Atlantic, where mariners used the device but inserted it within their own understanding of direction. In Northern Europe, for example, the English compass had thirty-two rhumbs, familiar to the English speaker today, such as north, north by east, and north-northeast. Some of these compasses also contained lunar times to help estimate high and low tides, since tidal variations were incredibly important to Northern Atlantic navigation (Ward 2009: 131–8). However, in the Mediterranean, direction was based on the windrose, and rhumbs were referred to as *vents* (winds) as late as the sixteenth century. Interestingly, the windrose in the Mediterranean, which was originally based on eight points of the Greek windrose, became more sophisticated in this period, and was further divided into sixty-four points (Taylor 1956: 98; Ward 2009: 132). The adoption of the compass in the Mediterranean also had other unintended and culturally specific evolutions. Once the compass became a prevalent instrument onboard Mediterranean ships in the latter half of the medieval period, Mediterranean navigators and cartographers started using rhumb lines on portolan charts to assist in determining their course, particularly in overcast and dark conditions, as seen in Figure 1.2. However, no such rhumb lines or charts have been found in the medieval Indian Ocean or China Seas tradition (Ronan 1986: 3:161).

It must be kept in mind that the importance of the compass is sometimes overstated in this time period, as it still had the potential for serious error and was not the highly accurate instrument that we know today. Nor did all ships have compasses, and many continued to use more traditional methods of determining their courses at sea. It is assumed that in places with clear visibility such as the western Indian Ocean, the majority of navigators continued to use stellar rhumbs for bearings and only relied on the compass when necessary. That said, it was an invaluable aid for finding direction in unfamiliar seas or when the skies were overcast, and it was to have a significant impact on increasing the efficiency of commercial shipping. Collectively, the development and refinement of navigational instrumentation during the medieval period, along with the emergence of literature that codified maritime knowledge, fostered a dramatic increase in oceanic navigation and laid the foundations for the subsequent age of global maritime expansion in the early modern period.

CONCLUSION

In conclusion, it is apparent that there were a series of developments in maritime knowledge during the medieval period that transcended local and national boundaries. In the field of navigation, these led to an increased reliance on the compass, the development of new instruments and techniques for latitude sailing, and an increased production of navigational literature. By the end of the medieval period, much of this information was systematically organized and transcribed for later generations of navigators. Our historical sources, though sporadic, reveal that sophisticated systems of navigation developed in disparate parts of the world, and that the knowledge and technologies that undergirded these systems spread across cultural and geographic boundaries as diverse communities of mariners traversed the seas. This is not to say that a universal maritime culture existed by the end of the medieval period but rather that the era witnessed a significant expansion in maritime knowledge due to the emergence of "a heterogeneous fretwork of contact zones, aversions, and transmissions between sophisticated and acquisitive cultures" (Chism 2009: 624) in the maritime realm, which appears to have increased significantly during this period.

There is still much more work that needs to be done in the field of maritime knowledge in the medieval period to better understand these larger networks of knowledge production and transmission. Most studies of medieval maritime knowledge still suffer from a profoundly regional focus, understandably due to limitations of linguistic requirements to authoritatively compare such diverse sources. Those that provide a more universal focus, such as Lincoln Paine's (2013) and Filipe Fernández-Armesto's (2006) global maritime surveys primarily rely on a variety of secondary literature and published translations of primary sources from a variety of different regions. The notable exceptions to this, such as Hyunhee Park's (2012) comparison of mapmaking and navigation in Chinese and Islamic societies in this period, are still relatively rare in the field. One suggested avenue of future potential research is to create collaborative projects in which scholars specializing in different regional and disciplinary areas of maritime knowledge work together to provide alternative frameworks for analyzing and discussing knowledge of the sea in this time period. At the moment, there is a plethora of detailed regionally specific studies, but a comprehensive conceptualization of medieval maritime knowledge on a more global scale is still required.

CHAPTER TWO

Practices

Cultures and Communities of Fishing between the Medieval Indian Ocean and North Atlantic

STEPHANIE WYNNE-JONES AND JENNIFER HARLAND

CONNECTED WORLDS: THE INDIAN OCEAN AND NORTH ATLANTIC

The expansion of the maritime landscape during the medieval period makes this a fascinating setting for considering cultural interactions with the sea. Yet, as well as long-distance travel, navigation, and trade, this was also a period during which coastal communities flourished, inhabiting shores and harbors, exploiting marine resources in increasingly intensive ways. Fishing communities have always existed; in the medieval period they became the bedrock of larger maritime communities across the world. From approximately the eighth century onwards, overlapping worlds of maritime interaction grew in the North Atlantic and the Indian Ocean world. These very different environments were each the setting for a growth in maritime activity based on the international trade in luxuries. At the widest scale, there are hints from material culture of objects, ideas, and people carried between them and over massive distances; here we use these two oceans as the setting for a comparative discussion of fishing practices and communities through the medieval period. Fishing and shellfish collecting are predictably important to coastal communities and are a crucial way in which people have always engaged with the sea. They bring with them a world of maritime technologies, skills, and knowledge, as well as access to secondary products such as shell or oils from fish and marine mammals. In the medieval period, fishing was also affected by the developing world of maritime commerce that drove new contacts and markets. In this chapter, we focus on fishing as a practice, providing a window into what was certainly the most widespread and enduring medieval engagement with the sea but one that nevertheless found little opportunity for self-representation in high literature or art.

The Indian Ocean and North Atlantic are at first glance very different environments and situations but some common features emerge. In particular, both regions are places where we can view fisherfolk as enmeshed in "communities of practice" that transcend cultural, ethnic, and linguistic boundaries and instead relate to common networks of knowledge and skill (Lave 1991; Thomas 2009; Wenger 1998). During the period between *c.* 800 and 1500 dynamic changes in both regions accompanied some parallel historical trends. Throughout much of the period, the seasonal rounds of agriculture and fishing reacted to changing climate, shifting political allegiances and trading links, and changing demand. At the start of the medieval period, *c.* 800, the Vikings had just started to spread throughout the North Atlantic region while in the Indian Ocean a series of new coastal communities was beginning to exploit the opportunities of the monsoon trade from small and often ephemeral settlements. By the end of our period of interest, around 1450, permanent settlements had become firmly embedded into the local landscapes and seascapes of both oceans.

The eighth century and the eleventh century marked moments of transition in the scale and shape of maritime commerce that shaped both regions; these are also moments of transition in fishing practices. In the North Atlantic, the period after 1100 witnessed the incorporation of fish and fishing into this more commercial world, while in the western Indian Ocean the commercialization of fishing was more limited. In both regions, fishing practices and fish consumption rarely make an appearance in written histories, even where marine food sources provide the majority of the protein consumed by coastal populations. Instead, our knowledge of these communities is largely reconstructed through archaeology: particularly zooarchaeology, the study of animal bones from archaeological contexts. From these, we see that the technologies associated with fishing communities were deeply embedded in social changes such as growing commercial production networks, trade, and religious practice. We therefore use the comparison between these regions as a way of exploring differing responses to large-scale trends and attempt to account for these through discussion of varied relationships with commercial networks, hinterland communities, and sources of social power. In doing so, we explore a world of practice that is largely absent from economic and cultural histories and yet was the foundation for activity and maritime communities across the world.

HISTORIES OF CONNECTION AND COMMERCE

The Indian Ocean was central to the increasing connectivity experienced across the Old World from the eighth century onwards (see Figure 0.1). Not only was the region deeply interconnected by Islamic networks of faith, migration, and trade but also that interaction drove developments across Eurasia, including the expansion of trade communities through western Russia to the Baltic as discussed by Shepard in this volume; overland routes through Central Europe; and the development of trans-Saharan trade routes linked to emerging kingdoms in West Africa (Abu Lughod 1989; Beaujard 2005; Wink 1990–2004). The North Atlantic region also felt the effects of this growth in commercial networks through the trade in furs, slaves, and exotica that were traded from the Baltic through eastern European networks to the Islamic world. Our two regions were thus interconnected, although they had their own trajectories and local dynamics.

The Indian Ocean monsoon trade connected the east coast of Africa, the Gulf, South Asia, and ultimately Southeast Asia and China. Commodity networks from the mid-eighth century onwards ensured the flow of luxuries between the Abbasid court at Baghdad and Tang China as well as more mundane transactions between partners across the region. Yet they were also based on older patterns of connectivity that are less easily represented in the archaeological and historical record. Evidence for early plant translocations between Asia and Africa points toward maritime connections from at least the first millennium BCE, although the sites associated with this trade are elusive (Boivin et al. 2014).

The ways that sailors used the monsoon winds to move from port to port are detailed by multiple historical sources (see Staples in this volume, and Figure 1.2). The Belitung wreck, a ninth-century Arab vessel that sunk off the coast of Indonesia, provides a material embodiment of this phenomenon (Heng 2019; Krahl et al. 2010). The boat was of sewn-plank construction, a technique associated with the western Indian Ocean, and had a hull constructed from African hardwood. The ship carried a cargo made up principally of Chinese ceramics as well as fine goldwork and other goods relating to the multiethnic crew onboard. Figure 2.1 shows a scale model of the original ship, as reconstructed from the shipwreck timbers. The wreck thus provides testimony to the coasting trade of this period, when ideas and materials from around the ocean were drawn upon by travelers and traders over long distances and voyages that took them far from home. This history of interconnectivity has given the ocean its specific character, with an Indian Ocean identity drawn from long interaction between the peoples of the various coasts (Pearson 2003). Yet there are other environmental characteristics that may be more important in terms of fishing and subsistence practices. These are more local, as the ocean is home to an immensely varied marine ecosystem, focused on the resources

FIGURE 2.1 Scale reconstruction of the Belitung wreck, in the ArtScience museum, Singapore. © SEAArch Southeast Asian Archaeology (southeastasianarchaeology.com).

of the coral reefs that fringe much of the Indian Ocean coast, as well as more specific systems of mangrove and lagoon that create rich near-shore worlds for exploitation (Beech 2004; Lane and Breen 2018).

During a similar time period, areas of the North Atlantic were connected through the raids and subsequent settlement that characterized the Viking Age (see Figure 0.7). From the late eighth to the mid-eleventh century, Scandinavian raiders and sailors created links between coasts that had been long-settled, such as northern Scotland including the Northern Isles (comprising Orkney and Shetland) and Western Isles (the Hebrides), and those with minimal or no previous human settlement, such as the Faroes and Iceland, settled in the ninth century. Later settlements in Greenland, in the tenth century, and Newfoundland were ultimately short-lived. As Eric Staples discusses, these Nordic settlers brought with them an excellent understanding of the sea. Evidence of their shipbuilding technology is apparent from excavated iconic examples such as the eleventh-century Skuldelev 2 longship, built in Ireland but eventually sunk in Denmark where she was later excavated. The Scandinavian diaspora was by no means limited to the North Atlantic, other regions included England, Ireland, and Russia. After the "Viking Age" came to an end in the mid-eleventh century, the regions of the North Atlantic settled by the Norse continued to be maritime-oriented and politically connected.

One of the contributing factors behind the Viking diaspora was the favorable climatic condition of the North Atlantic region. The Medieval Climatic Anomaly or MCA (also referred to as the Medieval Warm Period) was a sustained period of more favorable temperatures and conditions for settlement, including less sea ice, across the North Atlantic. This was followed by the Little Ice Age (LIA). Although the MCA was a worldwide trend, it was subject to regional variation—we know of little impact in the Indian Ocean area, for example, although this may reflect a lack of data—and its extent and impact in the North Atlantic remains controversial. The settlement of Greenland appears to coincide with general warming, and its subsequent demise by the sixteenth century is due in part to a failure to adapt to the onset of cooler conditions (Dugmore, Keller, and McGovern 2007). In contrast to the reef and mangrove shores of the Indian Ocean, the moderately shallow continental shelves around the North Atlantic teemed with marine life and fish in particular, marine mammal populations too would have been plentiful at the start of the Viking Age.

SOURCES

These are, then, two regions where the medieval period was profoundly shaped by maritime connectivity and commerce. This brought with it a growing importance for coastal settlement also, with towns developing along the littorals of both regions. These settlements relied on fishing as an important part of their subsistence economy and yet, history deals poorly with this world of fishing. Here we use primarily data from archaeology—specifically zooarchaeology, that is, the study of excavated animal remains, exemplified by the mixed assemblage of fish bones shown in Figure 2.2—to reconstruct those practices, which were simultaneously crucially important to coastal groups and yet generally beneath mention in written histories. Of course, zooarchaeology brings its own biases, notably where excavations have been conducted and with what focus, whether excavated deposits were sieved to retrieve smaller bones and fragments, and the conditions of preservation particular to each site.

Animal bone and shell preservation is generally good for the coastal regions of Scotland and much of the coral geology of the Indian Ocean, although areas with more acidic soils tend to have poor bone survival. Modern excavation methods typically include fine sieving, a necessary requirement to get an unbiased record of the fish remains. Within the North Atlantic, traces of smaller fish such as herring or eel will rarely be seen while excavating and even the smaller bones from large cod and ling can easily be missed. Sieving to at least two millimeters—that is, using a sieve with perforations as small as two millimeters square—is now standard practice and has been so since the 1980s. However, older assemblages excavated by hand collection are still a valuable contribution to our understanding of fishing and fish consumption, as long as biases are acknowledged.

FIGURE 2.2 Mixed assemblage of archaeologically retrieved fish bones from the medieval North Atlantic. © J. Harland.

Fish and shell remains are identified using good, comprehensive reference collections, not always an easy undertaking for remote areas; for the whole Indian Ocean only a few exist. Taxonomy, the science of classification, identification, and nomenclature, plays an important part in the analysis of zooarchaeological remains, with finds classified to species level wherever possible, or to family level if not. Element (the part of the skeleton the remain comes from), butchery, and depositional history are also typically included. Identifications also need to include fish size, determined by measurements and regression equations or by broader comparison with reference skeletons. Determination of the animal's approximate size at death is important for the reconstruction of likely fishing grounds and thus likely fishing methods, a process undertaken using fisheries literature, including fishbase.org (Froese and Pauly 2019) and ethnographic studies of premodern fisheries (e.g., Fenton 1978). More recently DNA analysis has allowed archaeologists to trace cod excavated in Germany back to Arctic fishing grounds (Star et al. 2017). Direct archaeological evidence of fishing gear does exist but is rare in comparison to the substantial quantity of fish remains found. Fishing weirs and traps along coastal areas can survive well although

FIGURE 2.3 Uzio fish weir at Vanga, Kenya. © Eréndira M. Quintana Morales.

they can be difficult to date. Organic nets and lines rarely survive, although fishhooks and fishing weights are occasional finds including in shipwrecks where onboard fishing clearly took place during journeys. Ethnography can also contribute valuable information, the uzio fishing weir at Vanga off the Kenyan coast shown in Figure 2.3 is the kind of traditional fishing practice to which ethno-archaeologists might turn in order to reconstruct historic methods.

FISH AND DIET: FISH IN THE INDIAN OCEAN

Systematic zooarchaeological study of fish bones in the Indian Ocean has been confined to a few areas and sites, which have nevertheless drawn slightly different pictures. Along the eastern African coast, a recent turn toward systematic zooarchaeology has begun to return evidence for a consistent pattern of marine exploitation with a marked change in practices around the eleventh century. This was first outlined for the northern site of Shanga in the Lamu archipelago, based on data from excavations during the 1980s (Mudida 1996; Mudida and Horton 1993). Many thousands of fish bones were retrieved from excavations there and analyzed as part of a broader zooarchaeological study that remains a landmark both for its chronological scope (eighth to fifteenth centuries) and also for its consideration of contextual and taphonomic features, that is to say, understanding of the way that organisms decay and are preserved. Of the 6,009 fish bones identified to species level at Shanga, the majority were emperor fish (Lethrinidae) and parrotfish (Scaridae) although the range and variety was enormous. Notably, the fish that dominate the assemblage throughout are from the shallow waters of the surrounding reef, not deep-water fish. Archaeologists Mark Horton and Nina Mudida suggested that significant exploitation of deep-water or pelagic fish such as shark and barracuda began only from the eleventh century (Horton and Mudida 1996: 380). They also linked the fish remains to particular areas within the site and possibly to different human groups living within them. Notably, at Shanga they distinguished between a southwestern area with cattle but few fish remains, and a northern area that contained a mixed assemblage of fish and domestic animals. Horton (1994) has interpreted this as being evidence for the presence of pastoralist groups at Shanga, who may have maintained a fish taboo despite moving to the coast, alongside fishing and fish-eating groups. This is to some extent supported by ethnographies in the area, where the Katwa coastal group still refuse to eat fish; it is unclear how applicable these findings may be to other parts of the coast. At Shanga, fish was an essential foodstuff and domestic animals begin to outnumber fish in the faunal record only from the eleventh century onwards.

Systematic comparative analysis of fish remains from sites along the East African coast has begun to expand this as a more general model. Previous work had remarked upon the dominance of fish remains at sites from Lamu (Wilson and Omar 1997), Zanzibar (Horton and Clark 1985; Kleppe 2001), and Mozambique (Badenhorst et al. 2011; Sinclair 1982). Zooarchaeologist Eréndira Quintana Morales (2013) has compiled these records and analyzed newly excavated materials from sites on the Kenya coast, Zanzibar (Prendergast et al. 2017), Mafia (Crowther et al. 2016), and Songo Mnara (Quintana Morales 2013). In all of these cases, zooarchaeological identifications have returned a majority of reef fish throughout all periods, reflecting a broad use of near-shore resources. Larger fish associated with deep-water habitats and requiring a different set of fishing technologies never dominated and only became common from the eleventh century onwards (Fleisher et al. 2015; McClanahan and Omukuto 2011; Quintana Morales and Horton 2014). The zooarchaeological record of sites from northern Kenya to Mozambique indicates that groups occupying these coastal locations were utilizing a range of wild resources, both terrestrial and marine. Fishing therefore sat alongside land-based hunting as a means of supplying subsistence needs (Badenhorst et al. 2011; Prendergast et al. 2016; Walsh 2007; Wilson and Omar 1997). This mixed strategy works well in the rich set of environments created by the coral coasts of eastern Africa. It is also a response to a particular set of challenges created by the coastal environment, where agriculture and the herding of stock can be more challenging pursuits. The growth in numbers of larger fish accompanies a shift toward domesticated terrestrial fauna, particularly cattle, at many coastal sites, as just mentioned in relation to Shanga. Although it is difficult to say exactly what drove the shift toward domesticated animals, the changes coincide with a shift in scale for Indian Ocean commerce as well as a broadening of oceanic connections (Fleisher et al. 2015). Exploitation of deeper waters accompanies what must have been a more consistent engagement with the wider ocean based on different boat technologies. It is also linked to the development of a coastal merchant elite, whose consumption practices would have shaped local demand.

On the Comores and Madagascar, zooarchaeological studies are less well developed but return a remarkably similar picture. Sites of the "Dembeni phase" of the eighth to tenth centuries on the Comores are associated with a mixed assemblage of marine and terrestrial species. On Madagascar some of the earliest sites from the eighth century onwards are coastal scatters containing fish bone and shell with only sparse ceramics (Dewar and Wright 1993: 431). From the eleventh century onwards, more permanent sites on the Bay of Ampasindava in the north (Radimilahy 1998; Vérin 1986) and in the southeast of Madagascar are associated with mixed assemblages of marine and terrestrial fauna. Developing research on the southwest coast seems to be returning a long time depth to patterns of exploitation based on near-shore resources. Although the most compelling data is from the last two hundred years, zooarchaeological analysis has shown a strong dependence on coral communities for protein (Grealy et al. 2016). It seems this may reflect a long history in this region of using local and near-shore resources (Douglass and Zinke 2015).

Elsewhere in the Indian Ocean world, there is a similar emphasis on reef resources but no sense of this chronological shift to deeper-water species: near-shore and pelagic species appear side by side. Zooarchaeological studies of the Gulf and the Red Sea region have instead pointed to striking continuity in the ways the sea was exploited for fish throughout the medieval period. A detailed study of the Gulf reports on only a handful of sites from the medieval period (Beech 2004), however, Siraf and Jazirat al-Hulaylah both have records from the pre-Islamic to late Islamic periods (*c*. fourth/fifth to early sixteenth century) and contain remarkably similar assemblages, containing both smaller inshore fish such as emperors and also larger pelagic fish such as tuna. The larger numbers of sites from the latter end of this sequence, such as Julfar, offer the same picture, with a very broad range of fish being exploited across both inshore and pelagic species. In general, Beech emphasizes the long-standing exploitation of all the many marine environments of the Gulf over the long history of settlement in this region (Beech 2004: 3). Little chronological change is reported, even during periods of urban growth at sites such as Siraf. This may reflect the nature of some of these archaeological sites, which are large urban tells and the assemblages may relate to high-status housing rather than fish-processing areas or rubbish pits.

The assemblage of fish remains from the Red Sea port of Quseir al-Qadim, formerly Myos Hormos in the Roman period, offers a picture of mixed exploitation of reef and pelagic fish. Here, though, reef fish were much more common, with parrotfish dominating assemblages throughout the Islamic period (Hamilton-Dyer 2011: 262). At Quseir, fish were caught for local consumption and massive quantities of bone recovered near the harbor reflects the fact that fish was filleted before cooking. Yet parrotfish were also an important resource for drying; they were sent to the network of desert settlements that supplied Quseir, including desert trading halts. Fishing would therefore have been an important economic industry at the site and perhaps at other Red Sea ports too. Curiously, this is not reflected in the historical records of trade and daily life, not in the Cairo Genizah, nor in the important corpus of thirteenth-century documents recovered at Quseir itself from the so-called "Sheikh's house" (Guo 2004). The latter offers a remarkably full account of commerce through the town, with receipts and outgoings recorded in full. Many foodstuffs are listed, including honey and meat, but fish does not appear at all in the records. Dried parrotfish may have been processed for use as shipboard provisions but whatever explains its absence from the written records, this is a powerful illustration of the ways that fish and fishing practices could be simultaneously crucial to the subsistence economy and also beneath mention in documentary records. Similarly, although dietetics and cookery were important written genres in the Islamic world, fish-based recipes hardly feature here either as both are the product of landed urban elites at some remove from the coastal communities under discussion here.

It is often difficult to reconstruct how fish was cooked as part of what we might call "dishes" within larger meals. Larger reef fish such as parrotfish can yield sizeable fillets, as the processing at Quseir has revealed, and these cuts were probably consumed in stews, fresh or rehydrated. Smaller, bonier fish, are more easily cooked whole and their meat picked off by hand afterwards. Grilling on an open fire is a common cooking method, as seen in Figure 2.4, a photograph of fish grilling on the beach at Songo Mnara, Tanzania. As shown, the coconut-fringed shores of the Indian Ocean provided abundant and ready fuel for cooking.

FISH IN THE NORTH ATLANTIC

Contrary to expectations, fish was rarely eaten in the North Atlantic region before the Viking Age. In general, the period saw minimal exploitation of marine foodstuffs and in some places this may have amounted to a taboo on eating fish, since quantities consumed in England and around the North Sea were so low (Dobney and Ervynck 2007; Russ et al. 2012). Coastal communities in Scotland ate some fish, but much of this was from near-coastal and inshore habitats. Juvenile saithe (Pollachius virens) are common, along with an assortment of

FIGURE 2.4 Fish grilling over coconut shells on the beach at Songo Mnara, Tanzania. © Eréndira M. Quintana Morales.

others including the cod family (Gadidae), ling family (Lotidae), flatfish, and wrasse family (Labridae). Slight suggestions of deeper water fishing for large, mature fish are starting to appear from sites excavated with modern recovery methods (e.g., Harland 2016, 2019), leading to the suggestion that boat technology was more advanced prior to the Viking arrival than has hitherto been assumed. These larger fish include mature cod (Gadus morhua), which inhabit depths of 150 to 200 meters, and ling (Molva molva), which prefer 100 to 400 meter depths (Froese and Pauly 2019). The few Scottish sites with fish remains from the centuries before 800 indicate a low impact on marine resources; these communities fished occasionally but ate insufficient marine protein for it to impact on the isotopic composition in their bones, as is often found among communities eating high levels of marine foodstuffs (Barrett and Richards 2004). When they did fish, they primarily used coastal resources that would have been seasonally abundant, fishing directly or using fish traps and weirs. The pristine environments of Iceland and the Faroes were relatively untouched at the time of initial Viking settlement; anthropogenic activity in the first millennium CE on the Faroes was present but minor and unlikely to have had a profound impact on the marine environment (Church et al. 2013).

The significant increase in maritime connectivity that occurred across this region with the Viking Age was accompanied by an enormous increase in the scale of marine fishing, seen across the region in the zooarchaeological assemblages. During the ninth and tenth centuries, coastal locations became home to significant fishing communities, marked by rich fish middens. These fish were also traded onwards to inland locations, such as York (Barrett, Locker, and Roberts 2004; Harland and Barrett 2012). In coastal locations such as the Scottish Northern Isles, dense midden deposits are found in coastal locations from Orkney and Shetland, and have often been identified because of coastal erosion; sites include Quoygrew, Westray, St. Boniface, Papa Westray, and Pool, Sanday (Cerón-Carrasco 1998; Harland and Barrett 2012; Nicholson 2007). These are shell-rich, the many limpets found within them presumably used for bait although there is some controversy over their consumption (see below for East Africa). Evidence from Viking Age Iceland shows that fish remains were present in large quantities from the earliest settlements onwards. When sites were located inland these fish could include freshwater and migratory Salmonidae, including salmon, trout, and char, but marine fish and particularly cod were more common and were even brought some distance inland, for example to sites in the Mývatn region (Perdikaris and McGovern 2009). In Iceland salmon were fished using nets and contested ownership of river banks (riparian ownership) has left historic records, but these fish were much less important than the cod and ling families. Faroese evidence suggests fishing was part of subsistence living, alongside agriculture, throughout much of the Viking Age and medieval period (Dufeu 2018).

Yet the largest increase in the exploitation of marine fish in this region occurs around the year 1000. During the later years of the tenth and the early eleventh centuries, the quantities of fish found at inland settlements increases markedly (Barrett, Locker, and Roberts 2004). This chronological moment has been dubbed the Fish Event Horizon (FEH) due to the consistent and compelling evidence for massive growth in ocean fish exploitation at this time. Archaeologist James Barrett suggests that this was the origin point for historical practices of over-fishing that have led toward contemporary population scarcity in these waters. In the Northern Isles, a proto-commercial fishery is in evidence during the eleventh century. The fish middens contain cod and related species such as saithe and ling, and together these comprise almost all of the fish taxa found. They are primarily larger, older fish of at least 80 centimeters total length, indicating a specialized fishery operating in open waters. From the eleventh century there is little change in the types of fish represented, but there is an increasing density of fish deposition at this time and an increase in the proportion of fish to mammal compared with earlier centuries. This intensification of fishing is contemporary with an increase in dairying (Critch, Harland, and Barrett 2018), a development that still requires satisfactory explanation.

In the Baltic islands, herring had long been the fish of choice, with the exploitation of herring shoals as old as settlement here (Benecke 1982; Enghoff 1999). Herring are biologically very different from the cod and ling families. They are small, young shoaling fish that are caught with nets, and because of their oil content, they need to be brined, salted, or smoked if not eaten when very fresh. In other areas, their exploitation increased during the eleventh century, as part of a more commercial pattern. They are almost completely absent from the Scottish zooarchaeological record for the Northern Isles. The Western Isles do have herring found archaeologically, and these then come to dominate in the thirteenth century and for the remainder of the medieval period as at Bornais Mound 1 and Mound 3 (Cartledge et al. 2012; Ingrem 2005). At this time herring begin to be found in inland assemblages in some quantities, as part of a trade in preserved fish that relied significantly on gadids (cod and herring). This was part of a significant shift for inland subsistence that saw a move away from freshwater fishing (perhaps due to overexploitation) and toward marine fish in the diet of urban populations. Barrett, Locker, and Roberts (2004) trace a transition at multiple centers across the British Isles around these years, including York, London, Southampton, Norwich, and Northampton. At all these sites, the quantities of marine fish consumed increase massively during the eleventh and twelfth centuries. This must reflect a shift among fishing communities, both toward exploiting deeper waters using different technologies and toward fishing for commercial purposes. It is a shift that is mirrored in urban assemblages across Europe, with sites in northern France, Belgium (Van Neer and Ervynck 2003), and Poland giving a similar picture. This growth in cod and herring fishing and the blossoming of a marketized economy in marine fish enters the written historical record more slowly. The herring fairs of the Sound, the Baltic, and East Anglia are documented in the eleventh and twelfth centuries (Barrett, Locker, and Roberts 2004: 624–5), but most historical data on the fish trade dates from the thirteenth century and beyond. By the thirteenth century, fish and fishing practices can be seen in legal frameworks, with herring ranked alongside salmon and above cod according to thirteenth-century law (Dufeu 2018: 154). In visual art too, a new familiarity with fish species becomes evident, for example in the representation of fish from the Northumberland Bestiary, produced in northern England around 1250 to 1260.

FISHING TECHNOLOGIES

Fishing technologies in eastern Africa have been understood through the lens of recent ethnographies (Nakamura 2011; Prins 1965). These point to a wide range of fishing and trapping technologies exploiting the variety of coastal habitats and species (see Quintana Morales and Horton 2014: table 2 for summary). In applying these to the region's medieval past, Quintana Morales and Horton (2014) have made the case for small-scale net and basket trapping on the reefs during the earlier period (seventh to tenth century); they associate the shift to pelagic fish from the eleventh century with a shift in fishing technology toward larger boats and drift nets; this in turn is tied to increasing wealth differentiation.

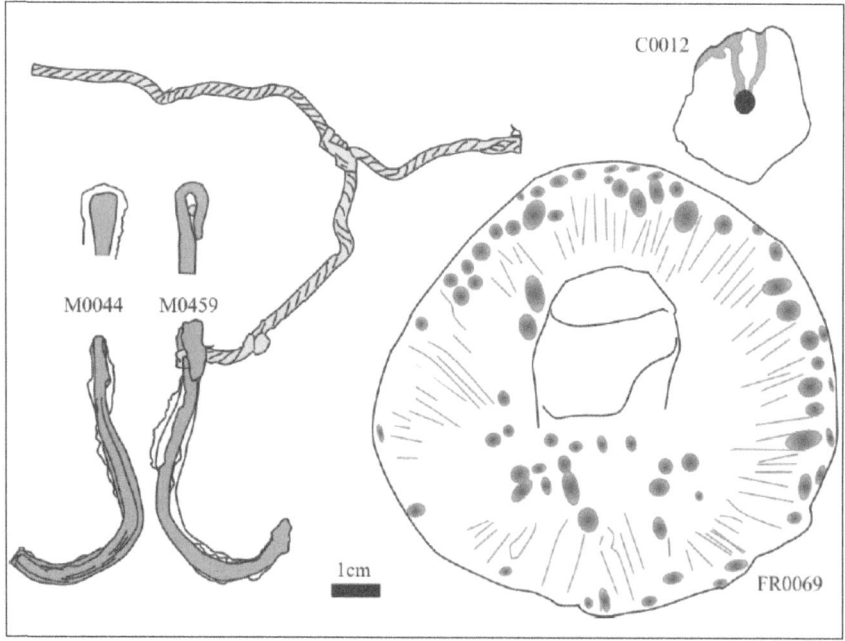

FIGURE 2.5 "Fishing technology from the Islamic layers of Quseir al-Qadim, Red Sea," from Peacock and Blue (2011: ch15). © R. Thomas.

Archaeologically, direct evidence for fishing equipment is not abundant in the western Indian Ocean. Fish hooks have been found at sites on Pemba, at Shanga, and on Madagascar but are few in number. The evidence from Quseir al-Qadim is much more abundant, and due to the wonderful preservation conditions at the site it includes a broad range of materials (Thomas 2011). Metal fish hooks, as seen in Figure 2.5, and ceramic net weights are complemented by surviving fishing line and nets of camel hair and fine mesh. Overall, these suggest that line fishing was more common than net fishing (Thomas 2011: 218), yet this is at odds with the zooarchaeological data for a majority of noncarnivorous fish; these do not take bait so need to be caught by net (Hamilton-Dyer 2011: 265). Yet by far the most common fishing objects are wooden gorges (88 of 128 artifacts). These would be attached to a line and laid at the bottom of the sea to be swallowed by fish. This technology was also widely used in the Gulf during all periods (Beech 2004). In both locations, the general pattern is of a diverse set of strategies deployed to gain maximum benefit from a range of environments. This resonates with ethnographies of small-scale communities today and speaks to a dispersed and skilled workforce without central control.

The large, mature cod, ling, and related species found in the North Atlantic were caught using lines, often made from twisted horsehair (Fenton 1978: 244, 534), with multiple baited hooks. Nets for these species were first mentioned historically with the opening of the Newfoundland fishery in the fifteenth century (Nedkvitne 2014: 526), and there is no evidence of nets being used in the medieval North Atlantic for cod and related species prior to this period. However, herring are relatively small, shoaling fish and their capture does require netting. In those places where herring were exploited, we must infer that nets were in use.

Knowledge of medieval boats in the North Atlantic comes, for the preChristian period, from boat burials and occasional though iconic finds of larger ships, including the Skuldelev 2. Boat burials include the Ardnamurchan boat burial of the early tenth century on the west coast of Scotland, 5.1 meters in length (Harris et al. 2017), and the late ninth/tenth century Scar boat burial on Orkney of 7.2 meters in length (Owen and Dalland 1999). Excavations of Viking Age pre-Christian boat burials in Dysnes, Iceland, indicate lengths of at least 6 meters (Gestsdóttir et al. 2017). These are typical of the small boats of less than 7 or 8 meters, which make up most of the known Viking Age and medieval vessels (Owen and Dalland 1999). These small boats were easily dragged ashore where they were stored in "nausts," simple earthen enclosures that provided shelter; many of these survive today. Scottish yoles are a direct continuation of Norse building styles: these are small, open boats of between 5.8 and 7.3 meters length, typically with two pairs of oars (Miller 2008: table 5.3, 107). Larger boats with three pairs of oars developed in Shetland for mature cod, ling, and related species with long lines in the Northern Isles, and similar boats were used for the herring net-based fishery around the Highlands (107–10). These boats were all small, open vessels, holding only small numbers of fishers who were skilled at navigating the sea and the tides, making repeated trips to bring home very large fish.

SHELLFISH: BAIT, HARDSHIP FOOD, AND TABOO

As emerges from the discussion above, shellfish represent another important coastal resource and played an important role as bait. Nevertheless, in spite of being a consistent substrate of the faunal assemblage in both areas, their exploitation remains poorly studied as an aspect of coastal subsistence and many questions remain about their consumption. At Quseir, there is a vertiginous decline in shellfish exploitation from the Roman to the Islamic periods. Hamilton-Dyer suggests this might be related to food taboos and that shellfish might have been a *haram* foodstuff (2011: 265). In fact, while the meat of scavenger animals was forbidden in Islam, as in Judaism, shellfish represented an exception, at least in Sunnism where their consumption was "discouraged" (*makrūh*) but not forbidden. Only Twelver Shias formally prohibited the consumption of shellfish (Glassé 2001: 148). The persistence of shellfish in smaller numbers in the Islamic layers of Quseir might thus be attributable either to their continued consumption by a small number of Sunni Muslims undeterred by shellfish's designation as *makrūh*, or perhaps to the use of shellfish as bait in fishing.

Yet these explanations appear to be contradicted by evidence for the continued importance of shellfish in the diet of East African Muslims. At sites throughout the medieval period, remains from shellfish consumption are common on the Swahili coast (Quintana Morales and Prendergast 2018). Despite this they have rarely been the explicit focus of archaeological study and so the assemblages that can be quantified are few (Christie 2011; Faulkner et al. 2018; Fleisher 2003; Wilson and Omar 1997). On the Mozambique coast, an area admittedly beyond the main centers of Swahili Islamization further to the north, the shell middens associated with sites such as Chibuene (seventh to fourteenth century) are over 5 meters tall, reflecting an incredible intensity of collection and consumption that dwarfs the faunal record. Shellfish are often today regarded as a hardship food (Msemwa 1994) and this ethnographic categorization means they have been used as an index of dietary abundance and of status for the past; the assumption is that shellfish would have been avoided by groups with other options (Christie 2011; Douglass and Zinke 2015). Yet it seems likely that in the past shellfish held a less marginal status in relation to other protein sources. As mentioned, they are abundant in sites of all periods and their exploitation follows the chronology of fish exploitation more generally, with a peak during the seventh to tenth century and a decline thereafter as domestic fauna became more common in the archaeological record (Fleisher 2003). Nonetheless, shells of marine molluscs used for food remain abundant in the archaeological record of both small settlements and large, affluent towns such as Kilwa Kisiwani and Songo Mnara (Wynne-Jones and Fleisher 2016). Their association with low social status might perhaps need to be revised.

In the North Atlantic, substantial quantities of shells are often found in conjunction with fish remains, and limpets (Patella sp.) are frequently the most common of these, followed by common periwinkle (Littorina littorina). A variety of other bivalves and gastropods are also found in smaller quantities. Some areas show preferences toward certain species, perhaps reflecting local availability and cultural preferences. For example, common mussels (Mytilus edulis) are the most common taxa at the Icelandic site of Akurvík (Amundsen et al. 2005: table 5). Limpet usage is controversial: were they used for bait or deliberately eaten? Ethnographic accounts from Scotland describe limpets as both bait for inshore fishing (Fenton 2008: 99), as famine food (Fenton 1978: 542), and conversely also as "love meat or kissing meat," to be eaten as a special meal by the bride and groom on the evening before their marriage ceremony (Muir and Irvine 2005: 98). Their use as pig food has also been suggested (Sharples 2005: 159). Limpets were present in substantial quantities at the Norse site of Bornais Mound 3, in the Hebrides, even though the site is 2.5 kilometers from the nearest limpet-rich coastline—thus suggesting that there was a value in bringing back live limpets to the settlement. While the excavator believed this could be for human consumption—"having consumed limpets I can testify that they are not unpleasant eating" (159)—isotopic evidence from human bones does not evidence the wide-scale consumption of shellfish (Milner and Barrett 2012: 113). It therefore appears that most of the shellfish found archaeologically may have been used as bait for fishing, although small quantities may have been consumed by humans on special occasions.

COMMERCE AND SOCIAL ORGANIZATION

How did fish and fisheries contribute to the developing world of international commerce that characterized these centuries? When did farmer-fishers start to specialize and become part of commercial fishing practices? In this respect, the two regions differ immensely. This relates to the types of fish being exploited and the nature of terrestrial networks creating a demand for fish away from the coast. It may also reflect a different form of market economy.

The development of the marketized trade in consumables such as fish characterizes the high medieval period of Europe. Initial fishing practices throughout the North Atlantic were subsistence-based, and part of a seasonal round that included agricultural activities. The Fish Event Horizon in the North Atlantic and associated terrestrial regions seems to represent a shift toward commercialized fishing practices, differing in scale, nature, and social organization. These took place within a maritime culture, one that featured boats, landing places, and maritime knowledge (Westerdahl 1992, 2008), and fishing for large cod and ling family fish required considerable fishing skills. Land-based processing shows some of these large fish were air-dried to form a preserved product, alongside plentiful evidence for fresh consumption. Commercial fishing, in contrast, creates a surplus product that is sold to the ultimate consumer, often using intermediaries (Dufeu 2018: 58) and with an infrastructure that could include landing, processing, and storage facilities. The fishers creating these products might still be operating within the seasonal agricultural round, and the fishing technologies themselves may be unchanged from subsistence fishing, but a degree of intensification is expected at this stage. The preserved fish could be traded for luxuries or staples, to pay rents, tithes, and dues, and they could also enter into commercial economies.

Commercial fishing in Norway dates to the late eleventh century (Nielsen in Starkey et al., *History of the North Atlantic Fisheries*, quoted in Dufeu 2018: 29), and the intensification of fishing seen in contemporary middens in the Scottish Northern Isles from the eleventh century (Harland and Barrett 2012) gives further credence to the idea that commercial (or proto-commercial) fishing was probably operating from this time. An Icelandic regulation from 1200 states that fish—presumably cod—could only be sold fresh on the day it was caught, otherwise it could only be sold as fish that was dried at the homestead. Dried fish were given a recognized value from around 930 (when 15.3 fish were equal to a single silver eyrir, or about 27 grams of silver), and later values indicate dried fish became more valuable over time (Dufeu 2018: 84–5). Could this regulation and valuations indicate these dried fish were entering the commercial economy? Icelandic dried fish started to arrive in English ports in the early thirteenth century, though given that Iceland was starting to come under Norwegian control the origins and owners of the trading ships are questionable (88). Icelandic historic sources stated that commercial fishing for export started in the early fourteenth century, when customs revenues on processed dried fish started to be significant for the first time (16, 23–4, 27), a date that can probably be pushed back to the late thirteenth century, when textual evidence shows dried fish were traded for imported goods (Gardiner and Mehler 2007: 389). The fourteenth century is also a significant date for the development of commercial fishing in the Faroes (Dufeu 2018: 33). This trade continues today: the air-dried and salted cod from the North Atlantic region are used to make traditional *bacalao/bacalhau* recipes in southern European countries such as Italy and Portugal. The dried and salted fish is prepared by multiple soakings, and can also be beaten for softening. Medieval recipes include boiling, "stewed with ginger and saffron, with cream, onions and lard, or fried with nuts and almonds" (Wubs-Mrozewicz 2009: 187).

It is worth noting quickly that fish were not the only natural products exploited for maritime commerce. The Norse settlers of the North Atlantic had a huge range of marine resources available to them. Some of these were exotics and thus appear in the historical records, including the polar bear furs and walrus ivory and hides of the Norðurseta, the Northern Hunting Grounds of Greenland (Frei et al. 2015; Star et al. 2018), and live Icelandic gyrfalcons (Mehler, Küchelmann, and Holterman 2018) valued for their hunting prowess. Whales are not common finds in the archaeological record, but they would have been scavenged for food, oil, and raw materials (including bone) when stranded, and some limited hunting of smaller species was probably undertaken when needed (Szabo 2008).

The shift in urban consumption practices that drove this commercialization was complex and differed from place to place. Marine resources were, in places such as London, replacing freshwater fish types that had been overfished or become unsustainable as sources of protein for growing populations (Orton et al. 2014). Demand was driven by an emergent urban elite and their demand for fish like herring and cod. The Christian elite may also have been involved, and church involvement in controlling access to Iceland's riverine and marine fisheries is documented from the mid-twelfth century, seen to indicate commercial fishing (Dufeu 2018: 83). It is possible that taxes paid from Iceland and the Faroes to Norway from the early eleventh century were in the form of dried fish (96), perhaps firstly being caught and processed by subsistence fisher-farmers who used fish to pay rents and dues to their chieftains, who then entered into small-scale commercial trade to pay taxes to Norway. Icelandic and Faroese chieftains formed allegiances to Norway from the eleventh century, in return for privilege and power, even though both archipelagos were nominally still independent, they may have exchanged dried fish in return and "it can be argued that such allegiance led to a kind of commercial partnership or commonwealth between Norwegians and Icelanders" (99–101). In part, there may also have been influences from the Christian church at this time, due to the adoption of Benedictine fasting practices in the tenth century that would have created demand for fish on fast days. This explanation is, however, far from universally accepted with James Barrett and others (Barrett, Locker, and Roberts 2004) refuting this causality. Nevertheless, literary scholars such as Allen J. Frantzen are now integrating this archaeological material with their sources to interpret what this change signifies for Anglo-Saxon England and ultimately the cultural history of the sea (Frantzen 2014: 232–45).

The shifts in social organization that this produced for fishing communities are imagined by Westerdahl (2008) based on modern ethnographies combined with historical data. He describes multiple areas of activity, from the people who manned the port infrastructures to military and commercial sailors. He suggests that many of these categories date back to the Hanse sailors of the fifteenth century, while they rest upon a foundation of the "small" world of the fisherman/farmers (Westerdahl 2008: 196). This latter world provides a backdrop to contemporary cultures of the North Sea and Baltic regions and produces cultural connections and unity across a multilingual, multinational sphere. This is, Westerdahl suggests, due to a set of common preoccupations with the world of the sea: with directions, combinations of time and distance. Based on cultural and ethnographic evidence, labor was probably divided and while it is unlikely that women fished, they were involved in all aspects of preparing and processing (Dufeu 2018: 44; Coull 1996: 49–50).

Until well into the post-medieval period, farming and fishing were two aspects of the same economic system throughout the North Atlantic, a system aimed firstly at providing sustenance for immediate family, and secondly to provide surplus food products—fish, dairy—for payments and trade. Scottish evidence shows that fish middens accumulated within domestic farmsteads, illustrating the dual sea- and land-based economics. Iceland does have some evidence for both temporary and permanent fishing stations from the thirteenth century (Dufeu 2018: 149)—a logical solution given that inland farms could be some distance from the sea, and a solution not needed in Northern Scotland or the Faroes. Akurvík is one such example, a beach site with fishing "booths," probably seasonally occupied (189).

By contrast, in the western Indian Ocean, there is little evidence for the commercialization of fishing practice in the medieval period. Instead, fish and fishing continued to provide an underlying subsistence base to settlement here, while commercial activity focused elsewhere. This may perhaps have been caused by the limited possibilities for transporting and preserving fish in tropical climates, but was also probably linked to the arena in which interaction and commerce was occurring. The Indian Ocean rim was interconnected by trade in raw materials that were lacking in some regions and abundant in others—the movement of mangrove wood from eastern Africa to the treeless Gulf is one such example. A significant trade in luxury goods such as glazed ceramics, glass and glass beads, ivory, and gold was also the impetus for oceanic commerce. Fish did not fit either of these categories, as a staple foodstuff found ubiquitously across the region. A few historical mentions suggest that dried fish may have been moved around oceanic networks. A mid-fourteenth century late Yuan source, Wang Ta-Yuan's *Tao-i Chih-lueh*, mentions dried fish as a product of the Maldives and fish are mentioned alongside cowries as local Maldivian commodities in later, fifteenth-century, Ming texts (Ptak 1987: 677, 686). One important literary source is the *Mānasollāsa* (Delight of the Mind), a Sanskrit "mirror for princes" composed around 1129 to 1130 by King Someśvara III of the Western Chalukya dynasty based in India's western Deccan region, which includes an extensive discussion of the freshwater and sea fish consumed at court (Sadhale and Nene 2005). The source is, however, silent about the fishing communities and practices that produced these catches, and indeed about the networks of exchange through which these fish were acquired. In most coastal areas it appears that while fish were widely eaten, either fresh or preserved, they were not part of the repertoire of long or even middle-distance commercial goods. A twelfth-century list of luggage written in Malabar in India for a journey to the Yemen lists "two waterskins of *hūt* fish," likely some kind of dried fish, among the provisions (Lambourn 2018), but there is no evidence for a wider commercial trade in fish out of Malabar.

In contrast, other marine products sometimes became heavily commercialized. Ambergris, a heavily scented excretion produced in the digestive system of the sperm whale, is mentioned as an export commodity from Africa by al-Masudi in his tenth-century *Murūj al-dhahab wa-ma ʿādin al-jawhar* (Meadows of Gold and Mines of Gems). Shell was also used as key raw materials for manufacture and as objects for trade. On the eastern African coast, marine shell was used to make disc-shaped beads from at least the seventh century onwards. The scale of this industry is demonstrated by the evidence for bead-grinders: ceramic sherds with diagnostic grooves where they have been used to smooth cylinders of Anadara (sp.) shell that was subsequently cut into discs (Flexner, Fleisher, and Adria LaViolette 2008). It has normally been assumed that these beads were produced for onward transit to interior markets; this is to some extent supported by finds from sites hundreds of kilometers from the coast in central Tanzania (Walz 2010). This industry declined from the eleventh century as glass beads from South Asia became more easily available to coastal and inland markets. Cowrie shells seem still to have been used as beads into the later medieval period. At some sites they were so numerous as to suggest their use as a form of currency (Kirkman 1964). Cowries were also an item of trade, although recent research has suggested multiple routes by which they were acquired. Sources in the Maldives were mined for commercial purposes, being traded onward into trans-Saharan and West African markets as well as eastwards into Bengal and Yunan in China, while eastern African sites more commonly used local sources (Haour, Christie, and Jaufar 2016). Elsewhere, esoteric shell industries existed, such as the beads fashioned from aragonite (giant clam shell) found in the deposits of Kilwa region, notably at Songo Mnara.

As discussed by Roxani Margariti in this volume, these industries were dwarfed by the pearling industry, which provided an enormous economic focus to fishing activities in the Gulf and the Gulf of Mannar between Sri Lanka and southern India from prehistoric times until very recently (Carter 2005). The world of fishing and subsistence described by the archaeologies stands in contrast to the world of commercialized pearling in which seasonal workers were employed to dive for pearls by rich urban elites. In East Africa by contrast, small-scale producers fished for local requirements. Some of the larger fish types represented in thirteenth- to fifteenth-century Swahili merchant houses (Horton and Mudida 1993; Quintana Morales and Horton 2014) may represent the control of ships and fisherfolk by richer inhabitants. Yet the larger picture is similar to the world described by more recent ethnographies, which document fishing societies whose women, men, and children all work to collect shellfish and to fish for larger catches from canoes in the coral reefs of the Indian Ocean; their diet consists predominantly of fish and other marine resources. These ethnographies of communities from Madagascar (Astuti 1995) to the Andaman coast (Hope 2002) demonstrate how fishing can define and shape a coastal community. Subsistence practices do more than simply providing food, they bring a set of technologies, skills, and activities to the forefront of daily existence.

CONCLUSIONS AND FUTURE DIRECTIONS

The commercialization of fishing through the medieval period in the North Atlantic contributed to what currently appears to have been a key difference between the two regions being compared here. Archaeology provides data that written sources do not, demonstrating that around 1000 CE, the food culture of the British Isles and other regions of the North Atlantic substantially changed in perhaps as little as half a century. From eating no or little fish, Europeans became mass consumers of sea fish. But besides fundamentally changing food cultures, the production of fish for trade brings with it a wealth of infrastructure in the form of people, spaces, and technologies. It also seems to have created a more professional group of fishermen and sailors with their own world that brought with it particular knowledge and worldviews. With the exception of some evidence from Iceland (Wilson 2016), this was overwhelmingly a male world, although the entire community would have been included in the processing of the catch. It stands in contrast to the picture of fishing practices from the Indian Ocean during the same period.

Yet, in both regions we can see similarities across the period between 800 and 1450. These are created by the communities of practice formed by those participating in the world of fishing, which create groups that cross-cut national, linguistic, and political boundaries. Communities of practice collaborate over a long period of time, sharing ideas and strategies, creating solutions and building innovations. The fishing communities of the medieval period achieved this through the networks of maritime knowledge and skill, their shared engagement with the sea, over long periods and across regions connected by water rather than by sociopolitical categories. These communities were dynamic, they responded to shifting political and economic circumstances, increasing demand, or to commercial possibilities in the form of dried herring, or pearls from the Gulf. They also created some of those shifts, through the creative ways they engaged with the oceans. The medieval period is often characterized by its increasing interconnectivity, the opening up of new routes and connections between places. The maritime space was crucial in this dynamic and it was carried on the backs of the fishing communities that maintained and developed knowledge of tides, currents, and winds, who pioneered the struggles with the sea that would come to shape the world. A bigger question nevertheless remains about the extent to which East Africa is paradigmatic of the wider Indian Ocean littoral where zooarchaeological data is currently sparse and only literary texts and a few documentary sources fill the void, if at all. While premodern literary references paint a consistent picture of fish consumption around coastal India (Achaya 1994), in these regions, for the moment, we have little detail about the species consumed, their preparation, or indeed their wider trade before the fourteenth or fifteenth centuries. Although all the archaeological layers at the early port site of Bhanbhore in Sind in present-day Pakistan are reported to be teeming with fish remains, these remain unrecovered and thus unstudied. The material and findings from the Red Sea and East African coast will hopefully spur greater attention to the systematic recovery of zooarchaeological remains during excavations elsewhere around the Indian Ocean, allowing far more extensive comparison between the Atlantic and Indian Ocean worlds and with it a better understanding of Europe's apparently very distinctive food culture.

CHAPTER THREE

Networks

Thicker and Quicker by Water

JONATHAN SHEPARD

Networks comprise persons scattered amidst disparate societies but sharing kinship, beliefs, or material interests and communicating in some way, or exchanging goods. Varying in degrees of intensity, and strung between multiple nodes, networks can be understood through the theoretical modeling of the diffusion of "weak links" of information, goods, and ideas leapfrogging distances between nodes, and also far-flung elites maintaining their collective identity through connectivity (De Weerdt 2016; Granovetter 1983; Sindbæk 2007). Data for our period is, however, seldom sufficient to sustain such models. One may simply view networks as a spectrum. At one end are exchanges between opposites, as in the silent trade, whereby commodities are exchanged without face-to-face meetings (Bonner 2011; *Russian Primary Chronicle* 1953: 184). At the other are networks whose participants forge cultures of their own—flexible cultures not entailing total commitment.

It is no accident that silent trading took place on land, whereas maritime networks and riverways harbored hybrid cultures. Long sea voyages were chancier, often requiring port cities. Some of these cities lay inland, such as Jenne Jeno on the Inland Niger Delta between the savannah of the Sahel and the wooded and wetter climes further south; from the Sahel, desert-caravans made for the Mediterranean. Such interconnectedness also features at Fustat, for example.

Maritime networks were not easily policed and they were—literally—well placed to transport commodities long distances. Deluxe goods made for the most profit, but other indispensable items such as salt and iron, lacking in some locales, had to be shipped in, sometimes from afar. Water transport was generally cheaper, especially for bulky goods, even if held up by the weather (Duncan-Jones 1982: 367–8; Horden and Purcell 2000; Walsh 2014: 64–7; Preiser-Kapeller 2015); slaves, heavy yet pricey and self-propelling, could cover vast distances (Shepard 2021).

Exotica provided a stimulus to long-range communications, especially of elites intent on exchanging "prestige goods" with others. Gift exchanges could stabilize relationships or, if one party's gifts outshone another's, signal the latter's inferiority. Crafted goods were thought to partake of their makers' extraordinary abilities—all the more so for coming from over the horizon, "Out-There" (Helms 1993). Among items long sought after was "incense," a term covering myrrh and frankincense, for worship and other rites invoking unearthly powers. From Southern Arabia and East Africa, incense traveled around the Indian Ocean and Mediterranean (Biedermann 2010; Groom 1981; Peacock and Williams 2007). Notions of a higher order "beyond the sea" feature among the Rus who, according to the *Russian Primary Chronicle*, invited such a prince to come and govern them (*Russian Primary Chronicle* 1953: 59) or the Aztecs who reportedly took Cortes for an emissary of Quetzalcoatl, if not the god himself (Hassig 2006).

Maritime networks abound in Afro-Eurasia, partly thanks to geography: Australia has few rivers flowing into the sea; likewise the west coast of South America. And the vastness of the Pacific told against even spasmodic long-distance communications, impressive long-distance migrations notwithstanding (Figure 0.7). Oceanic coastlines lacking a shield, such as the Caribbean islands offered for Mayan seafarers (McKillop 2005), could still foster networks. Medium-haul nexuses encompassed the West African coast and rivers such as the Senegal, while the Niger led to different ecosystems and, ultimately, the Mediterranean (Oliver and Atmore 2001: 2–3; Green 2012: 31–3, 46–57). Conversely, the dearth of such waterways on Africa's eastern coast perhaps stimulated maritime communications, especially as seafarers benefited from key assets: waters were navigable even by simple craft, with the term dhow covering a miscellany of sailboats (Oliver and Atmore 2001: 5–6, 194–8). Secondly, other landmasses and islands lay within reach—the Arabian Peninsula and points in th east. Thirdly, monsoons put wind in vessels' sails on both outward and return voyages to places with diverse ecologies (Figure 1.2). This lessened—without ever lifting—ocean-crossing perils (Campbell 2016: 1–3). Moreover the Malay Peninsula's port cities offered regional produce and access to East Asian goods, while the Red Sea led toward inland seas washing several peninsulas belonging to a continent that is arguably one itself: Europe

(Ohler 2010: 3). It is, then, unsurprising if the only maritime network plausibly describable as "oceanic" was long that encompassing the Indian Ocean. Our survey traces stages of development there, in Eurasia's inland seas, and in the North Atlantic. Thanks to riverways, there was by *c*. 1000 interconnectedness of things, persons, and sometimes, ideas. As commerce expanded, routes tended to segment into circuits dominated by specialists. Networks of culturally introverted communities undertook long-distance commerce, while agrarian societies formed supply chains without participating in maritime societies. Yet port cities could, literally, harbor new cults and ambitions. Such contrasts are a feature of maritime networks.

c. 800–c. 1000: PROFIT, PORCELAIN, AND BELIEFS

Networks spanning the Indian Ocean rim around 800 were of long standing:

> It is the nature of people in this land [Persia] (to love exchange and) trade. They constantly sail ships […] into the southern ocean towards the Land of the Lion [Sri Lanka], to obtain all manner of precious things […]. They also sail their ships to Han territory, right up to Canton, to obtain such things as damask silk and silk floss.
>
> (Dudbridge 2018: 303)

The Korean-born author wrote from experience: heeding his Indian-born teachers in China, Hye ch'o sailed to their homeland along seaways constituting a single organic system. Seeking wisdom in Indian monasteries appeared desirable to Chinese Buddhist monks, with perhaps a year or two's stopover at a monastery in Srivijaya in south Sumatra. Pilgrims went this way too (Dudbridge 2018: 304).

In Hye ch'o's day Islam was still a newcomer. Yet the ocean was "an Arab Mediterranean" from the eighth century on (Wink 1990–2004: 1, 65), Islam reaching areas barely touched by Eurasian norms. Along the African coast settlements began to form, exchanging ivory, gold, rock crystal from the interior for deluxe goods. Local elites made the running, adopting the religion of the traffickers while seeing to overland supply chains. A hybrid language emerged: Swahili. Tellingly, the name derives from the Arabic *sawāhil* (coasts). The singular *sāhil* meant both "shore" and "entrepôt" and in the latter sense gave its name to the Sahel (Beaujard 2012: 2:102). Not that Africans were landlubbers, the dynamic of "the Swahili Corridor" came from the sea (Horton 1987; Horton and Middleton 2000: 52–64). Around the time Swahili-speakers began adopting Islam in the mid-eighth century, Zoroastrian and Jewish merchants were voyaging between the Gulf and China. Literary and epigraphic sources from either destination attest this (Guy 2017; Silverstein 2007). So does underwater archaeology.

Sometime around 830 a cargo vessel returning to the Gulf sank off Belitung Island. Its cargo comprised high-fired Chinese stoneware and porcelain, much of it from Changsha. On thousands of bowls were motifs catering for faraway tastes, pseudo-Arabic calligraphy, plants and birds (Heng 2019; Krahl et al. 2010). Direct sailing between the Gulf and Chinese ports ceased early in the tenth century, yet nexuses persisted. Innovations in glassmaking under Abbasid auspices prompted mass production of flagons and jars (Henderson 2016). Some were shipped to China, as two tenth-century wrecks of Southeast Asian build bear witness to (Guy 2019): the boats had been plying between Sumatra, Sri Lanka or South India, before sinking off Intan and Cirebon. The Intan wreck carried twenty thousand bowls made by Chinese potters, perhaps expatriates. Pearls and, probably, incense were aboard too (Stargardt 2014: 44–50). These cargoes attest journeys shorter than that of the Belitung wreck, segmentation being a process not uncommon with maritime networks.

The momentum from the mid-eighth century onwards came from the combined manufacturing and purchasing power of the Abbasid caliphate and Tang China. Their opulence owed much to tax revenues. Yet for all the Abbasid's resources, prosperity sprang essentially from an Islamic "single market" (Bessard 2020). This carried on whatever the turmoil amongst ruling elites. Maritime networks straddling the Mediterranean and Black Seas were peripheral. Byzantium and the Christian West belonged to the *dār al-harb*, the "land of war," against which believers must wage jihad. Navigation along the North African coast was fraught although feasible, whereas overland routes benefited from Roman road systems and Arab expertise with camels. Among the goods borne south were beads and glasswares manufactured in the Levant or points still further east. These have come to light at, for example, Jenne Jeno (Brill 1995; McIntosh and McIntosh 1981) and Ibgo-Ukwu (Nigeria) (Haour 2007: 44, 90–7, 103; Magnavita 2013).

One should not, though, dismiss the Mediterranean as a Dead Sea. Cultural and religious ties bound the Christian West to the Holy Land, seaborne pilgrimages never ceasing. Charlemagne provided for Holy Land shrines, even endowing a pilgrims' hostel (McCormick 2011). He also tried to seize Venice. Charlemagne's interest is a measure of commerce's resurgence after previous disruptions: finds of containers of wine and oil from Byzantium and the Levant proliferate in the Upper Adriatic from the early ninth century on (Gelichi 2018: 15–17; Budak 2018). Perishable imports left no trace, for instance, fruits and spices. But clues survive in cathedral treasuries: Byzantine and Muslim silks (Muthesius 1997). No less suggestive are the incense burners beginning to feature in Western sources (Mayr-Harting 1992; Thietmar of Merseberg 1957: 66–7). Indeed, the fact that raiding became rife, with venturers from al-Andalus taking over Crete as Roxani Margariti discusses in her chapter on "Islands and Shores," shows what spoils were attainable if raiding alternated with slave trading. Towns such as Amalfi and North African coastal centers prospered. It is no accident that Amalfitans were among the first Westerners to establish themselves in Constantinople, wheeling and dealing between Muslims and Byzantines (Horden and Purcell 2000: 117–18, 168; Magdalino 2000: 219–22; McCormick 2001: 420–1, 626–30).

In these conditions, the Byzantine government controlled communications between the Mediterranean and the Black Sea. For instance, when the Jewish vizier of the Umayyad court in al-Andalus sought information about Khazaria, the Judaizing polity on the lower Volga, his seaborne envoys were held up at Constantinople; only overland contact proved feasible (Golb and Pritzak 1982: 79–86). Conversely, networks linking Khazaria with the Islamic world and societies to its west thrived (Figure 3.1). The Abbasid caliphate and, from around 900, the Samanids in Central Asia struck millions of gold and silver coins, known as dinars and dirhams. Many were bartered for northern produce; first and foremost furs, but also slaves, wax, and walrus ivory. Some 83,500 dirhams are known from Sweden (Gruszczyński 2019; Gruszczyński, Jankowiak, and Shepard 2021). Representing a fraction of the silver originally brought, they corroborate words put into the mouth of pirates in a saint's *Life*, spurning the citizens of Birka's attempt to buy them off, they declared: "any merchant has the means to pay at least 100 pounds of silver!" (Franklin and Shepard 1996: 18). This occurred not long before something happened to prevent a hoard weighing 67 kilograms and kept beneath a workshop floor on Gotland from being melted down (Östergren 2009). In 865 the Danes invaded England. Besides striking coins, the invaders brought dirhams: Abbasid and Samanid silver dirhams, as well as silver coins from as far away as eastern India, have been found across Britain. Figure 3.2 shows silver items from the Silverdale hoard, deposited around 900 in Lancashire, which included several Abbasid dirhams. Some hundred dirham fragments have been found in Torksey (Lincolnshire), site of the Danish winter-camp in 871/2. Two fragments struck respectively in 864/5 and between 866 and 868 took six or seven years at most to arrive from Central Asia (Blackburn 2011: 230; Woods 2021).

Networks leading to northwest Europe facilitated such speed. Ibn Fadlan offers a glimpse of them some fifty years later. He was dispatched by the Abbasid government to the Volga Bulgars, whose ruler had requested Islamic instructors, builders, and money. Ibn Fadlan went by caravan via the Samanid realm, now the prime source of the dirhams reaching the Baltic rim. But the Rus he met at the Bulgar capital on the Volga had come by boat. He saw them disembark and offer prayers to wooden idols: "Oh my Lord, I have come from a distant land, with such and such a number of young slave-girls and such and such a number of sables" (Ibn Fadlan 2012: 47–8). Their lifestyle culminated in what Ibn Fadlan describes as a leader's cremation with his slave-girl in a boat-burning. Certain rites, symbolizing her marriage to her late master, bear

FIGURE 3.1 Map of Central and Eastern Europe showing the river connections between the eastern Mediterranean, Black Sea, and Caspian with the Baltic and North Seas. © Sebastian Ballard.

FIGURE 3.2 Silver from the Silverdale hoard, including Abbasid dirhams, in Lancashire, England, deposited *c*. 900. © Portable Antiquities Scheme (public domain).

comparison with Viking-style weddings observed in the eighteenth-century Orkneys (Price forthcoming).

That Rus plying the Volga behaved like fellow Northerners far away is unsurprising in light of a tenth-century ship's ribs found at Rostov. Between 14 and 20 meters long, it recalls the cargo-vessel Skuldelev 1 excavated in Roskilde, Denmark; rivets from other boats of Scandinavian type have been found at Rostov. They came from the Baltic, dragged over portages between the Volga and riverways feeding into Lake Il'men. There stood the foremost powerbase of the land of Rus, Riurikovo Gorodishche. Its role as river port is captured by its Norse name: *Hólmgarthr* (Island Compound) (Franklin and Shepard 1996: 40–1; Nosov 2012, 108–9). Besides princes, Riurikovo Gorodishche accommodated workshops and markets. If glass beads excavated around the town attest exchanges with the Islamic world, other finds point west (Brisbane, Makarov, and Nosov 2012; Franklin and Shepard 1996: 33, 35; Nosov 2012: 111). A walrus tusk could come from anywhere in the North Atlantic, but symbols on it suggest the British Isles, notably the *triskelion*: three legs or lines radiating from a center. To the Celts of Ireland and Scotland this symbolized the sea-god Manannán mac Lir, skimming the waves. It seems likely that the *triskelion* was carved somewhere in the Hiberno-Norse world long before the tusk ended up in Rus—perhaps Dublin, where walrus ivory was worked (Leont'ev and Nosov 2012: 384; Shepard forthcoming). So was amber, and beads have been unearthed in Dublin and other Hiberno-Norse sites, along with segmented glass beads (Harvey 2014; Wallace 2016: 289–96, 365). Such glass beads also occur in Scotland, besides Ribe and Hedeby. They are of Islamic or perhaps Byzantine manufacture (Cropper 2014; Hilberg and Kalmring 2014: 240). Tens, if not hundreds, of thousands are known from settlements in the Upper Volga region, indicating indigenous populations' barter of beads or dirhams (often in fragments) for the furs and other northern produce they gathered (Shepard 2016: 391–4; Zakharov 2012: 223–33).

It is a moot point how far Islamic ideas followed the beads. Ibn Fadlan's encounter with the Rus shows how traders of different cultures looked to their own idols. A Rus trader would pray for "a rich merchant with many dinars and dirhams who will [...] not haggle!" (Ibn Fadlan 2012: 47–8). Yet Islamic norms had some impact: weight standards predominating in the Viking world in the ninth and tenth centuries were taken from their Islamic trading partners. Weights found at Torksey were imported from the caliphate or modeled on examples current there; examples found in Yorkshire at Aldwark even carry pseudo-Arabic inscriptions (Williams 2015: 110–14; Woods 2021). Their meaning was probably lost on users, but cultural "fallout" occurred nearer the Islamic world. Islam came under consideration from the Rus prince Vladimir, when choosing which religion to adopt in the mid-980s, he sent for instructors from Chorezm, on the Aral Sea (Franklin and Shepard 1996: 160–1). Byzantium's brand of Christianity was, however, his final choice, and Eastern Christianity has characterized the states (Russian Federation, Ukraine, and Belarus emerging from his polity) ever since.

c. 1000–c. 1250: DEEP-SEA FISHING AND PROLIFERATING NETWORKS, HINGING ON EGYPT

Both North Atlantic and Indian Ocean saw changes in the uses to which the sea was put. From around 1000, bigger boats were built and sea fisheries became significant, as Wynne-Jones and Harland discuss in this volume in "Practices." In the Atlantic, this was another by-product of the Viking diaspora. Place names bespeak a nexus from Bergen to the Orkneys and Shetlands, and down the Irish Sea to Normandy's Cotentin. Modern names of capes and rocks signal the routes. For example, *kerling*—Old Witch in Old Norse—designates mountain profiles and rock-formations from the Orkneys to Normandy. Norman French words deriving from Old Norse for walrus and whale-hide rope imply ventures far into the Atlantic (Ridel 2009). Icelandic engagement in trading is suggested by glass beads. They abound at Hrísbrú, a site in the Mosfell Valley just northeast of modern Reykjavik, casual losses from a high-status farmstead (Hreidarsdóttir 2014: 135–7, 140). Some types—eye beads and metal-foil beads—point to the Caspian Sea or the Near East; they recall finds at Hedeby where "an astonishingly high fifty per cent of the sampled glass [...] contains soda ash," suggesting eastern, perhaps Byzantine manufacture. At any rate, such glass is "not common in ninth-tenth century Western Europe, where soda lime and wood ash glasses dominated" (Hilberg and Kalmring 2014: 239–40).

The networks looping round the British Isles and reaching Central Asia encompassed circuits less spectacular but of greater volume: besides dried fish, high-quality wool was exported from the Northern Isles and Eastern England. Scandinavians put the lands they occupied to new uses, even introducing a new breed of sheep with wool for dyeing to their taste (Faith 2012: 683). Wool may be the prime reason for eleventh-century England's abundant silver. Its richest parts were mostly those best suited for sheep raising: the silver arrived as payment by Flemish and German merchants, probably having been mined in Germany (Sawyer 2013). Regulations for London's markets around 1000 give "the men of the emperor"—German-speakers—special rights, with merchants from Cologne enjoying permanent premises (Sawyer 2013: 104–5; Huffman 1998).

Thus networks arising from the Viking diaspora had ramifications. Dried fish helped nourish townsfolk in the Flemish conurbations, full-time craftsmen and craftswomen working cloth made of wool from the British Isles. This did not just stimulate commercial ties. It fostered lifestyles less attuned to agrarian rhythms. Those engaging in the new crafts were apt to share outlooks. Freethinking among Flemish and other textile-workers threw up questions about God, opening the door to dualist beliefs emanating from the Byzantine world (Roach 2005). New maritime networks formed: an unintended by-product of Henry II's marriage to Eleanor of Aquitaine in 1152 was the Gascon wine trade, herring being shipped south in exchange (Barrett 2016: 254, 258). Bulk deliveries were facilitated by innovations of possible Viking inspiration. Ships such as the Skuldelev 1 only needed a crew of five to seven men, while a vessel from Hedeby could carry 60 metric tons (Bill 2008; Englert 2015: 50–60, 271–6, 284–5). Possible itineraries are suggested by the Skuldelev 3 ship, built of oak from Leinster in Ireland around 1042, yet found in Denmark and capable of carrying slaves as well as warriors (Crumlin-Petersen and Olsen 2002: 183–93). Dublin's prosperity, owing much to slave trading, tallies with the tenth- to late-eleventh-century import of silks to Dublin and ports such as York and Lincoln (Holm 1986; Wincott Heckett 2003). Of Byzantine manufacture, some perhaps Islamic, the silks probably arrived along a route commonly known as the Way from the Varangians to the Greeks, which connected the Byzantine world with the Baltic and North Sea through river systems (Figure 3.1). So did the silks and gold brocade excavated at market sites in Rus such as Gnezdovo (near Smolensk), along with Birka and Hedeby (Franklin and Shepard 1996: 128–9, 141–2; Hägg 2016; Murasheva forthcoming). They were exchanged for furs and other northern produce, alongside slaves.

Slaves and warriors traveled in their hundreds or thousands from northwest Europe through the riverways of Rus. It was a point of pride for Swedish nobles to have sailed to Byzantium. Reportedly, they preferred waterways to any land route as being safer. Heading the other way were traders: at an emporium in the Oder estuary "Greeks" were a feature, one of their commodities being known locally as Greek Fire (Shepard 2019: 358). But perhaps commonest among northwards-bound passengers were churchmen and monks with icons and devotional apparatus, alongside messages whose seals have been unearthed near riverways (Bulgakova 2004; Ivakin, Khrapunov, and Seibt 2015). So ready were priests from the Byzantine world to officiate in Iceland that a twelfth-century law-code sought to prescribe which religious rites they could perform (Garipzanov 2012: 5).

The persons, things, and ideas moving into northwest Europe were few compared with the land of Rus. Vladimir's adoption of Byzantine Christianity bolstered the networks traversing his realm. The cities where archbishops were installed, Kiev and Novgorod, lay over 950 kilometers (600 miles) apart, however, portages linking the Dnieper with northern river systems facilitated traffic. Birch-bark letters from Novgorod attest the concerns of this network's citizens. For instance, a certain Giurgii wrote to his Novgorodian parents: "Sell the house and come down here to Smolensk, or Kiev: bread's cheap!" (Franklin and Shepard 1996: 283). Riverways and valleys led westwards too, and the sheer volume of Western wares matched or even outweighed imports from the Byzantine world. But the latter's goods had cachet—silks but also oil and wine for worship and feasting (Noonan and Kovalev 1997–8). Trading with the south became segmented with, for example, *grechniki* specializing in the route to Constantinople. A series of ramparts shielded Kiev from steppe-nomads and, before heading down the Dnieper, ships would assemble in a fortified harbor (Franklin and Shepard 1996: 170–1, 325).

Things were different in the Indian Ocean rim. Religious cults requiring the study of texts and fostering pilgrimages had long been spinning networks. The rim was ahead, in that segmentation of trading occurred in the tenth century. Boats with greater carrying capacity allowed port cities and coastal communities to expand, along with conurbations further inland. There was no single cause behind the changes. The Song dynasty's zeal for foreign trade prompted medium-haul voyages by merchant associations; Chinese quarters arose in port cities, on the Malay Peninsula, in Sumatra and Java. Their junks were imitated by local boatbuilders, strengthening hulls with layers of planking. Change was afoot across the ocean too: inhabitants of the Swahili Corridor now ventured offshore. Towns such as Manda and Kilwa expanded, their elites building mosques and madrasas with blocks from coral. Smaller settlements mushroomed too. Population growth along the coast went with a reorientation of culture toward the sea. Symbolic is the *mtepe*, a boat of sewn-hull construction yet managing long-haul voyages. Although documented only in modern times, its significance is attested by graffiti, as in the Great Mosque at Kilwa (Fleisher et al. 2015: 105–7).

Kilwa's mosque symbolizes Islam's spread among local elites and the upwardly mobile. The value, material and spiritual, of ties with "Out-There" is shown by Islamic-style pillar tombs set with Chinese porcelain dotting the coastline from the eleventh century on (Zhao 2015: 5, 35–6) (Figure 3.3). The mystique of

FIGURE 3.3 Mambrui pillar tomb with inset Far Eastern ceramics, near Malindi, Kenya. © S. Wynne-Jones.

the sea is encapsulated in Swahili foundation myths of the brothers sailing from Shiraz in southern Iran and founding towns along the coast (Pouwels 1984: 251–8). Meanwhile Islam won devotees among city-state elites around the Java Sea; by the eleventh century, their dead were commemorated with Arabic epitaphs (Guillot and Kalus 2008). Cults straddling an ocean could be supplemented with blood-ties, as witnessed by Abu al-Abbas. He spent forty years in China managing his ten-ship fleet, assigning his seven sons to seven ports. Although nine ships were lost to a storm, the survivor's cargo of porcelain and aloes wood (for incense) was enough to restore his fortune (Lombard 1990: 31). Societies virtually living at sea could do the business too. Thus *Orang Laut* (Sea Peoples) crewed vessels bearing spices across the Java Sea from the Moluccas to Srivijaya with each family manning one boat in home-waters (Sather 1997: 327). But associations geared to longer-distance enterprises often had religious strands. Such were the guilds in Sumatran and Javanese port cities, of essentially Indian heritage yet admitting local dealers and Buddhists and Hindus of both sexes (Beaujard 2012: 2:226–7). These functioned alongside centers of piety, such as Srivijaya's monasteries.

Religious obligations illustrate a paradox: tight-knit communities in touch across vast distances made for the most resilient of networks. Thus Jewish texts circulated between scholars along with kinsmen's messages, interlacing the commercial with the personal. Letters from the Cairo Genizah and other texts offer snapshots of partnerships across the Eastern and Central Mediterranean. Merchants' trading horizons were sometimes—as in the eleventh century—narrower than their ties of family and religious community (Goldberg 2012). Yet such ties alerted traders to hazards or market opportunities, adjusting to change. They fostered self-policing within one's community (Greif 2006: 58–62, 83–8, 278–9). Reputational damage arising from breaches of trust, let alone contracts, served as a deterrent, supplementing legal action (Forrest and Haour 2018: 203–4, 206, 208; Greif 2006: 61–71).

The Genizah's earliest documents date from the mid-tenth century. Egypt throve as a hub between the Indian Ocean and inland seas. Incense from the Moluccas had long smoldered in Egyptian religious rites and spices sold in its markets. But exchanges intensified thanks to the new dynasties' promotion of trade from either side of the Ocean, the Fatimids and the Song (Wade 2015: 57–68). Commerce still boomed in the Gulf but purchasing power shifted to Egypt, which Fatimid Caliphs took over in 969 (Jacoby 2000: 30–1). The "Fatimid miracle" (Goitein 1967–93: 1, 33) owed much to entrepreneurship, with top officeholders supervising sectors such as agriculture yet encouraging independent operators too (Brett 2017: 92–4, 200). Their treaty with Byzantium in 988 provided for delivery of all commodities the caliph requested, with Egyptian merchants residing in Constantinople; they could attend Friday prayers in a mosque there (Jacoby 2000: 36).

This was around the time Prince Vladimir adopted Byzantine Christianity and communications eased. Jewish communities, long ensconced in Kiev and communicating with Egypt (Golb and Pritsak 1982: 10–15), became involved with exporting linen southwards. Among the Genizah's documents are proceedings of a lawsuit of 1097 to 1098, featuring linen from Rus. Part of a consignment due for re-exporting, half to India, it was in fact sold with all the other textiles at a Red Sea port; prices were high there, said the merchant responsible (Goitein 1954a: 189, 191–5). Jewish traders may also have seen to importing Rus furs to Fustat, where they had long dealt in silk; their links with East Africa and India facilitated ivory working too (Fuʿad-Sayyed and Gayraud 2000: 153). Meanwhile gold flowed in from the Niger basin via Sijilmasa on the Sahara's northwestern fringes, supplementing gold shipped up the East African coast. As with the waterways from Rus, trans-Saharan communications benefited from Jewish networks, with close relatives residing in Sijilmasa, Aden, and Southeast Asia (Fauvelle 2018: 112–13).

Networks such as these crisscrossed with regional ones. Finds from the Serce Limani wreck, a ship wrecked off Asia Minor's west coast in the 1020s, give some idea of their workings. Operating like a tramp steamer, the ship sailed from port to port in the Levant and, laden with glass cullet, was most probably heading for the Sea of Marmara. Small-time traders were aboard, several seemingly Bulgarians (Shepard 2015: 226–7; Van Doorninck 2009: 3–4). Such supply chains across the Eastern Mediterranean tally with maps in *Kitāb gharāʾib al-funūn* (The Book of Curiosities) (discussed in this volume by Emanuelle Vagnon), which cites "the wise merchants who cross the seas." In the case of routes to Islamic shrines, the Fatimids provided a fillip. Intent on legitimizing their overlordship of Mecca and Medina, they stationed a fleet at Aydhab to supply grain en masse to pilgrims performing the hajj. Pursuing worldwide ambitions for their brand of Shi'ism, they took effective command of the Yemen and sent missions to Oman and beyond, gaining a foothold in western India (Brett 2017: 108–9, 223–5).

Christian pilgrimages to the Holy Land grew apace, too. While Byzantines flocked to Jerusalem by land and sea, Constantine IX (1042–55) saw to the mosaic decoration of the Church of the Holy Sepulchre. Pilgrims also came down the Way from the Varangians to the Greeks. Young men of means were apt to serve in the imperial forces. Their exposure to Byzantine Christianity left its mark on Swedish commemorative inscriptions. The wording "God help the soul" recalls standard Byzantine invocations. The list of places visited on one runestone is evocative: "the Greeks, Jerusalem, Iceland, Saracen-land" (Mel'nikova 2001: 299–300, no. B-III.4.7). Cherson was a center of the cult of St. Clement, which spread beyond Rus (Crawford 2008). Cherson's citizens voyaged far, judging by mussel shells excavated there. Datable to the eleventh or twelfth centuries, they are pilgrims' emblems brought back from Santiago di Compostela (Jašaeva 2010: 485).

Long voyages could lead to cross-fertilization. Thus Fulk Nerra, Count of Anjou, introduced the cult of St. Nicholas to Angers, after the saint averted a shipwreck off Asia Minor, heeding his Byzantine shipmates' prayers (Bachrach 1993: 151, 165–6). Piety could blend with commerce as the Amalfitans show. Already prominent among Italian merchants frequenting Alexandria in the 990s, they founded a monastery on Mount Athos; this may have been how a copy of St. Benedict's Rule reached the Holy Mountain (Von Falkenhausen 2010: 27–8). Amalfitans promoted Jerusalem pilgrimages, founding a house there around 1060, and another hospice at Antioch, which boasted an Alley of the Amalfitans. By the later eleventh century Jerusalem's patriarch owned land in Southern France donated by pious Westerners.

Harassment of pilgrims increased once Turcomans overran Byzantine provinces and Syria, and Jerusalem's Christians grew apprehensive (Riley-Smith 1997: 32; Shepard 2017: 773–4). Emperor Alexios I Komnenos counted on Christian ranks closing against the "infidel," urging, along with the Jerusalem patriarch, "the entire Christian people" to send aid. Peter the Hermit was one bearer of these messages, probably after a pilgrimage. The upshot was the First Crusade. Byzantium's long-standing ties with Amalfi and Venice meant that neither city looked likely unilaterally to aid the Crusaders. Alexios's relations with the ruler of Sicily, Count Roger, were also amicable (Shepard 2017: 759–62, 775–8, 781–2).

If Alexios reasoned that he could control Crusader communications, he miscalculated. Western maritime powers proved equal to the task of supplying the Crusaders at Antioch, especially the Genoese. Spotting opportunities, they helped capture the ports along the Levantine coast. Reward came in the form of commercial privileges. They were, for example, granted the port city of Gibelet (Jubayl): the Embriaco, a leading Genoese family, took over administration. Assistance came from the Pisans too (Mack 2018: 474–6). The resultant networks, familial and commercial, enriched Pisa and Genoa. The Pisans were simultaneously supplying Egypt with timber, docking at Alexandria in greater numbers than anyone else. By 1150 the city housed a Pisan *fondaco*, the earliest such Western trading factory in Egypt. One attraction of the Egyptian markets was their spices' cheapness in comparison with those in Constantinople. A Genoese merchant visiting Egypt and Constantinople around 1135 was asked by his wife to bring back spices bought in Egypt (Jacoby 2000: 56–9). However, the most elaborate network was the Venetians', dominating routes between Venice, Constantinople, and Alexandria and much of the carrying trade between Byzantium's regional markets.

In 1171 Emperor Manuel I, apprehensive of their militaro-commercial weight, expelled Venetian merchants and seized their goods. Yet in the 1180s, Isaac II Angelos reached an agreement with Saladin whereby, after expulsion of the Crusaders, the Byzantines would govern Jerusalem and the Syrian coast while the Venetians fended off offensives from the west (Magdalino 2007). However, the project came to nothing. Barely a decade later, Doge Dandolo contracted to convey the Fourth Crusaders to Egypt, preparatory to recapturing Jerusalem. Upon the Crusaders' defaulting on payments due, Dandolo made an arrangement that ended up in the Crusaders' sacking of Constantinople in 1204 and installation there of a Latin emperor and a Venetian-born patriarch (Phillips 2004).

This train of events shows the magnetism of Egyptian wealth and how maritime networks could metamorphose into thalassocracies. The Venetians took over Crete and Negroponte along with a stake in Constantinople (Jacoby 2019: 759, 762). Although uninvolved with the Crusade, the Genoese began expanding trade in the Black Sea, vying with the Venetians for furs and other produce from the far north. Grain, too, was in demand and fetched high prices. Lasting partnerships across the Mediterranean were taken for granted. Thus a Pisan manual of 1202 sets a mathematical problem involving two business partners: one lives in Alexandria for over five years while the other's residence is Constantinople (Jacoby 2000: 74).

Three port cities—Venice, Genoa, and Pisa—now dominated the Mediterranean, with the waning of the Almohads. The Venetians' maritime awareness was symbolized by the annual Marriage to the Sea, the Doge throwing overboard a consecrated ring. The Genoese, for their part, acknowledged their ties with the Crusader states: their city's chronicle opens with their part in the First Crusade, written up by a participant (Hall and Phillips 2013: 49–56; Mack 2018). Whether cross-fertilization necessarily occurred is questionable. *Fondaco*, the Italian for "trading factory," derives from the same word as the Arabic *funduq*, but these compounds let Westerners follow their own customs. The networks' role is epitomized by the incense burners manufactured in the West from the early twelfth century onwards. Burning aromatics from East Africa or Southern Arabia, they share elements in design and decoration with Eastern Christian lamps and burners (Westermann-Angerhausen 2014: 50–1, 99–101, 104, 131–2).

Not that exchanges were wholly confined to commodities, or pilgrims. Port cities saw cultural cross-fertilization. Crusader Acre held out until 1291—a redoubt, yet accommodating exchanges of views and texts between Western and Eastern churchmen, and housing Jewish scholars (Rubin 2018). Early in the thirteenth century, Beirut's Frankish lord Jean d'Ibelin commissioned a palace overlooking the harbor. The fountain and hall drew on Islamic and Byzantine motifs to convey his status to his subjects, including non-Christians (Hunt 2015: 279–86).

c. 1250–c. 1450: INTERSECTING CIRCUITS, WITH OPENINGS TO THE ATLANTIC

For the first hundred years or so of this period, maritime networks follow familiar patterns. They straddle circuits interlinking the Mediterranean, the Indian Ocean, Central Asia, and China: what Janet Abu-Lughod dubs a "world system" (1989: 8–18). Disruption and reconfigurations were ever possible, though. No two circuits worked alike and, at the start of the period, the Pax Mongolica emerging from the Mongols' conquests made travel across Eurasia safer and trade more profitable. If, as is likely, maritime traffic across the Indian Ocean faltered around the same time (Wade 2013: 95–6, 102–3), this goes to show how interconnected networks were. In any event, the volume of trafficking remained high, thanks to the adaptability of the ocean's commerce. This in turn benefited from other nexuses carrying on regardless of profit.

The Indian Ocean rim took in three circuits. The westernmost reached from the Red Sea to western India and Sri Lanka, overlapping with one encompassing India, Sumatra, and the Malay Peninsula. The latter two places came within the third circuit, alongside China and the Philippines (Abu-Lughod 1989: 251–9, fig. 10). Precisely because regional ports within these circuits kept in touch for social and religious reasons, the segmentation of the "Maritime Silk Road" (Kauz 2010) into circuits proved cost effective. Cargoes could comprise high- and low-value goods, as witnessed by a thirteenth-century wreck in the Java Sea. Its items ranged from resin for Buddhist ritual and fine-glazed Chinese ewers to green-glazed bowls, dishes and suchlike everyday wares, besides its Indonesian crew's belongings (Flecker 2003: 395–402). Networks of compatriots and coreligionists—Muslim, Jewish, Buddhist, Hindu—and their dealings with more localized merchant guilds and wealthy traders kept up circulation around this "commercial ecumene" (Hall 2011: 196–207; Wade 2013).

Undeniably, change was underway. Islam appealed to urban communities and aspiring potentates in maritime Southeast Asia. From the early fifteenth century onwards, a Sultanate presided over the Malacca Straits. Meanwhile, from their vantage point, many Chinese merchants saw in Islam the surest pathway to benefits in this world and the next. There was, however, variation amongst the branches of Islam, as of Buddhism. Parallel networks and cults betokened pluralism and syncretism, Sufism blending with traditional beliefs in rural areas and Hindu-Buddhist shrines alike (Reid 2007: 7–8). Thus the kings of Majapahit entrusted control of trade to priesthoods while cultural traditions upheld women's status there, as across Southeast Asia. In fact, the Pasai sultanate in Sumatra came under women rulers for three decades.

Comparable syncretism was in play across the Indian Ocean with the Chinese-made porcelain on Swahili pillar tombs (Figure 3.3), as also on Madagascar (Beaujard 2012: 2:243–4, 474–84, 502–9, 548–9).

A booster to the Ocean's westernmost circuit came from the axis two formidable powers forged. On India's Malabar coast arose a polity under "the king of the Seas," centered on Calicut. This attracted Muslims from the Red Sea with trading privileges, together with Jewish merchants and, nearer home, Gujaratis. Devising this nexus was facilitated by the blow the Mongols dealt to markets looking onto the Gulf: in 1258 they sacked Baghdad and put paid to the Abbasid caliphate. Meanwhile, the Mamluks took over Egypt and Syria. Like their Fatimid precursors, they sought to maximize revenues from commerce, favoring elite merchants known as *karīmī*. Of diverse origins, Iraqi as well as local, they dominated commerce in the Red Sea, especially the spice trade, without going themselves beyond Aden. These "merchant-princes" personify maritime networks lacking corporate status yet well financed and well connected. Thus when Egyptians took the Yemeni sultan prisoner in the Hijaz, it was the *karīmī* who intervened and saw to his ransoming (Abu-Lughod 1989: 229–30; Beaujard 2012: 2:269–70, 275–6).

The downside to Egypt's position between the Indian Ocean and the inland seas is highlighted by the route taken by the Black Death. The *Yersinia pestis* was almost certainly borne by humans or other creatures from breeding grounds in Central Asia. Populations around the Indian Ocean were hard hit. Judging by genetic data, the plague spread from India down the Swahili-speaking coast, leading to the decline, if not abandonment, of Shanga, Tumbatu, and Kilwa (Green 2014: 44–5, 48–51). That Egypt suffered higher mortality than, say, Syria is understandable, given its transit trade. More strikingly, the plague-bearers reaching Alexandria in the autumn of 1347 had embarked on an Italian vessel on the Black Sea's north coast (Abu-Lughod 1989: 236–9; Beaujard 2012: 2:156–7, 276). Ironically this route map registers a network that enriched the Italians and brought Mamluk Egypt its lifeblood—slave warriors, leadership, and its modern name. It also helped restore and maintain a Byzantine emperor on the throne (Amitai 2008).

Several aspects of this nexus are noteworthy. First, an agreement between Michael VIII Palaiologos and the Genoese before his seizure of Constantinople in 1261 gave them customs exemptions in those ports under his control. Among other privileges was the Galata trading quarter on the Golden Horn. Its revenues were put at some six times the customs dues of Constantinople by a mid-fourteenth-century observer (Nikephoros Gregoras 1829: 841–2). Secondly, exploiting their newfound advantage, the Genoese consolidated in the Black Sea, making Caffa on the Crimea their stronghold. From such bases, and islands like Chios (occupied in 1304), the Genoese could compete with the Venetians. Thirdly, Michael VIII came to an agreement with the Mamluk sultan of Egypt, assuring shipping safe passage through the Bosphorus but also customs dues for himself (Holt 1995: 122–8). Slaves from the steppes and beyond were a prime cargo: besides providing military manpower, slaves of either sex fetched high prices in Egyptian markets (Amitai 2008: 350–2, 357–65; Favereau forthcoming). Fourthly, Genoese commitment to the Mamluk cause was less than wholehearted. One measure is their preparedness in the 1290s to build a fleet for the Mamluks' archenemies, the Mongol Il-Khans: the plan was to sally forth against the Mamluk axis with India (Amitai 2008: 367).

Fifthly, the Venetians were no less agile. Even before losing pole position in Constantinople in 1261, Venetian merchants saw opportunities in the Pax Mongolica, notably Marco Polo's father and uncle: he would join them for a subsequent venture, ending up in China. Marco justifies skipping the Black Sea: "it is very well known to many people" (Polo 1976: 335, ch.9), reflecting the Venetians' establishment at Tana in the Don estuary. What Venice did *not* do was devise networks inland. State policy was to leave territorial matters to the Khans of the Golden Horde whose interests generally converged with theirs. Venetian alertness to this is shown by the embargo mounted jointly with the Genoese in 1343 to try and halt Khan Janibeg's assaults. This episode also illustrates the Genoese's different outlook: less disciplined, they eventually came to blows with Venice over the refusal of Caffa's citizens to observe the embargo (Di Cosmo 2010: 97–100; forthcoming). Although debarred from Tana for a while, the Venetians reinstalled themselves there, slave trading and exchanging textiles and wool for silks (Stahl 2019: 359–62).

The network operated by the Genoese (competing with the Venetians) between Mamluks, Byzantines, and the Golden Horde was geared to commerce, not culture. Yet it facilitated a network encompassing Rus whose Christians, now under Mongol overlordship, still looked south for an ecclesiastical lead. Thus the painter Theophanes began working at Constantinople, including for the Genoese in Galata. He did further painting for their churches in Caffa before moving to Novgorod and, eventually, Moscow's Kremlin. Genoese of varying classes took to Byzantine cults and iconography. The revetted image of Christ's face donated by John V Palaiologos to a sea captain in charge of Galata eventually became a talisman for Genoa, while a wonder-working icon of Mary gained a popular following (Shepard 2012: 76–80, 86). Genoa was open to French and Islamic cultures too, as can be seen in its cathedral's styles.

Most striking, though, is the travel between the Byzantine lands and northern Rus, mainly by water. This became common enough to warrant a Greco-Slavonic handbook targeting monks and other pious Rus. It provides words for shipwreck, seasickness, and tricky situations: "the brothers have arrived [...] they want to eat, there is nothing to eat!" (Anonymous 1922: 63). An Athonite monk named Dionysios arrived in Moscow and later, upon becoming abbot of a monastery in the Vologda region, introduced a rule from Athos. There may even have been reciprocal arrangements between Byzantine houses and monasteries in Novgorod. A Byzantine emissary staying on in Novgorod was led by a vision to found another monastery in Lake Onega; this later attracted at least one monk from Athos (White forthcoming). Commerce drove exchanges between Byzantium and the far north too, but religious commonalities provided a pulse, reminiscent of what took Buddhist trainees from China to Indian monasteries. Furthermore, the riskiest part of the journey, across the Black Sea, was often done in Italian vessels.

The waterways crisscrossing Rus linked it with another network. The Hanseatic federation had a trading factory in Novgorod known as "the German compound." In return for furs, wax, and honey from the interior they sold metalware and, above all, textiles: the Novgorodians gave top- and medium-quality cloth names of Germanic origin. Yet here, again, trafficking did not make for cross-fertilization. Juridical norms were observed in Hanseatic dealings with the Novgorodian authorities, but a grandee could undergo rough justice at the hands of the town assembly (Lukin 2014: 252, 278, 406–16, 425–6). Hanseatic codes of practice prevailed for the merchants' internal affairs, aligned with those of Lübeck. This city lay near a key transit point between the southern and eastern Baltic's German-speaking ports and cities such as Hamburg and, up the Rhine, Cologne. Trading factories were also set up in Bruges, London, and Bergen.

Although communications were slow and firms mostly small scale, the towns were capable of acting in concert, as when they beat King Valdemar IV and forced him to grant 15 percent of Danish trading profits in 1370. By this time assemblies were meeting in Lübeck, but not all towns sent representatives. Its decisions were not binding, and Hansa membership was voluntary. Bonds were, rather, cultural. Encouraging consensus over fair dealing was a language, Low German. The lingua franca in the Baltic and the North Sea, it was not far-removed from non-Germans' speech. Frisian long remained comprehensible to southern Englishmen and vice versa, as witness the Dutch name for Plymouth, "Pleimuiden" (Mostert 2020: 187–8).

One mechanism invaluable for long-range enterprises was reciprocal arrangements of the sort Hanseatic traders made. A businessman sending a cargo load to a distant merchant needed assurance that he would both maximize profits and remit the proceeds after deducting true costs—quite a tall order. If that same agent played the part of principal, sending goods for the aforementioned businessman to sell, constraints were in place. Hence contracts seldom needed to be put in writing. At the same time, marriage ties and convivial reunions served an ulterior purpose: fraud or, simply, sharp practice was unlikely to pass unnoticed, with the reputation of the whole community—not just the family—at stake. In other words, fears of reputational damage made for self-policing (Ewert and Selzer 2016: 35–7, 41–57, 150–2).

These goings-on shed light on other networks, vibrant and not necessarily peaceable, where ties of culture and kinship could do more than institutions to govern behavior. Beside the Jewish networks—now prompting scholarly controversy (Ewert and Selzer 2016: 154–6)—and those arising from the Viking diaspora, the Swahili, and "the Sea Peoples" stand out, but others may have functioned in less-documented parts of the world. The reciprocity mechanism was, after all, not so very different from gift exchange. It worked for Hanseatic outfits communicating by sea, whose hazards were mitigated by the cogs they sailed: spacious, sturdy, and relatively cheap to construct. The Hanse also exemplifies the paradox that networks can thrive on a conservative, inward-looking culture. One observes few drives to proselytize and some sense of identity (Scales 2012: 437–43). Nor did members show appetite for waters beyond the North Sea.

Certain networks were alert to opportunities. The Genoese are our prime example, with their readiness to build a fleet for the Indian Ocean. Thus the Zaccaria family took over Chios and alum mines at nearby Phocaea for half a century and, in 1354 the piratical Francesco Gattilusio received Lesbos along with the Byzantine emperor's sister in marriage (Wright 2012). The Gattilusio and their associates straddled routes running from Caffa to Alexandria. Multiple Genoese slave traders dealt with the Turkish beys now dominating Western Asia Minor. But it was the Giustianini family and associates who thrived, supervising export of mastic and alum via Chios, alongside the Gattilusio. Indispensable for fixing dye in cloth, alum was shipped to Genoa, but also directly to Flemish manufacturers. To carry this heavy commodity, the Genoese took to using cogs, square-rigged sailboats resembling Hanseatic vessels and needing few crewmen to weather Atlantic storms (Balard 2019: 847–50). Bringing Flemish cloth to Mediterranean markets, their flotillas forged lasting links between the Atlantic, the inland seas, and the Indian Ocean. As Emmanuelle Vagnon discusses in this volume in "Representations," it was in this period too, in 1346, that Jaume Ferrer, a seafarer from Majorca, sailed in search of western Africa's river of gold, and his voyage is pictured and noted on the later Catalan Atlas of 1375 (Figure 7.6).

Such links were unprecedented. They facilitated the accounting methods of the Italian bankers now installed in London and Flemish cities and also gave a fillip to those Portuguese merchants already shipping wine and oil northwards in return for badly needed grain. By 1300 Bruges had a "Portuguese street." Based well inland, Portuguese farmers exported their produce through the port cities of Lisbon and Porto, where Genoese and Florentine bankers were installed. This network functioned effectively without Portuguese traders venturing further afield: even in the fifteenth century, only a minority of the population had much to do with the sea (Ferreira de Miranda 2013).

Portugal's rulers were more restless. John I favored trade with England but also sought fresh income streams, less exposed to the Hundred Years War or to Castile, already contesting Portuguese claims to the Canaries (discovered apparently by Genoese voyagers). In 1415 John marshaled a fleet to capture Ceuta, incurring losses for Portuguese merchants and upsetting Genoese interests there. Yet over time his zest for profit in the name of Crusading won

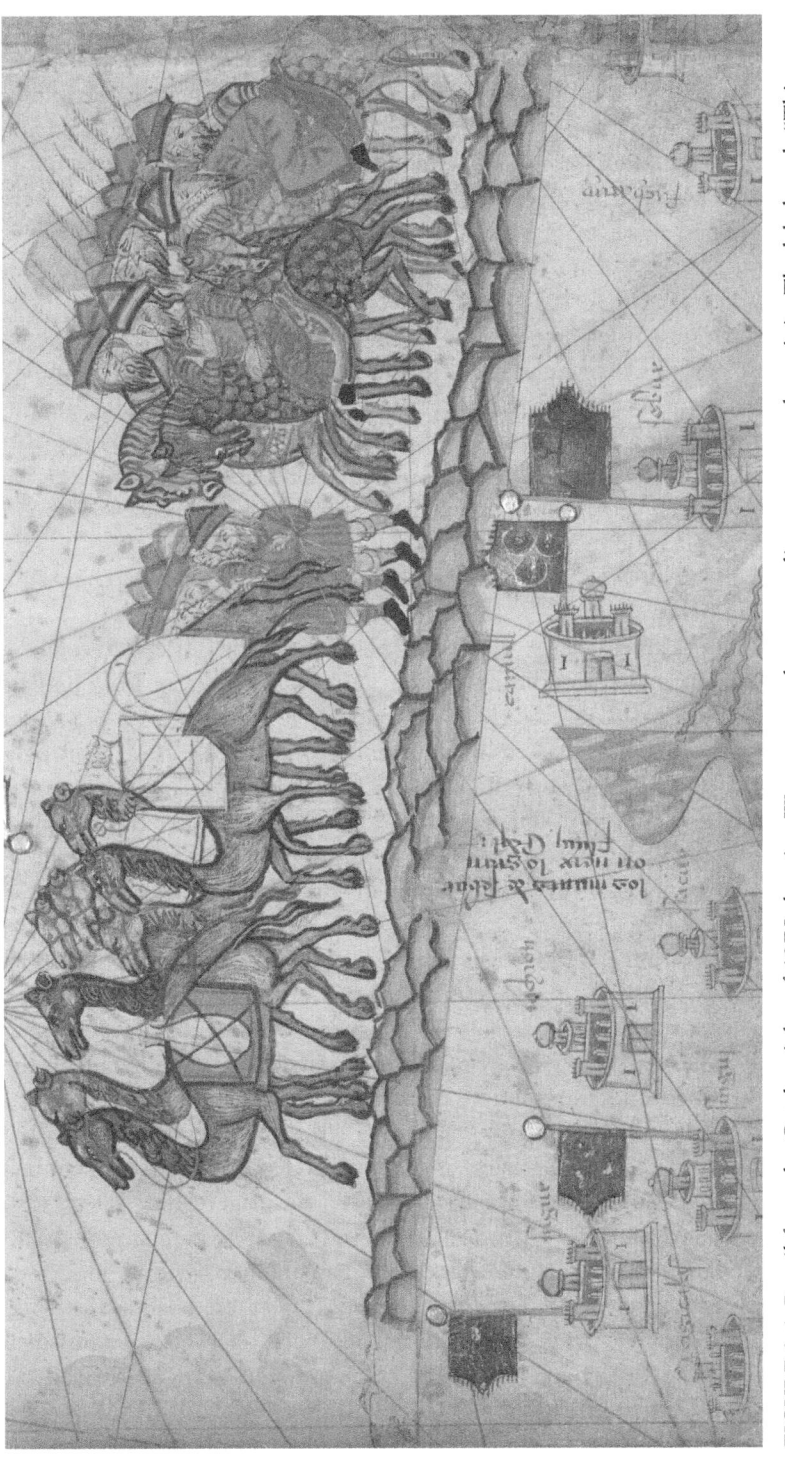

FIGURE 3.4 Detail from the Catalan Atlas of 1375 showing Western merchants traveling across northern Asia. The label reads "This caravan has departed from the Empire of Sarra [Kipchak] to go to Alcatayo [Cathay]." Ink, silver, and gold on vellum and wood. Paris. © Bibliothèque nathionale de France, Espagnol 30.

their backing. Probing Africa's northwest coast, John and his son, Henry the Navigator, broke with tradition. Whereas Muslim geographers knew little of the ocean (Fauvelle 2018: 164), Henry sponsored cartography and expeditions, harnessing trade winds to source the gold long since borne across the Sahara. Overcoming fiascos such as the Tangier expedition, royal patronage saw to the occupation of Madeira from 1420. Within thirty years the Portuguese were shipping gold and slaves from Senegalese entrepôts; before long, sugarcane cut by slaves on Madeira, Cape Verde, and the Azores was in Flemish markets (Disney 2009: 147; Green 2012: 69–99, 185).

It was, apparently, the Genoese who introduced sugar to Madeira (Benjamin 2009: 75), illustrating their significance in linking up oceanic worlds. Geography and flexible networks favored their shipping of alum alongside Oriental luxuries to northwest European markets. Persistent long-haul voyages of this sort went against the general trend toward segmentation of a route, once trading intensified. The busy Afro-Eurasian networks of the period are encapsulated in the heavily peopled routes depicted throughout the 1375 Catalan Atlas (Figure 7.6). Figure 3.4 shows a detail from the atlas in which Western merchants are seen traveling the overland route to China.

Genoese interest in oceanic ventures mounted in the fifteenth century, because of deteriorating conditions in the Eastern Mediterranean. Conflicts between the successors of Timur (Tamerlane) after his death in 1405 upset overland traffic along the Silk Roads, while the Venetians posed fresh challenges in the Aegean, and the network the Genoese had been operating between the Black Sea, Constantinople, and Egypt unraveled. Slaves were still shipped south. Indeed, the series of Mamluks now ruling were known as "Circassians," signaling their origins. However, intervening in commerce and fixing prices, the Mamluks disrupted the Genoese network, to the advantage of their Venetian rivals. Egypt's position as a hinge was all the more glaring, in light of the Indian Ocean's vitality in the fifteenth century. If this registers dislocation to the Central Asian routes, it also indicates the interconnectedness of routes by land and sea and how swiftly networks reacted. Long since willing to dabble in the Persian Gulf and beyond, the Genoese knew of the Maritime Silk Road. Nor was the Ocean's prosperity lost on the Portuguese whose traders, frequenting the Maghreb, were briefed on its affairs. One of Vasco de Gama's first encounters at Calicut in 1498 was with an unenthusiastic Tunisian merchant: "Devil take you! Who brought you here?" (Brotton 2002: 168). That Portuguese rulers and attendant merchants laid plans to bypass the Egyptian hinge by rounding Africa is unsurprising. Scarcely more so is the quest of a Genoese-born sea captain, convinced of a shorter route to "the land of spices," for Portuguese royal patronage, spending years in Madeira in preparation (Green 2012: 180–5). That captain was Christopher Columbus, and his three-master *Santa Maria* that eventually sailed west seems to have had lines reminiscent of a Genoese cog.

CHAPTER FOUR

Conflicts

Connected Histories of Maritime Violence in the Western Indian Ocean

ELIZABETH LAMBOURN

INTRODUCTION

Like many of the cultural histories explored in this volume, the cultural history of conflict at sea in the Middle Ages, such as it currently exists, is scattered across disciplines and by no means evenly spread. The topic benefits from a well-established core of scholarship, often developed within naval history and centered on the seas around Europe and the Mediterranean but suffers from much thinner and sometimes nonexistent coverage beyond this. Outside this core, still very little research is carried out on this period, very little is written, as an explicit contribution to the cultural history of maritime conflict. For the South Atlantic, the Indian Ocean, and the Pacific, with few exceptions relevant material must be hunted down in single articles or chapters contributed to encyclopedias, edited volumes, journals, and special issues of larger temporal or thematic scope, or indeed within other disciplines. Some monographic studies do exist for the medieval period, but they are few and far between (Fahmy 1948), and marked by a noticeable emphasis on East Asia (Conlan 2001; Dars 1992; Delgado 2010; Lo 2012; Shapinsky 2014).

This chapter hopes to begin to change this pattern by offering an insight into the data, scholarship, and future opportunities for the study of violence at sea in the western Indian Ocean. Synthesis is extremely challenging in a field as rich but fractured as this, and the discussion that follows inevitably skips over in a sentence or two regional traditions or particular themes that have occupied scholars their whole lifetimes. No slight is meant. As for other Indian Ocean themes and topics Connected History approaches—emphasizing work across written evidence in multiple languages; across written, visual, and material sources; and across regional and disciplinary boundaries—amply repays the effort (Lambourn 2016b).

WAR—CONFLICT—VIOLENCE: DISCURSIVE FRAMEWORKS

The evolving title of this chapter within this Bloomsbury set—first entitled "War," renegotiated by the premodernists among us to "Conflict," and now discussed in this chapter under the label "violence at sea"—is a reflection of the various ways in which violence in a maritime context has been framed within different disciplines and methodologies, and our own debates as editors about the best manner in which to cover this within a cultural history framework and across the long timeframe of these six volumes.

As several comparatively recent titles bear out—Williams's *Viking Warfare and Military Organisation* (1999), Hattendorf and Unger's *War at Sea in the Middle Ages and the Renaissance* (2003), or Susan Rose's *England's Medieval Navy, 1066–1509: Ships, Men, and Warfare* (2013)—the study of violence at sea continues to bear the formative imprint of its origins in European and American military and naval history (Lambert et al. 2010). This naval ancestry continues to determine methodologies, discourses, and thematic interests. Many studies still examine violence at sea as "war" or "warfare" within the framework of state sea power, in terms of "fleets" or "navies" and their associated logistics, and of battle strategy and tactics or maneuvers. For many this discursive mode is not only alien, it fits uncomfortably with the medieval evidence and new models of maritime territoriality. Yes, "wars" fought by state-supported fleets on the water or on shore, in purpose-designed craft manned by specialist combatants were a feature of some regions and periods. The state-supported fleet of oared galleys operated by Venice in the eastern Mediterranean fits this model and belongs to a long and particularly well-studied system and set of technologies going back via Byzantium to the Roman Empire (see Volume 1 of this series). Throughout the medieval period northern European states sporadically invested in purpose-built fleets—if only to let them rot away afterwards. However, this was by no means the only model either in the Mediterranean or in the waters around Europe, and it was particularly unsuited to larger maritime spaces such as the North Atlantic, Indian Ocean, or Pacific where sailing was often highly seasonal or involved long distances.

European naval historians and medievalists interested in war at sea are the first to acknowledge that formal, standing navies rarely existed at this period. Standing navies were expensive to build, crew, and maintain in permanent readiness with the result that medieval "navies" often consisted of commandeered merchant or fishing vessels crewed by ordinary seafarers. The series of treaties associated with the so-called Cinque Ports in England from the mid-eleventh century is one of the better-studied examples of the formalization of this common practice (Rodger 1996). Growing evidence for the Indian Ocean and western Pacific (China and Japan) similarly suggests that premodern polities only intermittently built and maintained permanent fleets, opening the way for more comparative research into the role of seafarers and mercantile communities in what we might conveniently label "sea power." In Philip Steinberg's *The Social Construction of the Ocean*, a foundational study of ocean space, it is noted that the use of the sea as a battlefield "has not been constructed universally; some societies that used the ocean for shipping and resource extraction failed to develop the concept of the sea battle" (2001: 16). Steinberg's use of the word "failed" is a telling reminder of the pervasiveness of modern European and North American naval models in the discussion of maritime cultures, by implication it regards the sea battle as the norm from which other societies—Steinberg's footnote refers to Micronesia and the Indian Ocean—deviated. Two decades on we can begin to present data that counters this statement.

If scholars retain modern naval terminologies it is arguably to allow the medieval to keep a place at the table of modern warfare studies and the institutions and publication series that support it. Many major monographic studies, including those just cited, continue to be published as part of warfare-focused series such as Routledge's "Warfare and History" founded in 1998, The Boydell Press' series of the same name, or Brill's "History of Warfare." Terminologies always reflect thinking and in turn shape it, and as the discipline itself has been aware since the 1990s, in retaining this approach and the audiences that come with it, naval history risks stagnation and even extinction. Notwithstanding the absorption of naval history into the academy in the 1960s under the broader banner of Maritime History, and its belated formal recognition as a subdiscipline by the American Historical Association in 2008, deep problems remain (Hattendorf 2012). As several "state of the field" studies have explored, there remains, as Maria Fusaro expresses it "a certain element of intellectual snobbery on the part of the historical profession" due to the "consistent and rich engagement of non-professional historians, and the lure of the narrative charms of swashbuckling adventures and derring-do" (2010: 267). The field's interest in "the history of operational and technological developments" and its continued adherence to national perspectives (267) are other factors that have tended to alienate it from a historical profession increasingly interested in theoretical approaches and transnational histories. Yet there is no denying that violence, including its more formalized expression as "warfare," is a persistent and powerful part of all human societies and that naval historians have made important contributions to this field, in part precisely because of their practical experience of the sea. Rila Mukherjee makes the point that water histories have their origins in the maritime history of the 1960s even if it was "primarily a naval history of Europe, being a palette of 'discoveries' in a nautical canvas concentrating on the period between 1400 and 1800" (2014: 89). Fusaro's article argues for maritime history's place within global history (2010).

There is certainly no place for the snobbery Fusaro speaks of, from either side, and this chapter hopes to show a way that, particularly for the premodern world where modern naval frameworks are already acknowledged to sit uneasily, cultural history and naval history might work together whilst respecting the distinctive histories, expertise, and discourses of each.

New labels rarely solve deeper methodological problems, why then try on yet another one? "Violence" as an interpretive concept has been well established within cultural history since the 1970s and the pioneering work of Natalie Zemon Davis on religious riots in sixteenth-century France (1973). While it has been pointed out that after almost half a century of use "violence" risks becoming an under-theorized "catch all" (Dwyer 2017: 8–9), from the standpoint of this volume, the term still offers many advantages. Freed from an ill-fitting modern naval history framework, the study of violence at sea offers better opportunities to engage the complexity of actors, particularly non-state actors, reflected in the medieval evidence and it certainly discourages the sort of "great man" narratives often favored in classic naval history. Above all, the term and its history encourage us to think beyond the "when, where, who" to the "how" and the "why" of violence at sea. Freed from the "operational and technological" focus of naval history, the term encourages consideration of a wider range of forms of violence than the "naval battle" per se and the technologies that support these. Above all, cultural history approaches to the study of violence (as opposed to social science/criminological approaches, see Dwyer 2017) aim to understand the meanings of violence and the symbolism attached to it. The large body of research on cultural histories of violence built up over half a century, together with new critical reassessments of it (Dwyer 2017), offer ripe ground for exploration, even if maritime violence as such has never been a primary focus. The term is entering Indian Ocean studies—for example in phrases such as "purveyors of maritime violence" (Margariti 2008) or "regimes of maritime violence" (Prange 2013)—as an alternative to "piracy" but there remains ample room to explore and develop this approach beyond or alongside the question of piracy.

"NOT AS IN OTHER SEAS"?: NORMS AND EXPECTATIONS

Questions of warfare, violence, navies and fleets typically enter historical discourses about the Indian Ocean only with the arrival of European powers, particularly the Portuguese, at the tail end of the fifteenth century. Early Indian Ocean scholarship such as George Hourani's classic *Arab Seafaring in the Indian Ocean in Ancient and Early Medieval Times* (1951) conceptualize it as a "sea of peace" (Hourani 1995: 61) and as a binary opposite to the bellicose Mediterranean where the new Islamic Empire quickly adopted Mediterranean practices of maritime warfare. In the Indian Ocean, by contrast, peaceful seas enabled "a great expansion of commerce" (55). With the exception of occasional references to "pirates" and "piracy," the dominant narrative for the pre-Portuguese Indian Ocean has continued to be that of a peaceful sea with an overwhelmingly commercial focus (Alpers 2013; Pearson 2003; Sheriff 2010). The easy equation of peace with commercial expansion is, of course, amply contradicted by the example of the Portuguese Estado da India, and the later commercial policy of almost every other European power involved in the newly global world of trade after 1500. Violence and commerce are by no means anathema and there are in fact a growing number of examples from across the medieval Indian Ocean to bring into the discussion. Odd references indicate that merchant vessels might carry armed men. As Roxani Margariti presciently wrote in 2008 "the prevalent picture of a virtually conflict-free pre-modern Indian Ocean obscures both the dynamics of mercantile life and the nature of medieval maritime states in the region" (547).

One obvious way to rebalance the established narrative is to demonstrate that the seas of the Indian Ocean before 1500 were also "battle grounds." Framed as "naval warfare" and as "sea power" the Indian Ocean can fight for a place at the table of naval history studies. It has done so in the past: historian of China Jung-Pang Lo (d. 1981) produced early pioneering articles on Sung and Yuan sea power and navies (Lo 1955, 1969), culminating in the posthumously published monograph *China as a Sea Power, 1127–1368* (2012). With "Les flottes islamiques de l'océan indien (VIIe-XVe siècles): une puissance navale au service du commerce" (The Islamic Fleets of the Indian Ocean (7th–15th Centuries): Naval Power in the Service of Commerce) (2017) historian Éric Vallet provides an important survey of the material, executed firmly within the frameworks and terminologies of naval history. Another, complementary approach, however, and one explored here, is to broaden the discussion away from naval history's favored focus on "technological and operational" matters by applying cultural history approaches and questions. This enriches naval and maritime history but it also builds important bridges with other historical fields, demonstrating that the maritime is also a part of "mainstream" history. My discussion of Indian "hero stones," which interweaves Jean Deloche's technological readings of these images with Cynthia Talbot's work on the "martial ethos," demonstrates the value of this dual approach, at least for certain bodies of material.

Before engaging with these questions more fully, however, I want to return briefly to Hourani and his comparative discussion of the Arab Mediterranean and Indian Ocean (1995: 53–61). Hourani makes the point that "the situation in the Mediterranean was not as in other seas. Here it was a necessity of defense to the new empire to create a naval power" (55). Hourani's passing comment is deeply insightful, effectively pinpointing the singularity of the Mediterranean. The Arab conquests in the eastern Mediterranean and across North Africa brought the Islamic polity into direct conflict with the Byzantine Empire and, with it, long-established ideas about, and technologies for, the control of maritime space. The ship types—essentially oared galleys—and the tactics associated with them are not generally included among the many knowledges and technologies—scientific, medical, administrative—inherited by the Islamic world from classical antiquity, but they deserve to be. In response to this new environment, as Hourani points out, Islamic polities around the eastern and southern Mediterranean built and maintained fleets of galleys (shawānī or 'ushāriyāt, in Arabic) largely manned by professional sailors. This Mediterranean tradition was maintained into the early modern period, particularly by the Ottomans, and through them even entered the western Indian Ocean where Ottoman fleets provided some of the strongest resistance, sometimes the only resistance, to Portuguese seaborne expansion (Casale 2010). Rather than accepting Mediterranean practices as the norm, we might usefully think in terms of a "Mediterranean tradition of violence at sea." The continuity of practices seen in the Islamic Mediterranean has enabled it to participate with success in the "naval" lineage of maritime history. Although it has remained a subspecialization within medieval maritime and Islamic history, since the 1940s and Aly Fahmy's pioneering monograph *Muslim Naval Organisation in the Eastern Mediterranean from the Seventh to the Tenth Century A.D.* (1948) a number of books and articles have appeared dedicated to, or substantially covering, Islamic navies in the Mediterranean—notably Fatimid (Bramoullé 2007, 2012; Hamblin 1986; Lev 1984)—and aspects of "naval warfare."[1] Christophe Picard's *La mer des Caliphes* (*The Sea of the Caliphs*) (2015; English translation 2018) offers one of the first synthetic overviews of caliphal policy across the entire Mediterranean basin up to the twelfth century with an integrated discussion of the fleets and admiralties properly speaking. Synthetic studies such as Picard's are especially valuable for demonstrating the way that hard naval history can form part of a much broader historical narrative and analysis. Nevertheless, recognizing the formative role of Mediterranean technologies of maritime violence in shaping scholarly expectations and approaches to other seas is a necessary first step toward a more vigorous and inclusive discussion of violence at sea in its many forms.

FINDING FLEETS IN THE MEDIEVAL INDIAN OCEAN

Picard makes the point that Abbasid caliphal interests were overwhelmingly focused on the Indian Ocean as a source of profitable commerce (2018: 19). Unlike the Mediterranean, few campaigns during the Arab conquests of Sassanian Iran and the Arabian Peninsula were in any way maritime. Given the extent and long timeframe of Arab expansion, the only examples from the western Indian Ocean are: for the seventh century, the prolonged maritime siege of Sassanian-held parts of the Gulf coast, activities in the Red Sea as well as three strategic raids against major ports in western India (overview in Agius 2008: 247–8; Vallet 2017: 755–8). For the eighth century, phases of the conquest of the greater Indus Delta in Sind would appear to have been more dependent on sea power than is generally recognized, although the written sources and archaeology are difficult to work with. The activities in South Asia are particularly poorly documented as by the time the Islamic conquest narratives (*futūh*) were penned in the ninth century under the Abbasids these regions had either dropped out of Islamic control entirely or seceded from the empire. This marked early differentiation between the Sea of the Romans (*bahr al-rūm*) and the Sea of the Persians (*bahr al-fārs*), as the two seas were known in Arabic, justifies Hourani's moniker "sea of peace" for the period he discusses. However, the situation changed markedly in the eleventh and twelfth centuries. As Abbasid central control fragmented, coasts and ports often took on a new importance within seceding regions as transport hubs and sources of revenue either from taxes on transiting goods or the direct exploitation of maritime resources. As regional circuits of exchange were consolidated, many polities around the Indian Ocean rim, both Muslim ruled and not, increasingly used violence to control ports and shipping lanes and developed close relationships with local seafaring communities, fishing and mercantile, as agents of violence.

One of the most cited naval engagements in the medieval Indian Ocean is the attack in November and December of 1135 by the ruler of Kish Island (Qays) in the Gulf against the port of Aden at the mouth of the Red Sea. A perfect storm of sources make this one of the few acts of maritime violence that can be discussed in any detail—and yet the sources have been underexploited since they were first edited and published in 1954 by S.D. Goitein. Roxani Margariti's work on Aden's topography and the siting of the engagement (2007: 76–83) is probably the most exhaustive study to date although there remain ample opportunities for further analysis from a military history angle. This is not a task I propose to undertake here, but I will discuss what we currently understand of the attack both as an example of naval engagements at the period and as an example of the methodological issues historians face in working on violence in the medieval Indian Ocean world.

The attack against Aden is best known through the fortuitous survival in the Cairo Genizah of two eyewitness accounts of the event (Goitein 1954b) and the later, early thirteenth-century, account of the Iranian traveler Ibn al-Mujawir, which must have relied on local oral memories of that time (Ibn al-Mujawir 2008: 143–5). The attack was initiated and directly supported by the ruling dynasty of Kish and, if we follow contemporary accounts, it is apparent that this was well prepared. Kish sent fifteen ships of very specific types: three *shaffāra*s, a type of streamlined fast vessel often described as a galley that typically accompanied and defended larger ships; ten *jāshujiyya*s, a type of troop carrying "launch used in warfare, especially for landing operations" (Goitein and Friedman 2008: 341n26, 342n27); and two recognizably commercial vessels, *burma*s, named after a type of rounded pot, very probably used to transport supplies. Together they carried around seven hundred troops, a sizeable force. Roxani Margariti's topographical work has established that the fleet stopped and assembled at Aden's main anchorage, *al-mukalla* in the sources, an area she identifies as just off the rocky island of Sira. We have no contemporary maps or realistic representations of Aden itself, however, the basic topography of the site can be seen in the sixteenth-century view shown in Figure 4.1. Sira island, by now fortified, can be seen on the left while at the center is Aden's main town nested at the base of the extinct volcanic crater known as Jebel Shamsham. Margariti's research indicates that the bay (known now as Front Bay) would have been substantially deeper and closer to the crater in the twelfth century since the shoreline has advanced since then. In spite of this, the image provides a helpful context for the discussion of this earlier attack. Just as the Portuguese fleet

FIGURE 4.1 View of Aden's main town and anchorage in the mid-sixteenth century, from Georg Braun and Frans Hogenberg's *Civitates Orbis Terrarum*, vol. 1 (Cologne, 1572). Heidelberg University, VD16-B7188.

moored off the main town, this is where Kish's ships anchored and apparently stayed put for two months with only limited attempts at landing. The ships were finally dispersed by force after the arrival of two ships belonging to a merchant from the rival Gulf port of Siraf who maintained strong trade networks in Aden. The expedition was part of a systematic strategy by the rulers of Kish to control shipping routes and ports, particularly in the Gulf and in western India, in their favor. That this tactic should be extended to the major entrepôt at the mouth of the Red Sea, nearly 1,700 nautical miles (over 3,100 kilometers) away, already bears testament to the oceanic scale of Kish's strategy and its fundamentally maritime focus. This much is clear.

Nevertheless, important questions remain about the original strategy and the later development of the campaign. Eyewitness accounts describe Kish as wishing to take a part of Aden, suggesting a plan for a long-term physical occupation of the port, a tactic that would certainly have necessitated seven hundred troops, however, what unfolded was, as Margariti suggests, more like a two-month-long naval blockade. The operation occurred "at the beginning of seafaring time (*fī awwal al-waqt*)," the start of the northeasterly monsoon that brought vessels into Aden from the Gulf and western India. This would have provided the favorable winds needed for the 3,000-kilometer journey from the Gulf but also allowed the fleet to reach Aden before any other incoming shipping had arrived, thus effectively blockading the port. Indeed, the sources state that Aden had no ships in port at this period. Yet if the intention was to blockade the port and divert shipping coming from India to the Gulf, or even to destroy the ships of rival merchants, it failed as the sources report that no ships arrived for two months. If the intention was to lay siege to Aden and physically claim it, engagements between Yemeni troops and those from Kish appear to have been relatively limited during these two months. As the prominent merchant and community leader Madmun b. Hasan Japheth related in his account "we faced each other, but they did not dare to land, while the people of the town had no vessels for attacking their ships. Thus each was afraid of the other" (quoted in Goitein 1954b: 256). The stand-off appears to have taken a turn when Kish troops landed and took Sira Island (see Figure 4.1) and then entered the abandoned town. They were repelled by local forces, in some cases the townspeople themselves; some were decapitated while the rest fled back to their ships. Shortly afterwards two vessels belonging to the merchant Ramisht of Siraf reached Aden's port (*bandar*) and were rapidly loaded with some of the two thousand government troops that had now assembled in Aden. No major sea battle took place, the Kish fleet decided to retreat and eventually sailed away.

Whether siege or blockade, the forces from Kish appear to have underestimated the duration of the operation, and during those two months troops are reported to have died of thirst or hunger. One may wonder whether the landings at Sira (apparently unfortified at this time) and subsequent fighting in the town came about as troops searched for provisions and water in the abandoned houses, or perhaps tried to reach the strategically important rainwater cisterns located in the volcanic crater above the town. Aden was infamous for its poor water supply and seven hundred troops would have required an enormous amount of provisions over two months. Many more points of topography and strategy remain to be disentangled, notably from the slightly divergent later account in Ibn al-Mujawir, and no doubt by a much more thorough grounding of this event within historical sources from the Gulf and the practices of maritime violence that developed there. Connected history is an essential prerequisite for future study.

These are questions for future research, what I want to underline here is how exceptional this campaign was, not necessarily because it represented an especially unusual event—historical sources make repeated mentions of seaborne attacks on ports around the western Indian Ocean—so much as because it is one of the few engagements for which we have sufficient details to be able to apply military and naval history approaches with their particular emphasis on logistics and geography (Agius 2008: 251–3; Goitein 1954b; Margariti 2007: 76–83; Vallet 2017: 758–9). It is a reflection of the problems faced by the field as a whole that this engagement finds little mention in Yemeni histories or administrative documents but is relayed instead in letters and travel accounts, types of written sources whose survival is generally ad hoc. On the whole the written sources for the western Indian Ocean offer few opportunities to develop any advanced understanding of ship technologies or strategies. In addition to this, and unlike Western Europe, visual iconographies are much rarer (Nicolle 1989) and we have almost no well-preserved medieval shipwrecks in the western Indian Ocean to offer detailed material evidence.

Yet a more focused analysis of the few sources we do have certainly repays the effort. These written sources reveal unique maritime terminologies. The term *jāshujiyya* was unknown until read by Goitein (1954b: 253) in one of the Genizah letters describing the attack. As Dionysius Agius discusses in *Classic Ships of Islam*, his exhaustive etymological study of ships in the Islamic world, the identification of this as a transport ship is a guess, based on the very context in which the term appears in our source and its derivation from the Persian *chāshū*, meaning sailor (2008: 343). Goitein was similarly unable to identify the term *shaffāra* in any dictionaries or in any source beyond the Cairo Genizah (1954b: 253); in this case, however, the Arabic root-verb /sh.f.r./ meaning "to cut," indicates "a galley that 'cut[s] the waves'," a streamlined and one assumes fast ship (Agius 2008: 343). There is nonetheless nothing to indicate that these were oared vessels, indeed Madmun discusses the wind as a critical factor in the maneuvers of the Kish ships suggesting that they were dependent on sail power alone.

Together these sources do, however, indicate that confrontations at sea took place. Aden we are told could not confront the fleet when it first arrived because no ships were then in harbor, however, once Ramisht's vessels arrived they were loaded with troops to go and engage the Kish ships directly. The language of Madmun's account also employs a distinctly military vocabulary: troops and townspeople engaged in battle, whatever supplies or material was left behind on Sira when the troops left was taken as booty. The eyewitness and travel accounts also give us brief but tantalizing insights into the nature of violence at the period. The mention in both Madmun's account and that of Ibn al-Mujawir that troops were decapitated en masse is striking, the scale of the killing reportedly gave its name to the area of Aden where this happened, as skulls remained visible for decades afterwards. According to Ibn al-Mujawir, it was known as al-Jamājim, the skulls of the *chāshū* (2008: 145). While Mongol practices of erecting skull towers is well documented, this deliberately casual attitude to enemies' bodies is exactly the kind of detail that opens the way for investigation within histories of violence with their emphasis on the social-symbolic significance of particular forms of violence.

The events in Aden hint perhaps too at the existence of very different traditions of maritime violence at this period between the Gulf and polities such as Aden, located directly on the shores of the far larger expanse of the western Indian Ocean. The fleet of Kish comprised a variety of specialist craft: ships for transporting large numbers of armed sailors, nimble and fast defensive craft, and supply ships. Ibn al-Mujawir describes the inhabitants of Kish as "real sea dogs. The lord of the island has neither horses nor soldiers" but many seagoing vessels (2008: 288), an equation that suggests that his "army" was composed of ships, a navy of sorts. By contrast Aden appears to have had no standing fighting vessels since the sources note that there were no ships in harbor with which to engage the force. As so often in Europe, during the attack by Kish, assistance came in the form of cargo vessels transformed into troop carriers.

HERO STONES: SOURCES OF TECHNOLOGICAL AND OPERATIONAL INFORMATION

The western Indian Ocean is nevertheless likely to have been home to a wide and evolving set of cultures of maritime violence. One important visual source for South Asia are so-called hero stones, relief carved and sometimes inscribed memorials that "commemorated many forms of noble behavior [...] such as death in battle, fights with wild animals, or death while protecting other people or cattle" (Storm 2013b: 61). Feats of animal bravery, notably canine and equine, and even a pet parrot, are also commemorated as is the sacrifice by self-immolation of widows (sati). Hero stones are found at sites across South Asia and over a wide timespan, roughly the fifth to thirteenth century. Those depicting death in battles at sea are concentrated as one might expect on the Indian coast but almost exclusively on the western coast where they are associated with the medieval period and coastal dynasties such as the Kadambas of Goa (ca. 906–1310) and the Silaharas (ca. 765–1215) based at Thana near modern-day Mumbai (Tripati 2005). Figure 4.2 is a detail from a twelfth-century Kadamba example, showing the hero fatally pierced by a spear from an oared fighting ship. In the upper panel, not shown here, he is seen being transported to heaven by apsaras (heavenly nymphs), his status marked by the two *chatr*s or ceremonial umbrellas over his head and the fly-whisk bearer to his left. Another well-known group of maritime hero stones is still in situ at Eksar, in what are now the suburbs of Mumbai, and broadly dated to between the ninth and thirteenth centuries during the time of the Silahara dynasty. The lower registers typically show rows of oared and rigged vessels sailing in orderly formation with battle scenes and the hero's ascent above this (Deloche 1987). First published in 1987 by Jean Deloche in the context of a study of Indian transport, these and other maritime hero stones have been eagerly exploited for the technical information they offer about medieval fighting craft in the absence of shipwreck or other visual evidence. I cannot better Deloche's technical analysis of the Eksar stones that

> show planked craft, sharp ended, with a long projecting bow strongly raked. In some of them the gunwale, fore and aft, does not seem to be continuous but forms in the middle a low waist on which is fixed a weather screen of

FIGURE 4.2 Relief-carved panel from a Kadamba hero stone showing close combat on a ship, ca. twelfth century. Goa State Museum. Drawing by Ariadni Ilioglou after a photograph by P-Y Manguin.

matting [...]. They are all propelled by oars, positioned at a single level, which pass through holes cut below the gunwale along each side. Of these wooden instruments (their number varies from 9 to 12) we don't see the blade, nor the loom; only the shaft is visible. The oarsmen row sitting and facing backwards as in Europe (Chinese sailors do it standing and facing forwards). The steering gear is not seen; in the central part, between the two lines of rowers, is probably a raised platform on which the warriors fight. All the ships carry one mast held firm in the deck and secured in place by shrouds running from the masthead to deck level on the ship's side. At the masthead is a platform, or a kind of cage used as a fighting top. The sail is absent. The size of these vessels is not easy to determine. If we assume there is 1 metre between each oar and 4 metres for bow and stern, the length of the hull would be from 13 to 16 metres and the oars would be 4 or 5 metres long.

(Deloche 1987: 166)

Caution is needed when using historical images as sources for the history of technology or warfare, however, other work on the representation of riding equipment in the art of the neighboring Hoysala dynasty (Deloche 1986) suggests that Indian artists were aware of, and responsive to, technological changes such as the introduction of the stirrup. We may thus rely on the more finely executed images of ships as visual sources. Ethnographic research has always been an important source for the study of ship technologies in the Indian Ocean area and it is not surprising to find Deloche remarking on the similarities between the ships depicted on the Eksar stones and larger craft built until recently on the coast around Mumbai, boats such as the macavà, batelà, and padàvà, although these were not oared.

Another important boat type represented on Kadamba period hero stones in Goa are "double-ended vessels having a banana shape in outline, with a longitudinal curve of the hull, and carrying soldiers armed with bows, spears and shields" (Deloche 1987: 166). Figure 4.3 shows another panel from one of these stones, of the thirteenth century, with three of these distinctively shaped boats visible in the bottom register. Deloche describes these as "vessels whose stem and stern are curved at the usual angle seen in dug-outs; they resemble the double-ended canoe-shaped fishing boats plying along the Korikan coast, being hollowed logs on which a series of strakes are raised and sewn till the dug-out is transformed into a fairly roomy boat" (167). Dugout canoes, *mash'iyya* in Arabic, are mentioned by the Muslim geographer al-Idrisi in his account of the resistance of Indian polities on the west coast such as Somnath to attacks by Kish in the twelfth century. *Mash'iyya* were, he reports, manufactured on the island of Qamar in southwestern India and each one was around sixty *dhirā'* or 27 meters in length and could carry, he reports, 150 rowers (cited in Agius 2008: 252). Given that this stone comes from Goa, boats of this type would

FIGURE 4.3 Relief-carved panel from a Kadamba hero stone showing an oared dugout canoe, ca. thirteenth century. Goa State Museum. Drawing by Ariadni Ilioglou after a photograph by P-Y Manguin.

appear to have been used along the entire western Indian seaboard, and beyond. Al-Idrisi reports that the rulers of Kish used the same dug outs and had fifty of them (252).

The detailed visual evidence from the hero stones suggests that certain coastal polities along India's western seaboard, in particular the Silahara and Kadamba dynasties, deployed specialist fighting vessels that must have belonged to something resembling navies. Although others probably relied on more ad hoc assemblages of fishing and cargo vessels. Grant documents are among the most important sources for medieval South Asian history and material from the Konkan and Malabar coasts points to some of the administrative structures and processes through which fighting ships were acquired and maintained. Probably the clearest example is a copperplate grant from Goa dated to the mid-eleventh century, which provides exceptional biographical detail about a certain Saddhan, grandson of Isma'il of the *Tajiyavamsa* or Arab community from the port of Chaul, just south of modern Mumbai, who has also been the port's Head of the Shipowners. Through an association with the Kadambas the family eventually moved south to Goa where the grandson, Saddhan, was appointed Chief Minister in Charge of Ships to Jayakesi I (r. 1050–80) of the Kadamba dynasty (Lambourn 2016a: 382–3). The post of superintendent of shipping and ferries is described much earlier in Kautilya's *Arthashastra*, a classic Indian treatise on government, and included, at least theoretically, responsibility for all forms of water transport and a large degree of government control over fishing and commercial transportation, as well as the destruction of pirate ships (Kautilya 2016). The *Arthashastra* does not mention state maintained fighting ships, however, this may have changed by the medieval period. Epigraphic records evidence a constant vying for control of ports and their revenues, and attacks by sea that may have warranted more direct state involvement in the construction and maintenance of fighting ships.

Although none of these sources describe skirmishes and battles off the Indian coast during this period in detail, the iconographic evidence from the hero stones indicates that, in the age before cannon, spears played an important role in maritime violence (Figure 4.2). In Aden too, one eyewitness account of the attack by Kish mentions how the ships "were thrust with spears" (Goitein 1954b: 256). As coveted military technology spear shafts, like horses, could be made a government monopoly and Ibn al-Mujawir noted that none of the people of Kish might "buy or sell […] spear shafts except the king himself" (2008: 290). Against this general dearth of written source material, early European travel accounts of India are sometimes useful in hinting and broader naval tactics. Marco Polo's account of "pirate" activity along the western seaboard describes how:

> their method is to join in fleets of 20 or 30 of these pirate vessels together, and then they call a sea cordon, that is they drop off till there is an interval of 5 or 6 miles between ship and ship, so that they cover something like a hundred miles of sea and no merchant ship can escape them.
>
> (1903: 2:392)

INTERPRETING HERO STONES WITHIN THE CULTURAL HISTORY OF VIOLENCE

Ship representations on hero stones clearly contribute to the "technological and operational" vein in naval history. Parallel to this, other scholars uninterested for the main part in maritime issues, have built up a considerable body of scholarship about the martial cultures of medieval India that challenges prevailing models by emphasizing the place of military action and training in South Asian society (Kloff 1990; Storm 2013a; Talbot 2001; Thapar 2003). Although not explicitly situated within the scholarship on cultural histories of violence, the material is in fact ready-made to contribute to this. The work of

Cynthia Talbot in particular on what she terms the "martial ethos" in medieval South Indian society as studied through the Kakatiya period of Andhra Pradesh suggests an immediate interpretive framework through which to understand the maritime violence seen at the same period but on India's western coasts and at sea.

Talbot makes the point that the models of Indian kingship favored by Western scholars—so-called "dharmic kingship," from *dharma*, "virtuous duty"—fail to take account of the truism that "political power has a physical basis in armed might" (Talbot 2001: 144). Talbot points to the work of Dirk Kloff (1990), which demonstrated that "military skills and weapons were widespread among Indian peasantry, many of whom took up occasional military service" (Talbot 2001: 68). Military service generated income but it also facilitated upward mobility, as Talbot observes "through success in battle, a warrior could move up in the world and even aspire to kingly status" (67), and helped to form socioreligious identities. The iconography of hero stones bears out the high regard in which different acts of violence were held and by implication the status they conferred. Although neither Talbot nor Kloff were focused on seafaring communities or maritime violence, their work provides valuable new models for these areas. In the present context they help us to understand that on the coast too, service of polities or sea lords was a source of revenue, of prestige and power as well as a dynamic generator of group identities amongst seafarers of all sorts.

What we might term "royal service" by seafaring communities cannot have been a medieval innovation. Already in the first century CE the *Periplus Maris Erythraei* (Periplus of the Erythraean Sea) describes the important role played by local seafarers in piloting merchant ships arriving at the mouth of the Gulf of Cambay and heading for the port of Bharuch:

> Local fishermen in the king's service come out with crews [sc. of rowers] and long ships, the kind called trappaga and kotymba, to the entrance as far as Syrastrene [Saurashtra] to meet vessels and guide them up to Barygaza. Through the crew's efforts, they maneuver them right from the mouth of the gulf through the shoals and tow them to predetermined stopping places; they get them under way when the tide comes in and, when it goes out, bring them to anchor in certain harbors and basins.
>
> (*Periplus Maris Erythraei* 1989: 79)

The accuracy of this account is borne out by the fact that the ship types mentioned have been identified in Jaina texts and correlated with representations of ships and inscriptions on clay sealings (Chakravarti 2002: 37–9, figs. 2.1 and 2.2).

Peaceful piloting services offered to arriving vessels, such as this, might easily slip into more forceful practices and one notes Marco Polo's observation that the port of Fakanur in Malabar "encouraged" passing ships to pull in and offer "presents," in effect port dues, to the ruler or face being chased down (Polo 1903: 2:233). Marco Polo's account also hints that these were formal arrangements between polities and local seafaring communities. Thus at Thana, Polo describes how its rulers (the port was now under Yadava control from Devagiri) had a covenant with seafarers he terms "corsairs" to procure much-needed war horses (2:330). Roxani Margariti has made the point that the use of terms such as "pirate" or "corsair" by contemporary authors and modern historians in association with coastal states has led to them being considered "marginal and exceptional" (2008: 545) when in fact they signal "a sustained bid to create a land-and-sea realm, to stake out a claim over littoral and maritime space and routes" (545). Margariti points to the comparative possibilities and parallels with maritime states in the contemporary Mediterranean (Tai 2005) and their weaving of relationships with different agents of maritime violence. In the Islamic world and South Asia, such practices may be seen as continuing at sea common landed practices of raiding and booty that were an integral part of kingship at a period when land borders too were fluid and ever changing.

Service at sea in its many forms brought income, social advancement, and prestige, and we should consider these activities an integral part of the medieval coastal economy of the western Indian seaboard. As in so many parts of the world these would have been seasonal activities, dependent on the monsoon and other coastal rhythms. In tandem with Wynne-Jones and Harland's exploration of fishing practices and fishing communities in northern European waters and along the Swahili coast, the South Asian evidence highlights the important role of these often invisible actors in various aspects of cultural history in the medieval period.

Fishing boats and cargo ships probably played a key role in what has become one of the most iconic "naval" expeditions of the medieval period in India: the series of Chola raids against Southeast Asian ports in 1025. The Chola dynasty (r. c. 848–1279) campaigned actively across southern India and Sri Lanka, involving their armies to some degree in maritime transport or strategy. The most ambitious of these, however, was the series of attacks against some thirteen Southeast Asian ports and polities along the Malay Peninsula and in south Sumatra. The subject of a dedicated edited volume *Nagapattinam to Suvarnadwipa. Reflections on the Chola Naval Expeditions to Southeast Asia* (2009), this study offers an important account of the expeditions situated within the larger political and social context, but it is also telling to see the tension in the analysis between the idea of a Chola "navy" undertaking "naval operations" and the available evidence. As Yellava Subbarayalu notes "very rarely is the Chola navy mentioned in inscriptions" (2009: 92), a silence amplified by an extensive body of epigraphic information on the organization and activities of Chola land armies. As he is forced to conclude: "it is possible that the *pattinavar*, the fishing community, of this coastal area [Thanjavur district] […] played a large part in the Chola naval organization" (93). While there may be some evidence of boatbuilding undertaken specifically for the expeditions, we have no information about the types of ships employed and it seems reasonable to infer that, as on the western seaboard, fishing and cargo vessels were the Chola "navy" and that these definitely played a large part in the expeditions. Navy or not, the South Asian material offers an important and powerful counter-narrative to lingering discourses about Hinduism's avoidance of the polluting sea (Bhindra 2002). The Indian Ocean was neither polluting nor peaceful.

MEDITERRANEAN-INDIAN OCEAN EXCHANGES IN THE RED SEA

Long before the Suez Canal, the Red Sea had been an area of repeated and unique interactions between the Indian Ocean world and the Mediterranean. The Indian Ocean penetrates so deeply into the Afro-Eurasian landmass at this point, and comes so close to the eastern Mediterranean and the Nile, that the portage of even large ships between the two systems had been undertaken repeatedly, if intermittently, since the Pharaonic period while at other times large canal infrastructure projects had aimed to link the two seas. The twelfth century was another period of interaction and it saw the establishment in Aden of the first state-sponsored galleys built with Mediterranean technologies. As historian of the Yemen Éric Vallet has underlined the arrival of Ayyubid galleys in Aden in 1173 durably changed regional shipping technologies and maritime strategy right through to the mid-fifteenth century, the end of the reign of the Rasulids (r. 1229–1454), the Ayyubid's successors (Vallet 2017: 760). Reinvigorated in the fifteenth century by fresh Ottoman technology and shipbuilding know-how (Fuess 2001), it was the Mediterranean galley tradition that eventually provided the most effective, and sometimes the only, resistance to Portuguese attacks in the Red Sea and western Indian Ocean during the sixteenth century (Casale 2010). Figure 4.4 shows the Portuguese attack on Jedda in 1517 and underlines in stark graphic form the very different naval technologies that came face to face in the Red Sea after 1500. While these events lie outside the timeframe of this volume, I finish by looking at the beginnings of this important technological transfer of Mediterranean vessel types to the Indian Ocean world, and the change in ideas about the nature of violence at sea that accompanied it.

Aden's Ayyubid galleys (*shīnī*; pl. *shawānī* in Arabic) were another local particularity picked out by the traveler Ibn al-Mujawir for the entertainment of his readers. The "Zuray'id rulers," he writes, "had no knowledge of galleys and remained [ignorant of them] until Shams al-Dawlah Turan Shah b. Ayyub arrived together with a whole fleet of them" (Ibn al-Mujawir 2008: 158). There is perhaps a hint of derision in his concluding comment that after the conquest these galleys were initially left in Aden "rotting in the sun" (158) until

FIGURE 4.4 Ottoman galleys pictured in the middle ground defend Jedda from Portuguese attack in 1517. © FLHC Maps 16/Alamy Stock Photo.

a change of policy in 1183 under a new governor. The "whole fleet" actually consisted not of fighting ships as such but transport vessels that had served to bring provisions from Aydhab on the Egyptian Red Sea coast while the Ayyubid foot soldiers had traveled to the Yemen overland through the Hijaz (Vallet 2010: 485n73). This Ayyubid strategy followed predictably Fatimid models. While the Fatimids kept large fleets of fighting galleys in the Mediterranean, the Red Sea was largely a home sea and it emerges from the Fatimid sources as a place where merchant shipping might require protection from attack and pillage, notably by the Sultans of Dahlak (Margariti 2008), but that troops and cavalry only needed to cross safely rather than fight on (Bramoullé 2012). The Mamluk historian al-Qalqashandi later recorded that the Fatimid's Red Sea "fleet" consisted of just five ships, and later only three, supervised from Qus on the Nile, and that it was mainly responsible for accompanying merchant ships in the southern sector of the Red Sea, between Aydhab and Suakin (cited in Vallet 2010: 485n70).

Yet these forgotten Egyptian galleys clearly marked historical memories in Aden. Whether they were indeed left to rot for a decade as Ibn al-Mujawir suggests is not clear, they may have been used locally, however, they seem to have been in good enough condition in 1183 to be redeployed to protect Adenese shipping along the Indian coast, and deemed technologically significant enough to be copied by Yemeni shipbuilders. Ibn al-Mujawir ascribed this change to the arrival of a new Ayyubid governor, however, the timing merits deeper analysis.

In the early twelfth century Crusader states began to take an interest in access to the Red Sea. In 1116 Crusader forces took control of the important port of Aylah in the Gulf of Aqaba integrating it into the Oultrejourdain. But the full possibilities this access offered were not explored until the late 1170s and early 1180s under Renaud de Châtillon Lord of Oultrejourdain. As William Facey records, in 1182 to 1183 Renaud de Châtillon used Aylah to launch a naval campaign deep into the Red Sea, attacking the port of Aydhab and then threatening Medina. Although hardly recorded in European sources, his actions are agreed by historians of the Islamic world to have sent a shockwave through the Middle East, a fact amply borne out by the many Arabic textual sources recording these events (see Facey 2005; Margariti 2008: 567–9).

Having lost Aylah to Salah al-Din in 1170, Renaud's first step was to retake the port, he then had five prefabricated ships transported overland from the Mediterranean to be assembled on the Red Sea coast. Three ships, carrying around three hundred men in all, set sail for Aydhab where they destroyed several merchant ships as well as local food stores, and then crossed to the port of Rabigh on the Arabian coast where part of the force set out to attack Medina. The Ayyubids rapidly portaged ships to the Gulf of Aqaba from Fustat and Alexandria and sailed to engage the Crusader ships in two confrontations off Aylah and Rabigh. Those troops already on their way to Medina were caught and executed (Facey 2005). As one chronicler reported, Salah al-Din ordered every one executed to "suppress all traces of what they had done so that not one of their eyes would remain to blink and no one would tell of the way of that sea or know of it" (Facey 2005).

Renaud de Châtillon's expedition shattered assumptions that the Red Sea was essentially a "sea of peace" where commercial vessels might be subject to, at worst, pirate attacks. It also highlighted the vulnerability of Mecca and Medina to attack though their Red Sea ports. As this last quote suggest, Salah al-Din acted to suppress any spread of knowledge about Red Sea navigation and topography. If the Ayyubids could portage ships, so could Crusaders. Renaud's raid underlined the potential of the Red Sea to become a space of naval confrontation and actual sea battles, something it did eventually become in the sixteenth century. It is surely no accident then that it was in 1183, the year of Renaud's abortive expedition, that the Ayyubid's decided to revive the use of the galleys stationed in Aden and in fact to build new ones locally along Mediterranean models using iron nails rather than the coir-rope usually used to secure planks in western Indian Ocean shipping. That these ships were first put into service to protect merchant shipping and in the western Indian Ocean signals a new Ayyubid awareness of the importance of sea power and of the Yemen's unique ability to control Red Sea access. Big set naval battles between large fleets of galleys as practiced successfully by the Fatimids in the Mediterranean did not reach the Red Sea until the sixteenth century and when they did, with the Portuguese and Ottomans, they did so in very different ships and with very different weapons. Nevertheless, the twelfth century transformed both technologies of, and attitudes toward, sea power in this sector of the Indian Ocean.

In the next century, armed galleys became intrinsic to Rasulid commercial strategy and accompanied merchant shipping both in the southern Red Sea and on the longer open-ocean crossings to southern India. The Rasulid state built and ran its own merchant fleet, giving it almost total control of shipping in the southern Red Sea. Thanks to rich historical documents and narratives many aspects of Rasulid naval activity, from shipyards via taxes to commercial policy, come into newly sharp focus (Margariti 2008: 569–72; Vallet 2010: 482–8, 127–8; 2017: 760–2). The change in the quality and quantity of the written evidence is not accidental but reflective of the fact that, as Margariti observes, "the Rasulid state in the days of al-Muzaffar [r. 1249–95] viewed maritime technology (meaning ships and shipping) as a crucial instrument of advancing state interests" (2008: 569). That history is currently written across multiple articles and smaller publications (see bibliography in the footnotes of Margariti 2008; Vallet 2010, 2017) and urgently awaits a synthetic monographic study.

CONCLUSIONS: LORDS OF THE SEAS

Brief as they are these insights aim to bring new material into the discussion of sea power and violence at sea in the Indian Ocean world, and into the "why" of it all. In naval history the "why" of naval battles is at its heart profoundly territorial, state sea power defends or expands control of seas and sea routes by landed polities. Naval battles are ritualized confrontations the outcome of which is agreed to determine maritime control. The material presented in this chapter certainly counters assumptions that the Indian Ocean was a "sea of peace" until the arrival of European powers. Patently it was not. More complex to counter or move on are arguments about the meaning and theoretical conception of maritime space and power in the medieval Indian Ocean. For Philip Steinberg, author of the seminal work *The Social Construction of the Ocean* (2001), the idea of maritime territoriality—condensed in the early seventeenth-century dialectic between Grotius's *mare liberum* and Selden's *mare clausum*—was specifically European. The Indian Ocean was a space apart, "few if any attempts were made to use ocean-space for projecting power" (Steinberg 2001: 47) and in the Indian Ocean world the deep sea was "*non*-territory" (40, my emphasis).

Two decades after Steinberg wrote, the idea of Indian Ocean *non*-territoriality cannot stand. Part of the problem is Steinberg's fluid, interchangeable use of the terms "ocean," "deep-ocean," and "sea," more fundamentally, however, at issue is the difference between theoretical conceptualizations of control and claims to this, versus actual practice. In a world before radar and air support, before submarines, and certainly before satellite imagery, at a time when the range, speed, and sometimes direction of ships was determined by wind or the endurance of their oarsmen, and navigation still relied overwhelmingly on sight, it is patently ahistorical to suggest that any form of control of any deep-ocean was possible. Europeans did not in practice control the deep Atlantic so much as control key ports and access points, even if theoretically they laid claim to the whole ocean. Put this way, Indian Oceanists can argue that the deep Indian Ocean was every bit as territorialized as the Mediterranean and the seas surrounding Europe. The "why" of violence may not be as different as it first seems at least at the level of polities.

Today, medievalists know much more about the use and conception of the sea by autochtonous polities and maritime communities in the Indian Ocean. Polities around the western Indian Ocean sought to control shipping lanes through naval expeditions that sacked or blockaded rival ports, they also sought to increase their coastal territory and access to maritime resources through seaborne attack. Few maintained permanent, formal navies, but if we examine the European sources the same is true here, merchant shipping always played a vital role in early "navies," and seafaring communities were frequently coopted.

Although not through written treatises, many of these polities also developed the idea of lordship over the sea. The titles of a number of Indian dynasties incorporated this idea: the Silahara sovereign, for example, was *Pashchimasamudradhipati* (Lord of the Western Ocean), Jayakeshi I of the Kadambas was *Padavalendra* (Lord of the Ocean). The sea forms part of notions of sovereignty in ancient and medieval India although the whole topic would benefit from further study of the rich epigraphic sources available. The wide spread of these ideas is reflected in the Genizah documents, thus Madmun b. Hasan Japheth, the Jewish head of merchants at Aden in the twelfth century, was characterized in one document as "trusted by all the lords of the seas and the deserts," a phrase S.D. Goitein interpreted as signifying that "he had agreements, in the interest of his clients, with the many petty rulers (or pirates) who controlled the routes of the Arabian and Indian seas" (Goitein 1966: 347). Goitein's use of the terms "petty" and "pirates" only serves to underline Roxani Margariti's point that maritime states have often been dismissed as marginal or exceptional.

Recognition of lordship over maritime spaces also encourages examination of the novel means developed for expressing and invoking this in the absence of durable territorial or maritime control. Raids and blockades, maritime violence in short, certainly operated to this end, but we may also be able to detect more culturally specific strategies. Sunni Muslim polities in the western Indian Ocean developed new uses of the Friday sermon (*khutba*) delivered in mosques across their territories, which traditionally included a section, *the da'wat al-sultān*, that allowed for the recitation of the name of the ruling sovereign. It can be no accident that some of the most active sea-raiders in the western Indian Ocean, notably the rulers of Kish and the Rasulids of Yemen actively encouraged their names to be recited by Muslim congregations living outside their territories in non-Muslim Indian port polities. While these Muslim rulers did not physically control ports and towns in India, the rhetoric in contemporary Islamic chronicles was that of transoceanic territorial control, of "rule" at these Indian ports (Lambourn 2008). In actual practice, we might think of this translation of the *khutba* to the Indian Ocean environment as a means of integrating these places and congregations into a larger symbolic Islamic territoriality based around shared faith and common commercial interests. The success of the practice is demonstrated by its continued use by different Islamic states with Indian Ocean interests right through to the period of Ottoman naval engagement in the Indian Ocean in the sixteenth century.

It has been a refrain of this chapter but one I will repeat once more: much more work remains to be carried out on the waters beyond northern Europe and the Mediterranean in the medieval period. Multidisciplinary approaches, as explored here with naval history and the history of violence, are essential to extract the maximum amount of information from historical sources that are consistently sparse and varied. Many written sources in multiple languages still remain to be identified, translated, and thoroughly interpreted across this area, as does new iconographic and material evidence. Freed from the idea that the Indian Ocean was a "sea of peace" scholars will hopefully listen for the violence in their sources, to subvert Sebastian Sobecki's entreaty that literary historians listen for the sea in their primary sources. This research will allow us to better grasp the variety of agents of violence and the different forms of violence that evolved in the maritime environments across this area. More importantly, it will help us to discover more about the sociocultural meanings of violence in the different regions that make up the Indian Ocean world.

CHAPTER FIVE

Islands and Shores

Janus-Faced Cultures at the Interstices of Land and Sea

ROXANI MARGARITI

INTRODUCTION

The centuries between roughly 800 and 1450 represent a transformative period in the long lives of seas, shores, and islands. World economies and societies saw significant and long-lasting changes that directly impacted life on islands and along coasts, as Wynne-Jones and Harland discuss for fishing communities in this volume. Exchange between the Indian Ocean and Mediterranean worlds quickened, as the two oceanic economies progressively integrated most of the Eastern Hemisphere into a single economic system; meanwhile, some of the most remote oceanic lands in the Pacific were being settled and exploited by humans in ways that have yet to be incorporated in scholarly views of the "Global Middle Ages" (see Introduction and Figure 0.7). In terms of geopolitics, for polities as structurally distinct as the Viking kingdoms of Scandinavia, the early Muslim caliphate and its successor states, the Italian maritime republics, and Tang and Song China, shores functioned at times as borderlands: symbolic ends and beginnings of states, zones dotted with fortifications and launching pads for expansion, political and economic. Islands shared with shores geopolitical ambiguity, and feature as claimed but often elusive territories, or at times as centers of independent land-and-sea realms, some procuring exceptional commodities to regional and transregional economies.

After a short account of the themes and concepts that guide writing about medieval shores and islands, this chapter explores the notions that in the Middle Ages coastal and insular spaces played various but often crucial roles in the definition of political territories; that the people inhabiting them participated in regional and transregional economies most decisively through the procurement of marine resources and often as the agents of intense networking; and that societies on islands and shores displayed cultural distinctiveness, producing a large part of the maritime cultural landscape. We will see that while maritimity does not necessarily define littoral and island spaces, as discussions of the Swahili make clear (Fleisher et al. 2015), the ever more intensive engagement with the maritime element in medieval times proved a generative force for distinct littoral and island cultures.

SHORES AND ISLANDS, EDGES AND MICROCOSMS

I begin with a short but complex episode in the millennia-long history of the big island of Crete, a quintessential story of shores as points of departure, crossing, encounter, and new beginnings, and islands as destinations and microcosms. While a voluminous and diverse literature about maritime places—with a full typology of islands and shores, more or less exotic—circulated in the Middle Ages and informs a distinct area of inquiry into representation and the imaginary, as James L. Smith's chapter in this volume traces, here we will focus on medieval shores' and islands' real cultural histories that both these and a variety of other sources help illuminate.

In the year 202 of the Muslim calendar—818 in its Christian equivalent—a long-simmering civil struggle between Cordoba's Umayyad rulers and factions of the city's learned class erupted in a celebrated revolt. Defeated and ousted, the rebels fled to the shore, in Arabic *al-'udwa*, literally "the opposite one"— meaning the shore of the Gulf of Cadiz, seen as the land across from the North African coast. From there some of the rebels made the approximately 60-nautical mile crossing to Morocco while others traversed the entire length of the Mediterranean, eventually landing more than 2,000 miles away in Alexandria. By 212/826–7, under the leadership of one Abu Hafs 'Umar b. Shu'ayb, the Andalusians took to their ships again and headed north to attack the Byzantine island of Crete. They met with little resistance, partly thanks to a rebellion that was occupying the bulk of Byzantine armed forces at the time. It is also reasonable to conclude that conquest was facilitated by the islanders' indifference as to which foreign ruler they would have to endure.

The Andalusian Muslim conquest and settlement included Crete's south, an important feat given that the newcomers must have traversed the imposing mountain chain forming an internal border in what Fernand Braudel would term in his foundational account of the role in Mediterranean history of islands a "miniature continent" (1972: 1:148). The eleventh-century Byzantine chronicler Ioannis Skylitzae claims that Abu Hafs burned the ships that had carried his army to Crete's shores so that there would be no chance of defections (Figure 5.1); he urged the men to focus instead on the island's natural bounty

FIGURE 5.1 The Muslims burning their own fleet. Illuminated manuscript of Ioannis Skylitzae, *Synopsis Historion*, twelfth century. Manuscript known as "Skylitzes Matritensis," Madrid, Biblioteca Nacional, VITR/26/02, fol. 39r. © Album/Alamy Stock Photo.

and female captives (Scylitzae 1973, 2010: 44–6). Apocryphal as this tale may be, island resources clearly played a role. The Iberians stayed and they became Cretans—islanders—themselves. The rule of Umar's descendants ended almost a century and a half later when a resurgent Byzantine navy evicted the Muslim rulers in 961. The year after the Byzantine reconquest an itinerant saintly renunciant visited the island and preached orthodoxy to the islanders (Vita Niconis 1987: 1, 83–9, 279–80). Reading between the lines of the *Vita* of Nicon Metanoeite—Nicon Repent, so named because of his relentless preaching to "errant" Christian audiences (83–9)—we catch a glimpse of an island population that had broken free from the enforced orthodoxies and hierarchies of the imperial mainland and did not show sufficient eagerness to return to the metropole's fold.

Historical study of shores and islands, topologically both places where land and sea meet, points to the common themes of boundary crossing, social encounter, and economic and political opportunity as well as danger, and ultimately of distinct cultural ways that variously combine the terrestrial and the maritime (Billig [1936] 2009; Braudel 1972; Dening 2004; Gillis 2012; Mack 2011; Sahlins 1985). Histories of medieval shores and islands have received less attention than those of ancient and early modern times but share these themes in fundamental ways. It is useful here to adopt an expanded version of Michael

Pearson's term "littoral society" (2003), and to use it to signal the economy, social organization, and networking of groups and individuals who live by the sea and, at least partly, from the sea. The medieval littoral too emerges as a distinct locus of history, at once not only "threshold" but also "capacious environment" at water's edge where people made their homes, as John Gillis shows in his important world history of shores (Gillis 2012: 3–8). In the case of islands, their littoral defines them. It is their shores that render islands of very different sizes and physical geography into a single geographical category. Shores confer to islands variable boundedness and connectivity that we might therefore call, with Mediterraneanists Horden and Purcell, "all-around connectivity" (2000: 225–6). At the same time certain islands and archipelaga have fruitfully been understood as frontiers in and of themselves. Not only Crete (Tsigonaki 2019) but also Sicily (Darley 2019), Socotra (Harpster 2019), and Sri Lanka, all large islands and archipelagic centers, and Jerba (Holod and Kahlaoui 2019), a small coastal island, have all been characterized as frontiers in the medieval period. Both shores and islands were in medieval times, as in other time periods, "janus-faced," looking at once landward and seaward.[1]

The following chapter explores these histories of edges, crossings, and maritime littoral worlds against the background of two overarching themes: the question of human agency, particularly with respect to maritime mobilization, and the geohistorical dynamics in the balance between isolation and connectivity. Agency in overseas migration, initial colonization of previously uninhabited lands, subsequent settlement, and processes of population and depopulation of shores and islands raise the conundrum of human motives for mobilization. As island archaeologist Atholl Anderson puts it, "one of the enduring questions about maritime migration is what impels it" (2006: 33). The Andalusians' *periplus* all the way to Crete was reportedly prompted by dramatic conflict, exemplifying one powerful motive for maritime mobilization that we are all too familiar with today. Conflict, of course, is not the only reason for going out to sea, whether collectively or individually, by compulsion or voluntarily: prospection for new lands and exploitation of marine resources, trade and other kinds of material exchange, and religious entrepreneurship and pilgrimage, all constitute responses to particular historical circumstances and to the "opportunities provided […] by the sea itself " (Purcell 2005: 115).

With regards to initial colonization and settlement of maritime lands, the period between the ninth and the fifteenth century covered in this chapter may be said to truly exemplify the middleness evoked by the term "medieval" with respect to islands and shores in the Atlantic, the Mediterranean, and the Indian Ocean—there seems to have been little or no new settlement of islands in these seas during these middle centuries, between the early human migrations of prehistory and the ancient world that first populated even some of the most remote islands, and the later occupation of some of the last uninhabited oceanic islands of the planet, such as the Mascarenes in the Indian Ocean, in the early modern era. In the Pacific, on the other hand, the fascinating and celebrated peopling of Polynesia's eastern archipelaga is now known to have taken place in two rapid spurts between the eleventh and thirteenth centuries. A cluster of recent studies have significantly revised and shortened the chronology of initial colonization and habitation of Eastern Polynesia, based partly on recently retrieved radiocarbon dates and partly on a reconsideration of the earlier evidence. Although not definitive, the argument is statistically powerful and convincing (Wilmshurst et al. 2011: 1815–20). We should not, in any case, think in linear terms of a progressive filling out of maritime islands across the globe through time. Regarding social history and its impact on maritime culture, it is in fact important to note the instances in which islands and shores sometimes became depopulated, indeed completely empty for periods of time. That an island as central and accessible as Malta should appear to have had a period of depopulation, when only hunters, apiary foragers, and fishermen landed on its shores (Dalli 2016: 371), speaks to the vulnerabilities of island, as well as littoral, societies to outside forces (Purcell 2013: 98–9). Purcell further conceptualized maritime mobilization as "the varying and changing ability of […] a larger or smaller state, a community, or a locally or more widely powerful individual, to marshal and concentrate the worlds of labor, of expertise, and of suitable materials which are necessary for the intensification of maritime activity" (96)—thus helping focus the lens of Mediterranean and other sea-centered histories on both the processes and the human agents responsible for the creation of maritime island and littoral cultures. In general, the phenomenon of maritime migration, displacement, and circulation between shores—including insular ones—leads to cultural specificities to be explored further in this chapter.

The second theme that the story of the Andalusian Amirs of Crete evokes is that of the balance between connectivity and isolation of maritime places, especially, but not only, physical islands. Conflict not only drove the Andalusians from the shores of the Guadalquivir to those of Crete but also afforded them shelter on the island, as outside forces proved too weakened by war to intervene. Somewhat insulated by geography as much as by a set of historical conjunctures, the routed rebel became rooted *amir*, and an island emirate took shape. This insulation was clearly contingent, however, and never meant that this or any other island was truly isolated from its forelands. In the case of Crete, there are glimpses of crucial ties with sea rovers from the shores of Tunisia as well as with smaller Aegean islands, one of which, the island of Naxos in the Cyclades, was paying tribute to the Cretan Amirs (Christides 2018: 1–4). Even in very different seas, where it is difficult to construe mainland shores as "opposite" in the sense of the intimately located places of crossing denoted by the Arabic *al-ʿudwa* or the Greek *he peraia*, and where islands have the most robust "aquatic perimeter" imaginable on this globe—such as the archipelaga of Oceania—we find evidence for interactions between islands and even with the distant South American shores in the circulation of obsidian, basalt, plants, and similarities of tool kits (Rainbird 2007: 112; Wilmshurst et al. 2011: 1819–20). Both older studies and the newer revisionist work agree on this point, though more recent work by Atholl Anderson and a number of other scholars reasserts the importance of remoteness and isolation, and points to the fact that some islands such as Rapa and Rapa Nui (Easter Island) were more remote and, for a variety of reasons that include remoteness as only one of several factors, more isolated (Anderson and Kennett 2012: 254; Martinsson-Wallin and Crockford 2001: 244–78). In sum, the ever-shifting balance between isolation and connectivity is a crucial variable in the history of shores and islands, and in the period under consideration here it plays out in the growing intimacy of many different cultures with the maritime world just as it does in the development of particular island imaginaries and visualizations.

Finally, how do histories of shores and islands help us make sense of the "medieval period"? The term medieval was developed for European history. More recently, the notion of the Global Middle Ages has sought to free the term from its Eurocentric heritage, but understandably headway has still to be made in integrating large areas of the globe; for example and most importantly for a chapter on coasts and islands, the great expanses occupied by Pacific islands or the Caribbean are not usually included in medieval histories even though archaeological data from both contexts dates to the very same "medieval" centuries. In contrast, modern thalassography, the historical approach that since the mid-twentieth century privileges maritime spaces and decenters terrestrial frames of inquiry, has focused primarily on the Mediterranean but has more recently also engaged substantively with the Indian Ocean, the Atlantic world, the Caribbean, and the East China Sea. In both global medievalist and thalassographic approaches, a focus on islands and the littoral helps define the diversities and connectivities of the globe in the premodern period, and addresses the limitations of historiographical regionalism. The centuries covered in this chapter witnessed significant transformations in which shores and islands played pivotal roles. In economic terms this period is characterized by increasing integration of the Indian Ocean and Mediterranean systems, as well as the expansion of human endeavor in the Pacific. In environmental terms, this same timespan encompasses two sets of complex climatic phenomena, the Medieval Warm Period (or Medieval Climate Optimum) and the onset of the so-called Little Ice Age. The former, associated with warmer conditions and rising sea levels, saw a host of attendant changes in food production and resource exploitation; though far from halting the economic integration, the onset of the Little Ice Age may have caused local downturns and depopulation of more fragile littoral and island environments, such as those of the important maritime corridor of the Red Sea where droughts and food insecurity has been linked to political instability in early modernity (Serels 2018). Furthermore,

ISLANDS AND SHORES

as Emmanuelle Vagnon discusses in this volume, at the same time this period witnessed the development of new ways of picturing maritime space, of mentally and visually connecting distant shores through mapping, and particularly of describing islands, of cognitively, discursively, and visually "islanding them." Medieval geographic and cartographic renditions of the Mediterranean, the

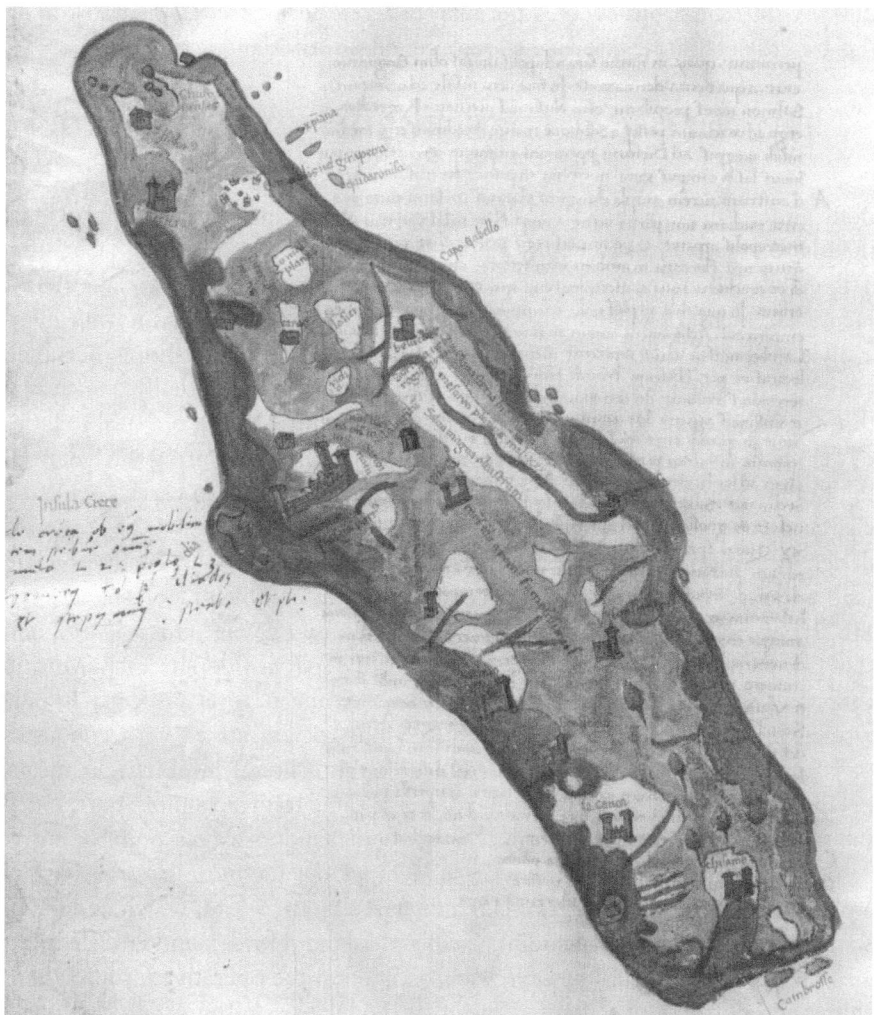

FIGURE 5.2 Detail of the island of Crete from a copy of Cristoforo Buondelmonti's *Liber insularum Archipelagi*, c. 1465–75. Gouache on paper. © Bibliothèque nationale de France, Département Cartes et plans, GE FF-9351 (RES).

Indian Ocean and East China Sea depict marine space as a world of islands; see, for example, the view of the Indian Ocean from the eleventh-century Egyptian geographical compendium the *Kitāb gharā'ib al-funūn wa-mulāh al-'uyūn* (The Book of Curiosities). The new literary genre of the *isolario* or atlas of island maps, a geographical genre devoted exclusively to islands, distinguishes the Middle Ages as a time when islands and shores came to be systematically imagined as a geohistorical reality. The earliest example is Cristoforo Buondelmonti's *Liber insularum archipelagi* of 1420 (Buondelmonti 2018; Legrand 1897; Tolias 2007) with renderings such as the map of Crete in Figure 5.2 demonstrating the greater detail now afforded to representations of island geography.

THE POLITICAL EDGE: BORDERS, STATES, AND STATELESSNESS

Both under the short-lived Muslim principality and as a Byzantine province, the island of Crete functioned as a border in the middle of sea, to use Christina Tsigonaki's felicitous characterization of late antique Crete (Tsigonaki 2019). Henri Pirenne (1937) famously presented the medieval Mediterranean as a divided and dividing sea, with its northern and southern shores occupied respectively by Christian and Muslim states and cultures, mutually constituted through antithesis and hostility. Indeed, shores feature in the political realities of the medieval period somewhat differently than they did during the height of the Roman Empire. The Arabic term *'udwa* for the shore can carry a semantic charge of confrontation. Furthermore, the Arabic term *thaghr* that came to designate borderlands and especially ports and coasts of the Mediterranean (and only later of the Indian Ocean) conjures the notion of antagonism between the "House of Islam" (*dār al-islām*) and the "House of War" (*dār al-harb*), and thus points to the currency of a vision of a divided world. The early Muslim caliphates and their successors fortified Mediterranean ports and early Islamic historiography devotes often separate sections to war at sea with conquests of islands particularly emphasized. But at a more literal level, *thaghr* means opening or entry point, and metonymically it came to mean simply port, much the same way that the Latin term *portus*, denotes a doorway, a point of entry. Also, the semantic range of the term *'udwa* includes the more neutral sense of a place across from another, similar to the Greek term *peraia*, which designates shores across from a vantage point, usually an island (Horden and Purcell 2000: 133). Moreover, the Arabic *sāhil*, "coast," is often the operative term for both shores and ports. In the Mediterranean, as the history of Alexandria can attest, ports and shores were edges of diplomacy as much as they were contentious or marginal borderlands. Thus, without adopting Pirenne's notion of a rigid temporal break at the rise of Islam or an overdrawn boundary between realms, people, and cultures, we can still point to political disunity of the late antique and medieval Mediterranean world as an important dynamic for the political status of littoral places in the centuries before the early modern period.

While construed in the medieval Mediterranean-centered imagination as borders separating the *dār al-islām* and the *dār al-harb*, however, littoral and island space of the Mediterranean and other seas were often politically ambiguous. In the earlier Middle Ages, the tenure of expansive, imperial, land-based states, particularly the Abbasid Caliphate (750–1256) or Tang China (618–907), on the coast was never entirely firm, and the political liminality of places on the shore is a more common reality than tight and centralized government. Shores and islands were often no state's land, a politically ambiguous zone often out of the reach of terrestrial political authority. In the later Middle Ages, the Rasulids of Yemen (1229–1454), a dynasty whose realm straddled critical crossroads of global trade and who presided over a transregionally connected state, may be said to have pursued a "transoceanic policy" (Vallet 2005, 2010), yet their direct control over their own coasts and islands of the Southern Arabian seaboard appears to have been minimal. Instead the littorals were under the purview of tribal entities, in contact but not coterminous with the powers further inland.

This phenomenon of fragmented sovereignty was often more pronounced in the case of islands; just like shores they were not usually within easy reach of land-based powers and imperial entities. In the twelfth century, the Kadamba dynasty of present-day Karnataka erected some of the few maritime-themed hero stones in India and in inscriptions a sovereign boasted of being ruler of the Western Ocean and of having conquered Sri Lanka over a bridge of ships (Tripati 2005: 4–5, 7). The mythic element in these boasts of conquest and possession is paralleled in a variety of metropolitan mainland discourses notably in East Asia and across the Islamic world, that conversely distance islands and the maritime. As discussed by James Louis Smith in this volume, the repository of medieval Arabic wonders literature is replete with islands ruled by utopian or dystopian regimes (Lauri 2013; Toorawa 2012), and shares with both European and Chinese models the particularly fascinating tradition of islands ruled by women (Toorawa 2012). The remoteness, inaccessibility, and alterity that characterize all these fictional islands may also reflect the difficulties that land-based metropolitan powers faced in attempts to master maritime lands. All the way through the Middle Ages to the latter-day eponymous utopian tale of Thomas More's *Utopia* in the dawn of early modernity, islands could be imagined in mainland contexts as political and social laboratories precisely because they were beyond the reach of mainland politics. As the compiler of Indian Ocean geographical fact and fiction Abu Zayd al-Sirafi put it, addressing what was probably a literate but non-littoral audience in the tenth century, "the sea is full of countless stories like this, of forbidden islands that the sailors cannot find, and of others that can never be reached" (*Akhbār al-sīn wa-l-hind* 2014: 28–9).

Partially as a correlate of their political liminality, shores could serve as hideouts and escape routes, while islands offered themselves as ideal refuges for political dissidents and upstarts alike, as in the genesis of the Cretan Emirate. Prisons and places of exile also abounded on shores and islands. This was as much a topos of mainland imaginings of islands as bounded and controllable spaces as it was a reality propelled by the contours of political geography discussed above; if states could not control actors, it was easier to expel them to "prisons" in inaccessible places. Thirteenth-century traveler Ibn al-Mujawir provides a list of what he calls the "prisons of the kings" (Ibn al-Mujawir 2008: 138); featured among these places of incarceration ostensibly used by both mythical and historical sovereigns are Dahlak, Aydhab, Siraf, and Aden, all at water's edge and the most important maritime hubs of the Red Sea and the Gulf before the thirteenth century. While cultivating notions of sacred and utopian islands, in Tang, Song, and Yuan times Chinese imperial practice also included exiling dissidents or disgraced officials to islands (Luo and Grydehøj 2017). We should probably take such references to island and littoral prisons with a grain of salt: in premodern times, before the enhanced transportation and surveillance technologies, these were not cases of confinement of prisoners in surveilled spaces. Medieval island prisons were no Robben Island or Alcatraz; they were places of banishment, where mainland powers could hope that their undesirables would languish outside networks of connectivity or at least remain beyond the perimeter of state sovereignty.

If the construct of exemplary prisons demonstrates the edges and limitations of state sovereignty, however, a second and in some ways opposite phenomenon implicates shores and islands in politics: the creation of independent or semi-independent polities at water's edge. Describing the sovereign of a bicoastal polity of the Gulf in the tenth century, historian al-Thaʿlabi calls the Ridwan b. Jafar Al Julanda Lord of the Waters and Master of the Fort of Huzu, the latter a stronghold that also functioned as a maritime observation tower (Williamson 1973: 25). A variety of polities, holding onto water's edge include the Zurayids of Aden and, of course, the Italian maritime republics of Pisa, Genoa, and Venice. In Spain, post-Umayyad polities such as the *taifa* of Denia, also distinguished themselves from their neighbors—whether allies or adversaries—further inland. Port city states in Southeast Asia and shoreline client kingdoms in South Asia also fall under this category of maritime regional states. The self-contained nature of medieval polities that developed on different kinds of islands and island complexes—Crete, Sicily, the Dahlaks, Pemba, Zanzibar, the Maldives, Sri Lanka, Hainan—signals the ramifications of connectivity for political economies and the realities of sovereignty within islands and between islands and mainland shores. A practical reality of sovereignty emerges, not one enshrined in the kind of legal thinking about free or dominated maritime space that Grotius and Selden outlined in the early modern era, but one practiced through effective control of resources and circulation across specific land-and-sea realms, that we might call, using a geographical term that seeks to describe the spatial extent of particular island and maritime cultures, maritories (*merritoires*) (Fleury 2013; Needham 2009).

THE ECONOMIC EDGE: MARITIME BOUNTIES, COMPLEMENTARY ECONOMIES AND CROSSROADS OF TRADE

As Wynne-Jones and Harland discuss in their chapter on "Practices" in this volume, products of the sea constituted one of the distinguishing features of littoral economies and cultures, from diets and the staples that sustained littoral peoples and their activities to delicacies and other marine specialties that connected them to trade networks and markets. The travel-writers, such as Ibn al-Mujawir and Ibn Battuta, to whom we turn for the less fabular descriptions of the Indian Ocean littoral, for actual island and maritime peoples' economic and cultural practices, give us a good sense of how these populations related culturally to the bounties of their maritime realm. But while travelers and other authors who approach the shores from a metropolitan and mostly landlubber perspective insist on the predominance of the aquatic fare—what to them and/or their audiences would have seemed in various ways exotic—brief references in these same accounts and the archaeological record examined by Wynne-Jones and Harland suggest the various ways in which most littoral people pursued quintessentially mixed diets, variously combining fish, mollusks, and aquatic birds with terrestrial mammals and other animals and plants. In other medieval contexts, even the intrepid seafarers who populated the island world of Outer Oceania and the Norse who reached the coasts of North America, settled near the coast to farm. These activities too were part of the mixed economies that characterized the shore and that exemplifies the various maritories' substantial combination of the aquatic with the terrestrial.

Complementarity of maritime and terrestrial subsistence and commercial economy often imposed on the life of littoral people a marked seasonality as well as a division of labor along gender lines. Pearl fishing is best practiced during the end of spring and beginning of summer in the Persian Gulf, suggests the Muslim polymath Abu'l-Rayhan al-Biruni (1936–7) in the eleventh century, while in the Gulf of Mannar good pearl-fishing years alternated with others when the banks yielded little and fishing became unviable, according to Francis Xavier in the sixteenth century (Schurhammer 1977: 2:312). Surely the workforces performing these tasks—just as in later, ethnographically recorded times—spent the rest of the year, or years of no returns, in other maritime activities and/or tending flocks and date trees on land. In medieval England, the seasonal migration of fish along the coast was mirrored by the staging of fairs on land where prodigious catches were sold—in fact the very word fair is etymologically derived from the word for voyage (Kowaleski 2010: 118–22) and clearly also suggests seasonality.

Beyond subsistence, diet, and cuisine, the medieval littoral and, especially, island populations procured a variety of products to markets further afield. These goods meant for islanders, as Braudel put it, "well-earned reputations" (1972: 1:157). Island commodities that circulated beyond the confines of the islands themselves included exceptional natural resources produced primarily or exclusively in ecologically unique insular microenvironments—think of the mastic of Chios (Bakirtzis and Moniaros 2019), Socotra's aloe and "dragon blood" (Biedermann 2006: 48–9), or the nutmeg, mace, and cloves of the "Spice Islands" as medieval examples—or more common goods enhanced by their insular place branding such as wines, cheese, metals, and pottery. Before the age of imperialism and protocolonialism in early modernity, the paradox of island products' "curious prominence, far beyond their intrinsic worth" (Horden and Purcell 2000: 227) appears to have worked more often than not to the benefit of island peoples and to speak to their participation in regional and transregional networks. This is to be contrasted to the well-known cases of intensive island monocultures exploited by outsiders—the sugar islands of the Atlantic and the Indian Ocean constituted just one such example—that, as Braudel noted, proved to be detrimental for the island societies that procured them (1972: 155–7).

Ultimately what distinguishes and unites island and mainland littoral economies more broadly speaking is their concatenation through predominantly maritime networks and the procurement of marine products. In addition to the fishy delicacies discussed by Harland and Wynne-Jones and the chanks examined by Lambourn in her Introduction to this volume (see Figure 0.6), in the medieval period the bounties of the sea that were converted into specialty goods included pearls, mother-of-pearl and other nacreous shells, cowries, tortoiseshell, coral, ambergris, purple and odoriferous shell opercula. Pearls take pride of place, confirming the famous observation by al-Biruni about their universal appeal (al-Biruni 1936–7). The importance of pearls and pearling to wider Indian Ocean trade is subtly hinted at in the iconography of a Rasulid coin minted at their port of Aden, the only coastal mint in their domains (Figure 5.3). While fish occasionally feature in Islamic coinage as part of the zodiacal signs Pisces or Virgo, the motif here of two fish circling a pearl is a pointed reference to the maritime focus and source of wealth of this port. Pearls and mother-of-pearl as well as comparable nacreous surfaces of other seashells were indeed a product of littoral laborers that most ubiquitously ended up in

FIGURE 5.3 Fish swimming around a pearl on a Rasulid silver *dirham* from the mint of the port city of Aden, 791/1384–5. Copenhagen, The David Collection, c268. © Pernille Klemp. The David Collection.

non-littoral realms and transferred the texture and imagery of the sea from the shores to their hinterlands, on the monuments, furnishings, and clothing of urban metropoles.

But how did littoral people themselves relate to the prized products they procured? One glimpse appears in the thirteenth-century story of a Yemeni fisherman who, mid-ocean, came across a large piece of ambergris; he picked up the precious flotsam without knowing its worth and returned to shore where, lacking firewood, he burned it to keep warm, earning the preposterous nickname "the man who burns ambergris in his hearth" (Ibn al-Mujawir 2008: 145–6). That ambergris was generally procured by fishermen as much as beachcombers is clear. This piece of folklore also conveys something of the contrast between life on the shore and life at the places where the littoral products were consumed. In the Central Andean kingdom of Chimu (*c*. 900–1470), the dazzlingly colored *Spondylus* shell featured in luxury objects, as it did in many other cultures of precontact Central and South America, and pointed to long-distance trade networks along coasts and between coasts and inland sites (Pillsbury 1996; Velázquez Castro 2017). Scenes of *spondylus* divers at work (Figure 5.4) point intriguingly but elusively to this very distance between littoral procurers and

FIGURE 5.4 Chimu gold earspool from the Central Andes with a maritime scene of divers working from a boat to collect the prized spondylus shell, thirteenth to fifteenth century. Atlanta, Michael C. Carlos Museum, 1992.015.261A/B. © Michael McKelvey, Michael C. Carlos Museum, Emory University.

consumers (Pillsbury, Potts, and Richter 2017: 93, 171, 200). But conversely, there are cases of coastal elites using shells and other marine luxuries in ways that parallel their valuation in inland metropoles. It is well established that cowries served as a form of currency across regions from the Bay of Bengal to the Atlantic and in many places in between, particularly inland West Africa and Yunnan in China during the late Middle Ages and early modernity (Hogendorn and Johnson 1986). Harvested in the Maldives, they appear in archaeological contexts in the archipelago (Haour, Christie, and Jaufar 2016), as well as in the text of al-Sirafi who reports already in the tenth century that they were used locally as money and even stored by the island queen in an early example of sovereign wealth (*Akhbār al-sin wa-l-hind* 2014: 24–5). The circulation of goods such as cowries and chanks and of their symbolism begs the question of the mechanics of connectivity between shores, hinterlands, and forelands. In this respect it is important to consider that certain denizens of shores specialized in connectivity by becoming themselves hubs. Moreover, littoral material culture and cultic practices demonstrate that the maritime infused shore and island cultures in distinct ways. The next two sections explore these two aspects of littoral culture.

ENCOUNTERS AT THE EDGE: TRANSIENTS, OPPORTUNISTS, AND LITTORAL GO-BETWEENS

In the thirty-ninth "session" or chapter of the *Maqāmāt* (Assemblies) of belle-lettrist al-Hariri's celebrated work of Arabic versed prose, the hero, Abu Zayd of Saruj, talks his way onboard a ship anchored at Basra and about to sail. Working in the first half of the thirteenth century, two illustrators of this much-copied work chose to depict the very scene, intrigued, perhaps, by the energy and pregnancy of the moment of embarkation and the vivid juxtaposition of shore, sea, and ship that the human figure bridges (Figure 5.5). The text goes on to describe the trickster's promise to those onboard of a special blessing for travelers, as well as the misadventures that follow on the high seas and the subsequent deliverance of all on the shores of an unknown island. Thus the images visually highlight the shore's nature as the interface of land and sea, while text and image in tandem conjure the beach as the domain of "castaways, gods, and madmen" and more generally "liminal characters," to borrow from

FIGURE 5.5 The trickster Abu Zayd on shore talking his way onto an ocean-going ship. Illuminated manuscript of al-Hariri's *Maqāmāt* (Assemblies), early thirteenth century. St Petersburg, Institute of Oriental Manuscripts, Russian Academy of Sciences, Ms. c-23, fol. 260. © Heritage Images/Getty Images.

John Mack's important essay on beaches (2011: 166–72). The character of Abu Zayd is the quintessential liminal figure, the *ibn al-sabīl* or "son of the road" (al-Hariri 1898: 2, 95), a veritable vagabond as he self-identifies in the text, a trickster whose prowess at transformation and the crossing of boundaries unfolds over this and the other adventures told in the *Maqāmāt*.

Through text and image, then, Abu Zayd reminds us of beaches as escape routes and zones of transition often inhabited by transients and outsiders. There was opportunity for reinvention and new beginnings in such spaces, even as the risks associated with exile and alienation lurked. One group of people whose presence on shores was fraught with danger and painful transition were the enslaved. By examining legal and documentary materials, Hasan Khalilieh has described the dynamics of the legal status of slaves onboard ships (Khalilieh 2010), and more broadly geographies of medieval slavery suggest that crossing shores was a common experience of enslaved people in the Middle Ages. Material vestiges of those passages are not as prominent as the later Atlantic slave trade's built infrastructure along that ocean's shores, and overall the archaeological vestiges of slavery are very slim for the period (Insoll 2003: 54), but in one medieval example the large number of cisterns on the island of Dahlak Kebir has been linked with textual sources attesting to the transfer through the islands of slaves from the Horn of Africa destined for the Yemen, Egypt, and beyond in the Indian Ocean and the Mediterranean (Insoll 2003: 54–6). It is important to note that perilous crossings, even those associated with the structures of enslavement, did not inexorably lead to singular fates, and the stories of those who found opportunities in movement stand out in the historical record and play out on and across shores. A remarkable example implicates the very same shores and islands of the Southern Red Sea: in the late eleventh century three brothers, sovereigns of an Abyssinian slave dynasty ruling the coastal lowlands of the Tihama in Yemen, were ousted from their territory by highland rivals. They fled across the water to the Dahlak islands where they liaised with the local sovereign, regrouped and from there staged their return. Ousted a second time, one of them, Jayyash bin Najjah, ended up fleeing to the Yemeni port of Aden, crossing the Arabian Sea to the shores of Western India and returning, along with an Indian enslaved concubine who soon became queen mother to the next ruler of the Najjahid state (al-Umara 1892: 81–93). Set at the crossroads of increasing maritime trade, and as told by the chronicler of Yemen in the following century, this is a story of crossings and opportunities in the world of the medieval Indian Ocean while also reflecting on the fluid and diverse structures of slavery in the Middle Ages.

Opportunities existed in more routinized crossings as well, especially in the kind of transregional trade incidentally involved in the story of Abu Zayd's voyage and amply evidenced in a variety of other sources for the medieval period. Cross-cultural trade, that is trading across geographical, political, ethnic, linguistic, and religious divides, happened in particular spaces and required mediators (Curtin 1984), and Greg Dening's (2004) metaphorical use of "the beach" to speak about spaces and even agents of negotiation fits well the context of increasing transregional, transoceanic connectivities among diverse peoples in the Middle Ages. It is important to note the many reported modes of negotiation on and across medieval shores. Silent trade, a shoreline encounter in the classic report of the phenomenon—Herodotus's account of trading exchanges between the seafaring Carthaginians and their trading partners on the African Atlantic coast in the middle of the first millennium BCE—also has its medieval examples. In one case, Abu Zayd al-Sirafi compiles accounts of trade with the islanders of the Nicobar Islands in which ambergris, coconuts, and other goods are exchanged for iron and clothing, the whole negotiation taking place through gestures (*Akhbār al-sin wa-l-hind* 2014: 5–6, 9). On the face of it, silent trade appears to require a minimum of contact and thus, whether real or imagined, conveys a maximum of cultural distance. At the same time, in some of the better-documented examples, the practice suggests shared ideas about reciprocity and fair exchange as well as a basic interdependence (Bonner 2011; Sacks 2014: 65–85).

A different and much more generalized mode of exchange was the domain of specialists who mediated between the different players along the maritime edge, at port cities and elsewhere. In the study of medieval transregional trade, a lot of attention has been paid to such individuals, embedded at points of crossing and facilitating trade and acting as cross-cultural brokers in the sense developed by Philip Curtin (1984) in his classic work on cross-cultural trade. Attested in a variety of literary and documentary sources across the Afro-Eurasian world is an array of titles for such facilitators, who translated, accommodated, and negotiated for others, the most prominent among them coming from the Arabic linguistic sphere stretching from the Mediterranean to the Southeast Asian world of trade—*wakil al-tujjar*, "representative of the merchants," *amir, kabir/rais/malik al-tujjar*, variously Chief or Prince of the merchants, and *shahbandar*, Lord of the Port (Goitein 1967–93; Goldberg 2012; Margariti 2007; Prange 2018). These titles denoted littoral social capital as well as institutional arrangements that may have ranged in degrees of formality but all functioned at the interface between individual traders arriving for the most part from overseas and communities or governments of polities at the receiving shores.

In the Middle Ages and in the context of the increasingly globalized world, that interface generally grew denser and the institutions that it generated have parallels into the onset of the modern world. "Brokerage institutions and commercial sponsorship," writes Miran with reference to the nineteenth-century port of Massawa, were particularly prevalent in "settings such as commerce orientated city-states, where in the lack of a strong centralized and regulating bureaucratic government, brokers played the role of facilitating international commercial relationships" (Miran 2009: 114). Noting the affinity among such institutions in commercial cultures across the Western Indian Ocean, Miran concludes that "the appearance of an assertive and centralizing modern-type administration" (114) under successive colonial regimes transformed and diminished the role of the resident brokers who had operated in earlier periods. It is the presence of go-betweens in medieval port cities that render the latter integral pieces of the shore in both the literal and metaphorical sense, precisely because they were hubs of encounter and negotiation.

LITTORAL CULTURAL LANDSCAPES: MATERIAL CULTURE AND RITUAL PRACTICES

Shores and islands anchor the maritime cultural landscape, a term developed by Norwegian archaeologist Christer Westerdahl to signify the "unity of remnants of maritime culture on land as well as underwater" (1992: 5). While the nature and distinctness of the maritime cultural landscape may remain somewhat disputed, the emphasis on the view from the sea has proven very useful. Maritimity is not a ubiquitous force in the cultures of island and littoral populations. But because islanders and littoral people can be shown to draw their "understandings of the world through associations with the sea as much or more than the land" (Rainbird 2007: 49), the maritime cultural landscape is a distinctly generative force and a point of convergence in their histories, just as proximity and easy access to the sea, reliance on maritime transport and the seaborne circulation of goods and modes of subsistence substantially linked to maritime food resources distinguish their material basis (Crumlin-Pedersen 2010). Expressions of the maritime cultural landscape from the vantage point of shores and islands vary, but some commonalities emerge in architecture and the built environment, maritime imagery on a variety of objects and expressions, and ritual and funerary practices, thus encompassing materiality, visuality, and spirituality.

Starting with materiality, building material collected, extracted, or scavanged along the shore distinguishes the built landscape of several medieval littoral places. Along tropical and subtropical seas, habitations, sea- and city-walls, and monumental edifices were built of coral quarried live underwater or fossilized on the shoreline, as archaeological investigations of sites on the Red Sea, the East African coast, and the Maldives demonstrate (Horton 1996; Insoll 2003). Ibn al-Mujawir—offering one of those rare textual descriptions of the mundane material culture of the littoral—lingers on the use of coral blocks (Ibn al-Mujawir 2008: 235), clearly because in his eyes it characterized the culture of the Red Sea, thus foreshadowing the use of the term "Red Sea Style" by architectural historians today (Um 2013). Another example of a maritime building material is the timber of mangrove, a truly amphibious tree that grows in tropical marine estuaries and protected shallows. Mangrove wood was used not only in terrestrial structures—mangrove poles feature in buildings at medieval sites across the western Indian Ocean from Shanga in the Lamu archipelago to Siraf in the Arabian Gulf—but also in shipbuilding along with other timbers that traveled long distances, thus, literally as well as metaphorically connecting distant shores.

Shipwreck timbers that end up in the hands of littoral people and may be ultimately reused in built environments constitute a special category of distinct material culture. The materiality of shipwreck reuse evokes the border of land and sea and the "recursivity" that characterizes the movement across it, while the discourse that often surrounds such reuse—accessible in the form of stories reported about the edifices constructed—exposes what that evocation may have meant for littoral people. That shoreline populations build whole lives out of flotsam washing up on their shores is well documented across the globe from various periods, but the kinds of uses to which flotsam was put and the associations it engendered in any one instance speaks to both the practical interests and the range of spiritual concerns of littoral people at the time. Medieval instances of reuse are visible through a variety of sources. On the practical side, a twelfth-century legal record of testimony from the document repository of the Cairo Genizah incidentally reports on widespread interest in, and collection of, shipwrecked timbers along the southern shores of Yemen (Margariti 2015). In the particular case recorded, the presence or absence of shipwrecked timbers belonging to a particular ship on its maiden voyage became evidence necessary for establishing the fate of the passengers and adjudicating the status of their surviving properties. But between the lines of the confirmation that "brand-new timbers" had washed up on certain segments of the Yemeni shore, we discern both the practice of collecting by and the extent of networks of littoral peoples.

Timbers collected at water's edge could be reused as structural elements in a variety of on- or offshore constructions—from grave coverings and houses to slipways and underwater barriers—or could be recycled back into shipbuilding. Reuse of older shaped timbers in boatbuilding is attested not only in arid and timber-poor regions but also in regions within close proximity of shipbuilding timber-rich forests, such as the Baltic and North Seas. Reused ship timbers in onshore constructions are attested as grave coverings at the Red Sea site of Quseir al-Qadim dating from the twelfth to the fifteenth century (Blue 2006: 279–81) and as "shelves, lintels and roof beams" at the site of Al-Balid in Oman (Belfioretti and Vosmer 2010). In Viking-era Denmark, timbers were reused in boatbuilding as well as in barriers to navigational channels (Crumlin-Pedersen 2010; Hinkkanen and Kirby 2013: 92). However, the most spectacular cases of recycling emerge in stories about the establishment of shrines and the building of places of worship with the remains of shipwrecked ships and other extraordinary flotsam washing up on island and other shores. During a famous incident in the life of the Prophet Muhammad that took place before the onset of his prophetic mission, the roof of the Ka'ba was rebuilt with timbers scavenged from a Byzantine ship wrecked off the coast of the port city of Jeddah (Ibn Ishaq 1955: 84). The story is reported both in the earliest biography of Muhammad, composed in the eighth century and redacted in the ninth century, as well as in the earliest history of the city of Mecca, written in the eleventh century (Peters 1994: 48–9), thus firmly attesting to the entanglement of the maritime with a desert context, one that has been regarded, notoriously if entirely wrongly, as hostile to the sea. According to a tradition that may well originate in medieval times, St. Thomas, the evangelist of India, dragged a giant floating timber out of the sea onto dry land and there used it to build the first Christian shrine in the subcontinent (Schurhammer 1977: 2:582). In the Maldives, work on the Hukuru Miskit or Friday mosque on Male in the 1960s revealed a restoration inscription dated 1337 from an earlier mosque that had been carved on a 3-meter-long teak plank whose shape and drilled holes and other cuttings clearly point to its first use in the hull of a sewn ship (Kalus and Guillot 2005: 27–36, figs. 3 and 4). Furthermore, Eastern Christian hagiography preserves the story of coffins bringing saintly bodies to the shores of the eastern Peloponnese all the way from Iberia; having been martyred at the hands of invading Muslims and subsequently having traversed the length of the Mediterranean, the relics of the saints Eulalia, Valerius, and Vincent of Barcelona were received by local communities who made of the miraculous flotsam the center piece of subsequent shrines (Kalligas 2010: 13).

Partly driven by the concerns of that view from the sea, the shores come to host shrines and graves that clearly look out to sea. Lines of sight and shelter visible from the sea are important in the placing of the large numbers of "island and shore-hugging archipelago chapels" registered either through texts or through the material record of medieval Scandinavia (Westerdahl 2012). Because orthodoxies of tightly governed places may not have applied, but also because of the compelling appeal of sheltered littoral waters, shrines on shores and especially on islands sometimes became places of shared worship. Examples include the Marian chapels found on small islands and shores across the medieval Mediterranean, where Latin and Greek Christians worshipped en route but also in rooted ways from land, and the island of Lampedusa where Muslims and Christians were, by the sixteenth century, venerating their respective holy protectors in a single shrine (Remensnyder 2018). In the central and eastern Indian Ocean shores, shrines to Boddisattva Avalokitesvara, a protector against dangers at sea, as well as a host of related imagery track the eastward expansion of Buddhist networks (Bopearachchi 2014; Ray 2003: 258–68). Graves and burial sites, an additional element of what Westerdahl calls the maritime ritual landscape, also reflect the concerns of both rooted communities of the littoral and those crossing it (Westerdahl 2012).

Thus, while outsiders create literary and conceptual topoi of island simulacra both positive and negative—prison islands, islands of exile, sacred islands, islands of bliss—real island, littoral, and maritime people in medieval times created their own sacred landscapes, responding to the maritime natural world and the maritime networks that sustain them. Considering these responses it might even be possible to pinpoint the kind of dialectic between mainland and maritime imaginations that island theorists have detected elsewhere (Baldacchino 2008; Luo and Grydehøj 2017).

Ultimately, island and coastal histories of the Middle Ages can instruct us on the question of the "alterity of the ocean." Surveying geographical and interdisciplinary approaches to the high seas, Camille Parrain (2012) characterizes the ocean as a "difficult terrain"; the alterity is generated by its immensity, mutability, and complexity, and we are reminded that the oceanic realm differs from the coastal one. Conversely, Nicholas Purcell, emphasizes certain classical authors' hostility toward the sea, without drawing a strong distinction between coastal, insular, and open waters. Yet, in spite of the discursive othering of shores and islanding of islands, engagement with the maritime element becomes progressively more visible in the medieval period, and we might even say that it is possible to trace a growing intimacy with the sea. As Christian Fleury notes, in the present-day intensification of maritime communications, development of sophisticated maritime technology and growth in geographical knowledge of the sea does not result in greater proximity with the maritime element (2013: 1–2); indeed, the operation of twenty-first-century remote lighthouses, twentieth-century supertankers, and nineteenth-century steamships testifies to the exact opposite, to a distancing of humans from the multidimensional nature of the aquatic. As we have seen, people in the Middle Ages engaged with the sea ever more intimately and in myriad ways, ever more intensely inhabiting those most maritime stretches of terra firma, shores and islands.

CHAPTER SIX

Travelers

Texts and Contexts

SHARON KINOSHITA

In both history and fiction, medieval travelers—merchants, pilgrims, crusaders, and others—crossed the seas with surprising frequency and regularity. Yet relatively rare are the accounts left to us of their shipboard experiences. As Elizabeth Lambourn writes of the Jewish merchants who plied the sea lanes between Aden (near the mouth of the Red Sea) and the Malabar coast of southwest India: "It is as if the simple act of embarkation put travelers and everything accompanying them into a state of suspended animation from which they only awoke upon arrival" (2018: 33). To be sure, maritime wandering has a substantial role in the development of medieval romance, particularly those derived (however indirectly) from ancient Greek sources. Like its late antique counterpart, the medieval *Apollonius of Tyre*, for example—attested first in a mid-twelfth-century fragment in Old French and notably in a Castilian Spanish version from the mid-thirteenth century—is structured by the protagonist's maritime journeys with the vicissitudes of sea travel precipitating its many plot twists (Gingras 2006: secs.8–9; Kinoshita 2014: 320–1). In some cases, accounts of ships and sea voyages represent continuations of the ancient literary topos of the *navigatio vitæ*, as in the maritime imagery in the poetry of Charles d'Orléans, near the end of the Middle Ages (Noacco 2006). In such examples, the spiritual focus perhaps explains why observational details of sea voyages feature so passingly. The present chapter focuses, then, on the problematic absence of the voyage itself; it takes up the challenge of recovering the shipboard experiences of medieval travelers, both real and literary. My examples are primarily European (including texts by non-Christian authors from Spain such as Benjamin of Tudela and Ibn Jubayr, a court secretary to the Muslim king of Granada) in addition to a few South Asian examples.[1] It is not always easy to predict where such accounts might appear: of two writers recording similar journeys, one might include details of life at sea and the other none at all. In general, our authors show little interest in accounts of life onboard ship for their own sake but only to the extent that they feed the larger aims—political, cultural, theological, dramatic—of the narrative that contains them.[2] This includes the narrative literature of the Islamic world, which appears focused on topoi rather than observational detail until well into the seventeenth century (Hassan 2014; Zargar 2014). Famous image cycles such as the Indian Ocean ships illustrated to accompany certain thirteenth-century copies of al-Hariri's *Maqāmāt* (see Figure 5.5) accompany only the most passing textual descriptions of sea travel itself and operate above all to reinforce the narrative's emphasis on the exotic nature of the Indian Ocean world and its peoples.

A case in point is provided by Marco Polo, the most famous traveler of the European Middle Ages. From a family of Venetian merchants, Marco left home around 1271 at the age of seventeen; with his father and uncle, he traveled overland to the court of the Great Khan Qubilai, just as the Mongols were completing their conquest of Southern Song China. Marco spent the next two decades or so in Qubilai's service, crisscrossing his empire and visiting allied or tributary states. The Polos returned to Venice in 1295; four years later, Marco, by then captive in a Genoese prison, collaborated with an Arthurian romance writer named Rustichello of Pisa on a work they called the *Devisement du Monde* (*The Description of the World*) (Polo 2016)—usually, if misleadingly, known in English as *The Travels*.

Despite medieval Venetians' strong association with control of the Mediterranean—their overseas possessions were collectively known as the Stato da Mar—most of the travels logged by Marco were land miles. Maritime portions of *The Description of the World* are limited to "The Book of India," describing the sea route from southeast China, through the Indonesian archipelago, westward across the Indian Ocean; this corresponded in part with the sea route the Polos took home to Venice—only because the land route was temporarily blocked by wars among the rival Mongol khanates. Even here, the sea as such garners only a few passing mentions. Java, Marco reports, is the largest island in the world, "according to [...] good sailors [...] who know it well [....]. The Great Khan could never have it on account of the long and fearsome way of sailing there" (Polo 2016: 149). Between Sardan and Condur, two islands in the South China Sea off the coast of modern-day Vietnam, the water is so shallow that "large ships passing there raise their tillers" (150). In southern India, the Coromandel coast, he mentions the use of small boats for pearl fishing (157). Throughout, Polo shows great interest in port cities such as Zaytun (Quanzhou), Qa'il (Kayalpatnam), Hormuz, and Aden: their density of merchants, the volume and variety of goods traded, tariffs and customs regulations. The only seaborne phenomenon he treats expansively is piracy, as in his account of the "great robbers of the sea" operating off the coasts of Malabar and western India who do "great harm to merchants" (174). After describing the tactics adopted both by the corsairs and their victims, he adds this interesting anecdote:

> When these bad corsairs capture merchants, they make them drink tamarind and seawater so that the merchants get sick and throw up everything in their stomachs. The corsairs gather everything the merchants throw up and go through it to see if there are pearls or other precious stones, for the corsairs say that when merchants are taken, they eat the pearls and other precious stones so that the corsairs won't find them.
>
> (175)

All told, these passing mentions of maritime life occur in only a dozen or so of *The Description of the World*'s 233 short chapters. Otherwise, as elsewhere in his text, Polo gives his attention to describing the different kingdoms—their rulers, commodities, local customs, and other curiosities.

In "The Sea," one of the episodes in the *Maqāmāt* (Assemblies) of the early twelfth-century Andalusian writer al-Saraqusti, the trickster figure Abu Habib, addressing an audience in the Omani port of al-Sohar, alternately argues against and praises travel by sea. "What impels you to sail this raging sea, and to traverse this swelling flood when, on land, you have a wide enough expanse and room enough to wander? In contrast to that, before you lie the quagmires and the fears provided by the terrors of the sea!" (al-Saraqusti 2002: 149–50). On the other hand, the sea

> contains the watercourses and torrentbeds of human livelihood, pearls and coral, and gatherers and harvesters of its fruit. The sea generously produces clouds that put white silk and cotton to shame [...]. In the sea, one is safe if one is prudent; one takes or leaves its contents, endures the galloping speed at which it chooses to flow, while being spared the rigors of a swift camel-pace and trot.
>
> (153–4)

DEPARTURES: TREPIDATION AND PAGEANTRY

Sea journeys were a frightful prospect. In 1358, the Italian Humanist Francesco Petrarch declined an invitation to accompany his friend Giovanni Mandelli to the Holy Land; despite self-consciously casting his life in the Augustinian

tradition of life-as-pilgrimage, not even the glory of that ultimate experience—
"O blessed journey and sight to be coveted by the Christian soul!" (Petrarch
2002: Proem 2)—can tempt him. "Although numerous causes hold me back,
none is more powerful than fear of the sea" (Proem 3); he elaborates:

> I fear slow death and nausea worse than death itself, not without reason
> but from experience. How many times do you think I have challenged that
> monster in the hope that habit would defeat or soften nature? You ask if
> it did any good? I tell you I have not reduced my fear but rather by sailing
> redoubled the torment.
>
> (Proem 5)

French knight Jean de Joinville expresses the same fear in *The Life of Saint Louis* (c. 1309), his hagiographic biography of King Louis IX. Writing over a half-century later, he vividly recalls the experience of setting sail from the port of Marseille on the Seventh Crusade in 1248:

> Before very long the breeze had filled our sails and wafted us out of sight of
> land, so that we saw nothing but sea and sky around us, while each day the
> wind carried us farther and farther from the land where we were born. I give
> you these details so that you may appreciate the temerity of the man who
> dares, with other people's property in his possession, or in a state of mortal
> sin himself, to place himself in such a precarious position. For what voyager
> can tell, when he goes to sleep at night, whether or not he may be lying at the
> bottom of the sea the next morning?
>
> (Joinville and Villehardouin 1963: 196)

Mostly, however, accounts of major expeditions such as the Crusades emphasize not the writers' trepidation but the pageantry surrounding their departure. In his chronicle of the Fourth Crusade, the northern French knight Geoffrey of Villehardouin, one of the Crusade's organizers, underscores the splendor of the fleet's departure from Venice in 1202: "shields were hung round the bulwarks and round the castles fore and aft, while banners, many and beautiful, were quickly hoisted aloft [...]. No finer fleet of ships ever set sail from any port" (Joinville and Villehardouin 1963: 46). Robert de Clari, a simple knight who also penned an account of the Crusade in vernacular French, is more expansive. In his words, the lead galley belonging to the doge (duke of Venice):

> was all vermilion [with] a canopy of vermilion samite spread over him, and
> there were four silver trumpets trumpeting before him and drums making
> great noise [...]. And all the pilgrims [crusaders] had all the priests and clerks
> mount on the high poops of the ships to chant the *Veni creator spiritus*. And
> everyone, great and small, wept with emotion and for the great joy they had
> [...]. When they were on that sea and had spread their sails and had their
> banners set high on the poops of the ships and their ensigns, it seemed indeed

as if the sea were all a-tremble and all on fire with the ships they were sailing
and the great joy they were making.

(de Clari 1996: 42–3)

A riot of color, sound, and emotion, the excitement and celebration of this scene form a contrast to the tedium, the novelties, and the dangers of the sea journey ahead.[3]

SHIPBOARD ROUTINE: FROM MARITIME VISTAS TO LOVE SICKNESS

Between departure and arrival, the time spent at sea could be long and harrowing. Absent such dangers as storms, shipwreck, or pirate attacks, however, it is not unusual for our texts to pass over the journey itself with little or no comment. After the fanfare of their departure, Geoffrey of Villehardouin is content merely to mark the stages of the Fourth Crusaders' crossing: from Venice to Zara, Zara to Corfu, Corfu to Negroponte, Negroponte to Abydos, and Abydos to Constantinople. Benjamin of Tudela, a Jewish merchant from the Christian Iberian kingdom of Aragon who traveled to the eastern Mediterranean and Persia in the 1160s, recorded his transit between stops in such minimal detail that it is sometimes difficult to know whether he was traveling by land or by sea. In a contemporary literary example, Chrétien de Troyes's Old French romance *Cligés* (c. 1180), the Greek prince Alexander leaves Constantinople to win his spurs at King Arthur's court. Embarking on a "peaceful and calm sea" with a "gentle wind and calm air" (de Troyes 1994: 58, lines 244–5), his departure is accompanied by great fanfare, focusing on the sadness and concern of the people left behind; in contrast, the voyage from Byzantium to Britain is narrated in six short lines: "They were at sea all of April and part of May. Without great danger and without worry, they came to port at Southampton one day between vespers and nones. They cast anchor and docked at the port" (58, lines 270–5).

Ironically, one of the most vivid descriptions we have of a routine crossing is Petrarch's account of a voyage he never took. Having declined to accompany his friend Mandelli to the Holy Land, he proceeds to offer him a guide to what to see and expect. This *Itinerarium* (journey) begins with taking ship in Genoa; after leaving the port, Petrarch advises, "see that you do not take your eyes off the land that entire day. Many things will appear to them" to admire: beautiful valleys, running streams, hills of momentous ruggedness, strong castles on the cliffs, very large villages (Petrarch 2002: sec.2.5). Here Petrarch affords us a view of the Mediterranean practice of *costeggiare*—sailing close to shore—from the passenger's perspective. Like a tour guide standing at the ship's prow, Petrarch points out what to look for as the vessel skirts the coast: passing the mouth of the Arno, "Florence is certainly too far away to see, but the commander will show you Pisa from the deck of the ship, an ancient city which nevertheless has a modern and pleasant aspect" (7.0). He calls Mandelli's attention not just to the mainland but to the islands to the west. After passing Livorno, "if you turn to the right, you will have in front of you Gorgona and Capraia, two small islands under the control of the Pisans [...] If you look carefully you will also see the uncultivated island of Corsica, abundant with herds of wild animals" (7.2). As in all travel accounts, real or constructed, the narrative is shaped by the writer's frame of reference.

Once Petrarch has "guided" Mandelli south of Rome, his geography is transformed from that of current knowledge or observation—"two small islands under the control of the Pisans"—to that the classical world, of Roman history and legend. Avernus is "the immense home of the Cumean Sibyl, half ruined by age and uninhabited but full of nests for birds of very kind" (9.4); nearing Naples, one finds "Inarima, [...] an island noted for the praise of poets that the people today call Ischia, beneath which, it is said, the giant Typhoeus was buried by the will of Jupiter" (9.1); traversing the straits between Reggio Calabria and Messina, in Sicily, "one encounters those infamous marvels, most feared by navigators, Scylla and Charybdis" (12.2). Then, after crossing the Adriatic and coasting "the Achaean shore," Petrarch returns to his present with Crete, "which is now (observe the instability of things!) a Venetian possession; it was once the kingdom of Jupiter and was the source of every pagan belief" (14.1). Once the itinerary reaches the Holy Land, biblical and sacred history take over; the seascape through which Petrarch guides his friend Mandelli traverses millennia and multiple civilizations.

Focusing exclusively on the land visible from the deck of the ship, Petrarch pays no attention to the water itself. One rare description of the sea comes from the *Akhbār al-sīn wa-l-hind* (Accounts of China and India).[4] The lone surviving manuscript, missing its initial folios, opens in medias res with the sea creatures to be found in the Gulf of Oman, including one that

> often raises its head above the water, and then you can see what an enormous thing it is. It also often blows water from its mouth, and the water spouts up like a great lighthouse. When the sea is calm and the fish shoal together, it gathers them in with its tail then opens its mouth, and the fish can be seen in its gullet, sinking down into its depths as if into a well. The ships that sail this sea are wary of it, and at night the crews bang wooden clappers like those used by the Christians, for fear that one of them will blunder into their ship and capsize it.
>
> (*Akhbār al-sīn wa-l-hind* 2014: 3, 1.1.1)

At the other end of the text, the author-compiler assures us that he has offered "the best part of what my memory has been able to recollect at the time, given the wide range of accounts of the sea," and underscores the critical judgment he has used in selecting his sources:

I have avoided relating any of the sort of accounts in which sailors exercise their powers of invention but whose credibility would not stand up to scrutiny in other men's minds. I have also restricted myself to relating only the true contents of each account—and the shorter the better. And God it is who guides us to what is correct.

(69)

In the Mediterranean at least, the relative paucity of descriptions of shipboard experiences undoubtedly reflects the routinization of sea lanes. However hazardous and unpredictable maritime journeys might be, medieval sailors plied routes largely predetermined by topography, currents, and seasonal winds. In the mid-twelfth-century French romance *Floire and Blancheflor* the titular hero, a Saracen prince in pursuit of his sweetheart, a Christian slave who has been sold overseas, takes ship with some merchants who precisely time their journey from Iberia to Alexandria to coincide with the annual ritual held by the sultan of Babylon (Cairo); their crossing takes nine days, with Floire one stop behind Blancheflor every step of the way (Kinoshita 2006: 90). In the Old Norse-Icelandic *Íslendingasögur* (Sagas of the Islanders), voyages from Iceland to Norway are described briefly and formulaically, with mentions of "a smooth passage" or favorable winds that bring protagonists to their destination at the appointed time and place serving as a narrative bridge providing continuity between episodes. Deviating from this route (usually for political reasons) and thus having to brave the open seas rather than hugging the coast can, in contrast, expose the travelers to "unfavorable winds" and rougher sailing (Barraclough 2012: 2). On the other hand, on westward voyages from Norway—typically recounted as part of migration myths of the ninth-century *landnám* (land-taking or settlement) of Iceland—the drop in winds as ships near the coast reflects "a sense of supernatural interaction with the meteorological and oceanographic conditions, working in concert to welcome them and to create an effortless entry into the country"—part of thirteenth-century Icelanders' "fierce desire to define and legitimize a strong sense of Icelandic identity particularly in opposition to Norway" in a moment of high political tension (4–5). In contrast, voyages to Greenland are characterized by turbulent seas—"difficult currents, disorienting winds, darkness, and glaciers" (7), an accurate depiction of meteorological and oceanographic conditions—and the sense of sailing into the unknown.

Interestingly, Lambourn's conceit of the ship as a space of suspended animation (2018: 33) is literalized in some French romances of the twelfth and thirteenth centuries. In Marie de France's Old French *lai* (short verse narrative with Celtic motifs and settings) *Guigemar* from the second half of the twelfth century, the titular hero, grievously wounded in a hunting accident, nevertheless manages to cross woods and plain until he comes to a sheltered harbor. There he finds a ship that is "very well equipped [...] caulked outside and inside:

no man could find a joint there. There was no peg or closure that was not all made of ebony; under heaven there is no gold that is worth more. The sail was all made of silk, very beautiful when unfurled" (Marie de France 1990: 34, lines 153–60, Sharon Kinoshita's translation). Though utterly empty, the ship is lavishly furnished—its centerpiece a marvelous bed "of Solomon's work" crafted of gold, cypress wood, and ivory with bedclothes of sable swathed in Alexandrian silk. Guigemar, feeling his wound, lies down on the bed. By the time he gets up, he cannot leave: "the ship is already on the high sea" (36, line 192) being carried along by "good weather and a gentle wind" (36, line 194); that evening, the ship deposits him below the ancient city, capital of that land, where Guigemar will meet and fall in love with the (married) woman who will cure him of his wound.

The mundane details of life at sea are in general harder to come by. In *Las Siete Partidas*, a law code compiled under King Alfonso X of Castile in the mid-thirteenth century, the section on War at Sea specifies that ships should carry copious provisions, including "biscuit, which is a very light kind of bread, for the reason that it has been cooked twice and lasts longer than any other, and does not spoil," along with "salt meat, vegetables, and cheese which is food of such a kind, that a little of it can sustain a large number of people; and garlic and onions to prevent them from experiencing the bad effect of the sea air and of the impure water which they drink" (*Las Siete Partidas* 2001: 2:467).

The travel account of Ibn Jubayr, a court secretary to the Muslim king of Granada, who made the *hajj* to Mecca between 1183 and 1185, suggests that commercial passengers had access to a more varied diet. On his return journey, his ship has been out at sea for twenty-two days and the provisions travelers have brought with them have begun to run low; luckily, however, their ship is like

> a city filled with all commodities. All [the travelers] might wish to buy could be found: bread, water, and all kinds of fruit and victuals, such as pomegranate, quince, water-melon, pear, chestnut, walnut, chick-pea, broad-bean raw and cooked, onion, garlic, fig, cheese, fish and many other things it would be too long to describe.
>
> (Ibn Jubayr 2013: 329)

An anecdote related by Jean of Joinville in his *Life of Saint Louis* likewise seems to address shipboard diet and provisions. On the king's homeward journey, as the fleet nears the island of Pantelleria, the queen, Margaret of Provence, "begged the king to send three galleys there to get fruit for her children" even though the island was inhabited by "Saracens" subject to the kings of both Sicily and Tunis (Joinville and Villehardouin 1963: 324). This request, however, turns out to be the trigger of a much graver episode: the king consents, but when the galleys dispatched to the island fail to make their appointed rendezvous, they are presumed captured by the Saracens. The king orders the fleet to prepare for battle, causing the queen to wail, "Alas! this is all my doing!" In fact, the missing ships soon reappear—delayed, it turns out, because six young Parisians onboard "had lingered in the gardens, eating fruit," and the crews of the ships had not wanted to leave them behind (324). As punishment, the king orders the six put aboard the longboat "where murderers and thieves are stowed," despite their protests that they will be "for ever disgraced." Forced to remain there for the duration of the journey, they are subjected to great danger and discomfort: "when the sea rose high the waves flew over their heads, and they had to remain sitting all the time for fear the wind might sweep them off into the water" (325). We are not told whether the fruit over which they had incurred such punishment lost any of its appeal for the queen and her children.

Over the course of the high Middle Ages (*c.* 1000–1500), as long-distance sailing in the Mediterranean was increasingly monopolized by Latin Christians— Pisans, Venetians, Genoese, and Catalans— it was not unusual for Jewish and Muslim travelers such as our two twelfth-century Iberian contemporaries Benjamin of Tudela and Ibn Jubayr to cross the sea in Christian ships. For them, things that would have seemed routine or passed beneath the notice of their Christian counterparts aroused curiosity or elicited comments. Ibn Jubayr— more expansive, as we have seen, than Benjamin of Tudela—provides a couple of examples. Sailing onboard a Genoese vessel, he describes the "festival for the Christians" observed by "non-Arabs" on All Saints' Day:

> They celebrated it with lighted candles. Hardly one of them, big or little, male or female, but carried a candle in his hand. Their priests led them in prayers on the ship, then one by one rose to preach a sermon and recall the articles of their faith. The whole ship, from top to bottom, was luminous with kindled lamps.
>
> (Ibn Jubayr 2013: 328)

When passengers—either Christian and Muslim—died at sea, their bodies were cast into the water. In such instances, reports a scandalized Ibn Jubayr, the captain inherits their goods, "for such is their usage for all who die at sea. There is no way for the (true) heir of the dead to gain his inheritance, and at this we were much astonished" (2013: 329).

In literary texts, the time onboard ship is mentioned only when it serves the plot; mostly, as we shall see, this involves the hazards of maritime travel: storms, shipwrecks, pirate attacks, and the like. Occasionally, however, the sea sets a stage for occurrences less likely to take place on land. In *Cligés*, as we saw above, Alexander's five- to six-week journey from Constantinople to Southampton is narrated in a scant six lines. Not long after his arrival, Arthur decides to move his court from Winchester to Brittany. In contrast to the brevity of the long-haul journey, the short hop across the Channel consumes over 120 lines, from the first mention of Arthur's ship (de Troyes 1994: 68, line 441) to the moment it comes to port (76, line 565). In between, Alexander and Arthur's niece, Soredamors, are seized with love for one another—the episode inflated by the fact that each suffers in silence, neither one daring to confess their true feelings.

> The queen [Guenevere] took notice and saw the two of them frequently flush and grow pale, sigh and tremble, but she did not know why and attributed it to the sea [*la mers*] over which they sailed. Surely she would have recognized the cause had the sea [*la mers*] not deceived her; but the sea [*la mers*] tricked and deceived her, so that she could not recognize love [*l'amor*] on the sea [*en la mer*]. For they were on the sea [*en la mer*], but bitter [*amers*] pain caused their suffering, and love [*amor*] was their malady. But of the three [love, bitterness, and the sea] the queen knows only to blame the sea [*la mer*], for the two of them denounce to her the third and by the third the two are excused, though they are guilty in the matter.
>
> (de Troyes 1991: 129–30)

This precious wordplay between "la mer" (the sea) and "l'amor" (love), "amer" (to love) and "amer" (bitter) self-consciously evokes the famous episode from the Old French *Romance of Tristan*, in which a powerful love potion mistakenly consumed during the sea passage between Ireland and Cornwall locks the young protagonists Tristan and Iseut in an adulterous love that will indeed prove bitter (and in some versions, fatal) to both. In *Cligés*, there is no such obstacle: Alexander and Soredamors are in fact perfectly suited to one another and will soon be married under the auspices of the king and queen. Meanwhile, the interlude on the sea allows the author to display his poetic virtuosity, recoding the intertextual reference to *Tristan* to play on the impossibility of distinguishing love-sickness from sea-sickness. If the long-haul brings the Greek emperor's son to the Arthurian court, the short channel hop facilitates the union of the lovers who will become the parents of the titular protagonist.

HAZARDOUS SEAS: STORMS AND SHIPWRECKS

The most frequently reported, because the most terrifying and dramatic, incidents that took place on the high seas were the storms that could strike with such sudden intensity. The abundant literary and indeed documentary material about storms and shipwrecks across European (Cerrito 2006; Fern 2012; James-Raoul 2006) and other sources (Acri 2019; Margariti 2015; Shaw 2012, 2013; Vijayalekshmy 2014) has engendered a comparatively rich and theoretically informed bibliography within the cultural history of the sea.

On Ibn Jubayr's outbound journey, his ship is hit with a wind off the coast of Sardinia, "throwing the sea into turmoil and bringing rain and driving it with such force that it was like a shower of arrows" (2013: 27). On his return journey, "waves like mountains [...] tossed [the ship] like a tender twig [...]. With the darkening night the buffeting increased and our ears were smitten by the bellowing" (331). In the case of King Louis IX, his outbound journey—despite Joinville's misgivings—is largely uneventful; on the return journey, however, a sudden wind forces the king's ship back to Cyprus. The sailors drop anchor, and "no one dared to remain [on the upper deck] for fear the wind might sweep him off into the sea" (Joinville and Villehardouin 1963: 321). The queen, Joinville relates, comes looking for her husband to "ask him to make a vow to God, or to His saints, to go on pilgrimage so that the Lord might deliver us from the peril in which we were; for the sailors had said we were all in danger of drowning" (322). Joinville advises her:

> Promise that if God brings you back to France, you will offer a ship of silver, worth five marks, for the king, yourself, and your three children. Then I guarantee that God will bring you back to France; for I myself made a vow to Saint Nicholas that if he saved us from the peril we were in last night, I would go from Joinville, on foot and unshod, to visit his shrine at Varangeville.
>
> (322)

The queen goes off to find the king but soon returns, saying: "Saint Nicholas has saved us from our present peril, for the wind has fallen" (322). Once safely back home, the queen, Joinville reports, fulfilled her vow, commissioning a votive ship with herself and her family, the sailors, rudder, and rigging all crafted in silver, which Joinville duly delivered to the shrine of Saint Nicholas in Varangeville, as promised. Although few such votive pieces survive the subject of Saint Nicholas calming the storm was common.

On the coast between Rome and Naples, Petrarch encourages his friend Mandelli to seek "a more favorable navigation" by visiting "the sanctuary of St. Erasmus [Elmo], who according to a well-established belief, has in the past assisted people who encountered dangers at sea" (Petrarch 2002: sec.9.0). In Marie de France's twelfth-century Old French *lai Eliduc*, the ship of the titular protagonist, a knight sailing home to Brittany with the daughter of the king of Exeter, is caught in a sudden storm.

> They had a good wind and good weather
> and completely reassuring conditions.
> But when they were about to land
> they met a storm on the sea
> and a wind rose before them
> that threw them far from the harbor;
> it broke and split their mast
> and tore away their whole sail.
> They call devoutly on God,

Saint Nicholas and Saint Clement,
and my lady St. Mary,
that she seek help for them from her son,
that he should keep them from perishing
and that they should reach the harbor.
One moment backward, another forward,
they they were skirting the coast;
they were very close to shipwreck.

(1990: 308, lines 813–29)

Alongside God and the Virgin, Eliduc's crew, like Joinville and Queen Margaret, appeal to Saint Nicholas, the fourth-century bishop of Myra (in Asia Minor) widely venerated as a patron of sailors, and for good measure, Saint Clement, a first-century pope who (according to legend) was martyred by being tied to an anchor and cast into the Black Sea. These prayers, however, fail to produce the desired effect—because, one of the sailors accuses, Eliduc, although already married, is bringing home another woman, "contrary to God and contrary to the law, contrary to rectitude and contrary to faith" (Marie de France 1990: 310, lines 837–8). "Let us throw her into the sea!" he urges. Instead, Eliduc clubs the offending sailor with an oar and throws his body overboard and "the waves carry his body away" (310, lines 839, 864) while the princess faints dead away at learning her lover already has a wife. With that, they come safely to port.

Appeals to God and the saints for protection against hazards at sea are a staple of European maritime travel narratives but also feature prominently across Buddhist hagiographies, Sanskrit Sūtras, the classical Malay chronicle the *Sejarah Melayu*, and Jain literature from South Asia. In Buddhism certain bodhisattvas developed into saviors to be called on during times of distress and Avalokitesvara—known also as Padmapani, Guanyin in China, and Kuan Yin in Japan—later became the bodhisattva most commonly associated with mercantile and maritime communities (Rao 1991; Ray 1994: 153).[5] Literary protagonists, of course, typically survive even the most terrifying storms to continue their adventures. In the *Romance of Eneas* (a mid-twelfth-century Old French adaptation of Vergil's *Aeneid*) our titular hero survives the storm that batters his ship but vicariously experiences the terror of a watery death by witnessing the destruction of his fleet and the foundering of one of his ships:

Its helm was shattered and its mast and sail plunged into the sea. It spun about thrice in a very short time. A wave dashed over it, striking it so hard on one of its sides that it smashed and splintered the timbers. The bolts and the seams burst, and the water poured in through the cracks and filled it suddenly. In a moment it had sunk. These men have finished their suffering: they will never more fear any tempest; no land will ever be conquered by them, nor castles burned, nor towers besieged. The wind attacks the other ships; masts, sails, and yard-arms are torn to pieces and scattered over the sea, and Eneas wonders greatly. He thinks he will never come to port: both sky and sea promise him death.

(*Romance of Eneas* 1974: 60–1)

Yet he does not die, and his ship eventually brings him safely to shore in Libya for his fated rendezvous with Dido.[6]

Though most dramatic and violent, storms are not the only hazard encountered on the sea. As King Louis's ship nears Cyprus on his return journey to France (1254), "a mist rose from the land and spread from there down to the sea," causing the sailors to miscalculate their position and the ship to strike a sand bar under the sea. The shock of the collision causes Brother Raymond, a Templar in charge of the crew, to tear his beard and cry, "We're lost! We're lost!" Happily, the ship is eventually disengaged from the sand bar. When Brother Raymond goes to tell the king, however, "he found him lying prostrate on the deck in front of the Body of Our Lord on the altar, his arms stretched out to form a cross, barefoot, in his tunic only and with his hair uncombed, like a man who fully expected to be drowned" (Joinville and Villehardouin 1963: 319–20). On the one hand, the collision with the sand bar saves the ship from the greater danger of "a great mass of sunken rocks, where our ship would have been dashed to pieces" (319). On the other hand, the keel is extensively damaged, and even though his men all urge the king to procure a new, safer ship, Louis insists on placing himself, along with his wife and children, "in God's hands" (321) rather than to abandon the more than five hundred other passengers who are left to trust themselves to the old ship's hasty repairs.

Fog and mist likewise play a role in a curious episode from the *Orkneyinga Saga*, an Old Norse history of the earls of the Orkney Islands (in northern Scotland). In the mid-twelfth century, after Earl Rognvald's fleet passed the straits of Gilbraltar on his way to the Holy Land to fight in the Second Crusade, they encountered unusual conditions in the western Mediterranean:

On they sailed, east over the sea beyond the land of the Saracens, and came close to Sardinia though they did not know there was land there. The sort of weather they had was like this: for long periods there was dead calm, with fog and sea mist, so they could see little from the ships, and progress was slow. Then one morning the fog lifted and when they got up and looked around they saw two islands, but when they looked again later on, one of the islands had disappeared.

(*Orkneyinga Saga* 1978: 155)

But the earl immediately opines that what his crew had seen were not islands at all but "the kind of ship people in this part of the world use, called a dromond.

From a distance, they seem as big as small islands" (155). "They must be merchants of some kind" (155) he suggests: if Christian, he is prepared to "give them the chance to make peace with us," but if, as seems more likely, "they're heathen," then he is ready to engage them in battle and give a fiftieth part of the loot taken to the poor (156). Such sightings must have been fairly routine in the western Mediterranean; where other authors might have passed over this incident without comment, it merits special notice for the interlopers from the North Sea.

Of course, which sea matters. The Mediterranean, *Mare nostrum* to the Romans, was well known to the sea-faring peoples of its shores, such as Marco Polo's Venetians or their great rivals the Genoese; the Indian Ocean, though much vaster and marked by even stronger seasonal winds and currents, had also been known since antiquity. On the other hand, in the Middle Ages,

> The western sea [the northern Atlantic] had no end, or its limit lay out of reach, and only a resolute ship could breach the unknown and draw near infinity. In the literature set on the open sea of the western *Occean* (itself a name for the West), this mélange of the barely possible with the undiscovered generated an early mirror-image of what is now called "science-fiction."
>
> (Sobecki 2003: 194)

This perilous sea at the northwestern margins of Europe served as a backdrop to the genre of *immram* (rowing about)—Irish maritime voyage tales closely related to the *Navigatio sancti Brendani*, a Latin hagiography of the sixth-century Irish saint Brendan, which cast the sea, a "liquid desert," as the Irish permutation of the Christian space of solitude and temptation (Sobecki 2003: 199–200).[7] From this material, Sebastian Sobecki has argued, the *Voyage of Saint Brendan*, a text in Anglo-Norman French composed in the early twelfth century, "creates a transitional insular sea of romance which supplied a model sea for the first generation of Anglo-Norman courtly narratives before being ultimately subsumed by the growing uneasiness towards the deep" (195). Recasting the sea as a locus for marvels, it shifts the focus from spirituality to adventure—an emphasis taken up by the nascent genre of vernacular French romance in land-bound as well as maritime settings.

ARRIVALS

Even at the end of a long and possibly harrowing journey, arrivals remain uncertain, subject to the vicissitudes of the elements. Guiding Mandelli past Cyprus to the Syrian coast, Petrarch is "happy we have reached land" but cautions: "I don't know where you will disembark since there are many ports available. The opinion of the commander, the consensus of companions, the winds, the sea, the days, the place and opportunity will tell you what is best to do" (2002: sec.16.0). The uncertainty of the landing has little to do with the length of the journey. Having safely crossed the Mediterranean from Ceuta to Alexandria, Ibn Jubayr dwells on the much shorter passage across the Red Sea. The *Akhbār al-sīn wa-l-hind* (Accounts of China and India) had earlier underscored the difficulties of navigating the Red Sea on account of

> the numerous rocks that protrude from its waters [...] ships sailing this sea must look for a place to take shelter every night, for fear of the rocks in it, so they sail only by day and anchor at night. It is a dismal, hostile, and malodorous sea, and there is no good to be found in its depths or on its surface.
>
> (*Akhbār al-sīn wa-l-hind* 2014: 64; sec.2.16.3)

Ibn Jubayr's journey lasts three days "because the wind was light" (2013: 7); as his vessel finally nears land, "the sight of the birds from the Hejaz coast circling in the air" is replaced by a sudden storm that "filled the air so that we knew not which way lay our course. Then a few starts appeared and gave us some guidance" (67). But the trial is not over: as Ibn Jubayr's craft navigates within sight of the Jedda coast, they drop anchor for the night at a small island: "we had met many reefs which had broken the water and made it laugh" (68). An unfavorable wind causes them to remain an extra day on this island, called the Obstacle of Ships, until they are able to sail on "quietly in a calm sea that seemed to the beholder to be a dish of blue crystal" (68). Nor is the return without its tribulations: of the westward crossing, Ibn Jubayr writes that "the journey from Jiddah to 'Aydhab is most calamitous for pilgrims, save those few of them whom Great and Glorious God preserves, for the wind takes most of them to anchorages on the desert far to the south of 'Aydhab" (64) where they were prey both to the harsh conditions and to the predations of the local inhabitants.

At the end of a long and potentially harrowing journey, arriving safely in port calls for celebration, both on the part of passengers and those there to meet them. When the Fourth Crusaders (after a series of diversions, serendipitous or calculated) finally arrive before the great Byzantine capital Constantinople, Robert de Clari offers a curiously detached account of the scene, emphasizing the reciprocal gazes of the Latin Christians aboard the ships and the Greek Christians lining the city walls—each side struck silent with wonder:

> When the whole fleet and all the vessels were come together, they arrayed and adorned their vessels so finely that it was the most beautiful thing in the world to see. When they of Constantinople saw this fleet which was so finely arrayed, they gazed at it in wonder, and they were mounted on the walls and on the houses to look upon this marvel. And they of the fleet also regarded

the great size of the city, which was so long and so wide, and they marveled at it exceedingly.

(de Clari 1996: 66–7)

Landings could be difficult if there was no friendly harbor. When Louis IX's galley arrived at the Egyptian port of Damietta, recalls Jean de Joinville:

> we found the full array of the sultan's forces drawn up along the shore. It was a sight to enchant the eye, for the sultan's arms were all of gold, and where the sun caught them they shone resplendent. The din this army made with its kettledrums and Saracen horns was terrifying to hear.
>
> (Joinville and Villehardouin 1963: 201)

Despite the enemy forces arrayed in plain sight, the crusaders clamor to make their way to shore: some crowd onto longboats so eagerly and in such numbers that the longboats begin to sink; one of the galleys beaches itself in the sand—the knights onboard leaping out "well armed, well equipped," and planting the king's standard on the strand.

> When the king heard that the standard of Saint Denis was on shore he strode quickly across the deck of his ship [...] and leapt into the sea, where the water came up to his armpits. He went on, with his shield hung from his neck, his helmet on his head, and lance in hand, till he had joined his people on the shore.
>
> (Joinville and Villehardouin 1963: 204)

For Joinville, the boldness of the king better known for his piety than his martial valor, literally jumping into the sea against the protestations of his vassals in his pursuit of crusade, exemplifies the sanctity of the saint-king who would be canonized in 1297, twenty-seven years after his death.

THE DECAMERON: A MEDITERRANEAN CASEBOOK

A vernacular Italian frame-tale collection composed by the Florentine writer Giovanni Boccaccio in the wake of the Black Death of 1348, *The Decameron* (*c*. 1350–70) offers a virtual casebook of Mediterranean actors and themes. In the frame story, a group of ten young friends—seven women and three men—withdraw to a country villa to escape the contagion ravaging their city. To pass the time, each tells a story on ten successive days (*Decameron* being derived from the Greek for "ten days"), each taking turns presiding over the proceedings and selecting a theme for his or her "day." Like his illustrious predecessor Dante, Boccaccio is strongly associated with Florence, and many of the intercalated tales, along with the frame itself, are set in that city or its environs. However, as the son of an agent of one of Florence's famous banking companies, Boccaccio spent his formative youth in Naples—then the capital of a French-ruled (Angevin) southern Italian kingdom and a hub of Mediterranean maritime trade. A substantial minority of the *Decameron*'s one hundred tales are in fact set in this maritime Mediterranean. Interestingly, several of these tales cluster in Day 2, devoted to "people who after a series of misfortunes attain a state of unexpected happiness" (Boccaccio 2010: 72) and Day 5, on "lovers who, after unhappy or misfortunate happenings, attained happiness" (366), where maritime hazards such as storms, shipwrecks, and pirate attacks—along with the risks and rewards inherent in long-distance trade—are the narrative forms into which sudden changes of fortune are poured.

As in our other narratives both historical and literary, many of the *Decameron*'s protagonists traverse the Mediterranean with little or no mention made of the passage. In tale 2.9, madonna Zinevra, the spurned wife of a Genoese merchant, cross-dresses and takes ship with a Catalan captain; all we learn of the journey is that she "served him so efficiently and so properly that he became very fond of her" by the time they "happened to dock at Alexandria" (Boccaccio 2010: 173–4). In tale 10.9, Saladin, the sultan of Egypt, wishing to reconnoiter Christian preparations for the Third Crusade, "set[s] out on his way" (769) and, after traversing various Christian provinces, arrives in Lombardy—we are not told how; traveling in the opposite direction, Messer Torello, setting out from Pavia, "reached Genoa [...], boarded a galley, and sailed away. In a short time he reached Acre [the last Crusader outpost on the eastern Mediterranean mainland, which fell to the Mamluk Egyptians in 1291], where he joined the rest of the Christian army" (776). On the one hand, these examples conform to the principles we earlier identified: the plot calls for characters to shuttle between northern Italy and Egypt; if nothing about the crossing itself interrupts or inflects the journey, then there is no need to describe it—in fact, Messer Torello later returns to Pavia on a magical bed supplied by Saladin! On the other hand, these examples perhaps also reflect the near-routinization of the maritime routes plied by the Genoese and the Venetians across the Mediterranean in their mercantile journeys to the great port of Alexandria in Mamluk Egypt and, in the centuries preceding Boccaccio, to the Crusader ports of Outremer, literally "overseas," the French name for Latin Christian possessions in the Holy Land.

An intermediate example is provided by the tale of three sisters from Marseille who flee their home with their lovers (tale 4.3 in the *Decameron*); after having equipped their getaway vessel,

> they all went aboard the brigantine, gave orders to weigh anchor, and off they sailed, without stopping anywhere until the following evening, when they reached Genoa, where the new lovers first took joy and pleasure from their love. After taking on all the provisions they needed, they set sail, going from one port to another, until on the eighth day, without any difficulty, they arrived in Crete.
>
> (Boccaccio 2010: 317)

This passage provides a beautiful illustration of the practice of coastal sailing—*costeggiare* or "tramping," as Fernand Braudel calls it in his seminal text on the Mediterranean (1972: 1:103–4). Interestingly, the text implies that the three pairs of lovers wait to consummate their relationship on land— presumably reflecting the limitations of sleeping arrangements onboard ship; meanwhile, mentions of the eight-day journey, with stops and reprovisioning in each port, open a narrative space for, without explicitly filling, our imagination of the romantic interlude enjoyed by the six young people before reaching Crete, then a Venetian possession, where their real adventures will begin.

In a handful of tales, on the other hand, adventures encountered on the high seas change the course of the protagonists' lives. In tale 2.7, the ship carrying Alatiel, the daughter of the sultan of Babylon (Cairo), to marry the king of Algarve hits "contrary winds" in the western Mediterranean. By the third day, "the sailors did not know where they were, and they could not determine their position by calculation or by sight, for the heavens were pitch black from the clouds" (Boccaccio 2010: 129). When the vessel springs a leak, the crew members abandon ship, fighting each other for places in the lone lifeboat that, overloaded, sinks, taking them all down with it. Meanwhile the ship, now with only the princess and her ladies-in-waiting onboard, is driven violently to the coast of Mallorca: "The shock of the crash was so great that the ship lodged itself tightly in the sand about a stone's throw from the beach, and there it remained all night, battered by the sea, but resistant to the force of the wind" (130). Thus begin Alatiel's adventures. Rescued by a local nobleman who is immediately captivated by her beauty, she passes from the hand of one man to another, each ready to kill or swindle Alatiel's current master to possess her. Eventually brought back to the eastern Mediterranean among people who speak her language, she falls into the company of a Cypriot merchant sailing from Rhodes to Cyprus on a Catalan ship. For her protection, they agree she should pose as his wife; they are given "a small cabin in the stern" where, "to keep up the pretense, the merchant and the lady slept together in a rather small bed" (143), with predictable results.

Alatiel is not the only protagonist to survive a shipwreck. In tale 2.4, the failed merchant-turned-pirate Landolfo Rufolo from Ravello (overlooking Amalfi, one of the four great medieval Italian maritime republics) is taken captive and set onboard a Genoese ship. "Toward evening a gale began to blow, causing high seas"; off the coast of Kefalonia in the Ionian Sea, the ship

> struck a sandbank [...] with a tremendous crash, splitting apart, breaking up into small pieces like glass smashed against a wall. As is usually the case in such accidents, the sea was now strewn with floating cargo, chests, and

planks, and although the night was pitch black and there was a heavy swell, the unfortunate wretches who had been on the ship and knew how to swim began to cling to any object that happened to float by.

(Boccaccio 2010: 96)

Rufolo is one of those survivors, thanks to a chest floating on the waves that he at first tries desperately to avoid, "afraid that it might hit him and drown him"; eventually, however, he drapes himself over it and, after two days "without anything to eat and far more to drink than he might have wished," he is blown ashore on the island of Corfu. Rescued by a village woman, he discovers that the chest is full of precious stones. Struck by this sudden upturn in his fortunes (in keeping with the theme of the Second Day), he returns to Ravello and, "without ever again wishing to practice the trade of a merchant, he lived splendidly the rest of his life" (Boccaccio 2010: 99). For Rufolo, seafaring is the source of risk (of destitution or death) and reward (in the form of prosperity) in equal measure—exemplified by his successes and failures as a merchant, pirate, and shipwreck survivor. Martuccio Gomito from the island of Lipari, off the northern coast of Sicily, takes to piracy to win enough wealth to earn the hand of the noble Gostanza. When his ship is captured and sunk by "Saracens," he is taken captive to Tunis; rumor reaches Gostanza, however, that he drowned with the rest of his crew. In despair but unable to take her own life by more conventional means, she steals off and finds

> a small fishing boat [...] equipped with a mast, sail, and oars. And since like most women on the island she was somewhat familiar with the rudiments of navigation, she quickly climbed aboard and rowed out into the sea. Then she set the sail, threw away the oars and the rudder, and completely abandoned herself to the wind, calculating that what was bound to happen was either that the boat without a cargo or a pilot would be capsized by the wind, or that it might strike some reef and be smashed, in which case she had no choice but to drown; and wrapping a cloak around her head, she lay down upon the deck of the boat and wept.
>
> (Boccaccio 2010: 379)

Throughout the *Decameron*, storms and sandbars wreak havoc on vessels more seaworthy than Gostanza's fishing boat. Given the theme of Day Five, however, a gentle north wind brings her safely to shore near Sousse, on the north African coast. She is eventually reunited with Martuccio, who in the meantime has prospered in the favor of the king of Tunis. With the king's permission, the two "embarked on a small boat [...] and accompanied by a favorable wind they sailed back to Lipari" (Boccaccio 2010: 385) where they are married and live happily ever after.

BY WAY OF CONCLUSION

An exception that proves the rule of the relative paucity of descriptions of life at sea comes from the pen of Felix Fabri, a Dominican from Ulm who at the very end of the fifteenth century composed an expansive account of his two journeys to the Holy Land and surrounding regions in 1480 and 1483. Called *Evagatorium* (Wanderings) and intended for his fellow Dominicans, Fabri makes a point of covering the kind of information and minutiae that would be taken for granted by an experienced merchant but of compelling interest to the neophyte traveler. Reflecting his clerical training and Latin education, his presentation of the sea and the dangers of maritime travel amalgamates passages from the Bible (Genesis, Psalms, Jonas, Matthew), *Speculum maius*, a thirteenth-century encyclopedic compilation by Vincent of Beauvais, and various classical sources. To these textual authorities he adds practical experience under the rubric "Some useful information for understanding a sea voyage." This includes the dangers of navigation: shipwreck, winds, the fragility of ships, becalmed seas; more unusually, he alerts his fellow monks to the particularities of shipboard life: the hierarchy of the crew, the administration of justice onboard, how the offices are celebrated onboard, distractions, meals, the awkwardness of finding the opportunity to relieve oneself. He gives a series of warnings about things the novice passenger should look out for: do not sit on the rigging (lest one get tossed up in the air); guard one's money and possessions from theft; and this piece of very practical advice: "May the pilgrim also take care to sit down prudently so as not to stick to the place where he is seated, because the entire ship is covered in pitch: when this is liquified by the heat of the sun, he who sits on it gets up all dirtied" (Chareyron and Tarayre 2006: 18).

Fabri also includes a long and astonishing description of the plight of galley slaves: at first he compares them to horses straining to pull a heavy load up an incline, whipped even as they are putting out their best effort; then:

> It disgusts me to write it and I am horrified thinking of the tortures and punishments these men endure: never have I seen beasts beaten in the awful way they are beaten [...]. Most [...] are slaves bought by the owners; sometimes these are men of low condition, prisoners, people who have fled their lands, have been chased out or exiled, or men so miserable that they cannot live on land and are unable to feed themselves. When it is feared they might flee, they are chained to their benches. In general, they are natives of Macedonia, Albania, Achaea, Illyria, or Slavonia; sometimes there are Turks or Saracens among them, but they hide their customs.
>
> (Chareyron and Tarayre 2006: 20)

Contemporary with the voyages of Columbus, the *Wanderings* of a Dominican monk from the landlocked German imperial city of Ulm pulls back the curtain on the dark side, as well as the trials and tribulations, of medieval and early modern sea travel.

CHAPTER SEVEN

Representations

Painting, Mapping, Reinventing the Seas of the World

EMMANUELLE VAGNON

INTRODUCTION

How was the sea represented during the Middle Ages? What was the relationship between knowledges and perceptions of the seas and oceans, on the one hand, and their visual representation, on the other hand? At the heart of these questions lie the difficulties of translating a natural phenomenon into a visual representation through artistic mediation. The sea is not just a landscape; in painting the sea, artists took into account not only physical perceptions but also a host of knowledges, imaginaries, and practices of maritime space. Maritime cartography, as it developed within different human societies, features prominently among the many types of visual representation possible, at the intersection of science, the conceptual and the experiential, that is to say, seafarers' experiences. The dialectic between the imaginary and real-life usage, between theory and practice, would seem to underpin every study of humankind's interaction with maritime spaces.

Particularly at stake in cultural histories of the sea is the question of the relationship between representation and control, the extent to which the representation of the sea implies control over that space. In his introduction to the multi-volume history *The Sea in History* the historian of the medieval Mediterranean Michel Balard underlines the extent to which relations with the sea have been integral to the development of human societies. In every historical period the fascinating but terrifying power of the sea has threatened the functioning of commercial ports and the incessant to-ing and fro-ing of pilgrims (Buchet and Balard 2017). Thus, in Mediterranean cultures, the perception of the sea during the Middle Ages oscillates between apprehension, a fundamental and ancient terror, and a familiarity bred of the gradual appropriation of maritime space through navigation techniques and mapping (Balard and Picard 2014: 211).

If the degree of appropriation of the sea varies across time, it also depends upon the scale at which it is considered since the term is broad, designating closed seas and salty waters, as well as the oceans that encircle dry land. For example, different visual conventions were applied to the representation of the ocean when it formed a part of a depiction of the earth, than to the depiction of a familiar "sea" as a locus of human activity. Generally speaking, representations of seas are not as common, and do not have the same cultural importance, in landed, continental societies as in littoral societies focused around fishing and navigation. Nevertheless, the presence or absence of representations of the sea may also have other causes: neither the Byzantine Empire nor the Vikings have left many iconographic traces of their respective relationships with the sea, however fundamentally maritime or connected to the sea they both were. Finally, every civilization developed its own particular representational conventions and techniques for depicting the form and movement of sea water whilst, at the same time, being open to the transregional circulation of concepts and images.

The cultural history of representations of the sea is based upon a wide range of sources: first among them is a vast body of medieval iconographic evidence in a variety of media, from painting and sculpture to stained glass or the seals and coats-of-arms of artistocrats and cities. It is worth remarking at this point that the sea is never a subject of painting or sculpture in and of itself, as in the modern period; works such as the marine seascapes of Horace Vernet or J. M. W. Turner, or even Hokusai's abstracted wave, find no medieval equivalents. The sea is represented in medieval art as the natural backdrop to an event, for example in a historical or biblical scene, where it might also carry a symbolic dimension. The seas and oceans are also depicted in scientific works dealing with the elements and nature. Finally, the sea, or rather coasts and seashores, are prominent in cartography.

Geographical maps should be approached as iconographic sources, they are culturally determined by specific contexts and conventions, as much as by the various technologies—for example the compass, as discussed later—that enabled knowledge of maritime spaces and physical action within them through navigation, exploration, or conquest. The representation of the extent and shape of the world's seas and oceans thus reflects simultaneously general geographical knowledge as well as the experience of the reality of that space. Cartographic conventions are neither obvious nor uniform and must be linked back to the wider history of perceptions and practices, and studied alongside both textual and archaeological evidence. Cartographic history as a whole has undergone a major revival since the 1980s, although the study of maritime cartography remains marginal in comparison to that of countries or continents, even when this focuses on maritime borders (Chekin 2006; Ducène 2018; Harley and Woodward 1987, 1992; Relaño 2002). Even today, there are in fact few monographs dedicated to the cartographic history of a specific sea or ocean, those that exist are often relatively old such as Kammerer's work on the Red Sea (1929–35) or Bagrow's on the Caspian (1956). The Indian Ocean has, however, recently been the subject of a dedicated study (Vagnon and Vallet 2017b). Nevertheless, even when such histories have been undertaken, it has frequently been from an essentially European perspective. Until recently then, cartographic history has generally approached its materials as an objective documentation of the progress of the age of exploration—in particular with regard to the representation of the Atlantic Ocean—while oftentimes neglecting the context in which such works were produced and the intentions of their makers.

It is important to understand that the seas and oceans as we define and name them today, have not always been so. Not only has empirical knowledge of these spaces changed over time but also their very nomenclature. Recent studies, initially focused on the Mediterranean, have highlighted the cultural component in the identification of maritime spaces (Lewis 1999). A whole historiographical trend, linked to the history of the sea as an ecosystem influenced by human society, has thus renewed the Braudelian approach of a "total" history of the Mediterranean Sea, although with a new emphasis on seas as spaces of connectivity (Horden and Purcell 2000). The rebirth of maritime history as the so-called new thalassology or thalassography, now extended to other seas of the globe, therefore belongs within global history, because it both steps back from traditional Eurocentric histories and is based not upon territories but rather, by definition, *relationships* between territories separated by shared waters. The study of the Mediterranean Sea has thus offered an example, or counter-example, for studies of other maritime spaces around the globe, in particular the Indian Ocean, which has been the subject of a considerable historiographical revival over the past few decades in the areas of economic history and anthropology (Alpers 2013; Beaujard 2012; Chaudhuri 1985; Pearson 2003; Ptak 2007b). The history of maritime cartography situates itself within this trend, as demonstrated by several recent publications (Couto and Taleghani 2006; Hofmann, Richard and Vagnon, 2012; Vagnon and Vallet 2017b), while maritime history conferences usually include at least one panel dedicated to maps.

This chapter therefore deals with three main aspects: the iconography of the sea in the visual art of the Mediterranean, modes of mapping the seas and oceans in Europe and the Islamic world, and finally other perspectives on the sea in East Asia and the question of their possible interactions with Western culture.

PART ONE: PAINTING THE SEAS. FROM EMOTIONS TO THE IMAGINATION

Studies of the historical perception and representation of the sea during the Middle Ages frequently insist on the terrifying and fascinating nature of maritime space for travelers and pilgrims, the latter forced to face the torments of a dangerous crossing to achieve salvation in the Holy Land. As the historian Christiane Deluz (1996) reminded us, "to leave is to die a little." The sea was a place of intense spiritual experiences and also the object of multiple religious and moral metaphors. The ninth-century Irish theologian John Scotus Eriugena even dramatically compared the rigors of intellectual work to a sea crossing:

> Let us spread sail, then, and set out to sea. For reason, not inexperienced in these waters, fearing neither the threats of the waves nor divagations nor the Syrtes nor rocks, shall speed our course: indeed she finds it sweeter to exercise her skill in the hidden straits of the ocean of Divinity than idly to bask in smooth and open waters, where she cannot display her power.
>
> (*Periphyseon* 4.744.AB; Erivgenae 1995)

In textual sources two emotions are thus frequently associated with maritime themes: fear but equally the courage to face and overcome the elements (Villain-Gandossi 2004a, 2004b).

In spite of the popularity of this theme, historical studies of the perception and representation of the sea have more often relied upon literary rather than visual sources, the latter often used simply to illustrate a chapter as opposed to being objects of study in their own right. Exhibitions such as *La mer, terreur et fascination* (Corbin and Richard 2004), *Mapping Our World: Terra Incognita to Australia* (2013), Institut du Monde Arabe and MUCEM's *Aventuriers des mers* (2016), or *Le Monde vu d'Asie* (Singaravélou and Argounès 2018) have played a major role in highlighting and broadening awareness of this iconography. Additionally, major libraries around the world—among them the British Library, the Bibliothèque nationale de France, the Vatican Library, and the Pierpont Morgan Library in New York—now provide free digital access to their collections, offering a rich mine of medieval manuscripts in which to locate representations of the sea. Nevertheless, many motifs and forms of maritime representation await synthetic and art historical study.

As one might expect, the greatest share of iconographic production among the three cultures that shared the Mediterranean basin—Western Europe, the Byzantine Empire, and the Islamic world—belongs to Western Europe, although representations of the sea also existed in the Islamic world and across the area in certain Jewish manuscripts. Biblical themes linked to the sea are, of course, shared by Judaism, Christianity, and Islam. The representation of the sea in Western Europe drew upon a common antique and biblical heritage, supplementing this with scenes from the daily life of seafarers. Medieval maps, themselves illustrated or accompanied by illustrations, also contribute in a broad sense to this body of maritime iconography.

THE SEA AS A NATURAL ELEMENT: THE COLORS AND NAMES OF THE SEAS

The first group of representations of the sea is linked to works on Nature and the Creation. The Book of Genesis was an inexhaustible source of iconography in the Middle Ages and offered the opportunity to comment upon, and illustrate, the relationship between land and water as well as the division of the earth between the sons of Noah after the Flood. Numerous paintings, frescoes, and illuminations represent God's primordial gesture of the separation of the waters from dry land, creating the seas and oceans and then populating them with sea creatures, as for example in the twelfth-century Souvigny Bible produced for Cluny Abbey. The illustrated Bibles known as "bibles moralisées" that appeared in France, and later other European countries, from the late twelfth century also offer numerous examples of this scene. The theme of God as Architect, master of the elements, populating the seas with marine creatures, featured equally in numerous illustrated manuscripts of French language Bibles, the so-called "bibles historiales," produced by Pierre le Mangeur (Petrus Comestor) and Guyart des Moulins from the twelfth century onwards. The story of Noah's Ark, by contrast, offered European illustrators the opportunity to represent the storm-tossed sea and the animals sheltering within the ark.

Medieval works of natural philosophy often contain diagrammatic maps of the terrestrial sphere as a whole or simply its inhabited regions, the Ecumene. Since the natural philosophy of the period built upon the commentaries of scientific texts from antiquity, the seas and oceans were considered forms of water, one of the four constitutive elements of the world alongside earth, air, and fire. The model of a double ocean encircling the world, first propounded in antiquity by Crates of Malos and later commentaried around 480 by Macrobius Ambrosius Theodosius as well as Martianus Capella, provided the source for a type of explanatory diagram first seen in the Carolingian Empire and later, from the twelfth century, across Western Europe. According to these ancient principles, the inhabited world (our ecumene) is bordered on the west and east by a circular meridian ocean linking the two poles, while an equatorial ocean running through the "torrid zone," characterized by its heat, delimits it on the south. It was the meeting of these two currents, it was believed, that caused the ebbs and flows that generated tides. Inland seas were considered to be gulfs produced by these circular oceans and the land masses thus appeared to float like islands in the midst of the oceans depicted in blue.

In the terrestrial representations inherited from antiquity, the encircling ocean penetrates deeply into the land like so many gulfs, each fed by river waters flowing down from the mountains. Nevertheless, in spite of all issuing from the same primordial ocean, the seas were perceived as having different qualities. "From the cold Baltic to the mysterious Red Sea, from the troubling Dead Sea to the much-disputed Mediterranean" (Questes Group 2018: 8), each has its own visual identity and particular character. More generally, the seas and oceans are liminal spaces, frontier zones between peoples, but also maritime spaces to be crossed in the discovery of new lands and worlds.

Techniques for representing the sea, and water more generally, vary across these different genres of illustration according to the painter and the sea depicted. Movement is evoked through undulations, convolutions, and spirals, with crests to suggest the movement of the waves. Notwithstanding the last example, the preferred color, since antiquity, has been green, as seen in the thirteenth-century world map from an English Psalter in Figure 7.1 or even earlier in the eighth-century Albi world map. Deep blue, a costly pigment, is only found in a few luxury maps such as the Catalan Atlas of 1375 (Figure 7.6, more details in Chapter 3, Figure 3.4) or later Fra Mauro's World Map of 1459 (Figure 7.7). Red was reserved for the ocean of the so-called torrid zone, or for the Erythrean Sea, what we now call the Indian Ocean. Red is also the color of the Red Sea (the ancient *sinus arabicus*) linked to the story of the Israelite's Exodus from Egypt and their crossing of that sea. This Bible passage, like that of Noah's Ark, forms part of the iconography of the three monotheistic religions. The appellation Red Sea is an interpretation of the Hebrew phrase The Sea of Reeds, which was translated in early Greek and Latin versions of the Bible as Red Sea by reference of the Greek Erythrean Sea. In numerous Western maps blue or green gives way to red for the coloring of the Red Sea, as for example in the English Psalter already mentioned (Figure 7.1). On the Catalan Atlas, the sea is colored red while a caption explains, as in many pilgrimage reports of the time, how:

> The sons of Israel passed through this passage when they fled Egypt. This sea is called the Red Sea which was crossed by the Twelve Tribes of Egypt. Let it be known that the water is not red, but the seabed is of that color. Through this sea come most of the spices arriving at Alexandria from India.

The convention of designating different seas according to their color also existed in Arab culture: the Encircling Ocean (*al-bahr al-muhīt*), comprising the Atlantic and Indian Oceans, is also termed the Green Sea (*al-bahr al-akhdar*), or again, to underline its terrifying character, the Dark or the Gloomy Sea (*al-bahr al-Zulumat*). In contrast, the Pontus Euxinus of antiquity, termed *Mare Maggiore* (Great Sea) in Italian in the Middle Ages, only took on the appellation Black Sea in the fifteenth century, perhaps from the Ottoman convention in which black designated the north.

FIGURE 7.1 World map from an English Psalter, produced after 1262. Ink and colors on vellum. British Library, Additional MS 28681, f.9. © Wikimedia Commons (public domain).

THE SEA OF BELIEVERS

We have already seen how the Books of Genesis and Exodus stimulated reflection about the nature of the sea and offered opportunities for its representation. Indeed, numerous religious iconographies include maritime motifs in one way or another, both as part of the natural backdrop to a particular story and as symbolic representations. Water is central to Christian symbolism through its role in the Sacraments and always carried contradictory meanings: the sea represents both fear and salvation, evil and purification, death and resurrection. The sea was perceived as a place of intense emotions and the Bible stories of the Flood, or of Jonah and the Whale, were an occasion to reflect humankind's fear of storms, of being engulfed by the sea and drowning, as shown in the scene from an early thirteenth-century French Psalter in Figure 7.2.

All three Abrahamic religions share the story of Jonah and that of Exodus. For Christians, the story of Jonas and the three days spent in the belly of the whale before being regurgitated prefigures the Resurrection of Christ after his three days in the tomb (Mt. 12:40) (Traineau-Durozoy 2017: 115–16). Sea water in this story also evokes Baptismal water, which for Christians marks their purification and rebirth into the faith. The representation of Jonah is very frequent in Romanesque art, and on a variety of supports: illuminated manuscripts, drawings, mosaics, stained glass, enamels, and on sculpted capitals in churches. Very often the iconography of the big fish with only a few waves painted around it represents metonymicaly the entire sea and its dangers. The Irish story of Saint Brendan also includes a variation around the story of Jonah, featuring as it does a giant fish and a symbolic act of navigation, for Brendan the sea voyage is a spiritual experience. Saint Brendan's voyage is, incidentally, one of the rare examples of Christian iconography to feature the Atlantic, or at least western and northern seas. In Islam by contrast, Jonah is held up as a model of patience and constant faith when faced with adversity, which perhaps explains the rather blank expression given to Jonah in the depiction of the scene from Il-Khanid Iran in Figure 7.3. Jonah emerges from the mouth of a large carp-like whale into swirling, crested waves inspired by Far Eastern art from the furthest ends of the Mongol Empire. Some pagan symbols related to the sea, such as the mermaid (with both its representation as a womanlike seabird or as a fish-tailed woman) are very often used in Christian iconography, especially Romanesque sculpture and manuscript painting. Such images are found across Europe. Art historian Jacqueline Leclercq-Marx suggests that the medieval mermaid embodies both the dangers of the sea and the temptation of the soul, thereby establishing a symbolic link between the sea and the female body (1997). More generally, the sea is perceived and represented as a parallel world, an inverted mirror of our terrestrial humanized space (Leclercq-Marx 2006).

REPRESENTATIONS 169

FIGURE 7.2 Depiction of Noah's Ark from the Latin Psalter of Saint Louis and Blanche de Castille, Paris, *c.* 1225–35. Ink, gold, and colors on parchment. © Bibliothèque de l'Arsenal, Paris, MS-1186 réserve, fol. 13v.

FIGURE 7.3 Jonah and the Whale, from a manuscript of Rashid al-Din's *Jawāmi' al-tawarīkh* (Universal History), Iran, early fourteenth century. Ink and colors on paper. Khalili collection MS 727, fol. 59a. © Image courtesy of the Khalili Collection.

Finally, Christian iconography frequently features the waters of Lake Tiberias or the Sea of Galilee in scenes where the Apostles are represented as fishermen in their boat or Jesus walks on the water to rescue a drowning Peter. Here again, the sea symbolizes death but also the trial that brings one closer to God. This symbol is also present in the iconography of the Virgin Mary, protector of ships, or in scenes depicting pilgrimages and shipwrecks. The Virgin is always invoked by Christian sailors and even identified with the Pole Star, the *stella maris*, which guides navigators at night and seems to attract the compass needle to bring them to safe harbor. Ex-votos, still found in certain churches, have long depicted a wild storm-tossed sea with the Virgin Mary above in the sky (Vauchez 2006). Venetian marine atlases of the fourteenth and fifteenth centuries are also encircled by pictures of the Virgin and saints to protect seafarers (Bacci and Rohde 2014). Lastly, the iconographies of certain saints depict the calm sea after a storm, as seen in the cycle of the life of Saint Nicholas. The scene belonged to a larger cycle of images from the saint's life that formed the predella, or bottom-most set, of a larger altarpiece to the Virgin and Child, painted for the church of Saint Nicholas in Florence (Corbin and Richard 2004: 84).

MARITIME ACTIVITIES

The representation of the sea is by no means limited to religious iconography. Numerous surviving representations, in particular of illustrated historical and literary texts, show human activities such as naval battles and sea journeys or crossings, as well as port and mercantile activities. Scenes with no particular religious connotation exist in both Western European iconography and, to a lesser extent, in Byzantine and Islamic art. Here again, European iconography is particularly rich, a characteristic going back to antiquity. Episodes from Homer's *Illiad* and the *Odyssey*, first depicted on Greek ceramics, were later illustrated in medieval manuscripts (Cerrito 2006; Leclercq-Marx 2017). Antiquity also inspired the astounding representations of Alexander the Great exploring the ocean depths with their strange aquatic creatures, as represented in color on the cover of this volume (Bellon-Méguelle 2006; Corbin and Richard 2004; Questes Group 2018). A group of illustrated manuscripts of the *Maqāmāt* (Assemblies) of al-Hariri produced in thirteenth-century Iraq offer scenes of Indian Ocean vessels altogether rare in the Islamic representational tradition until the sixteenth century. Unsurprisingly, the image of an sewn-plank vessel with billowing sail is among the most frequently reproduced images in studies of the premodern Indian Ocean world (Figure 5.5).

However, it was above all naval battles in historical works that provided the opportunity to paint a maritime landscape, beginning with the Battle of Troy. Crusader attacks against coastal Mediterranean fortresses in the thirteenth century or again the Ottoman siege of Constantinople also engendered famous images. One of the most famous battle scenes in Byzantine manuscript painting, from a twelfth century Sicilian copy of the *Chronicle* of Ioannis Skylitzae, depicts the use of so-called Greek fire against an Arab fleet besieging Constantinople. Maritime scenes also appear in travel accounts such as the *Devisement du Monde* (The Description of the World), which includes the accounts of Marco Polo and Jean de Mandeville. Justly famous is an early fifteenth-century miniature from a manuscript held in Paris depicting the use of a compass onboard a ship in the Indian Ocean, the first Western European representation of this navigational technology (see Figure 1.5).

As we have seen, the sea is frequently represented as a natural backdrop in medieval images, including world maps, where the sea encircles and delimits the land. It is therefore interesting, from an art historical standpoint, to analyze the challenge that the representation of the sea posed for artists, in addition to the evolution of their techniques over time and across production centers. As we have seen across the examples discussed thus far, the rendering of water's transparency, the shapes of waves, eddies, and foam, the depiction of currents and depths evidence changing conventions and new inventions. The sea as a natural element needed to be distinguished from the sweet water of rivers or the calm water of lakes, and certain artists attempted to render its depth, its more terrifying and mysterious aspects, and the constant movement that characterizes seas and oceans.

While the sea was considered a place of human activity, painters nevertheless frequently represented the sea as a symbolic component of the design without further elaboration. A few blue or green waves, sometimes nothing more than a coastline or a ship were enough, as a metonymy, to evoke an entire ocean. Cartography is different in this respect in that it aims to represent the shape of maritime space. In maps, space is not neutral, the sea is not simply a natural landscape but an ensemble of coasts and ports whose precise location is important. Maritime space is thus shaped by cartographic representation that names and delimits its contours.

PART TWO: MAPPING THE SEAS: REPRESENTATION AS CONTROL OF MARITIME SPACE

In geography the sea fulfills several functions: it defines land and often the borders between countries, as a navigable surface it is also a means of communication and it is, not least, an important economic resource. Mapping the seas is a way of knowing, discovering, and conquering maritime space; even more fundamentally, cartography is a means of inventing the world. To identify and name the oceans, the seas and their different parts, is to order the world and give its meaning. The history of this process antedates the globalization of the modern world and maps, as conceptualized across different cultures, in antiquity and during the Middle Ages. As a result, mapmakers had very different objectives, of very different scales. A primary aim was to know the world's oceans by naming and measuring them, but maps were also invented as tools of government and conquest, as reliable and efficient aids to navigation, and as means for representing maritime routes and commercial axes. These different functions varied and intermingled according to the type of representation and the cultural context in which a map was produced. Thus, before the thirteenth century medieval maps were long considered by historians to be purely didactic or symbolic schemata in which the actual positioning of land and sea were only of relative importance. The appearance of portolan charts during the twelfth or thirteenth centuries marks the first "modern" and exact representation of maritime space based upon the compass and mathematical measurements, technologies that supplemented the practical knowledge of seafarers. It is important to underline at this point that different modes of spatial representation—world maps, maritime maps, regional maps—were used alongside one another until the sixteenth century, even as each had its own particular uses (Gautier Dalché 1996b, 2002, 2017). Furthermore, it is simplistic to contrast an Islamic cartography descended from Ptolemy and supposedly founded upon mathematical principles with a Christian cartography that only became rational and "realistic" much later thanks to developments in navigation. Scholarly, administrative, and political uses of maps have always coexisted alongside actual experience of maritime space through voyages—often undertaken without maps, even in the modern period—or through direct intimate knowledge of the sea and maritime phenomena.

BETTER KNOWLEDGE FOR BETTER GOVERNMENT

However diverse, the world maps, or mappaemundi, of the Middle Ages define the relationship between land and sea on the surface of the globe (Woodward 1987). They might be simple diagrams, such as those illustrating treatises of natural philosophy mentioned earlier, or more detailed drawings showing territory. In the East as in the West these maps all conceive of land as surrounded by one encircling ocean and aim to represent the arrangement of lands and seas and their interactions. The ancient origins of these representations are still palpable in the Middle Ages although they developed differently in different cultures.

Few maps have survived from the Byzantine world. Those of Cosmas Indicopleustes, the sixth-century author of the *Christian Topography*, are simplified in the extreme and are primarily religious in significance. Nevertheless, the author's name, "the Indian traveler," suggests he was also interested in the connections between the Mediterranean and the Indian Ocean and all three surviving manuscripts carry diagrams representing a number of Red Sea ports such as Adulis (Wolska 1962). Furthermore, the works of Ptolemy had been preserved in Constantinople and studied, particularly from the thirteenth century onwards. Ptolemy's *Geography*, written in Alexandria in the second century CE, already offered a very detailed representation of the Old World from the Atlantic to China, although with little knowledge of more northerly seas or those south of the equator, and while Ptolemy's work was lost to the West for most of the Middle Ages, it continued to be used and interpreted in the Islamic world from the ninth century (Ducène 2017a; Gautier Dalché 2009; Pinto 2016).

In Western Europe, world geography and cartography mainly relied on Latin sources, as transmitted by medieval authors, notably Paul Orosius and Isidore of Seville (Woodward 1987). Thus, until the end of the thirteenth century, more or less detailed maps of the world were centered on the Mediterranean, the

Mare Nostrum of the Roman Empire, around which were situated the three major regions of the known world: Asia, Europe, and Africa. The other seas were laid out around this central basin and communicated with the encircling ocean on the basis of a geometry going back to Eratosthenes of Cyrene in which the Mediterranean is crossed by a parallel of latitude passing through Rhodes, while the remaining seas were laid out on several specific meridians. In this schema the Red Sea is located on the same north–south axis as the Black Sea while the Gulf is aligned with the Caspian Sea (Talbert and Unger 2008). This layout, of an encircling ocean with internal gulfs, is found in numerous Western medieval maps, from the eighth-century Albi map to the Hereford and Ebstorf (*c.* 1300) world maps. The Roman inheritance remained prominent even into the fourteenth century when the North Atlantic and the Caspian Sea were still poorly known and considered to be located at the edge of the world. The position of the Indian Ocean in world maps is more varied; it often merged, at the entrance to the Gulf and the Red Sea, with the encircling ocean, however, it was sometimes given a separate identity and extent. In a world map from an eleventh-century copy of Beatus of Liebana's *Commentary on the Apocalypse* copied at Saint-Sever, the entire Indian Ocean is given the classical name "Red Sea" (*mare Rubrum* in Latin, a direct translation of the Greek "Erythrean sea") and occupies the entire southern section of the map, separating the known world from the unknown lands of the Southern Hemisphere (Vagnon and Vallet 2017b: 41–56).

From the start in the Islamic world geographical knowledge integrated both classical Greek knowledge as well as Indo-Persian geographical traditions. As in the West, world maps represented the notion of an encircling ocean to producing a familiar, if nevertheless very varied, iconography (Pinto 2016: 79–146). Ptolemy's *Geography* followed in this ancient classical tradition and was translated into Arabic as early as the ninth century, under caliphal patronage in Baghdad, and subsequently incorporated into the work of Muslim scholars such as al-Khwarizmi (d. *c.* 850) and Ibn Hawqal (d. *c.* 990). As a consequence, geography earned a significant place in Islamic civilization much earlier than in the Christian West and embodied an inherently imperial agenda aimed at representing the extent of the Islamic world. The new Muslim empire was sea oriented from the very outset; in the seventh and eighth centuries the *dār al-Islām* expanded rapidly from the Indian Ocean as far as the western Mediterranean and the Atlantic (Miquel 1967–88; Picard 2018). Descriptive geography played an important administrative role from the early Abbasid period onward. Descriptions of the regions making up the Islamic world, a genre known in Arabic as *masālik wa-l mamālik* or "roads and countries," were often accompanied by maps depicting lands and shorelines. They were not used for navigation but transmitted information about coasts and islands, which were navigational and commercial nodes. The Islamic geographical tradition, built upon the model developed in ninth-century Baghdad, distinguished two maritime spaces: the Sea of Rum, that is the Mediterranean, a sea marked by conflict with Christian kingdoms, and the Indian Ocean and its two gulfs, the Red Sea and the Sea of Fars (the modern Gulf), a familiar sea of trade and exchange with South Asia. Geographical treatises produced from the tenth century onward by the Mediterranean caliphates—the Ummayyads of al-Andalus and the Fatimids in north Africa and Egypt—while not rejecting this Abbasid tradition, restored the balance by giving a greater place to the Mediterranean Sea as an essential region of the *dār al-Islām* (Pinto 2013; Picard 2018).

The biggest difference between these Western European and Islamic traditions lies in the very different balance accorded to land and sea. Whereas Western maps most often place the Mediterranean at their center, those from the Islamic world are centered on the Arabian Peninsula and represent the Mediterranean and Indian Ocean symmetrically to west and east. The Caspian Sea, part of the Islamic Empire and better known than in European cartography, is always depicted as a closed body of water, often rendered schematically and, in this example, somewhat decoratively as a perfect circle. The western Indian Ocean for its part was well known to the Islamic world, even if its immense central and eastern reaches remained comparatively unknown. The shape and extent of the Indian Ocean were a subject of speculation and variable representation from early on. Sometimes representations of the Indian Ocean departed from the Ptolemaic model of a closed sea bounded by land on the south, representing it instead, as in Ibn Hawqal's maps, extending to the east and opening into the encircling ocean. In one map by the Persian geographer al-Biruni the Indian Ocean is shown completely unbounded beyond Southern Africa and India with theoretically free circulation beyond these land masses (Ducène 2017a: 57–71).

Important new cartographic sources continue to come to light, one is the *Kitāb gharā'ib al-funūn* (The Book of Curiosities) discovered in 2000, which sheds interesting light on the ways in which the seas were conceptualized and represented in eleventh-century Fatimid Egypt (Bramoullé 2017; Rapoport and Savage-Smith 2014, 2018). As its anonymous author explains, he took inspiration from the descriptions of seafarers:

> We have only mentioned here what we have heard from trustworthy sailors, from which I selected and made my own judgments; and from what had reached my ears from the wise merchants who traverse the seas and from any ship captain who leads his men at sea, I mentioned what I have knowledge of.
>
> (Rapoport and Savage Smith 2014: 442)

The work, inspired in part by Ibn Hawqal, includes seventeen maps of which at least eight describe seas and islands. The sixth chapter devoted to "The representation of the seas, their islands and their harbours" includes the author's explanation of his cartographic method before offering a map of the Mediterranean and another of the Indian Ocean, the two maritime spaces essential to Fatimid commercial and political policy. The representation of the

Indian Ocean in the Book of Curiosities offers another variation, depicting it as a perfect, closed oval filled with islands (see Margariti in this volume). In both Mediterranean and Indian Ocean maps, sea water is colored dark green whilst the coasts are edged in red and islands located by means of circles. A fringe of labels and red dots locate ports or sometimes places and regions situated further inland. Analysis of these two maps by Yossef Rapoport and Emilie Savage-Smith, and by David Bramoullé, sees them as evidence for the ways in which the Fatimids understood and represented these spaces as closed and bounded, and so capable of being controlled (Rapoport and Savage-Smith 2014, 2018; Bramoullé 2017).

The representation of the Indian Ocean as a sort of gulf intruding between the South Asian and African landmasses and with Africa curved and stretched to the east is characteristic of the Balkhi school of cartography and was continued in the twelfth century by the geographer al-Idrisi in his Ptolemy-inspired

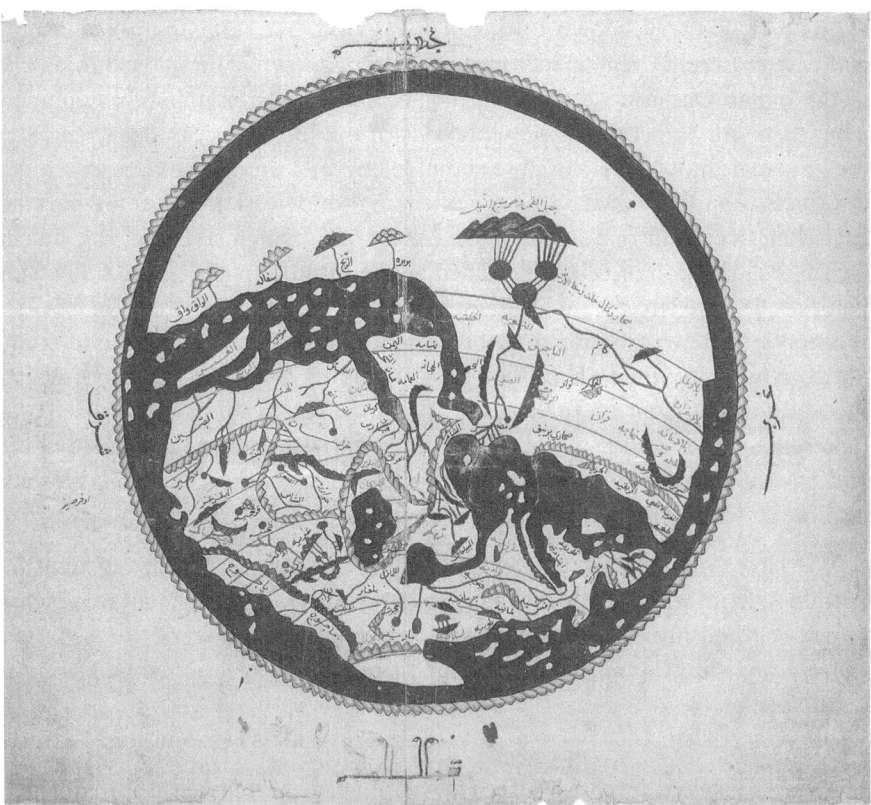

FIGURE 7.4 Double-page world map from al-Idrisi's *Nuzhat al-mushtāq fī ikhtirāq al-āfāq* (Book of Roger), composed mid-twelfth century, this manuscript copied in 960/1533. Ink and colors on paper, Bodleian Library Oxford, Pococke 375, 3b-4a. © Wikimedia Commons (public domain).

geography written for Roger II of Sicily (Figure 7.4). The circular world map at the start of the manuscript is followed by more detailed maps arranged according to the Greek system of climates but with names of towns, ports, and islands carefully indicated. It was this kind of map that the cartographer Pietro Vesconte took up and adapted for a Western readership in the famous world map presented in 1321 to Pope John XXII as part of Marino Sanudo's crusade

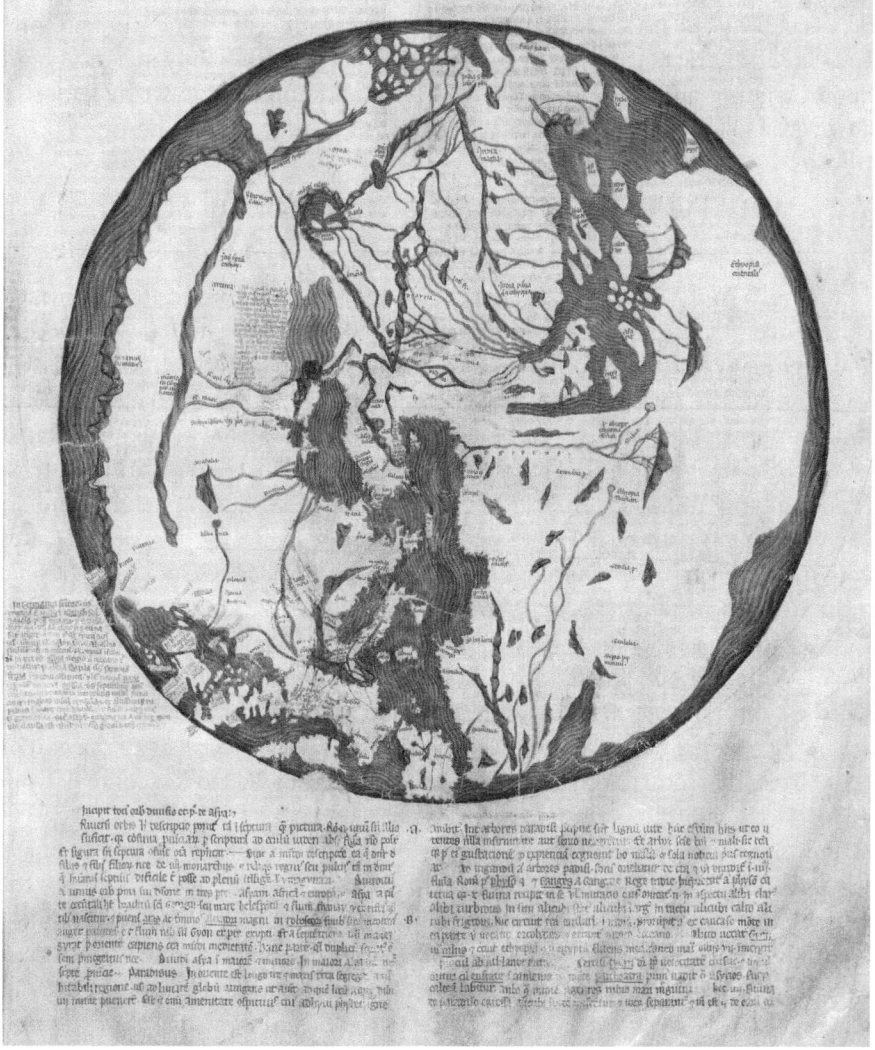

FIGURE 7.5 World map from Paulin de Venise's *Chronologia magna*, 1328–43, based on the earlier world map produced by Pietro Vesconte (1321) for Marino Sanudo's crusade project. Copied in Naples, ink and colors on paper. © Bibliothèque nationale de France. Département des manuscrits, Latin 4939, 9r.

project. This map was later reproduced in a historical work by Paulin de Venise (Edson 2004; Mauntel 2018; Schröder 2012; Vagnon 2013: 131–70) with the same eastward extension of Africa but with the oceans and seas arranged around the Christian focal points of Jerusalem and the Holy Land (Figure 7.5). Vesconte's world map was part of a larger body of cartographic material illustrating a complex plan for a naval blockade of Egypt aimed at weakening the Mamluk state and that allowed the viewer to understand, in one image, the interrelationships between the world's oceans and the axes of communication between Asia and the Mediterranean through which men and commodities circulated. The arrangement of the seas was particularly innovative and built upon seafaring and mercantile knowledge in addition to new written sources about Asia.

PORTOLAN CHARTS: A CHANGE OF SCALE

Pietro Vesconte's world map represents a major turning point in the history of cartography in the way that it connects what we might term the "ecumenically constituted" maps of the high Middle Ages with the more "practical," precise, and regionally focused maritime cartography seen in portolan charts, a form known since the thirteenth century (Campbell 1987; Pujades I Bataller 2007). Indeed, Vesconte is also the author of the oldest surviving signed and dated atlases of portolan charts. The origins of the form are shrouded in mystery, produced only in the Mediterranean and during the Middle Ages they find no equivalents in northern Europe, where navigation appears to have dispensed with maps, nor in the Byzantine Empire. They do not derive from cartographic techniques known in the Islamic world nor, as far as we know at the moment, from East Asian techniques. The oldest examples, namely the so-called Carte Pisane—discussed by Staples in this volume and illustrated in Figure 1.2—the Cortona and Lucques maps, as well as a chart recently discovered in Avignon, are neither signed nor dated but have been assigned by specialists to the end of the thirteenth century; the earliest example signed by Pietro Vesconte is from 1313.

Portolans, strictly defined, are textual objects, nautical instruction manuals developed to describe ports, harbors, and their access. These texts set out, for example, the distances between ports, their orientation and prevailing winds, and indicate features such as reefs, sand banks, or sometimes the depth of a channel. As Staples discusses in Chapter 1 "Knowledges," unillustrated portolan texts such as the *Compasso da navigare* and the *Liber de existencia riveriarum*, predate the surviving illustrated charts such as the Carte Pisane. Nevertheless, the medieval portolan charts that survive today were probably never taken to sea, they are luxury objects, illuminated, carrying coats-of-arms, illustrated with people, towns, and animals. Unlike other maps, however, in portlolan charts

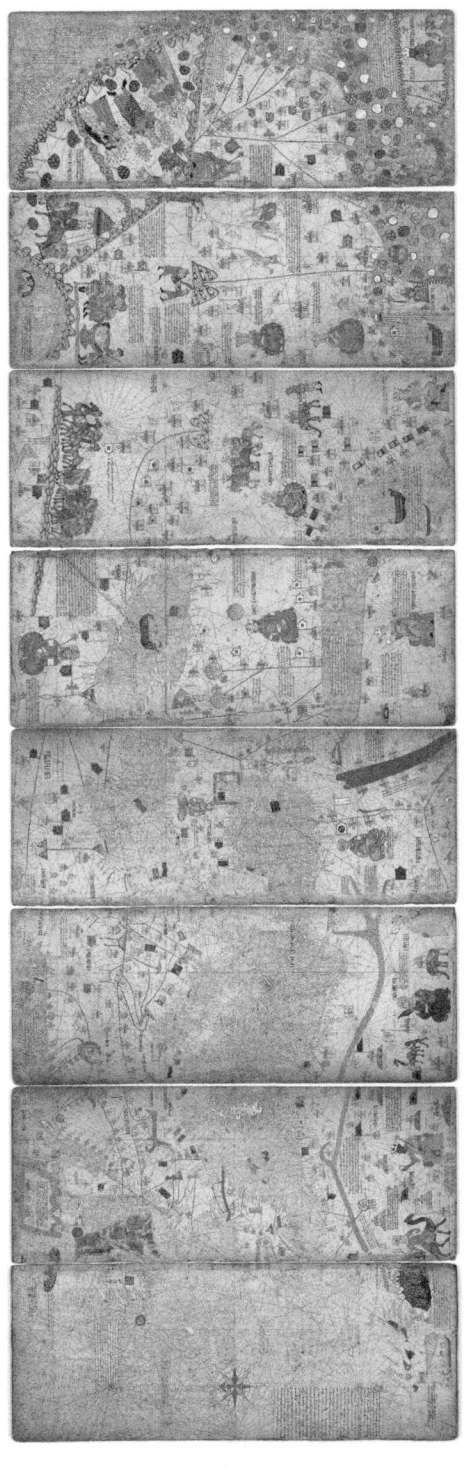

FIGURE 7.6 Composite view of the Catalan Atlas, produced in Mallorca, c. 1375. Ink, silver, and gold on vellum and wood. Paris, Bibliothèque nationale de France, Espagnol 30. © Bridgeman Images.

the land and sea are usually left as plain parchment with only a colored line to distinguish the coast. Much more than navigational aides these surviving examples need to be understood as geographical and political representations of the known world within which European merchants circulated, from the Black Sea to the Atlantic coast of northern Europe. The technical, navigational function of portolans was thus quickly supplemented by scholarly and political functions in which the representation of the inhabited world enabled merchants to visualize the spaces of maritime exchange as well as proving useful tools for the instruction of rulers.

An important document closely related to portolans is the so-called Catalan Atlas, attributed to Cresques Abraham (1375) and likely offered to King Charles V of France by the King of Aragon (Figure 7.6). The Atlas presents the known world of late fourteenth-century Europe from the Atlantic to China. Although it employs techniques derived from portolans and is furnished with numerous captions, the atlas was nevertheless conceived first and foremost as a geographical encyclopaedia allowing the viewer to locate lands and seas as well as peoples and their histories, natural resources, and the main axes of circulation between regions (see also Figure 3.4). Its coastal contours are relatively exact for western areas with a comparatively new attention to the detailed rendering of the Baltic Sea and the Hanseatic ports. The eastern section covers the Caspian Sea, the Gulf, and the Indian Ocean as far as Sri Lanka and Java. In a notable departure from portolan charts models, its illustrator colored the seas and oceans blue, with wavy lines to indicate waves. As in most Catalan charts, the Red Sea is colored red with a line marking the crossing point of the Israelites.

DISCOVERING THE WORLD'S SEAS

Marine cartography includes large swathes of the unknown, the ecumene is surrounded not only by *terrae incognitae* (unknown lands) but also by unknown seas. In a famous article the historian Jacques Le Goff described the Indian Ocean as "the oneiric horizon of the Middle Ages" (1977: 280) in reference to the marvels found in every travel narrative and legend about these distant seas, from Marco Polo to the *Thousand and One Nights*. As Smith underlines in this volume, following other writers such as Christiane Deluz (2005: 8–11), the marvelous is also found in the unknown seas of Western and northern Europe, for example, in the description of icefloes as the "frozen sea" (*mare concretum*) or the absence of snakes in Ireland (see Smith in this volume).

Cartography, however, presents a more nuanced image of these distant regions. Over the course of the Middle Ages these unknown seas increasingly became places awaiting discovery rather than impassable obstacles (O'Doherty 2011). One might even suggest that during the Middle Ages maritime spaces were perceived as interlinked, holding the potential for connectivity and the accommodation of exchange (Mauntel 2018). Already in the world maps of

Beatus of Liebana, which were copied from the eleventh century onward, and in the large thirteenth-century Hereford world map, the encircling ocean is dotted with islands, each one a potential waypoint for ships. The same can be said of islands in Islamic cartography. Thus, the maritime space of medieval maps is an inhabited place, even if such inhabitants are marvelous creatures such as the Waq-Waq of the east African coast (Ducène 2017b). This appropriation of the seas and oceans is particularly evident in Fra Mauro's large World Map (Figure 7.7), a synthesis of medieval Latin, Greek, and Islamic cartography produced in Venice in the 1450s (Cattaneo 2011: 118, 207–11; Falchetta 2006). The Indian Ocean, drawn on the basis of Marco Polo's decription but probably also informants familiar with the Middle East, is rendered as a space covered in exotic ships, a space of commercial routes and encounters between civilizations.

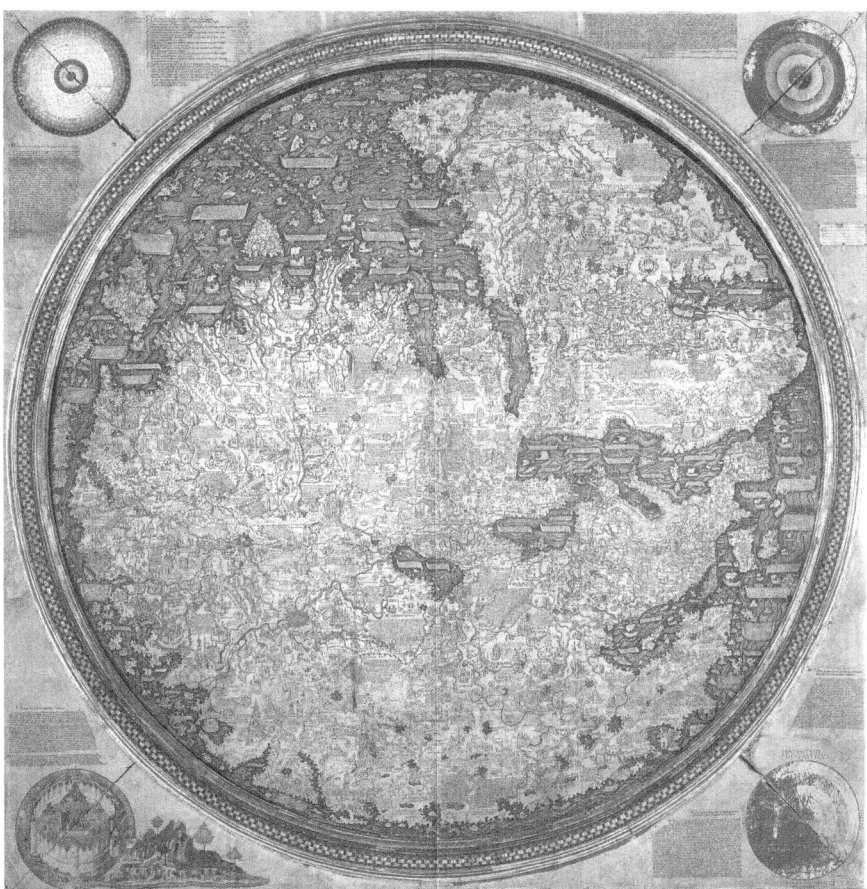

FIGURE 7.7 World Map by Fra Mauro, produced in Murano, near Venice, *c.* 1460. Ink, gold, and colors on vellum. Dimensions 240 × 240 cm. Venice, Biblioteca Marciana. © Wikimedia Commons (public domain).

In contrast to earlier descriptions and maps, the information gathered by Fra Mauro in Venice, then the preeminent European economic center of the mid-fifteenth century, is detailed and precise, a cartographic rendering of the textual information then available in that city-state, be it from merchant manuals, the *pratica della mercatura* literature, or descriptions of itineraries and commodities. The myth of Asia's limitless riches was thus revived and gave momentum to the oceanic explorations of the late fifteenth and early sixteenth centuries.

In Western Europe in the later Middle Ages two other types of map were to have a major influence on the conception and representation of the seas and oceans: new renderings of Ptolemy's geography and the *isolario* or atlas of island maps. The translation of Ptolemy's *Geography* from Greek into Latin by Jacopo Angeli da Scarperia, completed between 1406 and 1410, was later illustrated with a set of maps drawn by Francesco Lapacino and Domenico Buoninsegni, which provided the model for a large number of manuscripts, and after 1470, of printed copies too. After the world map, twenty-six maps—ten of Europe, four of Africa, twelve of Asia—focus on terrestrial geography, dividing up the seas and oceans according to the landmass or region to which their coastline belonged. Although this approach split the seas and oceans across maps, the scale of resolution allowed the mapmaker to specify the names of parts of the sea and gulfs much more precisely than in other systems. By the end of the fifteenth century in Florence, this tradition became fused with the new genre of the *isolario* (see Margariti in this volume and Figure 5.2) and the German geographer Henricus Martellus produced his *Insularium illustratum* (Illustrated Book of Islands) through a synthesis of Ptolemaic regional maps, Buondelmonti's maps of islands, together with portolan charts and some new marine maps, notably of the Caspian Sea. Martellus's work survives as a few large manuscripts on parchment (Bouloux 2012). Looking beyond the strict timeframe of this volume, these cartographic innovations were taken up in the Islamic world too, and particularly the Ottoman Empire, through the reception and translation of some of the European geographical works just mentioned.

The very end of the Middle Ages thus saw the emergence of a regionally focused maritime cartography centered around the description of coasts, harbors, and ports, which described the sea not only as a natural, wild space but also as a heavily inhabited space under human control. The portolan charts of the fifteenth century also hint at the growing momentum of oceanic exploration. The Catalan Atlas of 1375 mentions Jaume Ferrer's earlier navigation along the African coast in 1346 (Figure 7.6). The Canary Islands became part of these charts early on. As James L. Smith discusses in Chapter 8 "Imaginary Worlds," in antiquity and during the early Middle Ages the Blessed Isles had been considered to be somewhere at the edge of the known world and one of the locations of Paradise; now, newly identified as the Canary Islands, they became staging posts in the new exploration of the Atlantic. The cartography of Africa was also extended during the fifteenth century: Grazioso Benincasa's maps testify to the ports and islands explored by Portuguese and Italian sailors, in particular the Azores and the Cape Verde islands. Another mysterious island off the Atlantic coast was depicted in the chart produced by the Italian Zuane Pizzigano in 1424 where it is labeled Island of Antillia. This nomenclature, of uncertain origin, is found on several other late fifteenth-century planispheres and was eventually taken up again a few decades later to name the modern Caribbean archipelago. The history of cartography knows no neat boundaries and the further history of the representation of the Atlantic is continued in the next volume.

PART THREE: ASIAN REPRESENTATIONS AND EAST-WEST EXCHANGES

We have seen that cartography and iconographic representations of the sea around the Mediterranean and in the Islamic world had common origins and benefited from cultural exchanges at the heart of the Old World during the medieval period. What then of East Asian representations of the oceans, were they part of even more ancient traditions? Did this principally Chinese but also more broadly East Asian cartography interact with other cultural traditions, other ways of seeing and understanding the world? The current interest in Asian cartography also belongs within global history as Western historians attempt to shed Eurocentric paradigms, decenter their gaze, and adopt another viewpoint from which to study ancient maps. Comparative analysis by regional specialists within the Western academy encourages reflection on possible structural convergences in the representation of the world and, on the contrary, on their possible divergences due to the profoundly cultural nature of cartographic conventions and the interpretation of maps (for example, Mauntel et al. 2018; Pinto 2016). But European and American historiography is also increasingly challenged by booming Asian historiographies, particularly those of India, China, and South Korea, with their focus on maritime spaces less familiar to Western scholars such as the eastern Indian Ocean, the China Sea, the Sea of Japan, and, of course, the Pacific Ocean.

Studies of Asian technology and cartography have insisted heavily on the transfer of Chinese knowledge to the West, in particular after the thirteenth century when the Pax Mongolica facilitated the first European journeys to the East, for example those of Jean de Plan Carpin, Guillaume de Rubrouck, and Marco Polo (Needham [1959] 1979). Interactions in the reverse direction, from the Islamic world to East Asia, have generally been less well studied although Hyunhee Park's study, *Mapping the Chinese and Islamic Worlds: Cross-Cultural Exchange in Pre-Modern Asia* (2012) has gone a long way to rectifying this. In this volume the South Korean historian traces and contextualizes the travels of maps and concepts from the Islamic world eastwards as far as the Korean Peninsula and Japan. Her book offered the first in-depth study of exchanges between these areas to be based on primary sources in Chinese as well as

Arabic and Persian (Park 2012). Thus, East Asia was not only an ancient crucible of original, indigenous cartographic techniques but also a beneficiary of representations of the world returning via the maritime and terrestrial Silk Roads. The themes studied above in Mediterranean and Islamic societies are also illustrated in the maritime cartography of East Asian civilizations: the challenges of representing natural space, the desire to control space through mapping, the sea as a connective space and place of openess toward other civilizations. As a result, Chinese, and more broadly speaking East Asian, cartography offers a counterpoint to Western representations. Seen from East Asia, the Indian Ocean is a Western Ocean and the Mediterranean little more than a small lake at the other end of the world.

ASIAN TRADITIONS OF MARITIME REPRESENTATION

Chinese art had long concerned itself with the representation of nature, including water, through the depiction of landscapes of mountains, rivers, and lakes. Indeed, the Chinese word for "landscape" is made up of the characters "mountain" and "water." Landscape painting always communicated philosophical ideas and the idea of natural harmony, in these landscapes then water symbolizes the way of life, fluidity, while the mountain is a symbol of stability. Maritime waters, although less frequently depicted, feature in landscapes of estuaries and seashores. While such landscape paintings already existed during the Tang dynasty (618–907), water was particularly emphasized during the dynasty of the Southern Song (1127–1279) (Maeda 1971) whose territories encompassed much of China's eastern coast and whose capital was the port city of Lin'an (present-day Hangzhou). Perhaps the most magnificent examples of Southern Song waterscape painting are the work of Ma Yuan (c. 1160–1225), the founder of the Ma-Xia school (Edwards 2011). His series Twelve Views of Water (*Shi'er shui tu*) of 1222, explores the pictorial possibilities of water, as pictorial challenge certainly, but also, as in all Chinese representations of flowing water, as philosophical motif, a reminder of constant flow and change. Paintings such as *Clouds Rising from the Green Sea* (Figure 7.8) demonstrate a use of undulating brush lines and strokes to evoke the whirling, sinuous rhythms of turbulent water and waves quite unique within the representational repertoire of Eurasia at this period (Maeda 1971: 257). More than two hundred years later, in 1488, the Ming connoisseur Wang Ao (1450–1524) compared Ma Yuan's art to the paintings of two major earlier painters, Sun Whei and Sun Zhiwei, in the following words:

> Mountains and forests, great buildings, figures, flowers and trees, birds and animals, insects and fish – all have fixed forms. Only the transformations of water are not as one. All painters are faced with its difficulties […] Now I have seen Ma Yuan's paintings of water: water twisting and turning over level distances, coiling and counter flowing in skips and leaps, wind rippled, in moon-reflected

waves and in running waves under the sun – all transcending a foot of space with the appearance of a thousand li. Why should the two Suns [two earlier painters] be the only painters said to have exhausted the variations of water?

(Edwards 2011: 90–1; Maeda 1971: 256, with a different translation)

Another series of water studies, attributed to Ma Yuan but still of disputed attribution, is known as the Twenty Scenes of Water (*Hua shui ershi jing*) and includes famous water scenes such as studies of the Yellow River or the tidal bore at Qiantang (Lai 2014: 189). While it is not always possible in these studies to distinguish between riverine and maritime waters, the deep penetration of the Southern Song's territory by the estuaries of the Qiantang, Yangtze, and Pearl rivers, amongst many others, makes the point that the sea is often felt far inland from the seacoast as strictly delineated by modern maps. The fascination of other Song painters with the famous tidal bore on the Qiantang river at Hangzhou, the new Southern Song capital, notably in the work of Li Song (1166–c. 1225), led to the popularization of the tidal bore motif, as on the painted fan, later mounted into an album, in Figure 7.9. The Southern Song world was deeply maritime and this is reflected in its art.

Regarding maps, with the exception of coastal waters, East Asian maps only rarely represented the sea itself and this is in spite of the fact that we have evidence of communication by sea between China and other regions from an early period and appropriate cartographic techniques. Cartography

FIGURE 7.8 Ma Yuan, *Clouds Rising from the Green Sea*, painting from the series *Shi'er shui tu* (Twelve Views of Water), 1222, Song dynasty. Light colors on silk. Palace Museum Beijing, 26.8 x 41.6 cm © Wikimedia Commons (public domain).

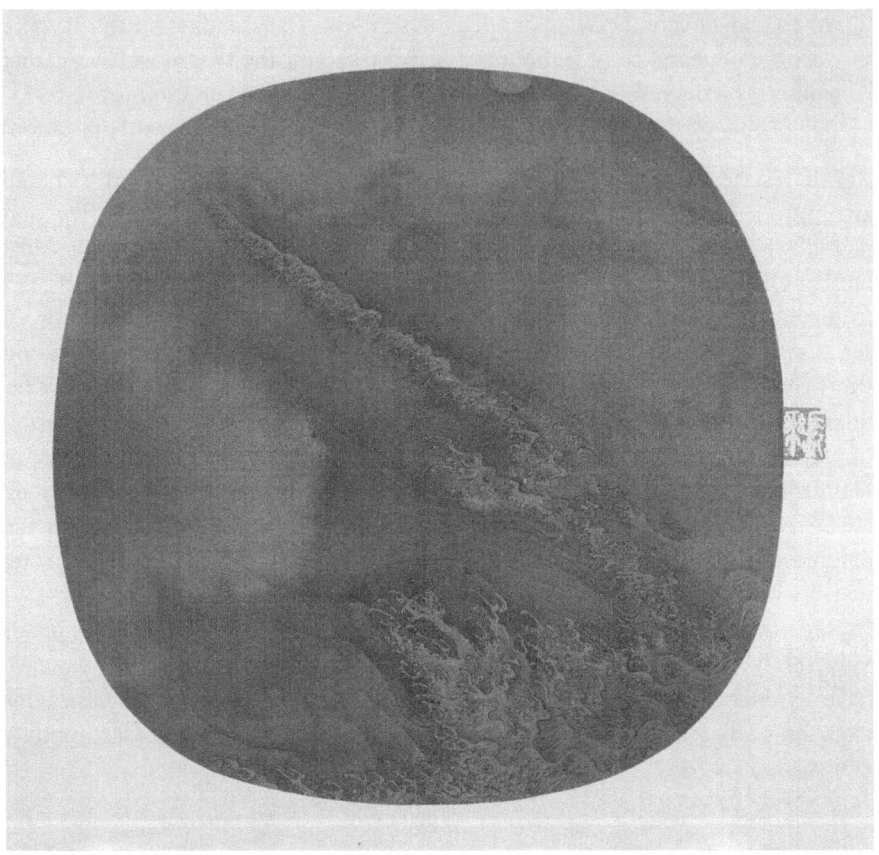

FIGURE 7.9 *Waters in the Moonlight*, inspired by views of the tidal bore on the Qiantang River in Hangzhou, Song dynasty (1127–1279). Fan mounted as an album leaf; ink on silk, 22.2 × 22.4 cm. Metropolitan Museum of Art, New York, 47.18.70. From the Collection of A.W. Bahr, Purchase, Fletcher Fund, 1947. © The Metropolitan Museum of Art (public domain).

was considered an art requiring observation and the naturalistic representation of nature through refined means such as engraving on stone, painting on silk, embroidery, calligraphy, and especially woodblock printing (Yee 1994: 128–69). Maps are varied, some come close to landscapes featuring the shorelines of lakes or indeed seas. In prints the sea is differentiated from the land, which is left blank, through the use of dark, closely spaced wavy lines, which form reliefs or patchwork effects, according to different artists (De Weerdt 2009: 158; Yee 1994: 158, 161, 168). In marked contrast to Western European and Islamic cartography with their interest in the marvels commonly associated with the sea, the sea of East Asian cartography is usually uninhabited, devoid of decorations, fish or other sea creatures.

Generally speaking, the anthropocentric idea of an inhabited world surrounded by waters with "other" imaginary worlds beyond has been common to many ancient civilizations, and is also a model found in South and East Asian cultures. In Indian, Chinese, Korean, and Japanese cartographies this conception of the world persisted until the early modern period, notably in maps based on Buddhist cosmologies, the oldest examples of which go back to the seventh century and which continued into the eighteenth century (Nanda and Johnson 2017: 55–9; Moerman forthcoming). These maps depict a landmass usually comprising China and India, and Japan as an island, centered on the mythical Mount Meru, and encircled by the outermost ocean. This type of map was introduced into Japan along with Buddhism in the eighth century and was known as a *Nansenbushu Bankoku Shoka No Zu* (Outline Map of all Countries of the Universe). One of the oldest surviving examples of this model is the impressively large, 177 centimeters by 166 centimeters, *Gotenjiku Zu* (Map of the Five Indies) drawn by the Buddhist priest Jukai in 1364 and now held in the Horyu-ji temple in Japan (Ledyard 1994: 255). Unlike simpler examples of the genre, the Horyu-ji map shows regions far beyond East Asia including Europe, notably France and the British Isles, and Africa, which is shown as an island, a reflection no doubt of the hugely increased trans-Eurasian connectivities stimulated by the earlier Mongol conquests.

Other map genres coexisted with this. Traditional Chinese cartography represents the world as composed of a central landmass, sometimes referred to as the "inside the seas" (*hainei*), surrounded by the "four seas" (*sihai*) (Dorofeeva-Lichtmann 2003). As with Buddhist-inspired maps, this model had a long life span (Nakamura 1947). An early geographical treatise known as *Shanhaijing* (Guideways Through Mountains and Seas), composed perhaps as early as the first century BCE, describes over 447 different mountains, as well as rivers and seas, all arranged in twenty-six lists of itineraries, yet still structured around the cosmographical system found in the world maps just mentioned (Dorofeeva-Lichtmann 2003, 2007; Strassberg 2002). The *Ch'onhado* (literally, Map of All Under Heaven), based on these ancient conceptions, was developed in Korea and continued to be reproduced for centuries afterwards, being especially popular in atlases of the eighteenth and nineteenth centuries produced under the later Choson dynasty (1392–1910) (Figure 7.10). These works, printed or hand drawn, are usually composed of thirteen maps, sometimes more, sometimes less. They open with the Korean "wheel map," which extends the traditional Chinese picture of the world to include another circle toward the lands "outside the seas"; this circle may, according to Vera Dorofeeva-Lichtmann, emulate the symbolic shape of the heavens suggested in the work's very title (Dorofeeva-Lichtmann 2019). Following this comes a map of China, then a map of Korea, based on a fifteenth-century prototype, and maps of the eight Korean provinces, Japan, and the Ryukyu islands, then an independent kingdom.

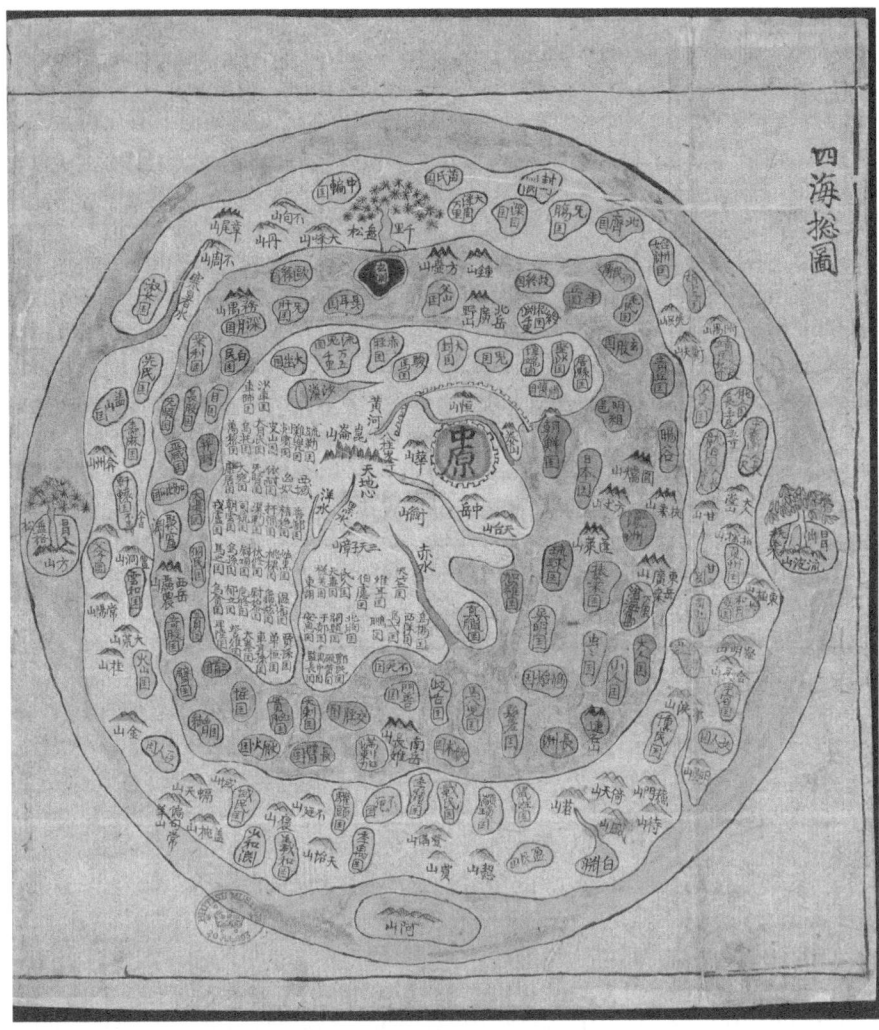

FIGURE 7.10 *Ch'onhado* (Map of All Under Heaven) showing China as the center of the world, according to the ancient Buddhist tradition. Korea, *c.* 1800. Colored print on paper. British Library, London, Maps.C.27.f.14. © Album/Alamy Stock Photo.

Just as West Asia represented the East and its seas, East Asia did not ignore western seas. The so-called Western Sea (*Xihai*), was considered one of the Four Seas and was represented cardinally oriented and in a largely conceptual manner. If the notion of a western region (*Xuyu*) was already established under the Han dynasty, it was only under the Tang dynasty (618–907), as contact between China and Western Asia intensified, that this became identified specifically with the northwestern reaches of the Indian Ocean (Park 2012: 29–30). As mentioned by Eric Staples in this volume, the Tang minister Jia Dan (729–805) supplied a detailed description of the sea route between Gangzhou and Iraq, and drew the *Hainei huayi-tu* (Map of Chinese and Non-Chinese Territories in the World) to accompany it. Unfortunately now lost, the oldest surviving Chinese maps to show countries on the periphery of the Chinese Empire date several centuries later, notably the *Yu ji tu* (Map of the Tracks of Yu), based on a square grid and which is dated between 1043 and 1048 during the Song dynasty (960–1276). The *Yu ji tu* was completed by the *Huayi tu* (Maps of the Chinese and Non-Chinese Territories), which lists foreign places on its margins according to Jia Dan's map. The two maps are known from engraved copies found on a stone stele of 1227, although obviously based on these older models (Chavannes 1903: 214–47; De Weerdt 2009: 151–5; Most 2011; Park 2012: 37).

As Hilde De Weerdt notes (2009: 145), under the Southern Song, maps acquired a new political significance, supporting the policy of restoration of the lost northern part of the empire as well as incorporating material reflecting their maritime commercial policy and contacts. It was during this period that the Song government established a naval force to protect the maritime trade and the Chinese shore (Calanca 2010: 25). Thanks to new technologies such as larger junks and, from the eleventh century, the compass, longer voyages became possible, which brought an expansion of geographical knowledge. This was bolstered by the arrival and settlement of foreign merchants in the main ports (24). Besides using the earlier *Zhufan tu* (Map of Foreign Countries) as a source, Zhao Rugua, the superintendent of merchant shipping in Quanzhou and a member of the Song imperial family, collected new information from these sources for his own geographic account the *Zhufan zhi* (Records of Foreign Countries) (Park 2012: 50–1). Among the list of the world's seas and oceans in Zhou Qufei's 1178 treatise *Ling wai daida* (Notes from the Land Beyond the Passes) we find two oceans, one to the east—the *Dong dashi hai* or Indian Ocean—and one to the west the *Xi Dashi hai* or Mediterranean. Toward the period 1265–70, a Chinese Buddhist scholar included maps of countries and seas in his chronicle *Fozu tongji* (General Records of the Founders of Buddhism); both the *Map of States of the Western Regions* in the Han Period and the *Map of the Five Indian States in the West* locate the Western Sea (*Xihai*) in their margins, to the west (Park 2012: 42).

Park concludes that the representation of the sea at this period corresponds with the increase in maritime exchanges with the Islamic world but remains limited to itineraries between ports rather than being included as part of a synthetic worldview. As she writes:

> The growing scale and importance of maritime trade between China and the Islamic world prompted Chinese to collect practical information about both sailing and markets, which included details about each country in the Islamic world that could affect travel or trade. Even though the Chinese geographers did not draw the full coastline between the two societies in the maps, the knowledge they did possess of these routes, and of the major

Indian Ocean port cities along these routes, placed the Islamic world in an expanded geographic framework. Chinese readers could imagine a series of ports that formed a line that stretched all the way to the Islamic world.

(2012: 54)

THE CIRCULATION OF MAPS IN THE MONGOL PERIOD: THE *KANGNIDO*

The Yuan dynasty (1260–1368) marks the apogee of Chinese relations with the West in the premodern period and it is the period at which new representations of the world appeared. For a little over a century China was the center of the Mongol Empire with its capital at Khanbaliq, the ancient site of Beijing. Scholarly exchanges with the Islamic world were particularly important in this period and showed interest in cartography as well as maritime spaces. A Muslim astronomer from Iran, Jamal al-Din, brought astronomical instruments to Kubilai Khan's court in 1267, among them a colored terrestrial globe engraved with a grid probably representing coordinates according to latitude and longitude. In 1285 the emperor Kubilai Khan commissioned a huge geographical compendium, the *Dayuan da yitong zhi* (The Treatise on the Great Unified Realm of the Great Yuan), finally completed in 1303, as well as a *Rāh-nāmah* (Book of Routes) based on seafarers's descriptions. During his stay Jamal al-Din combined several earlier maps to produce a new world map for the emperor that, although now lost, inspired several other surviving maps, notably the celebrated *Honil gangli yeokdae gukdo jido* (Map of Integrated Lands and Regions of Historical Countries and Capitals), usually referred to as the *Kangnido,* completed in Korea in 1402 and of which several late fifteenth-century copies presenting slight variations survive (Ledyard 1994: 243–7; Park 2012: 103–9) (Figure 7.11). The preface to the map refers explicitly to its sources, among them a work of the fourteenth-century scholar Li Zemin (*c*. 1380 for the prototype map), as well as to the conditions of its creation in Korea. For the first time in East Asia the *Kangnido* map shows parts of Western Asia, Europe, and Africa as well as the Indian Ocean. As seen in Figure 7.11 Africa is represented as a triangle, the Indian subcontinent disappears almost completely, and the countries of Southeast Asia are depicted simply as small islands in the sea. The Mediterranean Sea resembles a tiny lake in the upper western corner of the map, and a later copyist even mistakenly painted over the Straits of Gibraltar, effectively transforming the Mediterranean into a large lake. While details such as this indicate that the copyist did not know the regions he was copying, nevertheless, the detail of the map is oftentimes remarkable with even the far-away Mediterranean port of Marseille featured. Just as for the Western maps of Pietro Vesconte or Fra Mauro, the specific depiction of the sources of the Nile is reminiscent of the maps of al-Khwarizmi or al-Idrisi and thus indicative of knowledge exchanges with the Islamic world (Park 2012: 106).

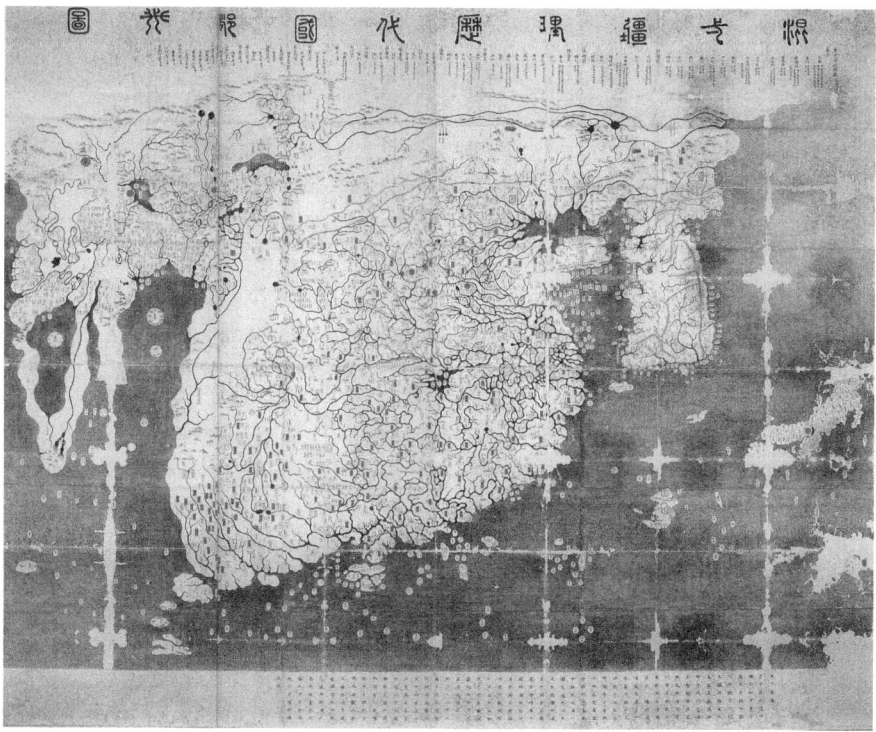

FIGURE 7.11 Yi Hoe and Kwon Kun, *Kangnido* world map, Korea, *c*. 1470, based on an earlier map of 1402. Ink and paint on paper. H: 220 cm; W: 289 cm. Honkoo-ji Tokiwa Museum of Historical Materials, Shimabara, Nagasaki Prefecture, Japan. © Wikimedia Commons (public domain).

Another map, the *Guanglun jiangli tu* (Map of the World's Regions) originally drawn in 1360—but known from the Ming dynasty work Ye Sheng's *Diary from East of the River* of 1474—shows several lines in the sea resembling sailing routes and provides concise long-distance navigation guidance for the most important ports. Thus a caption next to Quanzhou reads "Riding the wind from Quanzhou, one can reach Java in sixty days, Malabar in 128 days, and Hormuz in around 200 days" (Park 2012: 107–8). Such labels prove the existence of a maritime route linking the principal ports of China and the Gulf, namely Guangzhou and Quanzhou with Hormuz.

MARITIME ITINERARIES OF ZHENG HE UNDER THE MING

Maritime relations between China and the western Indian Ocean declined gradually under the Yuan's successors, the Ming (1368–1644). In a context of isolationist policies and to better control trade, in 1372 the court issued a maritime edict (*haijin*; literally, sea ban) prohibiting private navigation between

China and foreign countries. The ban remained in force, theoretically at least, until 1568. This was also the period at which a true maritime defense policy (*haifang*), particularly against the pirates of the sea of China, was introduced (Calanca 2010: 25). Yet at the same time, Yuan geographical knowledge continued to be diffused through copies of the *Kangnido*, of which several examples were dispatched to Korea and Japan. It was also knowledge of maritime routes and navigational technologies developed in China that made possible the seven extraordinary voyages led by the Chinese admiral Zheng He (1371–1433) between 1405 and 1433, under the Ming emperors Yongle, Hongxi, and Xuande. Zheng He was a Yunnanese Muslim of Bukharan descent who eventually became an imperial eunuch in the service of Yongle (r. 1403–24), the third emperor of the Ming dynasty. As one of the emperor's closest advisors, he was entrusted with the greatest project of maritime exploration yet undertaken by China. Beginning in 1405 Zheng He led a Chinese fleet of as many as seventy ships on seven voyages across the Indian Ocean area (Chan 1998). During the course of the first three voyages—in 1405, 1407, and 1408—the fleet sailed as far as maritime Southeast Asia and Calicut, on the southwestern coast of India, stopping at the most important ports along the way to establish treaties with those rulers who agreed to pay tribute to China. In 1412, Yongle ordered a fourth voyage to extend this process as far as Hormuz, then the most important port on the Gulf. In preparation for the voyage Zheng He recruited translators and Muslim seafarers with knowledge of routes in the area. Zheng He's voyages remain deeply embedded in Chinese historical memory, since 2005 his voyages are commemorated every July 11, as China National Maritime Day. Nevertheless, their ultimate purpose has engendered lively scholarly debate. Were these peaceful exploratory missions or demonstrations of Chinese military strength as Edward L. Dreyer has suggested in *Zheng He: China and the Oceans in the Early Ming Dynasty, 1405–1433* (an opinion criticized by Ptak 2007a)? Did Chinese navigators even round the Cape of Good Hope as some have suggested? Whatever the answers, these voyages bear witness to Chinese maritime technology and a continued Chinese interest in maritime routes and cartography.

Zheng He's expeditions are known in lively detail thanks to the *Ying-yai sheng-lan* (The Overall Survey of the Ocean's Shores), an account written by a translator on the voyages, Ma Huan, although without maps (Ma Huan 1970). Maps describing the various possible routes taken by Zheng He have nevertheless come down to us in the form of route maps later integrated into the Ming military manual *Wu bei zhi* (A Treatise on Armament Technology) compiled in 1621 by Mao Yuanyi, which were very probably drawn from marine maps used during the original voyages (Figure 7.12). A strip map divided into forty pages, including eight of West Asia and Africa, retraces Zheng He's expeditions, marking out a linear route from China to West Asia (Park 2012: 172–3). Rather than relying on a depiction of the coastline these maps provide

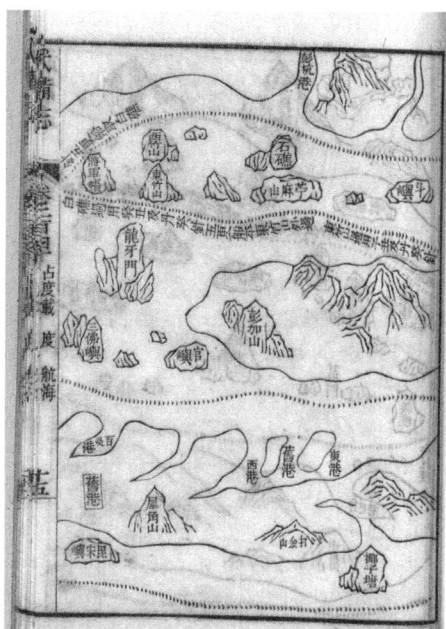
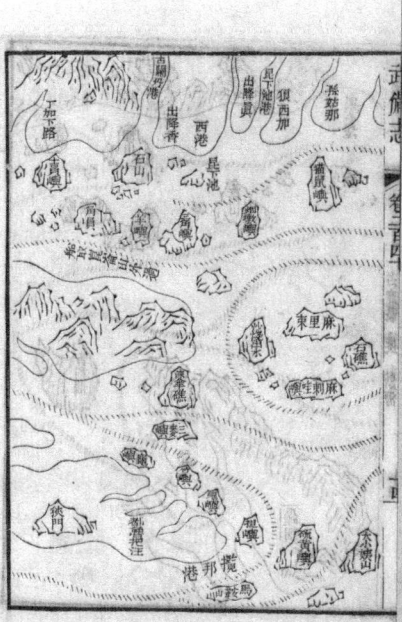

FIGURE 7.12 Headings and routes around southern Sumatra, map 13 of 22 from Mao Yuanyi's *Wu bei zhi* (A Treatise on Armament Technology), 1621, based on fifteenth-century route maps. Woodblock print. Library of Congress G2306.R5 M3 1644.
© Library of Congress (public domain).

precise headings, according to the directions of the compass (*zhenlu*), rendered by means of dotted lines connecting the main ports and anchorages. In so doing they provide the first visual representation of the relationships across the Indian Ocean between locations in South Asia and the Arabian Peninsula. Figure 7.12 shows routes around Southern Sumatra and through the Malacca Straits. The story of Zeng He (also named San Bao tai jian) was illustrated in a sixteenth-century novel by Luo Maodeng, *Xin kan quan xiang san bao tai jian xi yang ji tong su yan yi* (The Voyage of the Eunuch San Bao to the Western Sea), with engraved picures showing the admiral on his boat in the midst of the storm.

In the long run, however, after Zheng He's expeditions relations between China and West Asia continued to decline. By the end of the Ming dynasty, Chinese rulers paid much less attention than their predecessors over the last millennium to the benefits of international maritime trade. This phenomenon is visible in the Chinese maps of the period that revert to traditional Sino-centric models and gradually reduce the space devoted to the western Indian Ocean in spite of having had access to the new global geography through European planispheres and globes. Certain exceptions nevertheless stand out, with documents such as the so-called Selden map indicating that navigation practices and original cartography of the seas continued in China well beyond this period (Batchelor 2013).

CONCLUSION

The visual representation of the sea encompasses two complementary aspects that together enrich the cultural history of human relationships with maritime space. On the one hand, in the visual arts, the sea features as a natural element, as both landscape and economic resource. The study of this iconography can enrich environmental history and the history of human relations with nature, whether wild and dangerous or appropriated and tamed. On the other hand, in cartography, mapping the seas presupposes the identification of their contours, the irregularities of their coasts, their dangers and safe havens, as well the routes along and across them. The cartography of the seas allowed humans to situate maritime space in relationship to land, to enrich their knowledge of their world and, later on in the Middle Ages, to assist seafarers in their navigation. Nevertheless, one should not construct too radical an opposition between a medieval terror-inducing sea and a "useful" sea, tamed by mapping after the thirteenth century. Cartography enables knowledge and communication of coastal and sea routes but it is also a font of placenames and images. The sea always has symbolic potential, even when mapped, and early modern maps were inhabited by sea creatures, ships, and mythological allegories even more than those of the Middle Ages. These images have a long, shared history going back to antiquity: the encircling ocean, the Flood, sea monsters, mermaids, and other wonders. The sea is something shared by all peoples although perceived and conceptualized according to different sensibilities. The seashore bounds countries and continents, yet maritime space is at the same time lived and represented as a mean of communication and connectivity, as infinite sea routes toward new worlds.

Cartography is an essential source for the history of the world's seas, both diachronically and synchronically, since it builds upon ancient shared sources while at the same time combining often diverse medieval models. The study of maps evidences the fact that the representation and definition of maritime spaces were ultimately a collaborative effort based upon shared matrixes and exchanges. It is through maps, and in particular maritime maps, that human societies slowly constructed a representation of the entire earth, differentiating between regions and naming their parts. The seas and oceans were not impervious to this process of differentiation and classification even as it operated in different ways across medieval cultures. It is only relatively recently, in the modern period, that the model of European world geography, with its distribution of oceans and continents and their specific names, became the global standard and was integrated, but not without resistance, into the maps of other cultures around the world.

CHAPTER EIGHT

Imaginary Worlds

Plural Seas, Liminal Foundations, Contested Identities

JAMES L. SMITH

INTRODUCTION

History has been shaped by the powerful, and the cultural history of the sea as a space of imaginary worlds is no exception. Norms of description, such as taxonomies of difference and similarity, stifle our vision of the vivid internal heterogeneity of oceanic imaginations. Critical race theorist Sarah Ahmed has observed that "differences become congealed in entities; differences become sediment, heavy histories that weigh us down" (2015: 95). Ahmed's work reveals a sentiment that resonates across other intersecting categories of alterity. Maritime histories based on a canon of difference are not liquid like their subject matter. The tired and exotic tropes of medieval oceanic dichotomies such as "Self" and "Other" and an obsession with Orientalism are suffocating if attended to at the expense of other narratives, yet their cultural force is the foundation of European colonial hegemony and defines the history and heritage of both Europeans and those affected by colonization. As editor Elizabeth Lambourn has described in the Introduction to this volume, the work of establishing a comprehensive cultural history of the sea is a work in process and requires flexibility. A history of the *imaginary* sea is even more problematic, for it rests on ever-shifting liminal foundations and contested identities.

Late medieval literature and culture scholar Marianne O'Doherty describes this liminality well when introducing the Indies as a unit of medievalist analysis that is "neither a fixed, bordered entity that can be plotted on a modern map nor an abstract discursive construct without referent in the physical world or impact upon individuals" (2013: 5). Historicist arguments that instrumentally convert story into primary source material without nuance run the risk of trivializing the cultural heritage of already subaltern voices. The imaginary world exists at a threshold between categories of being. As in the literary genre of magical realism first deployed in the postcolonial Americas—in which the fantastical and the real seamlessly merge without division—the plural oceanic imaginaries explored in this chapter do not observe boundaries between *types* or *degrees* of reality, be they mythical, magical, or supernatural in nature (see Zamora and Faris 1995). By privileging multiple worldviews and cosmologies that mingle levels and forms of reality, these forms of knowing share perspectives made strange by the enforced boundaries of Western empiricism and rationalism. The medium of narrative transmission is of key importance, be it histories, texts, stories, material culture, or ideas percolating through the oceans of the world.

Claiming that themes and stories are part of a shared imaginary world should not be oversimplified or turned into a master narrative. Matthias Egeler, a scholar of Norse and Irish place, has pointed out that exploring mythmaking and storytelling as part of a "deep history" in cultures that are known to be historically connected is hazardous (2017: 15–16). It is necessary to look for "complex, non-trivial" correspondences rather than purely thematic similarities. Elements within mythologies should be compared within the context of their own time and place of creation and should rely on primary sources rather than claims made in secondary literature. As Egeler puts it, "the main aim of studying [...] contact is not a mere history of motifs, but a history of human encounters" (16). This is also true of imaginary worlds: studying their differences or similarities uncritically is not useful or culturally sensitive.

To understand the interactions within this chapter, imaginary worlds or otherworlds must be understood as a community of interacting individuals, cultures, and world systems, and not as a cascade of abstracted themes and motifs to be compared like a family tree. The fecundity and plurality inherent to the folkloric, mythic, spiritual, and literary visions of imaginary worlds within the oceans are unified by a form of culturally nuanced reading familiar to medievalists. The way visions of life, death, exile, or return are expressed is unique, situated temporally and culturally as a core strand of place and identity. There is not one sea but as many seas as there are cultures to experience them. In fact, as Sinophone island theorists Bin Luo and Adam Grydehøj posit, global imaginaries are co-implicated: historical Western island imaginaries bear strong resemblances to those in the East, and the cultural history of the sea implies a shared and interwoven history (2017: 25–6). As Luo and Grydehøj point out, "Russia, South Asia, Southeast Asia, the near-shore islands of Africa as a whole, and South America have been largely missing from island studies' worldview, thereby limiting our ability to engage in a truly informed and truly global island studies" (4). To ignore all of these regions to only study Europe continues a colonial epistemology in need of deconstruction.

Medieval minds were hypnotized by the whisper of myths in the waves and reworked them into new multi-thematic and multilingual confections (Smith 2016). Water is a different face of medieval literary and historical reception and adaptation, endowing the oceans of the world with the power to hold cultural meaning, acting as a laboratory of stories. As geographers Philip Steinburg and Kimberley Peters have described, "like the ocean itself, maritime subjects and objects can move across, fold into, and emerge out of water in unrecognized and unanticipated ways" (2015: 261). Cultural beliefs swirled through the waves in eddies and flows of medieval thought and its global contemporaries, teeming with afterlives, paradises, myths, and stories that make the sea restless with human story and identity. The worlds that emerged were both spatialized and supernatural, part of the urge that Egeler tentatively proposes as a cross-cultural trend that repeats across the oceanic world, for "the mere existence of narratives about otherworld locations has a tendency to motivate their real-world localization" (2017: 311–12). Imaginary worlds beg for a material existence and location.

If we go into the ocean looking for an objective sense of history, we may find layer upon layer of accreted happenings instead, an undetermined "deep map" of essayed place that refuses to conform (Bodenhamer, Corrigan, and Harris 2015). Cultural history, like these accretions, is composite in nature. As Portuguese and Brazilian specialist Zoltán Biedermann puts it, imaginary worlds emerge from the interweaving of our words, images, and ideas, rising from the depths of the imagination (2017: 223). Islands of rock, soil, and sand emerge as well as clumps of monsters, dreams, fantasies, and political ambitions. All are imaginary worlds. World-building theorist Mark J.P. Wolf situates these places in a process of "subcreation," spawning new adaptations, offshoots, and trans-authorial "dynamic entities" (2012: 3). Like a literary imaginary world—Ursula K. Le Guin's *Earthsea*, for example—these spaces grow dynamically and take on an independent and transtemporal life with medieval episodes for us to explore beneath.

These stories pass through the medieval but participate in the full scope of a longer cultural history beyond its remit. What is dreamt or imagined is destined to reoccur throughout history, a phenomenon of eternal reemergence. Once the imaginary world is conceived of, it is *reconceived* again and again "by those protagonists who occupy it and (frequently) by the reader, viewer, or player who experiences this transformation" (Graziadei et al. 2017: 240). As the imaginary world is modified by encounter, experience, or literary reception, it "undergoes a morphological shift—either geophysically, spatially, conceptually, figuratively, or, as is common, a combination of some or all of the above" (240). It becomes a complex repository of identity, a store-house of identity mapped on the moveable surface of the oceans, shaped by "how [a particular] ground, [or] country, amply holds both connections and ruptures between pasts, presents, and futures" (Jolly 2001: 455). Islands are an excellent example of these phenomena, as are the reaches of the oceans themselves. Archipelagic and oceanic identities blur and merge, flowing across the semipermeable membranes of shorelines and across the horizons of knowledge.

The absorbent oceanic waters are the pages on which the narratives of imaginary worlds are written and must be seen anew from a global perspective to be fully realized. For the influential postcolonial writer and anthropologist Epeli Hau'ofa, "the ocean is not merely our omnipresent, empirical reality; equally important, it is our most wonderful metaphor for just about anything we can think of" (2008: 55). Europeans have frequently forgotten the wild imaginative polyvalence of the sea, instead choosing to belittle the oceanic world. The sea was with Europe always, even if Europe was not with it. Thus, as literary scholars Matthew Boyd Goldie and Sebastian Sobecki (2016) have discussed in the context of the archipelagic Middle Ages, we must move from "islands in the sea" to a "sea of islands" where we are at home (Hau'ofa 2008: 31–2) and imagination can thrive. The growth of an "island logic" unmoored from neoliberal structures of power and spatialization can intervene "in ways that expose naturalized political structures and hierarchies and lay them open to contestation and rearticulation," as island studies scholar Otto Heim has proposed (2017: 927–8).

When attempting to historicize the imaginary ocean as history, empirical categories of description are problematic. Is oceanic knowledge "objectively" history? Is it cultural memory? Is it mythology? It is all these things, a substrate of cultural identity rich with internal diversity and contradictions. As medievalists Emmanuelle Vagnon and Éric Vallet describe in their study of the Indian Ocean, the knowledges of the oceanic world are formed from the generative "machine" (*fabrique*) that is the sea (2017a: 23), a term taken by the editors from early modern cartography referring to the globe as a divinely created and ordered *machina mundi* or machine of the world. No one group of people owns these stories, generated from the mass of the waters, and the oceans of the world do not divide into nation-states, cultures, or regions. They are a blue and fantastic commons, a generator of meanings. As I have argued elsewhere (Smith 2016), the separations of oceanic life have the paradoxical power of connecting us all. It is history always beginning, but it is a history of destabilization. Oceanic life is also a history of powerful and influential emotions, both individual and communal: curiosity, wonder, fear, ambition, greed, suspicion, and cruelty. These passions imbue the medieval seascape with the agency to link the world through the social science-inspired notion of the hydro-social arrangement (Linton and Budds 2014), a recursive link between water and society in co-creation. The blue humanities and new thalassology put forward by literary scholar Steve Mentz (2009) and historian Peter Miller (2013) require a capacious understanding of cultural interconnections, and the role of the wondrous and imaginary is not "out there" but at its heart.

Otherworlds exist within a political ecology with lasting effects. In the Western imagination, the monsters, islands, marvels, and myths discussed in this chapter were all waiting "out there" across the sea, and were actively spun into a political narrative of power and control. The results were brutal and genocidal, irreparably disrupting and reshaping the islanded cultures of the world in their image. The sea brought death and cultural suppression: in the age of empire, a shadow stretched out to touch the world, smashing the systems it encountered. The narrative qualities of the European medieval became the framework by which all other stories were understood. The current world order was built on their ruins, and a new order will inevitably displace our present. This is the ecology of imaginary worlds, and the Middle Ages was a period in which ancient and newly minted tales gained the beginning of what would be a centuries-long hold on the imaginations of billions.

INVESTIGATING IMAGINARY WORLDS

Over the last decade the exploration of imaginary worlds in academic scholarship has been plural and vibrant. The primary source materials covered here are equally diverse, ranging from manuscripts to oral history and mythology. The topic is inherently multidisciplinary and inexhaustible in meaning. An extraordinary range of scholarly accounts detailing European otherworlds have been published, yet providing a decentered global medieval account requires decentering the thickness of this scholarship. Drawing on the seminal work of Hau'ofa (2008), it has embraced a postcolonial global urgency (Grydehøj, Heim, and Zhang 2017; Heim 2017; Llenín-Figueroa 2012; Luo and Grydehøj 2017; McCusker and Soares 2011) and medieval cultural studies has been inspired by this discourse (Chism 2016; Davis and Puett 2016; Goldie and Sobecki 2016; Hiatt 2016; Mentz 2009, 2016; Smith 2016; Staley 2016). Critical theory has enriched the debate surrounding the mechanics of world creation (Graziadei et al. 2017; Hayward 2012; Pugh 2013; Wolf 2012) as well as medievalists' descriptions of genres such as the otherworld and the wonders of the East (Byrne 2016; Egeler 2017; O'Doherty 2013). These discourses merge with a rich array of medieval studies detailing the cultural history of the sea and of water in the West and within Christianity (Adão da Fonseca 2018; Biedermann 2017; Classen 2018; Jaspert and Kolditz 2018; Vagnon and Vallet 2017b), in the Asia-Pacific and Oceania (Grydehøj et al. 2017; Luo and Grydehøj 2017; Shaw 2012), and within Islam and in the Islamicate world (Alardawe 2016; Chism 2016; Ducène 2017a, 2017b; Hassan 2014; Lambourn 2018; Shafiq 2013; Zargar 2014). This chapter covers the intermingled mythologies of the

Asia-Pacific, Oceania, the Indian Ocean, the Islamicate world, and Europe in equal measure, moving from East to West. Its attention is to deliberately diffuse. In this chapter, you will also encounter a wide array of supplements from disciplines such as anthropology (Scott 2012), geography (Steinburg and Peters 2015), indigenous culture and materiality (Rosiek, Snyder, and Pratt 2020), and popular history (Tallack 2016) to name but a few.

The very mutability of imaginary worlds defines our experience of the sea, and the Middle Ages participated in this long thread of intermingling narratives, adding its own unique resonances that are with us still. The cultural reality of these powerful stories is strongly felt, and cultural imagination or ocean-going life cannot be conceived without their presence. They are part of what manuscript scholar Martha Rust (2008) has termed the "manuscript matrix," a mnemo-technical, imaginative and textual space in which the diverse material and embodied practices of manuscripts combine to form a world within a text. They are also oral history and storytelling, passed from generation to generation for millennia. They are machines of identity as medievalist Jeffrey J. Cohen (2003) describes it, spilling out of the body and into the world. Like Rust's matrices, environmental engagement creates a cultural symbolism without boundaries, it creates an embodied reading experience tying the environment to a long history of myth (Siewers 2009: 5–6).

To read the sea, one must be entangled in an assemblage of ocean, archipelago, coast, and hinterland in which different registers are spatially encoded and navigated. One must engage in a wet ontology that privileges the aqueous transactions of stories (Steinberg and Peters 2015). How can we reconcile the conflicting narrative forces at play? Postcolonial knowledge is more accommodating (see McCusker and Soares 2011). We might imagine the eddies and currents of oceanic knowledge *tidalectically*, as Barbadian poet Kamau Brathwaite did, rather than *dialectically*. Brathwaite scholar Anna Reckin describes the tidalectic as "a kind of recursive movement-in-stasis that is anti-progressive (the tidalectic) but also contains within it specific vectors" (2003: 2), such as the movement of the slave trade across the Atlantic. Mentz has added to the call for another path, arguing that "Geography may not quite be destiny, but in today's era of environmental uncertainty, a history that embraces nonhuman ecological systems seems essential" (2016: 562). Nonhuman history is never linear, singular, localized, or exhaustible in meaning.

Take the example of islands. Powerful repositories of the oceanic imaginary world, places and spaces where mysteries hide within the concealing bulk of the ocean, islands are a crucial actor in the stories to come. We might see these islands as existing within a network of both real and imagined waterscapes, corralled together into an "aquapelagic assembly"—defined by island and maritime cultures specialist Philip Hayward as "a social unit existing in a location in which the aquatic spaces between and around a group of islands are utilized and navigated in a manner that is fundamentally interconnected with and essential to the social group's habitation of land and their senses of identity and belonging" (2012: 5). European medievalists will be familiar with many insular exemplars—no European mythology is without them—especially those entangled with the legendary Irish saint Brendan. Gerald of Wales could not resist the temptation when assaying the topography of Ireland, he writes of an island to the West where "human corpses are not buried and do not putrefy, but are placed in the open and remain without corruption" (1982: 2.39, 61).

As the context of the imaginary world emerges, some further parsing is required. Two overlapping categories—otherworld and imaginary world—are often synonymous but require some definition for full effect. What is an otherworld, and how does it differ from an "imaginary" world? The simplest distinction that can be made is that an otherworld pertains to the boundary between life and death, natural and unnatural, spatializing the journey from birth to life and into death. All otherworlds are to some extent realms of the imagination, but not all imaginary worlds are otherworlds. Answering the question is notoriously difficult. One answer might be that an otherworld is a place where the normal rules do not apply, as medievalist Aisling Byrne has put it when attempting a definitive explanation. The quest for singularity reveals plurality, for an otherworld is "the next world, the world of the fairies, an imaginary fantastical realm, or, less frequently, far-flung corners of the globe such as the wondrous East or the Antipodes" (2016: 5). This list is both sufficient and superfluous: it explains what an otherworld *can* be but appropriately highlights its mercurial and floating signification. This puzzle is inescapable.

ISLANDED OTHERWORLDS OF OCEANIA

Belief in a maritime afterworld is a common theme in the mythologies and cultures of Oceania. Exploring this theme requires a more respectful engagement with indigenous approaches to materiality and nonhuman agency as well as time and myth (Rosiek, Snyder, and Pratt 2020). To do so here, we begin in the East and move to the West. Imaginary worlds and their cultural expression bear a striking resemblance to the narrative phenomenon of the "matter," described by anthropologist Michael W. Scott as "not the evolutionary precursors to so-called national epics—but the prolific, unsorted, unreconciled, living *prima materia*—both written and oral out of which such epics have sometimes been selected, arranged, and edited" (2012: 120–1). Matters are familiar to European audiences in the form of the "matter of Britain," the body of myths and stories surrounding legendary kings and heroes such as King Arthur.

Using the example of Makira island in the Solomon Islands, Scott describes "loosely cohering tales and traditions [that] are truly nebulous, consisting of undelimited tangents spinning off from and producing sacred centers, holy lands—motherlands and fatherlands—emotion-laden landscapes shaped by marvelous deeds and events" (2012: 121). Like the enfolding cloud of ideas that is a European medieval matter—the Brendan legend and its archipelago of wonders might also qualify—tales of the ocean are the substrate from which culture, identity, and myth are formed around a sea of islanded tales and identities. Pacific island cultures contain many islands with traits like those found in European myths: Tongan and Fijian mythology speaks of an "Island of Women" filled with beautiful but dangerous goddesses (*hotooas*) located somewhere to the northeast (Egeler 2017: 308). These stories may share qualities, but they represent separate manifestations of what Egeler terms a "willingness to locate otherworldly places of myth within coordinates of the real world" (308). Imagination in and with the ocean bonds stories together.

We begin in Aotearoa-New Zealand, where the island of Hawaiki occupies a notable premodern role in Māori history and myth as well as a continued living cultural importance. This insular narrative defies Western epistemes, existing beyond the restricting ambit of the word "imaginary." It is twenty-first-century culture and materiality, as alive today as in the past. European anthropologists and folklorists of the nineteenth century have belittled the mentalities and beliefs of Oceania's islanded peoples, understanding them as stories of half-remembered historical fact waiting to be "unpicked." This is inaccurate: a history that is a spiritual place and a myth that refers to historical events are more capacious than the term "imaginary world" allows. Taking steps to decolonize this mentality is a fundamental theme of twenty-first-century island studies.

European knowledge regimes have long clashed with the cultural complexity of Hawaiki: although accounts differed between the *iwi* (tribal groupings), early visitors to Aotearoa were told matter-of-factly that these islands were not the original home of the Māori. The story of how Aotearoa came to be peopled by Māori is filtered through an ancestral island known as Hawaiki, somewhere beyond the northeastern horizon. In the best-known version of the story, an explorer named Kupe from this place discovered a bountiful new home—at some point between *c*. 800 CE and an estimate of the fourteenth century CE— and named it Aotearoa, the land of the long white cloud in te reo, the language of the Māori. Kupe returned to Hawaiki, told his people of his voyage, and led a "great fleet" of canoes to the new land.

Recent archaeological research has supported this chronology. Radiocarbon dating reveals two distinct phases of expansion from Western Polynesia to the Society Islands and on to Aotearoa-New Zealand, the first between 1025 and 1121, the second from 1200 to 1290 (Wilmshurst et al. 2011). The discovery on New Zealand's South Island of parts of the hull of a sophisticated Polynesian voyaging canoe dated to *c*. 1400 CE (Figure 0.8) embodies the technologies of long-distance maritime travel that enabled these voyages (Johns, Irwin, and Sung

2014). The passengers of these canoes were the ancestors of the Māori people (Tallack 2016: 20). Orbell points out that the story represents a transposition of memory into myth, not a literal representation of "fact" as sought by European empiricists (1991: 8). The "matter" of Hawaiki is a spiritual repository for a spatially codified otherworld as well as a history. There is trivialization in the European collection and curation of myths and legends from across the world that must be challenged.

Hawaiki is an enduring substrate of the physical fabric of Aotearoa. Material traces are thought to dwell within the land: objects with remarkable powers or value might have come from there. Treasured tiki and pendants of greenstone owned by high-ranking *iwi* families were handed down from generation to generation from the first ancestors who had come to Aotearoa in their canoes. *Mauru*—stones, stone images of portions of soil or sand—contain the life principle of plants, animals, or sea life. Many had come from Hawaiki (Orbell 1991: 52) and were deposited in places where they could exercise their power. Their mana was supernatural because it was of a supernatural place, but the physical object was also from another place. As Dilys Johns and her coauthors remark in their analysis of the sea turtle carved on the Anaweka canoe (Figure 8.1), turtles are uncommon in Maori iconography but ubiquitous in East Polynesian art, myth, and ritual and carry a heavy symbolic and religious load (Johns, Irwin, and Sung 2014). As a largely pelagic species that nevertheless relied upon beaches to lay their eggs,

> sea turtles were known to make long migrations in open ocean. They came from the deep sea onto land and they also crossed symbolic boundaries. On occasion they could represent humans or gods. Turtles were associated with voyaging to the afterworld and assisted in a successful passage of the spirit after death […]. A sea turtle on a 600-y-old Polynesian canoe is a unique and powerful symbol.
>
> (Johns, Irwin, and Sung 2014: 14729)

In the Anaweka canoe Hawaiki is alive in Aotearoa, even several centuries after the island's first settlement.

In 1793, Chief Tuki Tahua was asked by Europeans to draw a map of the islands of Aotearoa, originally sketched on the floor in chalk it was later transposed to paper and then reproduced in later publications (Figure 8.2). He reproduced the islands with great accuracy and also included, as seen in the dotted lines on Figure 8.2, the path of a "spirits road" running the length of the North Island. The road led to Te Reinga Wairua, marked as "Terry-inga" on the map, a point at the extremity of the North Island to the northeast of Cape Maria Van Diemen, on Cape Reinga, where the *pohutukawa* or "leaping place of the spirits" was located. This was a place where each spirit would dive into the ocean and swim toward the other world and be reunited with Hawaiki.

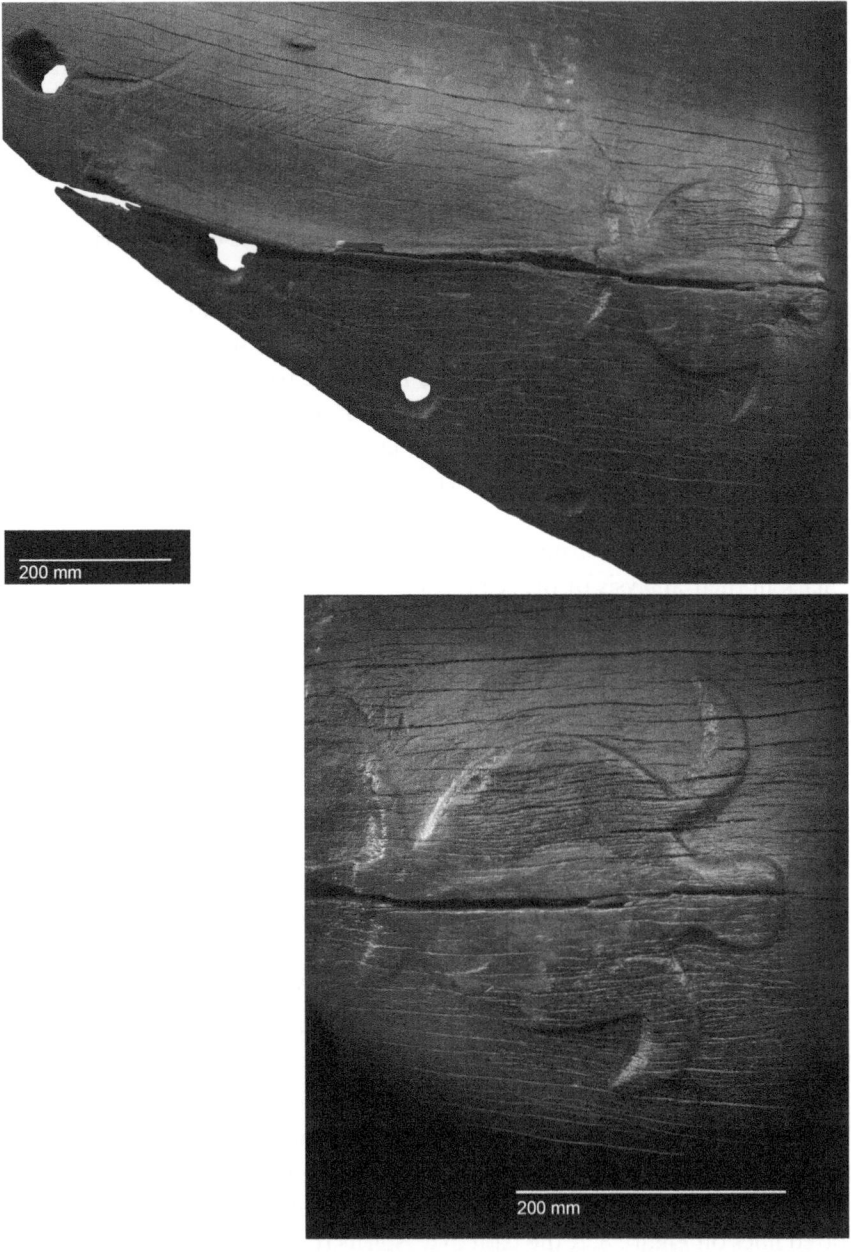

FIGURE 8.1 Low-relief carving of a sea turtle, from part of a much larger East Polynesian voyaging canoe excavated on New Zealand's South Island and radiocarbon dated to around 1400 CE. © Dilys Johns.

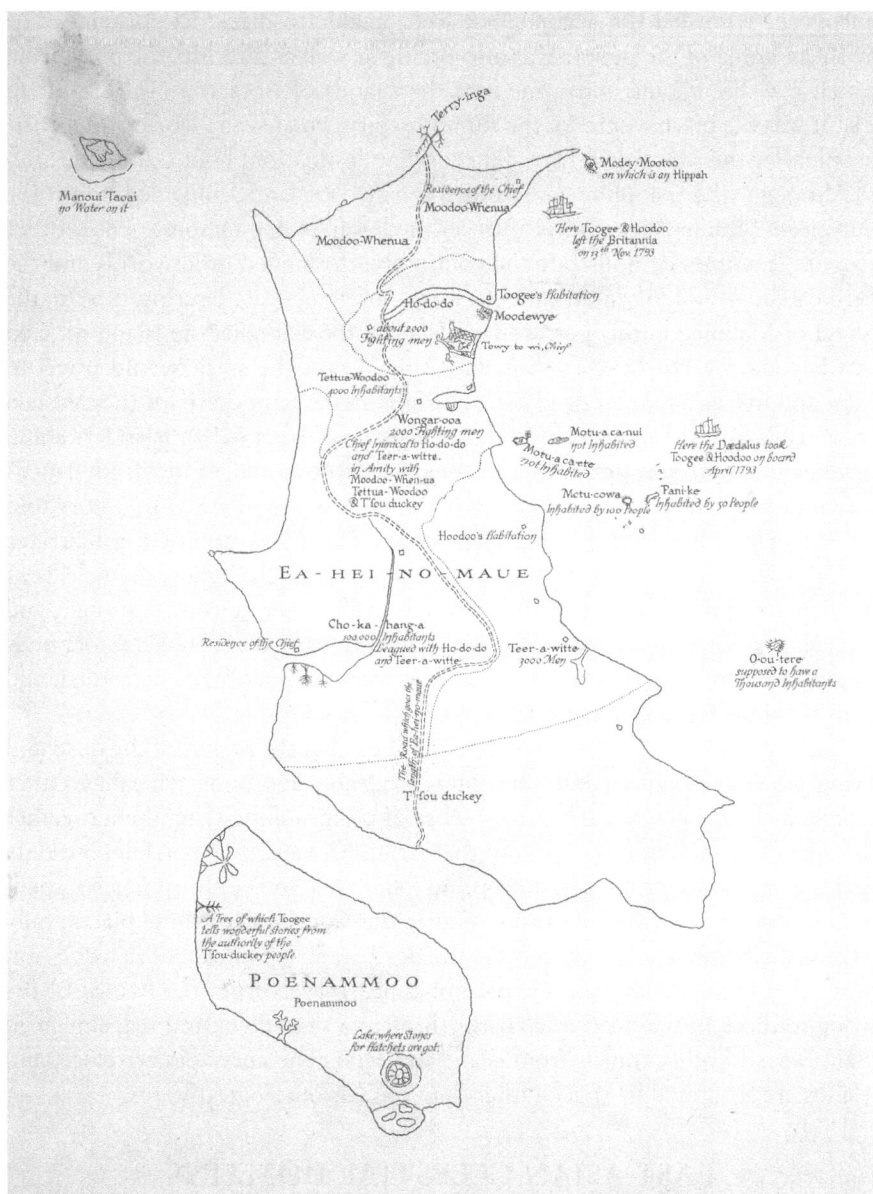

FIGURE 8.2 Engraved copy of the so-called "Tuki's map," originally drawn in 1793 chalk by the Maori chief Tuki Te Terenui Whare Pirau for Philip King, Governor of New South Wales and Norfolk Island. The spirit road to Te Reinga Wairua, marked "Terry-inga," is clearly visible at the top of the map. From Collins (1798). © Out of Copyright (public domain).

Europeans recorded the account but were unable to digest its episteme. The mythical home of the people was also prelife as well as afterlife, the place from which new life sprang and came into the islands of Aotearoa (Tallack 2016: 21). It was the place where Io, the supreme spirit, created the world and its first people. For the Māori *iwi*, Hawaiki is origin, destination, home, and afterlife.

Although the peopling of Aotearoa-New Zealand coincided with the European Middle Ages and is thus a "medieval" story in some sense, other cognate examples demonstrate the continuity of islanded otherworlds and the permeability—and often meaninglessness—of temporal descriptors. On the island of Mabuiag in the Torres Strait Islands, for example, the island of Kibu was beyond the North–West horizon. After death, the spirit would travel to Kibu and live as a *markai* or ghost, returning home temporarily if they wished or warring with the living if they chose (Tallack 2016: 17–18). Islanders could invoke the *markai* through divination or spirit consultation, or in "death dance" ceremonies held several months after someone had passed away. In a story told on Mabuiag, a handsome young man named Tabepa is promised in marriage to Ug of Kiba, a *markai* girl. After a courting process that spans the worlds of the living and the dead—with the spirit girl visiting her betrothed at night and returning to Kibu by day—Ug takes Tabepa to visit her on Kibu. The story ends tragically when Tabepa is killed by Baz, a *markai* jealous of Ug's betrothed, and joins the dead himself (Lawrie 1972: 105–7).

Island cultures of the Pacific share the notion that the realms of the dead and living are not wholly separate but interchangeable and semipermeable. Other mobile maritime practices share this sense of permeability, tying them together through the common membrane of the ocean. Movement is possible, but only under certain circumstances. European folklorists and anthropologists spent decades trying to rationalize and spatialize the "location" of these places, only to miss the point. The living can visit the dead, and vice versa, but this does not mean that these places exist in space or time. Travels from the islands of the living to those of the dead trace paths through a shared cultural sea, similar in many ways to other travels from island to island. The ancestors are close, and islands are separated by space rather than time or ontological status.

EAST ASIAN CELESTIAL DOMAINS

Moving northwest to elaborate East Asian literary cultures such as those of China and Japan, the ocean was the site of celestial courts and supernatural entities caught in wonderous versions of earthly disputes and politics. Their conflicts, interactions, and transactions were the fabric on which the mandate of heaven was written—they shaped what was ordered and what was disordered in the times to follow. In a parallel multilingual, polyvalent, and intertextual legendary spanning the European Middle Ages and unfolding over preceding millennia,

FIGURE 8.3 Section from a handscroll depicting the Immortals' islands of Fanghu, Yingzhou, and Penglai, part of the Isles of the Blessed, Ming dynasty, fifteenth century, artist unknown after Puguang (active c. 1286–1309). Ink and color on silk. Overall dimensions 31.5 × 970 cm. Royal Ontario Museum, 2005.22.1. This acquisition was made possible with the generous support of Mr. and Mrs. A. Charles Baillie. © Royal Ontario Museum.

literary culture shaped and reshaped its oceanic legends as it reinvented itself. It was not and is not dependent on European norms or standards for its reality.

The primary traits of otherworlds within the oceans of the Asia-Pacific imbue hidden islands and undersea realms with traits not found on land: immortality, perfection, timelessness, magic, elemental power. They beat the bounds of the possible, the correct, the moral, and the natural, setting up the world order. In Taoist myth, the divine Yellow Emperor Huangdi pacified the disordered waters by defeating Kuei, an ox-like creature found on Flowing Waves Mountain deep in the East Sea. Like many global myths of cosmogony, the exploits of Huangdi iteratively gave form to the natural order and its expected behaviors. Kuei was a rogue actor: his passage through the ocean caused terrible storms, and his voice created catastrophic thunder. Only by overcoming Kuei's elemental fury and defeating him could the Yellow Emperor advance his quest to balance the primordial world, creating the model for future kingship (Palmer and Zhao 1997: 50–2).

Elsewhere in Taoist narrative, the figures of the Eight Immortals cast a legendary shadow over the seascape and its wonders. They were said to live on Mount Penglai—known as Hōrai in Japanese mythology—and four other islands hidden within the Bohai Sea. Also known as the Isles of the Blessed or the Mystic Isles, this archipelago was the setting for legendary deeds, appearing on maps to haunt future generations and yet shaped out of mythology and deep time (Perry 1921: 158). The islands once floated with the tides, never fixed, but were eventually supported on the back of giant turtles (159). While cults dedicated to the Taoist Immortals date back as far as the Han dynasty of the third century BCE to first century CE, depictions of the Eight were first executed during the twelfth to thirteenth century under the Jin dynasty. Figure 8.3 shows a Ming copy of an originally late thirteenth-century painted scroll depicting *zhenren* or perfected beings borne by crane birds and clouds approaching the islands of Fanghu, Yingzhou, and Penglai. On these superlative isles, like their Western counterparts—the Irish Tír na nÓg of Land of Youth, for example—there is no pain, no winter, and no want. Food is plentiful and magical fruits grow that can cure disease, bestow eternal life, and raise the dead. Palaces are made from gold and platinum, everything is white, and jewelry grows on trees (Luo and Grydehøj 2017: 28–9). Figure 8.4 shows an island with its palace and blessed inhabitants. The painter's contrast of the mundanity of daily life on the islands with the surging, stormy seas that surround them communicates perfectly the extent to which these islands parallel the real world and yet remain unreachable, isolated from it, accessible only by cloud or crane. The sea itself and islands are remarkable for the absence of boats or mooring places. Although not always the subject matter of painting, the Isles of the Blessed are ingrained deeply into the religious and literary fabric of the religions and cultures that permeated the ocean, crossing the waters between Korea, Japan, and China and tying them together through their shared waters.

FIGURE 8.4 Detail of the handscroll of the Isles of the Blessed showing one of the seven islands of the human realm with its inhabitants, Ming dynasty, fifteenth century, artist unknown after Puguang (active *c.* 1286–1309). Ink and color on silk. Royal Ontario Museum, 2005.22.1. This acquisition was made possible with the generous support of Mr. and Mrs. A. Charles Baillie. © Royal Ontario Museum.

The desire to discover these islands stretched back to the beginning of China. The First Qin Emperor Shi Huang-Ti was obsessed with the secrets of immortality and sent an emissary—the alchemist Xu Fu—to locate the mystic islands to the east after a bird carried a strange plant with the power to revive the dead to the mainland. Xu Fu was dispatched to the island to acquire the herb. After finding nothing and returning to the Emperor in a panic, the alchemist lied instead, claiming that the Sea God of the Eastern Sea had demanded lavish tribute in exchange for the miraculous herb. Instead of being forced to undertake another impossible task, Xu Fu fled and founded the nation of Japan (Wang 2005: 8–9). In addition to forming a classic exemplar of how dishonesty only spawns more lies, these tales had a long-standing influence on the Chinese imagination of Japan. Like Europeans visiting the Americas and expecting to find Cathay, the Chinese expected to find the legendary civilization of Xu Fu in the Japanese Isles and behaved accordingly. Japanese mythology contains a similar story, with the character of Wasobiowe replacing Xu Fu (Egeler 2017: 309–10).

Below the sea, wonders and struggles continued. One prominent subaquatic world is the palace of Ao Guang, Dragon King of the East Sea (Luo and Grydehøj 2017: 33). In Japanese mythology there is Ryūgū-jō, the palace of Ryūjin, the dragon *kami* or spirit of the sea. Secure in his fortress beneath the waves, the dragon spirit was lord of all he surveyed, a powerful and fickle elemental force embodying the wealth and power of the East Sea. The skirmishes of the dragon spirits and the Eight Immortals express a kind of environmental psychomachia, giving voice to natural disturbances. In one tale, the dragons of the four seas create a tsunami to destroy their adversaries after a series of tit-for-tat conflicts between land and sea. The Immortals then retaliate by pushing Mount Tai into the sea and filling it with dirt, to which the dragons then respond by referring the Immortals to the High Court of Heaven and the Jade Emperor for crimes punishable by the law of heaven (Yuan 2006: 130). In Japanese folklore, a young man named Urashimotaro is taken by a turtle to the Dragon Palace at the bottom of the sea, and there he meets Princess Otohime and her maids. When he returns to the surface, he finds that three hundred years have passed (Kawai 1995: 107).

The ocean provides a refuge for the powerful spirits and gods of mythology and the disordered chaos beyond the mandate of kingship. Conflict and political antagonism are required before the framework of order can emerge. The modern form of these myths was often cemented and formalized during the period now known to Europeanists as the Middle Ages, inspiring art, poetry, literature, and the telling and retelling of folk myth, accompanied by folk practices honoring figures such as the Eight Immortals and the Dragon King. Luo and Grydehøj argue that a "truly decolonial island studies must go beyond simply considering 'local' reactions to island metaphors imposed by the West" (2017: 40): this is a lesson that this case teaches in abundance, and should be applied to all non-European imaginary worlds of the ocean. Acknowledging their force on an equal and parallel epistemic footing is an essential task for a global cultural history of the sea: East Asia has its own islanded imaginary, entangled with but independent of Western narratives.

A DROWNED TAMIL HOMELAND

India and Southeast Asia participated in the wider network of ocean-going narratives, part of the Buddhist religious world and the circuit of trade stretching across Asia. Their traditions were united by one of the great world circuits of the precolonial Indian Ocean world described by world historian Janet Abu-Lughod (1989), the Eastern segment of an Indian linchpin tying the Islamicate and East Asian worlds together. Buddhist studies scholar Sarah Shaw describes the Indian storytelling seascape as "a 'pool of signifiers' from which storytellers drew, applicable between traditions, as well as within them" (2012: 132). This pool, spanning the pluralistic traditions of Jainism, Hinduism, and Buddhism, was part of a wider Indian Ocean region teeming with variants on narrative.

As discussed in the "Introduction" to this volume, Hindu mythology is filled with powerful creation imagery in which the admixture of the oceans makes order from chaos. The Indian Ocean is a womb and a catalyst, a pool of creation and destruction. Our case study for this section comes from southern India and Sri Lanka, and mingles history, mythology, environmental catastrophe, medieval reception, and modern adaptation. Tamil mythology speaks of a lost continent known today to many as Lemuria, circulated through sword and sorcery, adapted in Europe by mystic sects such as the Theosophical Society and enduring in popular culture. First popularized in the late medieval *Kanda purāṇam* of Kachiappa Sivacharyara (Weiss 2009: 90), a Tamil version of the *Skanda purāṇa*—a gathering of Hindu religious texts—the legend draws on a long history of stories relating to lost land known as *Kumari kandam* between what is now Tamil Nadu in India and Sri Lanka. After transmission and adaptation by various medieval Tamil authors, the story was taken up by European scientists and ethnohistorical fantasists of the nineteenth century as proof of a "lost continent of Lemuria" and later became a powerful facet of Tamil history. It is part of a wider complex of stories depicting a land stricken centuries ago by *katalkōl* (seizure by ocean), a possible reference to a large tsunami (Ramaswamy 2004: 142). The symbolic significance of this drowning is keenly felt within Tamil culture: the antediluvian words and works of an ancestral homeland are not accessible. As cultural historian Sumathi Ramaswamy poignantly phrases it, "instead of sustaining Tamil homes and hearths today, their patrimony lies consigned to a 'watery grave' at the bottom of the Indian Ocean" (142). Oceans have the powerful affordance of absorbing cultural histories but preserving their memory, hiding them just out of sight to eternally reemerge from the waves into political and cultural discourse.

There were many medieval accounts of the Tamil Pandyan kings—various branches of whom ruled from the fourth century BCE up until the sixteenth century CE—losing a large tract of land to the ocean. Flood survival and loss is built into the cultural memory of the Southern Indian peoples, dating back to the mythical floods of Hindu mythology. Legendary accounts of lost lands, cities, temples, and shrines map a tenuous coastline prone to sudden shifts in topography and cataclysmic flooding. To imagine the loss suffered by the Tamil people, one would have to conceive of a large littoral chunk of what was once the antique or medieval European world being gone, disappeared beneath the waves. Something more culturally immediate than Atlantis, no more Greece or no more Italy, for example. Drowned Lemuria exists still in the cultural memory, but the sea has swallowed it up. As Ramaswamy concludes, this sense of loss became a fundamental element of an emerging Tamil nationalism, with complex interactions that shaped a sense of cultural history, sociopolitical loss, and contested vision. The amalgam of scientific and mythological claims to authority inherited by twenty-first-century Tamils are "incongruous and impoverished, meeting the demands of neither history nor fantasy" (Ramaswamy 2004: 226). When fact-finding and mythology combine, no observer is satisfied.

The legacy of European pseudo-history also had a long arm, influencing romantic deep-time racial fantasists such as Robert E. Howard, author of the Conan stories. In his essay *The Hyborian Age*, Howard imagined an antediluvian world of pure empires brought low by climate catastrophe, the canvas on which to paint his tales of sword and sorcery. In Howard's lurid imagination, "volcanoes broke forth and terrific earthquakes shook down the shining cities of the empires.

Whole nations were blotted out" (1936). Howard vindicates strong criticism of the mythmaking associated with lost continent theories by subsuming them into his notoriously racializing fantasies of human prehistory. As Ramaswamy puts it, the story has become "a staple among those freelance scholars in Europe and the United States who write about Earth's prehistory under the sign of 'lost continent'" (2004: 2). This genre of fantasist imaginary pseudo-scholarship seeks to "crack" the mystery of Easter Island, or of Machu Pichu, by resorting to stories of Atlantis, Lemuria, or another lost land known as Mu.

These discourses wholly deserve the scorn that they attract from Ramaswamy, but they also explain a great deal of the romance attached to imaginary worlds today. For these writers, it is not possible for the ocean to be a realm of living stories and plural histories. It must instead be a place of disappeared realms, lost cultures, and vanished races. As Ramaswamy points out (2004: 3), the question of *what it means* to categorize a place as "lost" is a more pressing question than if it ever existed. The symbolic capital of naming something lost shares a kinship to the naming of a place as imaginary: the past returns to haunt the present as "the disappeared, the vanished, the submerged, and the hidden." Every culture has a story that haunts it through the centuries, and the oceans of the world echo the call. The story of Lemuria is far from over, another manifestation of premodern literary culture birthing a repetitive and adaptable resonance.

MARVELOUS ISLAMICATE SEAS

Legends of the ocean from the Islamicate world will be familiar to Westerners through the Orientalist confection arising from the popular translations of the *Seven Voyages of Sindbad the Sailor,* found within the *Arabian Nights.* These tales are framed as an episodic attempt by a wealthy citizen of Baghdad seeking to recover his squandered wealth through adventure and are a made up of a mélange of fables thought to have been translated into Arabic in the ninth century. Its earliest constituent tales originate in Persia and India, and yet the text is a composite spanning many centuries (Shafiq 2013: 30–1) famously curated in a series of European translations between the eighteenth and nineteenth centuries. As we move toward the Islamicate world, we once again see the circuits in the medieval world system at work—the accounts of medieval navigators sailing from the ports of the Gulf and Red Sea span the length of the Indian Ocean from East Africa to the western Pacific fringe.

The pool of stories beyond European nautical travel was vast and can never be judged in contradistinction. Late medieval and early modern efforts to instrumentalize ocean knowledges and spatialize the imaginary seascape during the so-called age of exploration discovered only hubris and proto-empire. Islamic Qur'anic literature and poetry contained a rich collection of water symbolism and imagery that informed a rich intellectual and literary culture spanning the pre-Islamic *jahiliyyah* (period of ignorance) and the centuries following the life of the Prophet Muhammad (Alardawe 2016; Hassan 2014; Zargar 2014). The sea was abundance, opulence, growth, and generosity. The tropical climates and deserts of most Arab countries guaranteed its valorization, much like the desert mentality of Christianity and its Israelite roots (Hassan 2014: 133). The sea underscored divine providence.

In the medieval Arab world, we encounter *'ajā'ib* (singular, *'ajab*), the curiosities, marvels and wonders of nature. Whether these wonders were in the realm of scientific understanding or beyond it, they belonged in the collected wonders of God's creation (Shafiq 2011: 15). Many of the most vivid medieval marvels appear in the tenth-century *Kitāb 'ajā'ib al-hind* (Book of the Wonders of India) (16). In this text, we encounter a catalog of classical and medieval marvels that sketch out a rich Indian ocean world stretching across seven seas, a world that drew people of many cultures and faiths together in cohabitation and harmony in a rich and changing network (163). This world stretched from the South China Sea to the heads of the Red Sea and the Gulf, a string of ports and voyages enabling a flow of goods, stories, and ideas. The imaginative responses such places elicited are beautifully evident in the illustration to a shipwreck tale from the twelfth-century collection of stories the *Maqāmāt* (Assemblies) of al-Hariri illustrates (Figure 8.5). The illustrator of this particular copy, who worked in southern Iraq in the first half of the thirteenth century—and signed himself as al-Wasiti, that is originally from Wasit near Basra—chose to populate his island with exotic creatures such as parrots and monkeys as well as a harpy and a human-headed and winged feline, two motifs commonly used in metalwork and other decorative arts.

Nevertheless, as art historian Persis Berlekamp has proposed (2011: 10), it would be a mistake to understand wondrous tales using the models established for European texts such as the thirteenth-century pseudo-biographical travels of Sir John Mandeville. The European model of marvel explores the boundaries of familiarity and experience, the strangeness that lay beyond the familiar. Islamicate literature with superficially similar content read in this way would lack its full possible nuance: marvels should instead be seen as a systematic attempt to "induce wonder at God's creation and its order" (14). They are a sense-making and reiterative explanation of order and cosmology, even more so after the world-changing upheavals of thirteenth-century Mongol invasions and their reordering of once-solid power structures. The genre of *'ajā'ib* literature entrenches what is known rather than marveling at what is not.

The compendium of descriptions within the *Kitāb 'Ajā'ib al-Hind* and its fellows catalogs and marvels at the world in equal measure (Ducène 2018: 269; Shafiq 2013: 164). Seafaring beasts such as whales and giant fish make an appearance, playing with or attacking ships. In one account, three whales surround a reef-grounded ship. The only way for the crew to survive is to spend the entire night banging pieces of wood against each other and ringing bells (Shafiq 2013: 77–8). Elsewhere, there are flying fish capable of generating a

FIGURE 8.5 An eastern island, "Thirty-ninth Assembly," from the *Maqāmāt* (Assemblies) of al-Hariri, copied and illustrated by Yahya ibn Mahmud al-Wasiti, Iraq, 634/1236–7. Ink and colors on paper. Paris, Bibliothèque nationale de France, Ms. Arabe 5847. © Wikimedia Commons (public domain).

destructive hurricane (Ducène 2018: 269). In another tale giant lobsters appear, so large that their horns resemble two mountains in the sea and wreaking havoc with navigation by playing with anchors. The lobsters are rumored to turn to stone when reaching an island in the South China Sea, and their eyes are a sought-after medical remedy (Shafiq 2013: 79). In the isles of Waq-waq there were said to be trees bearing fruit the shape of small humans or human heads that exclaimed "waq-waq!" in alarming voices (Ducène 2018: 270).

As Berlekamp has argued, "the earliest illustrated wonders-of-creation manuscripts maintained a clear visual distinction between divinely created wonders, on the one hand, and notable features of geographical regions, on the other" (2011: 2–3). As time went on, the manuscripts came to be increasingly identified with explorations of wonders in cartographic form, gradually parsing geography into a genre separate from that of the illustrated *'ajā'ib* (4). The role of human agency is maintained throughout to varying degrees of emphasis, with later medieval texts more likely to frame wondrous content in the context of human travels and encounters rather than through their cosmographic frame. The *'ajā'ib* were part of a wider complex of nuanced concepts, including *makhlūqāt* (created things), *gharā'ib* (strange things [adj.] or oddities [n.]) (sing. *gharīb*), and *mawjūdāt* (things that exist), sitting within a complex ecology the *how* and the *what* of the created world (23).

It was in the ocean that variety, terror, wonder, and wealth mingled, first understood through divine provenance and later through the voyages required to behold them. Little wonder, then, that these tales were so appealing to the Orientalist imaginations of early translators: they combine both vivid content and detailed descriptions of travel and navigation. In the future, medieval cultural history must learn to see these stories as a diffuse and global community of narratives rather than glimpsing them through the romantic lens of exoticism, languor, and cruelty so famously called out by literature professor Edward W. Said in his seminal book *Orientalism*.

ELUSIVE INSULARITY IN THE EUROPEAN WEST

At the end of our journey, we return to better traveled and more familiar—and more culturally dominant—waters. Europe had a unique genre of imaginaries beyond its extremities. "Out there" to the east lay a land of dog-headed men, giants, and cannibals, the torrid south beyond North Africa was thought to be an impassable equatorial inferno. For historians of science Lorraine Daston and Katherine Park, European wonders "enlarged their readers' sense of possibility, allowing them to fantasize about alternative worlds of barely imaginable wealth, flexible gender roles, fabulous strangeness and beauty" (2008: 60). To the west, mediated by water, lay a sprinkling of islands, monsters, biblical marvels, and fantasies. Scholars such as medievalists Sylvie Bazin-Tacchella and Albrecht Classen have given excellent accounts of the sheer breadth of these marvels (Bazin-Tacchella 2002: annex 1, 99–120; Classen 2018: chs. 2–3, 53–88).

The seas of medieval Europe beyond the comforting encirclement of the Mediterranean were a *topos* of the unknown, an uncannily familiar stranger. They were beyond the land *and* beyond the world, existing in a space of wonders and mysteries (Adão da Fonseca 2018: 129–30). It is for this reason that Hau'ofa's (2008) observation that the European sea is not home becomes apt. The reason that we expect otherworlds and imaginary worlds within the medieval ocean is because medieval knowledge of the oceanic realm primed observers to expect their existence. Medievalist Sebastian Sobecki proposes that the "antithesis of land and sea permeates [European] civilisation, ranging from the basic, elemental dichotomy to more sophisticated literary contexts" (2008: 10). In the context of Britain, this means that, for example, the "liminal position of Britain and, therefore, of England, would contribute to narratives of Englishness that are inseparable from the sea" (10). The result was stories in rich profusion that cemented identity but also estranged the imagination.

The words used by Europeans to describe the lands beyond Europe are telling. Medieval historians Nikolas Jaspert and Sebastian Kolditz discuss the distinction in geographic thought of the Middle Ages between the *entre mers*, lands like Egypt "between" the Indian Ocean and Gulf on one side and the Mediterranean on the other, and the *outre-mer*, the lands "beyond the sea" such as Jerusalem and Palestine—the latter became the informal Norman name for the Crusader states (2018: 8). These naming strategies reveal that it is "the sea itself which forms the hinge holding lands isolated from each other together" (9). As Emmanuelle Vagnon discusses in her chapter on "Representations" in this volume, classical geography held that the Indian Ocean was in fact a vast inland sea, bounded on all sides (Adão da Fonseca 2018: 129), peripheral to European concerns but scintillating to its imagination. The reverse perspective flipped the picture, with al-Idrisi's twelfth-century *Kitāb nuzhat al-mushtāq fi ikhtirāq al-'afāq* (Book of Pleasant Journeys into Faraway Lands) describing the British Isles as distant and liminal land embraced by a "sea of darkness," the premodern Arabic name for the Atlantic (Chism 2016: 500).

Europe's imaginary worlds have attracted some of the sparkle and excitement of cultural Romanticism. There are many contenders for the most influential tradition: Mandeville, the Voyages of Brendan, or Marco Polo. Any of these bodies of textual material could form the focus of this section, and I have spent time discussing them in the past (Smith 2016). Irish culture has found itself front and center of this phenomenon. In the broader understanding of imaginary or other worlds within the ocean, imaginary islands emerge from the waters. Genres such as the Irish *echtrai* (pre-Christian heroic journeys) and *imramma* (Christian voyages) were staples of Irish and European myth (Westropp 1912). Journeys to places such as *Tír na nÓg*, the Land of the Young—and interactions with the supernatural and divine Tuatha Dé Danann, the People of the Goddess Danu, who call it home—evoke the wonder and mystery of the genre but are far from the entire story. The Norse, too, had their own "Islands in the West," including *Vinland* (Wine- or Vine-land), *Hvítramannaland* (the Land of White Men), *Glaesisvellir* (the Shining Fields), and *Ódáinsakr* (the Fields of Immortality) (Egeler 2017: 1–2). Large and taxonomic studies have long been devoted to studying the imaginary islands of the North Atlantic, typified by writer and poet William Henry Babcock's extensive 1922 study *Legendary Islands of the Atlantic; a Study in Medieval Geography*. They merge geography, cartography, and European mythmaking, shaped by modern fantasies of origin, and experienced a surprisingly long afterlife as a caption from the later fourteenth-century Catalan Atlas makes clear. Produced in the Western Mediterranean by a Mallorcan Jew, a large caption positioned in the North Atlantic, off the coast of Ireland, details the existence "out there" of

> many wonderful islands whose existence can be credible; among them, there is a small one where men never die, because when they are about to die of old age, they are transported outside the island. There are no snakes, frogs, nor poisonous spiders because the soil repels them given that this is where Lacerie Island [Cléire/Clear Island] is located. Furthermore, there are trees that attract birds like ripe figs. There is also another island where women never give birth because when they are about to give birth, they are taken outside the island as it is customary.
>
> (The Cresques Project n.d.: panel III.1)

In the Catalan Atlas, memories of Celtic myth coexist alongside classical geographies of the East sourced in the Alexander romance and historically attested explorations of the West African coast by Mallorcan mariners.

When understanding the proliferation of received and newly minted imaginary worlds known to medieval people, it is crucial to look beyond Europe. Furthermore, it is equally important to consider *why* these worlds populate the ocean as well as *what* the stories describe. Nationalistic mythmaking—like the Tamil narratives surrounding Lemuria discussed above—are also at the core of many European national identities and delimitations. This is well demonstrated by an Irish example. The thread of influence of premodern Irish Christian mythology and its romantic reception continued into the nation-making of the late nineteenth- and early twentieth-century "Celtic twilight." In his famous folkloric collection of the same name, the celebrated Irish poet W.B. Yeats was taken by the mystery and romance of Ireland's moveable islands. In these spaces, "he who touches shall find no more labour or care, nor cynic laughter, but shall go walking about under shadiest boscage, and enjoy the conversation of Cuchullin and his heroes" (1893: 157).

Yeats seems to capture the tidalectic eddies and flows of mythmaking: just as flotsam and jetsam return to land, so too do stories wash up on lonely shores. The mythical island of Hy Brasil is an eternal promise of something else to come, be it cultural upset, better times, or worse. Like the *matter* of Makira described above, its insular imaginary forms an expressive trope for a kind of active mythmaking, a place-making soaked with emotion, story, and wonder. As sociologist Barbara Freitag (2013) catalogs, the story of Hy Brasil, like many other European mythical isles, is the tale of myths interweaving, merging with cartographic error and speculation, and erupting into popular imagination, nation-building, and Irish exceptionalism. The Irish folklorist and antiquarian Thomas Johnson Westropp claimed rapturously that "the early Gael loved sea-tales" (1912: 226), and Irish Romanticists such as Yeats channeled this love—or their vicarious love—into ethno-national mythmaking. The result is a coalescing of Irishness, a bundling of shared experience by the imaginer in their role as curator of national identity.

This phenomenon can be extended to countless other European manifestations. When Columbus set off on his voyages to the Americas in the 1490s, his imaginary worlds came with him. As medieval intellectual historian Valerie Flint notably proposed, the Christian mythmaking of the New World drew on the energies previously held by faraway countries, "patterned with geographical pictures and descriptions as strange as they were elaborate, some drawn from the Bible, some from [stories about Christian seafarers and pilgrims]" (1992: xiii). As I have discussed in the past (Smith 2016: 534–5), Columbus encountered the legacy of imaginary worlds when he sailed to the West, populating the oceans with wild cartographic and mythological fantasies. When elements from different influential cultures, they create what Egeler terms *resonances* (2017: 291), leading to a composite cultural element that is changed but also strengthened. For example, the combination of the Christian Earthly Paradise, the Irish Otherworld islands and the Roman Blessed Isles merged to create Saint Brendan's Island, a composite with the cultural power to reach out through the centuries. Columbus believed it was "out there," part of an archipelago of imaginary loci formed from the constituent parts of their antecedents. As medieval literature and cartography scholar Alfred Hiatt (2016: 513) has argued, the European Middle Ages contained within it many competing and evolving notions of insular space, and these notions continued to morph and change beyond 1492, the medieval mingling with the modern.

CONCLUSION

As Abu-Lughod famously described the global interactions of cultures, "in a system, it is the *connections* between the parts that must be studied," for "when these strengthen and reticulate, the system may be said to 'rise;' when they fray, the system declines" (1989: 368, emphasis in original). Thus, historical change and social connectivity catalyze the waxing and waning of the links that shape the regional, and even global, Middle Ages (Davis and Puett 2016). The Middle Ages permeates the insular knowledges of the world for one simple reason: European premodernity was the lens through which all other stories were judged, and thus our reception of their meaning has been distorted into European forms.

By expanding our perspectives on the cultural history of the sea through comparative studies and a renewed appreciation of mutable plurality and diversity, we can arrive at new possibilities for interdisciplinary and collaborative research. By looking for resonances across cultures, spaces, and temporalities, new histories are possible. Together, imaginary worlds are a shared consciousness of the ocean and an archipelago of human experience. The sea of the Middle Ages concealed ideas, cultures, and peoples that we are familiar with today in our globalized world but were, at the time, spatially removed and thus intellectually wrapped up in the marvelous, the supernatural, and the atemporal. A long history of narratives from the familiar to the obscure attest to this legacy, and the story is paralleled in every ocean-going culture of the "Global Middle Ages."

What are we looking at when we gaze into the ocean and imagine that we understand it as history? Through a series of thematic case studies, this chapter has surveyed the global medieval reception and adaptation of imaginary worlds within the cultural history of the sea, ranging from afterlives and stories of gods to submerged coastlines, natural and unnatural marvels, and vanishing islands. Its source materials have been varied, emerging from folklore, myth, living cultural heritage, history, travelogue, literature, and cultural theory in equal measure. We can make sense of these imaginary worlds within the ocean as part of an age-old human preoccupation with the sea not as an objective historical entity but as a cipher promising history and yet delivering stories. Layered narratives and knowledges spring from the diverse cultures of the medieval oceanic world through copying, translating, retranslating, sharing, traveling, and adapting. This chapter has skimmed the surface, with the true depth of their meaning always waiting to emerge.

NOTES

Preface

1 This phrase is the title of a Walcott poem "The Sea Is History" (2007).

Introduction

1 Sobecki's work distinguishes itself from Kathy Lavezzo's earlier *Angels on the Edge of the World. Geography, Literature, and English Community, 1000–1534* (2006) by its maritime focus and explicit framing within the cultural history of the sea.
2 Gillis gives fifty thousand B.P (Before Present) (2012: 19); this date has been refined since.

Chapter 4

1 Tellingly, however, a large proportion of this literature is noticeably absent from of an important reference work in the field: Kelly DeVries's *Cumulative Bibliography of Medieval Military History and Technology* (2001) and its subsequent updates, notwithstanding dedicated sections on "Naval Warfare" and "Ships."

Chapter 5

1 For an excellent articulation of "janus-faced" qualities of littoral societies at the onset of modernity, see Jonathan Miran's study of the Red Sea port hub of Massawa (2009).

Chapter 6

1 I thank Elizabeth Lambourn for calling some eastern, especially South Asian, examples to my attention.
2 Tellingly, to describe life onboard ships in the Indian Ocean, Jan Qaisar (1987) was obliged to rely on sources of the sixteenth century and later.
3 In Indian romances such as Uddyotanasūri's eighth-century Jain novel, *Kuvalayamālā*, scenes of ships' departures were, as Christine Chojnacki notes, highly conventionalized (Uddyotanasūri 2008: 1:206).

4   This Arabic text was composed in two parts: the first in the mid-ninth century by an anonymous author and the second in the tenth century by a certain Abu Zayd al-Sirafi, charged with verifying and continuing the narrative.
5   See Andrea Acri's (2019) recent study of the trope of the wondrous aversion of a shipwreck in texts from the Buddhist and Hindu worlds.
6   In the *Eneas*, it is Juno who torments the protagonist for seven long years, "stirring up the sea most violently" (Romance of Eneas 1974: 59). A storm scattering the ships bearing its titular protagonists helps trigger the *dénouement* of the thirteenth-century Old French *chantefable Aucassin and Nicolette* (1971: 52).
7   The relative chronology and lines of influence of the *immram* and the *Navigatio* are a matter of scholarly disagreement (Sobecki 2003: 196–8).

BIBLIOGRAPHY

PRIMARY SOURCES

Ahmad, S. Maqbul (1989), *Arabic Classical Accounts of India and China*, Calcutta: Indian Institute of Advanced Study.

Akhbār al-sīn wa-l-hind (2014), *Accounts of China and India: Abū Zayd al–Sīrāfī*, ed. and trans. Tim Mackintosh–Smith in Philip F. Kennedy and Shawkat M. Toorawa (eds.), *Two Arabic Travel Books*, 4–161, New York: New York University Press.

Aucassin and Nicolette and Other Tales (1971), trans. Pauline Matarasso, Harmondsworth: Penguin Books.

al-Biruni, Abu'l-Rayhan (1936–7), *Al-jamāhir fī maʿrifat al-jawāhir*, ed. Fritz Krenkow [in Arabic], Hyderabad: Osmaniya Oriental Publication Bureau.

Boccaccio, Giovanni (2010), *Il Decamerone*, trans. Mark Musa and Peter Bondanella as *The Decameron*, New York: Signet Classics.

Buondelmonti, Cristoforo (2018), trans. and ed. Evelyn Edson as *Cristoforo Buondelmonti, Description of the Aegean and Other Islands*, New York: Italica Press.

Chaucer, Geoffrey (2018), *The Canterbury Tales*, ed. Larry D. Benson as *The Riverside Chaucer* [in Middle English], Boston: Houghton-Mifflin Co. Available online: https://chaucer.fas.harvard.edu/pages/general-prologue-0 (accessed October 19, 2020).

de Clari, Robert (1996), *La Conquête de Constantinople*, trans. Edgar Holmes McNeal as *The Conquest of Constantinople*, Medieval Academy Reprints for Teaching, Toronto: University of Toronto Press.

Erivgenae, Iohannes Scotti (1995), *Periphyseon (De Divisione Naturae): Liber Quartus*, ed. Edouard A. Jeauneau, trans. John J. O'Meara and I.P. Sheldon-Williams [in Latin and English], Dublin: Institute for Advanced Studies.

Gerald of Wales (1982), *Topographia Hibemica*, trans. John O'Meara as *The History and Topography of Ireland*, London: Penguin Classics.

Hall, Martin and Jonathan Phillips, eds. and trans. (2013), *Caffaro, Genoa and the Twelfth-Century Crusades*, Farnham: Ashgate.

al-Hariri, Abu Muhammad al-Qasim b. ʿAli b. Muhammad (1898), *The Assemblies of Al-Hariri*, trans. F. Steingass, London: Royal Asiatic Society.

Ibn Fadlan, Ahmad (2012), *Risāla*, trans. as "Mission to the Volga," in Paul Lunde and Caroline Stone (eds.), *Ibn Fadlan and the Land of Darkness: Arab Travelers in the Far North*, 3–58, London: Penguin.

Ibn Ishaq (1955), *Sīrat rasūl Allāh*, ed. and trans. A. Guillaume as *The Life of Muhammad*, Oxford: Oxford University Press.

Ibn Jubayr, Abu'l-Husayn Muhammad (2013), *Rihla*, trans. Roland Broadhurst as *The Travels of Ibn Jubayr*, New Delhi: Goodword Books.

Ibn Majid, Ahmad (1971), *Al-ʿulūm al-baḥriyya ʿinda al-ʿarab. Al-qism al-thani: musannafat Shihab al-Din Ahmad b. Majid b. Muhammad b. ʿAmru b. Fadl b. Duwayk b. Yusuf b. Hasan b. Husayn b. Abi Muʿalliq al-Saʿdi b. Abi Rakaʾib al-Najdi. Al-jizʾa al-awwal: Kitāb al-fawāʾid fī usūl al-ʿilm al-bahr wa-l-qawāʾid*, ed. Ibrahim al-Khuri [in Arabic], Damascus: Matbuʿat Majmaʿ al-Lughat al-ʿArabiyya bi-Damashq.

Ibn Majid, Ahmad (1993), *al-Nuniyya al-kubrā maʾa sitt qasāʾid ukhra*, ed. Hasan Salih Shihab [in Arabic], Muscat: Ministry of Culture and Heritage.

Ibn al-Mujawir, Yusuf ibn Yaʾqub (2008), *Taʾrikh al-mustabsir*, trans. G. Rex Smith as *A Traveller in Thirteenth-century Arabia: Ibn al-Mujawir's Tarikh al-Mustabsir*, London: The Hakluyt Society.

Joinville, Jean de and Geoffrey de Villehardouin (1963), *Chronicles of the Crusades*, trans. Margaret R.B. Shaw as *Chronicles of the Crusades*, Harmondsworth: Penguin Books.

Kautilya (2016), *The Arthashastra*, trans. L.N. Rangaranjan as *The Arthashastra*, New Delhi: Penguin Random House India.

Konungs Skuggsjá (1917), trans. Laurence Larson as *The King's Mirror (Speculum Regale–Konungs Skuggsjá)*, New York: American-Scandinavian Foundation; London: Humprey Milford; Oxford: Oxford University Press.

Ma Huan (1970), *Ying-yai Sheng-lang*, trans. from the Chinese and ed. Feng Ch'eng Chun with introduction, notes and appendices by J.V.G. Mills as *Ying-yai Sheng-lan, The Overall Survey of the Ocean's Shores (1433)*, Cambridge: Cambridge University Press.

al-Mahri, Sulayman b. Ahmad (1970), *Al-ʿulūm al-bahriyya ʿinda al-ʿarab. Al-qism al-awwal; musannafat Sulaymān b. Ahmad b. Sulayman al-Mahrī. Al-jizʾa al-awwal: al-ʿumdat al-mahrīyya fi dabt al-ʿulūm al-bahriyya*, ed. Ibrahim al-Khūrī, Damascus: Matbuʿat Majmaʿ al-Lughat al-ʿArabiyya bi-Damashq.

al-Muqaddasi, Shams al-Din Abu ʿAbd Allah Muḥammad (1906), *Kitāb ahsān al-taqāsim fi maʿrifat al-aqālīm*, ed. M. J. De Goeje, Leiden: Brill.

al-Muqaddasi, Shams al-Din Abu ʿAbd Allah Muhammad (2001), *Ahsan al–taqasim fi maʿrifat al–aqalim*, trans. Basil Anthony Collins [in English], Reading: Garnet.

al-Masʿudi, ʿAli b. Ḥusayn (1861–77), *Murūj al-dhahab wa-maʿādin al-jawhar*, 9 vols, ed. and trans. C.B. Meynard and P. De Courteille [in French], Paris: Imprimerie impériale.

Nikephoros Gregoras (1829), *Byzantina historia*, ed. Ludwig Schopen and Immanuel Bekker, vol. 2, Bonn: Weber.

Orkneyinga Saga (1978), *The History of the Earls of Orkney*, trans. Hermann Pálsson and Paul Edwards, London: Hogarth Press.

Periplus Maris Erythraei (1989), trans. Lionel Casson as *The Periplus Maris Erythraei: Text with Introduction, Translation, and Commentary*, Princeton, NJ: Princeton University Press.

Petrarch (2002), *Itinerarium ad sepulchrum domini nostri Yehsu Christi*, trans. Theodore J. Cachey, Jr. as *Petrarch's Guide to the Holy Land. Itinerarium ad sepulchrum domini nostri Yehsu Christi/Itinerary to the Sepulcher of Our Lord Jesus Christ. Facsimile edition of Cremona, Biblioteca Statale, Deposito Libreria Civica, manuscript BB.1.2.5*, Notre Dame, IN: University of Notre Dame Press.

Polo, Marco (1903), *Livres des Merveilles du Monde*, trans. and ed. Henry Yule and H. Cordier as *The Book of Ser Marco Polo the Venetian concerning the Kingdoms and Marvels of the East*, 2 vols, London: John Murray.

Polo, Marco (1976), *Livres des Merveilles du Monde*, trans. Ronald Latham as *The Travels*, repr., Harmondsworth: Penguin.

Polo, Marco (2016), *Livres des Merveilles du Monde*, trans. and ed. Sharon Kinoshita as *The Description of the World*, Indianapolis, IN: Hackett.

al-Ramhurmuzi, Buzurg b. Shahriyar (1929), *'Ajā'ib al-hind*, trans. Peter Quennell as *The Book of the Marvels of India* [based on the French trans. by L. Marcel Devic of the Arabic original], New York: Dial Press.

al-Ramhurmuzi, Buzurg b. Shahriyar (1990), *'Ajā'ib al-hind*, ed. Yusuf al-Sharuni as *'Ajā'ib al-hind: min qisas al-Milāhat al-'arabiyya* [in Arabic], London: Riad El-Rayyes.

Romance of Eneas (1974), trans. John A. Yunck as *Eneas: A Twelfth-Century French Romance*, New York: Columbia University Press.

Russian Primary Chronicle (1953), trans. S. Hazzard Cross and O.P. Sherbowitz-Wetzor, Cambridge, MA: Harvard University Press.

al-Saraqusti, Muhammad ibn Yusuf al-Tamimi (2002), *Al-maqāmāt al-luzūmīyah*, trans. James T. Monroe as *Al-Maqāmāt al-Luzūmīyah by Abū l-Tāhir Muhammad ibn Yūsuf al-Tamīmī al-Saraqustī ibn al-Aštarkūwī (d. 538/1143)*, Leiden: Brill.

Schurhammer, Georg (1977), *Francis Xavier: His Life, His Times*, vol. 2, *India, 1541–1545*, trans. M. Joseph Costelloe, Rome: The Jesuit Historical Institute.

Scylitzae, Ioannis (1973), *Synopsis Historiarum*, ed. Hans Thurn as *Ioannis Scylitzae Synopsis Historiarum*, Berlin: De Gruyter.

Scylitzae, Ioannis (2010), *Synopsis Historiarum*, trans. John Wortley as *John Skylitzes: A Synopsis of Byzantine History, 811–1057: Translation and Notes*, Cambridge: Cambridge University Press.

Las Siete Partidas (2001), ed. Samuel Parsons Scott and trans. Robert I. Burns as *Las Siete Partidas*, 5 vols, Philadelphia: University of Pennsylvania Press.

Strassberg, Richard E. (2002), *A Chinese Bestiary: Strange Creatures from the Guideways through Mountains and Seas*, Berkeley: University of California Press.

Thietmar of Merseberg (1957), *Chronik*, ed. and trans. Robert Holtzmann and Werner Trillmich, Darmstadt: Wissenschaftliche Buchgesellschaft.

Tibbetts, G.R. (1981), *Arab Navigation in the Indian Ocean Before the Coming of the Portuguese*, London: Royal Asiatic Society Books.

de Troyes, Chrétien (1991), *Erec et Enide, Cliges, Yvain, Lancelot*, trans. William W. Kibler and Carleton W. Carroll as *Four Arthurian Romances*, London: Penguin Books.

de Troyes, Chrétien (1994), *Cligès*, ed. and trans. Charles Méla and Olivier Collet as *Lettres Gothiques*, Paris: Le Livre de Poche.

Tudela, Benjamin of (2005), *Sefer Masa'ot*, trans. Adolf Asher as *The Itinerary of Benjamin of Tudela: Travels in the Middle Ages*, Cold Spring, NY: Nightingale Resources.

Uddyotanasūri (2008), *Kuvalayamālā*, trans. and ed. Christine Chojnacki as *Kuvalayamālā: Roman Jaina de 779, Composé par Uddyotanasūri*, 2 vols [in French], Marburg: Indica et Tibetica Verlag.

al-'Umara al-Hakami, *Ta'rīkh al-Yaman*, ed. and trans. Henry Cassels as *Yaman: Its Early Mediaeval History*, London: Edward Arnold.

Vita Niconis (1987), *Bios kai politeia kai merik thaumatn digsis tou hagiou kai thaumatourgou Niknos myroblytou tou Metanoeite* [The Life, Conduct, and Partial Narration of the Miracles of the Holy, Miracle-Worker Nikon Myrobletes the Metanoeite], ed. and trans. Denis Sullivan as *The Life of Saint Nikon: Text, Translation, and Commentary*, Brookline, MA: Hellenic College Press.

Zhao Rugua (1966), *Zhufanzhi*, trans. Friedrich Hirth and W.W. Rockhill as *Chau Ju-Kua: His work on the Chinese and Arab Trade in the Twelfth and Thirteenth Centuries, Entitled Chu-fan-chï*, New York: Paragon Book Reprint Corp.

SECONDARY SOURCES

Abu-Lughod, Janet L. (1989), *Before European Hegemony: The World System AD 1250–1350*, Oxford: Oxford University Press.

Achaya, K.T. (1994), *Indian Food: A Historical Companion*, New Delhi: Oxford University Press.

Acri, Andrea (2019), "Navigating the 'Southern Seas', Miraculously: Avoidance of Shipwreck in Buddhist Narratives of Maritime Crossings," in Marina Berthet, Fernando Rosa, and Shaun Viljoen (eds.), *Moving Spaces: Creolisation and Mobility in Africa, the Atlantic and Indian Ocean*, 50–77, Leiden: Brill.

Adão da Fonseca, Luís (2018), "Straits, Capes and Islands as Points of Confluence in the Portuguese Ocean Route between the Atlantic and the East (in the Fifteenth Century)," in Nikolas Jaspert and Sebastian Kolditz (eds.), *Entre Mers—Outre-Mer: Spaces, Modes and Agents of Indo-Mediterranean Connectivity*, 129–38, Heidelberg: Heidelberg University Publishing.

Agius, Dionisius (2008), *Classic Ships of Islam: From Mesopotamia to the Indian Ocean*, Leiden: Brill.

Ahmed, Sara (2015), "Race as Sedimented History," *Postmedieval: A Journal of Medieval Cultural Studies*, 6 (1): 94–7.

Alardawe, Rania Mohamdshareef S. (2016), "The Poetic Image of Water in Jāhilī and Andalusian Poetry; A Phenomenological Comparative Study," unpublished PhD diss., Durham University, UK.

Aleem, A.A. (1967), "Concepts of Currents, Tides and Winds among Medieval Arab Geographers in the Indian Ocean," *Deep–Sea Research*, 14: 459–63.

Alpers, Edward (2013), *The Indian Ocean in World History*, Oxford: Oxford University Press.

Amitai, Reuven (2008), "Diplomacy and the Slave Trade in the Eastern Mediterranean," *Oriente Moderno*, n.s., 88: 349–68.

Amundsen, Colin, Sophia Perdikaris, Thomas Howatt McGovern, Yekaterina Krivogorskaya, Matthew Brown, Konrad Smiarowski, Shaye Storm, Salena Modugno, Malgorzata Frik, and Monika Koczela (2005), "Fishing Booths and Fishing Strategies in Medieval Iceland: an Archaeofauna from the of Akurvík, North-West Iceland," *Environmental Archaeology*, 10 (2): 127–42.

Anderson, Atholl (2006), "Islands of Exile," *Journal of Island and Coastal Archaeology*, 1 (3): 33–47.
Anderson, Atholl and Douglas J. Kennett, eds. (2012), *Taking the High Ground (Terra Australis 37): The Archaeology of Rapa, a Fortified Island in Remote East Polynesia*, Canberra: ANU E Press.
Anderson, Jon and Kimberley Peters (2016), "'A perfect and absolute blank': Human Geographies of Water Worlds," in Jon Anderson and Kimberley Peters (eds.), *Water Worlds: Human Geographies of the Ocean*, 3–19, London: Routledge.
Anonymous (1922), *Ein russisch-byzantinisches Gesprächbuch*, ed. Max Vasmer, Leipzig: Markert & Petters.
Astuti, Rita (1995), *People of the Sea: Identity and Descent among the Vezo of Madagascar*, Cambridge: Cambridge University Press.
'Atwan, Hussein (1982), *Wasf al-bahr wa-l-nahr fī-l-sha'r al-'arabī min al-'asr al-jāhilī ilā al-'asr al-'abbāsī al-thānī* [Portrayal of the Sea and Rivers in Arabic Poetry from the Jahiliyya to the Second Abbasid period], 2nd edn., Beirut: Dar al-Jil.
Babcock, William Henry (1922), *Legendary Islands of the Atlantic; a Study in Medieval Geography*, New York: American Geographical Society.
Bacci, Michele and Martin Rohde, eds. (2014), *The Holy Portolano / Le Portulan sacré: The Sacred Geography of Navigation in the Middle Ages. Fribourg Colloquium 2013 / La geographie religieuse de la navigation au Moyen Age. Colloque Fribourgeois 2013*, Freiburg: De Gruyter.
Bachrach, Bernard (1993), *Fulk Nerra*, Berkeley: University of California Press.
Badenhorst, Shaw, Paul Sinclair, Annell Ekblom, and Ina Plug (2011), "Faunal Remains from Chibuene, an Iron Age Coastal Trading Station in Central Mozambique," *Southern African Humanities*, 23 (1): 1–15.
Bagrow, Leo (1956), "Italians on the Caspian," *Imago Mundi*, 13: 3–11.
Bakirtzis, Nikolaos and Xenophon Moniaros (2019), "Mastic Production in Medieval Chios: Economic Flows and Transitions in an Insular Setting," *Al-Masāq*, 31 (2): 171–95.
Balard, Michel (2006), *La Méditerranée médiévale: Espaces, itinéraires, comptoirs*, Paris: Picard.
Balard, Michel, ed. (2017), *The Sea in History: The Medieval World / La mer dans l'histoire: Le Moyen Âge*, Woodbridge: Boydell Press.
Balard, Michel (2019), "Latins in the Aegean and the Balkans (1300–1400)," in Jonathan Shepard (ed.), *The Cambridge History of the Byzantine Empire, c.500–1492*, rev. edn., 834–51, Cambridge: Cambridge University Press.
Balard, Michel and Christophe Picard (2014), *La Méditerranée au Moyen Âge: Les hommes et la mer*, Paris: Hachette.
Baldacchino, Godfrey (2008), "Studying Islands, On Whose Terms? Some Epistemological and Methodological Challenges to the Pursuit of Island Studies," *Island Studies Journal*, 3 (1): 37–56.
Baldwin, R.C.D. (1980), "The Development and Interchange of Navigational Information and Technology Between the Maritime Communities of Iberia, North-Western Europe and Asia, 1500–1620," unpublished PhD diss., Durham University, UK.
Barraclough, Eleanor Rosamund (2012), "Sailing the Saga Seas: Narrative, Cultural, and Geographical Perspectives in the North Atlantic Voyages of the *Íslendingasögur*," *Journal of the North Atlantic*, 18: 1–12.

Barrett, James H. (2016), "Medieval Sea Fishing, AD 500–1550," in James Barrett and David C. Orton (eds.), *Cod and Herring*, 250–72, Oxford: Oxbow.

Barrett, James H. and David C. Orton, eds. (2016), *Cod and Herring: The Archaeology and History of Medieval Sea Fishing*, Oxford: Oxbow.

Barrett, James H. and Michael P. Richards (2004), "Identity, Gender, Religion and Economy: New Isotope and Radiocarbon Evidence for Marine Resource Intensification in Early Historic Orkney, Scotland, UK," *European Journal of Archaeology*, 7: 249–71.

Barrett, James H., Alison M. Locker, and Callum M. Roberts (2004), "Dark Age Economics' Revisited: The English Fish Bone Evidence AD600 –1600," *Antiquity*, 78: 618–36.

Batchelor, Robert (2013), "The Selden Map Rediscovered: A Chinese Map of East Asian Shipping Routes, c. 1619," *Imago Mundi*, 65 (1): 37–63.

Bazin-Tacchella, Sylvie (2002), "Merveilles aquatiques dans les récits de voyage de l'époque médiévale," in Danièle James-Raoul and Claude Thomasset (eds.), *Dans l'eau, Sous l'eau: Le monde aquatique au Moyen Age*, 79–120, Paris: Presses de l'université de Paris-Sorbonne.

Beaujard, Philippe (2005), "The Indian Ocean in Eurasian and African World-Systems before the Sixteenth Century," *Journal of World History*, 16 (4): 411–65.

Beaujard, Philippe (2012), *Les Mondes de l'Océan Indien*, 2 vols, Paris: Armand Colin.

Beech, Mark J. (2004), *In the Land of the Ichthyophagi: Modelling Fish Exploitation in the Arabian Gulf and Gulf of Oman from the 5th Millennium BC to the Late Islamic Period*, Oxford: British Archaeological Reports.

Belfioretti, Luca and Tom Vosmer (2010), "Al-Balīd Ship Timbers: Preliminary Overview and Comparisons," *Proceedings of the Seminar for Arabian Studies*, 40: 111–17.

Belhamissi, Moulay (2005), *Al-bahr wa-l-ʿarab fi-l-taʾrikh wa-l-adab* [The Sea and the Arabs in History and Literature], Algiers: Manshurat ANEP.

Bellon-Méguelle, Hélène (2006), "L'exploration sous-marine d'Alexandre: un miroir de chevalerie," in Chantal Connochie-Bourgne (ed.), *Mondes marins du Moyen Age*, 43–56, Aix-en-Provence: Presses universitaires de Provence.

Benecke, N. (1982), "Zur frühmittelalterlichen Heringsfischerei im südlichen Ostseeraum - ein archäozoologischer Beitrag," *Zeitschrift für Archäologie*, 16: 283–90.

Benjamin, Thomas (2009), *The Atlantic World*, Cambridge: Cambridge University Press.

Berlekamp, Persis (2011), *Wonder, Image, and Cosmos in Medieval Islam*, New Haven, CT: Yale University Press.

Bernáth, Balázs, Alexandra Farkas, Dénes Száz, Miklós Blahó, Ádám Egri, András Barta, Susanne Åkesson, and Gábor Horváth (2014), "How Could the Viking Sun Compass Be Used with Sunstones Before and After Sunset?," *Proceedings: Mathematical, Physical and Engineering Sciences*, 470 (2166): 1–18.

Bessard, Fanny (2020), *Caliphs and Merchants*, Oxford: Oxford University Press.

Bhindra, S.C. (2002), "Notes on Religious Ban on Sea Travel in Ancient India," *Indian Historical Review*, 29 (1–2): 29–47.

Biedermann, Zoltán (2006), *Soqotra: Geschichte Einer Christlichen Insel im Indischen Ozean vom um bis zur Frühen Neuzeit*, Wiesbaden: Harrassowitz.

Biedermann, Zoltán (2010), "An Island under the Influence," in Ralph Kauz (ed.), *Aspects of the Maritime Silk Road*, 11–16, Wiesbaden: Harrassowitz.

Biedermann, Zoltán (2017), "Les îles dans la cartographie portugaise de la Renaissance," in Éric Vallet and Emmanuelle Vagnon (eds.), *La fabrique de l'Océan Indien: Cartes d'orient et d'occident*, 211–23, Paris: Editions de la Sorbonne.
Bill, Jan (2008), "Viking Ships and the Sea," in Stefan Brink with Neil Price (eds.), *The Viking World*, 170–80, London: Routledge.
Billig, Volkmar ([1936] 2009), *Inseln: Geschichte einer Faszination*, Berlin: Matthes and Seitz.
Blackburn, Mark (2011), *Viking Coinage and Currency in the British Isles*, London: Spink.
Blue, Lucy (2006), "Sewn Boat Timbers from the Medieval Islamic Port of Quseir al-Qadim on the Red Sea Coast of Egypt," in Lucy Blue, Frederick Hocker, and A. Englert (eds.), *Connected by the Sea: Proceedings of the 10th International Symposium on Boat and Ship Archaeology*, 277–84, Oxford: Oxbow Books.
Bodenhamer, David J., John Corrigan, and Trevor M. Harris, eds. (2015), *Deep Maps and Spatial Narratives*, Bloomington: Indiana University Press.
Boivin, Nicole, Alison Crowther, Mary E. Prendergast, and Dorian Q. Fuller (2014), "Indian Ocean Food Globalisation and Africa," *African Archaeological Review*, 31 (4): 547–81.
Bonner, Michael (2011), "The Arabian Silent Trade: Profit and Nobility in the 'Markets of the Arabs'," in Margariti Eleni Roxani, Adam Sabra, and Petra M. Sijpesteijn (eds.), *Histories of the Middle East: Studies in Middle Eastern Society, Economy, and Law in Honor of A.L. Udovitch*, 23–52, Leiden: Brill.
Bopearachchi, Osmund (2014), "Sri Lanka and the Maritime Trade: Bodhisattva Avalokitesvara as the Protector of Mariners," in Upinder Singh and Parul Pandya Dhar (eds.), *Asian Encounters: Exploring Connected Histories*, 161–87, New Delhi: Oxford University Press.
Bouloux, Nathalie (2012), "L'*Insularium illustratum* d'Henricus Martellus," *Historical Review / La Revue Historique*, 9: 77–94.
Bramoullé, David (2007), "Recruiting Crews in the Fatimid Navy (909–1171)," *Medieval Encounters*, 13: 4–31.
Bramoullé, David (2012), "The Fatimids and the Red Sea (969–1171)," in Dionisius Agius, John Cooper, Athena Trakadas, and Chiara Zazzaro (eds.), *Navigated Spaces, Connected Places, Proceedings of Red Sea Project V held at the University of Exeter September 2010*, 127–36, Oxford: Archaeopress.
Bramoullé, David (2017), "Représenter et décrire l'espace maritime dans le califat fatimide. L'exemple des cartes de la Méditerranée et de l'océan Indien," *Cartes et Géomatique, CFC*, 234: 55–68.
Braudel, Fernand (1972), *The Mediterranean and the Mediterranean World in the Age of Philip II*, 2 vols, trans. Siân Reynolds, New York: Harper & Row.
Brett, Michael (2017), *The Fatimid Empire*, Edinburgh: Edinburgh University Press.
Brice, William C. (1977), "Early Muslim Sea-Charts," *Journal of the Royal Asiatic Society of Great Britain and Ireland*, 1: 53–61.
Brill, Robert (1995), "Chemical Analysis of Some Glasses from Jenne-Jeno," in Susan McIntosh (ed.), *Excavations at Jenne-Jeno*, 252–7, Berkeley: University of California Press.
Brisbane, Mark A., Nikolai A. Makarov, and Evgenij Nosov, eds. (2012), *The Archaeology of Medieval Novgorod in Context*, Oxford: Oxbow.
Brotton, Jerry (2002), *The Renaissance Bazaar*, Oxford: Oxford University Press.
Buchet, Christian and Michel Balard, eds. (2017), *The Sea in History: The Medieval World / La mer dans l'histoire: Le Moyen Âge*, Woodbridge: Boydell and Brewer.

Budak, Neven (2018), "One more Renaissance?," in Mladen Ančić, Jonathan Shepard, and Trpimir Vedriš (eds.), *Imperial Spheres and the Adriatic: Byzantium, The Carolingians and the Treaty of Achen (812)*, 174–91, Abingdon: Routledge.

Bulgakova, Victoria (2004), *Byzantinische Bleisiegel in Osteuropa*, Wiesbaden: Harrassowitz.

Buschinger, Danielle and Wolfgang Spiewok, eds. (1997), *La mer dans la culture médiévale*, Actes du colloque Saint-Valery-sur-Somme, 20–23 mars 1997, *Speculum Medii Aevi, Zeitschrift für Geschichte und Literatur des Mittelalters / Revue d'Histoire et de Littérature médiévales* 3, Griefswald: Reineke Verlag.

Byrne, Aisling (2016), *Otherworlds: Fantasy and History in Medieval Literature*, Oxford: Oxford University Press.

Calanca, Paola (2010), "Perception et pratique de l'espace maritime par les fonctionnaires chinois (XIVe-début du XIXe siècle)," *Bulletin de l'Ecole française d'Extrême-Orient*, 97–8: 21–54.

Campbell, Gwyn (2016), "Africa and the Early Indian Ocean Exchange System in the Context of Human-Environment Interaction," in Gwyn Campbell (ed.), *Early Exchange between Africa and the Wider Indian Oceanic World*, 1–23, Cham: Palgrave Macmillan.

Campbell, Tony (1986), "Census of Pre-Sixteenth-Century Portolan Charts," *Imago Mundi*, 38: 67–94.

Campbell, Tony (1987), "Portolan Charts from the Late Thirteenth Century to 1500," in John B. Harley and David Woodward (eds.), *The History of Cartography, 1: Cartography in Prehistoric, Ancient and Medieval Europe and the Mediterranean*, 441–4, Chicago: University of Chicago Press.

Carter, Robert (2005), "The History and Prehistory of Pearling in the Persian Gulf," *Journal of the Economic and Social History of the Orient*, 48 (2): 139–209.

Casale, Giancarlo (2010), *The Ottoman Age of Exploration*, Oxford: Oxford University Press.

Cattaneo, Angelo (2011), *Fra Mauro's Mappa mundi and Fifteenth Century Venice*, Terrarum Orbis 8, Turnhout: Brepols.

Cerón-Carrasco, Ruby (1998), "Fish Bone," in Christopher Lowe (ed.), *Coastal Erosion and the Archaeological Assessment of an Eroding Shoreline at St Boniface Church, Papa Westray, Orkney*, 149–55, Stroud: Sutton Publishing in association with Historic Scotland.

Cerrito, Stefania (2006), "La mer dans le roman de Troie: les aventures d'Ulysse," in Chantal Connochie-Bourgne (ed.), *Mondes marins du Moyen Âge*, Actes du 30ème colloque du CUER-MA, 3,4 et 5 mars 2005, 79–93, Aix-en-Provence: Presses universitaires de Provence.

Chakravarti, Ranabir (2002), "Seafarings, Ships and Ship Owners: India and the Indian Ocean (AD700–1500)," in Ruth Barnes, and David Parkin (eds.), *Ships and the Development of Maritime Technology in the Indian Ocean*, 28–61, London: RoutledgeCurzon.

Chan, Hok-lam (1998), "The Chien-wen, Yung-lo, Hung-hsi, and Hsüan-te reigns, 1399–1435," in Frederick W. Mote and Denis Twitchett (eds.), *The Cambridge History of China*, vol. 7, *The Ming Dynasty, 1368–1644, Part 1*, 182–304, Cambridge: Cambridge University Press.

Chareyron, Nicole and Michel Tarayre (2006), "Le monde marin de Félix Fabri," in Chantal Connochie-Bourgne (ed.), *Mondes marins du Moyen Âge, Actes du 30ème*

colloque du CUER-MA, 3,4 et 5 mars 2005, 95–104, Aix-en-Provence: Presses universitaires de Provence.

Chaudhuri, Kirti N. (1985), *Trade and Civilization in the Indian Ocean: An Economic History from the Rise of Islam to 1750*, Cambridge: Cambridge University Press.

Chavannes, Edouard (1903), "Les deux plus anciens spécimens de la cartographie Chinoise," *Bulletin de l'Ecole Française d'Extrême Orient*, 3: 214–47.

Chekin, Leonid, S. (2006), *Northern Eurasia in Medieval Cartography: Inventory, Text, Translation, and Commentary*, Turnhout: Brepols.

Chism, Christine (2009), "Arabic in the Medieval World," *PMLA (Publications of the Modern Language Association of America)*, 124 (2): 624–31.

Chism, Christine (2016), "Britain and the Sea of Darkness: Islandology in Al-Idrīsī's Mushtaq," *Postmedieval: A Journal of Medieval Cultural Studies*, 7 (4): 497–510.

Christides, Vassilios (2018), "A Supplementary Investigation Tracing the Christians Under the Shadow of Muslim Rule in the Emirate of Crete (ca. 825/6–961 CE): The Case of the Treaty of Naxos in John Caminiates' Narration of the Sacking of Thessaloniki in 904 CE.," *Pharos Journal of Theology*, 99. Available online: https://www.pharosjot.com/uploads/7/1/6/3/7163688/article_26_vol_99_2018_-_unisa___greece.pdf (accessed October 20, 2020).

Christie, Annalisa (2011), "Exploring the Social Context of Maritime Exploitation in the Mafia Archipelago, Tanzania: An Archaeological Perspective," unpublished PhD diss., University of York, UK.

Church, Mike J., Símon V. Arge, Kevin J. Edwards, Philippa L. Ascough, Julie M. Bond, Gordon T. Cook, Steve J. Dockrill, Andrew J. Dugmore, Thomas H. McGovern, Claire Nesbitt, and Ian A. Simpson (2013), "The Vikings Were Not the First Colonizers of the Faroe Islands," *Quaternary Science Reviews*, 77: 228–32.

Chutiwongs, Nandana (2000), "Bronze Ritual Implements in the Majapahit Period: Meaning and Function," *Arts of Asia*, 30 (6): 69–84.

Clark, Alfred (1993), "Medieval Arab Navigation on the Indian Ocean: Latitude Determinations," *Journal of the American Oriental Society*, 113 (3): 360–73.

Classen, Albrecht (2018), *Water in Medieval Literature: An Ecocritical Reading*, Lanham, MD: Lexington Books.

Cohen, Jeffrey Jerome (2003), *Medieval Identity Machines*, Minneapolis: Minnesota University Press.

Conlan, Thomas D. (2001), *In Little Need of Divine Intervention: Tazeki Suenaga's Scrolls of the Mongol Invasions of Japan*, Ithaca, NY: Cornell University Press.

Connery, Christopher (2006), "There Was No More Sea: The Suppression of the Oceans, from Bible to Cyberspace," *Journal of Geographical History*, 32: 495–505.

Connochie-Bourgne, Chantal, ed. (2006), *Mondes marins du Moyen Âge*, Actes du 30ème *colloque du CUER-MA, 3,4 et 5 mars 2005*, Sénéfiance, 52, Aix-en-Provence: Presses universitaires de Provence.

Connor, Clifford D. (2005), *A People's History of Science: Miners, Midwives and "Low Mechanicks,"* New York: Nation Books.

Conrad, Lawrence (2001), "Islam and the Sea: Paradigms and Problematics," *Al-Qantara*, 23 (1): 123–54.

Corbellari, Alain (2006), "La mer, espace structurant du roman courtois," in Chantal Connochie-Bourgne (ed.), *Mondes marins du Moyen Âge*, 105–13, Aix-en-Provence: Presses universitaires de Provence.

Corbin, Alain and Hélène Richard, eds. (2004), *La Mer: Terreur et fascination*, Exposition de la Bibliothèque nationale de France, Paris: BnF/Seuil.

Coull, James R. (1996), *The Sea Fisheries of Scotland: A Historical Geography*, Edinburgh: John Donald.
Couto Dejanirah, Bacqué-Grammont Jean-Louis and Mahmud Taleghani, eds. (2006), *Atlas historique du golfe Persique (XVIe-XVIIe siècles)*, Turnhout: Brepols.
Crawford, Barbara E. (2008), *The Churches Dedicated to St Clement in Medieval England*, St. Petersburg: Axioma.
The Cresques Project (n.d.), "Panel III." Available online: https://sites.google.com/site/jafudacresquesproject/catalan-atlas-legends/panel-iii (accessed November 15, 2020).
Critch, Aaron, Jennifer F. Harland, and James H. Barrett (2018), "Tracing the Late Viking Age and Medieval Butter Economy: The View from Quoygrew, Orkney," in Jane Kershaw and Gareth Williams (eds.), *Silver, Butter, Cloth: Monetary and Social Economies in the Viking Age*, 278–96, Oxford: Oxford University Press.
Cropper, C. (2014), "Glass," in Ian Russell and Maurice Hurley (eds.), *Woodstown*, 282–3, Dublin: Four Courts.
Crowther, Alison, et al. (2016), "Coastal Subsistence, Maritime Trade, and the Colonization of Small Off-Shore Islands in Eastern African Prehistory," *Journal of Island and Coastal Archaeology*, 11 (2): 211–37.
Crumlin-Pedersen, Ole (2010), *Archaeology and the Sea in Scandinavia and Britain*, Roskilde: Viking Ship Museum.
Crumlin-Petersen, Ole and Olaf Olsen, eds. (2002), *The Skuldelev Ships*, vol. 1, Roskilde: Viking Ship Museum.
Cunliffe, Barry (2001), *Facing the Ocean: The Atlantic and its Peoples, 8000BC–AD 1500*, Oxford: Oxford University Press.
Curtin, Philip D. (1984), *Cross-Cultural Trade in World History*, Cambridge: Cambridge University Press.
Dalli, Charles (2016), "From Medieval Dar al-Islam to Contemporary Malta: raḥl toponymy in a Wider Mediterranean Context," *Island Studies Journal*, 11: 369–80.
Darley, Rebecca (2019), "The Island Frontier: Socotra, Sri Lanka and the Shape of Commerce in the Late Antique Western Indian Ocean," *Al-Masāq*, 31 (2): 223–41.
Dars, Jacques (1992), *La marine chinoise du Xe siècle au XIVe siècle*, Paris: Economica.
Daston, Lorraine and Katherine Park (2008), *Wonders and the Order of Nature, 1150–1750*, New York: MIT Press/Zone Books.
Davis, Kathleen and Michael Puett (2016), "Periodization and 'The Medieval Globe': A Conversation," *Medieval Globe*, 2 (1): 1–14.
Delgado, James P. (2010), *Khubilai Khan's Lost Fleet: In Search of a Legendary Armada*, Berkeley: University of California Press.
Deloche, Jean (1986), "Techniques militaires dans les royaumes du Dekkan au temps des Hoysala (XIIe-XIIIe siècle), d'après l'iconographie," *Artibus Asiae*, 47: 147–232.
Deloche, Jean (1987), "Etudes sur la circulation en Inde: VII. Konkan warships of the xlth-xvth centuries as represented on memorial stones," *Bulletin de l'Ecole française d'Extrême-Orient*, 76: 165–84.
Delumeau, Jean (1989), "Le protestantisme et la peur de la mer," in Alain Cabantous and Françoise Hildesheimer (eds.), *Foi chrétienne et milieux maritimes (xve-xxe siècle)*, 122–8, Paris: Editions Publisud.
Deluz, Christiane (1996), "Partir c'est mourir un peu: Voyage et déracinement dans la société médiévale," in *Voyages et voyageurs au Moyen Age: Actes du 26e congrès de la Société des historiens médiévistes de l'enseignement supérieur public*, 291–303, Paris: Publications de la Sorbonne.

Deluz, Christiane (2005), "Les mers merveilleuses au Moyen Âge," *Le Monde des Cartes: Revue du CFC*, 184: 8–11.
Dening, Greg (2004), *Beach Crossings: Voyaging Across Times, Cultures, and Self*, Philadelphia: University of Pennsylvania Press.
Dewar, Robert E. and Henry T. Wright (1993), "The Culture History of Madagascar," *Journal of World Prehistory*, 7 (4): 417–66.
De Weerdt, Hilde (2009), "Maps and Memory: Readings of Cartography in Twelfth- and Thirteenth-Century Song China," *Imago Mundi*, 61 (2): 145–67.
De Weerdt, Hilde (2016), *Information, Territory, and Networks*, Cambridge, MA: Harvard University Asia Center.
Di Cosmo, Nicola (2010), "Black Sea Emporia and the Mongol Empire," *Journal of the Economic and Social History of the Orient*, 53: 83–108.
Di Cosmo, Nicola (forthcoming), "From War to Peace in Medieval Steppe Empires," in Jonathan Shepard, Peter Frankopan, and Averil Cameron (eds.), *Byzantine Spheres*, Oxford: Oxford University Press.
Diffie, Bailey W. and George D. Winius (1977), *Foundations of the Portuguese Empire 1415–1580*, Minneapolis: University of Minnesota Press.
Disney, Anthony (2009), *A History of Portugal and the Portuguese Empire*, vol. 1, Cambridge: Cambridge University Press.
Dobney, Keith and Anton Ervynck (2007), "To Fish or Not to Fish? Evidence for the Possible Avoidance of Fish Consumption during the Iron Age Around the North Sea," in Colin Haselgrove and T. Moore (eds.), *The Later Iron Age in Britain and Beyond*, 403–18, Oxford: Oxbow.
Dorofeeva-Lichtmann, Vera (2003), "Mapping a 'Spiritual' Landscape: Representation of Terrestrial Space in the *Shanhaijing*," in Don Waytt and Nicola Di Cosmo (eds.), *Political Frontiers, Ethnic Boundaries, and Human Geographies*, 35–79, London: RoutledgeCurzon.
Dorofeeva-Lichtmann, Vera (2007), "Mapless Mapping: Did the Maps of the *Shan hai jing* Ever Exist?," in Francesca Bray, Vera Dorofeeva-Lichtmann, and Georges Métailié (eds.), *Graphics and Text in the Production of Technical Knowledge in China: The Warp and the Weft*, 217–94, Leiden: Brill.
Dorofeeva-Lichtmann, Vera (2019), "'Inversed Cosmographs' in Late East Asian Cartography and the Atlas Production Trend," in Tokimasa 武田時昌 and Bill M. Mak 麥文彪 (eds.), *East-West Encounter in the Science of Heaven and Earth* 天と地の科学, 144–74, Kyoto: Institute for Research in Humanities, Kyoto University.
Douglass, Kristina and Jens Zinke (2015), "Forging Ahead by Land and by Sea: Archaeology and Paleoclimate Reconstruction in Madagascar," *African Archaeological Review*, 32: 267–99.
Ducène, Jean-Charles (2017a), "Formes de l'océan Indien dans la cartographie arabe," in Emmanuelle Vagnon and Éric Vallet (eds.), *La Fabrique de l'océan Indien: Cartes d'Orient et d'Occident*, 57–72, Paris: Publications de la Sorbonne.
Ducène, Jean-Charles (2017b), "Merveilles de l'océan Indien dans la géographie arabe," in Emmanuelle Vallet and Éric Vagnon (eds.), *La fabrique de l'Océan Indien: Cartes d'orient et d'occident*, 269–72, Paris: Editions de la Sorbonne.
Ducène, Jean-Charles (2018), *L'Europe et les géographes arabes du Moyen Âge*, Paris: CNRS Éditions.
Dudbridge, Glen (2018), "Reworking the World System Paradigm," in Catherine Holmes and Naomi Standen (eds.), *The Global Middle Ages*, 297–316, Oxford: Oxford University Press.

Dufeu, Valérie (2018), *Fish Trade in Medieval North Atlantic Societies: An Interdisciplinary Approach to Human Ecodynamics*, Amsterdam: Amsterdam University Press.

Dugmore, Andrew J., Christian Keller, and Thomas H. McGovern (2007), "Norse Greenland Settlement: Reflections on Climate Change, Trade, and the Contrasting Fates of Human Settlements in the North Atlantic Islands," *Arctic Anthropology*, 44: 12–36.

Duncan-Jones, Richard (1982), *The Economy of the Roman Empire*, 2nd edn., Cambridge: Cambridge University Press.

Dwyer, Philip (2017), "Violence and its Histories: Meanings, Methods, Problems," *History and Theory*, 56 (4): 7–22.

L'eau au Moyen Âge (1985), Communications présentées au Colloque du CUER-MA, Aix-en-Provence février 1984, Aix-en Provence: Publications du CUERMA.

Edson, Evelyn (2004), "Reviving the Crusade: Sanudo's Schemes and Vesconte's Maps," in Rosamund Allen (ed.), *Eastward Bound: Travel and Travellers, 1050–1550*, 131–55, Manchester: Manchester University Press.

Edwards, Richard (2011), *The Heart of Ma Yuan: The Search for a Southern Song Aesthetic*, Hong Kong: Hong Kong University Press.

Egeler, Matthias (2017), *Islands in the West: Classical Myth and the Medieval Norse and Irish Geographical Imagination*, Medieval Voyaging, Turnhout: Brepols.

Elshakry, Marwa (2010), "When Science Became Western: Historiographical Reflections," *ISIS*, 101 (1): 98–109.

Enghoff, Inge Bødker (1999), "Fishing in the Baltic Region from the 5th Century BC to the 16th Century AD: Evidence from Fish Bones," *Archaeofauna*, 8: 41–85.

Englert, Anton (2015), *Large Cargo Ships in Danish Waters 1000–1250*, Roskilde: Viking Ship Museum.

Ewert, Ulf and Stephan Selzer (2016), *Institutions of Hanseatic Trade*, Frankfurt: Peter Lang.

Facey, William (2005), "Crusaders in the Red Sea: Renaud de Chatillon's Raids of AD 1182–3," in Janet C.M. Starkey (ed.), *People of the Red Sea: Proceedings of the Red Sea Project II*, 87–98, Oxford: Archaeopress.

Fahmy, Aly M. (1948), *Muslim Naval Organisation in the Eastern Mediterranean from the Seventh to the Tenth Century A.D*, Cairo: National Publication and Printing House.

Faith, Rosalind (2012), "The Structure of the Market for Wool in Early Medieval Lincolnshire," *Economic History Review*, 65: 674–700.

Falchetta, Piero (2006), *Fra Mauro's Map of the World: With a Commentary and Translations of the Inscriptions*, Terrarum Orbis 5, Turnhout: Brepols.

Falchetta, Piero (2009), "The Portolan of Michael of Rhodes," in Pamela O. Long, David McGee, and Alan M. Stahl (eds.), *The Book of Michael of Rhodes: A Fifteenth-Century Maritime Manuscript*, vol. 3, *Studies*, 194–210, Cambridge, MA: MIT Press.

Fatimi, Saiyid Q. (1996), "History of the Development of the Kamāl," in Himanshu Prabha Ray and Jean-Francois Salles (eds.), *Tradition and Archaeology: Early Maritime Contacts in the Indian Ocean*, 283–92, New Delhi: Manohar.

Faulkner, Patrick, Matthew Harris, Abdallah Ali, Othman Haji, Alison Crowther, Mark Horton, and Nicole Boivin (2018), "Characterising Marine Mollusc Exploitation in the Eastern African Iron Age: Archaeomalacological Evidence from Unguja Ukuu and Fukuchani, Zanzibar," *Quaternary International*, 471: 66–80.

Fauvelle, François-Xavier (2018), *The Golden Rhinoceros*, trans. Troy Tice, Princeton, NJ: Princeton University Press.

Favereau, Marie (forthcoming), "Byzantium and the Golden Horde," in Jonathan Shepard, Peter Frankopan, and Averil Cameron (eds.), *Byzantine Spheres*, Oxford: Oxford University Press.
Fenton, Alexander (1978), *The Northern Isles: Orkney and Shetland*, East Linton: Tuckwell Press.
Fenton, Alexander (2008), "Shellfish as bait," in James R. Coull, Alexander Fenton, and Kenneth Veitch (eds.), *Scottish Life and Society: A Compendium of Scottish Ethnology, Boats, Fishing and the Sea*, 90–102, Edinburgh: John Donald.
Fern, Carola (2012), *Seesturm im Mittelalter: ein literarisches Motiv im Spannungsfeld zwischen Topik, Erfahrungswissen und Naturkunde*, Berlin: Peter Lang Gmbh.
Fernández-Armesto, Filipe (2006), *Pathfinders: A Global History of Exploration*, Oxford: Oxford University Press.
Ferrand, Gabriel (1921–8), *Instructions nautiques et routiers arabes et portugais des XVe et XVIe siècles*, 3 vols, Paris: Librairie Orientaliste Paul Geuthner.
Ferreira de Miranda, Flávio (2013), "Before the Empire," *Journal of Medieval Iberian Studies*, 5: 65–89.
Flecker, Michael (2003), "The Thirteenth-Century Java Sea Wreck," *The Mariner's Mirror*, 89: 388–404.
Fleisher, Jeffrey (2003), "Viewing Stonetowns from the Countryside: An Archaeological Approach to Swahili Regional Systems, AD 800–1500," unpublished PhD diss., University of Virginia, USA.
Fleisher, Jeffrey, Paul Lane, Adria LaViolette, Mark Horton, Edward Pollard, Eréndira Quintana Morales, Thomas Vernet, Annalisa Christie, and Stephanie Wynne-Jones (2015), "When Did the Swahili Become Maritime?," *American Anthropologist*, 117 (1): 100–15.
Fleury, Christian (2013), "The Island/Sea/Territory Relationship," *Shima: The International Journal of Research into Island Cultures*, 7 (1): 1–13.
Flexner, James L., Jeffrey B. Fleisher, and Adria LaViolette (2008), "Bead Grinders and Early Swahili Household Economy: Analysis of an Assemblage from Tumbe, Pemba Island, Tanzania, 7th-10th Centuries AD," *Journal of African Archaeology*, 6 (2): 161–81.
Flint, Valerie J. (1992), *The Imaginative Landscape of Christopher Columbus*, Princeton, NJ: Princeton University Press.
Fontein, Jan (1990), *The Sculpture of Indonesia*, New York: Harry N. Abrams.
Forrest, Ian and Anne Haour (2018), "Trust in Long-Distance Relationships, 1000–1600," in Catherine Holmes and Naomi Standen (eds.), *The Global Middle Ages*, 190–213, Oxford: Oxford University Press.
Frake, Charles O. (1985), "Cognitive Maps of Time and Tide Among Medieval Seafarers," *Man*, 20 (2): 254–70.
Franklin, Simon and Jonathan Shepard (1996), *The Emergence of Rus, 750–1200*, London: Longman.
Frantzen, Allen J. (2014), *Food, Eating and Identity in Early Medieval England*, Oxford: Boydell and Brewer.
Frei, Karin M., et al. (2015), "Was it for Walrus? Viking Age Settlement and Medieval Walrus Ivory Trade in Iceland and Greenland," *World Archaeology*, 47 (3): 439–66.
Freitag, Barbara (2013), *Hy Brasil–The Metamorphosis of an Island: From Cartographic Error to Celtic Elysium*, Amsterdam: Rodopi.
Froese, R. and D. Pauly (2019), *FishBase*: World Wide Web electronic publication. Available online: http://www.fishbase.org/search.php (accessed October 20, 2020).

Fuʾad-Sayyed, Ayman and Roland-Pierre Gayraud (2000), "Fustat-le Caire à l'époque fatimide," in Jean-Claude Garcin (ed.), *Grandes villes méditerranéennes du monde musulman médiéval*, 135–56, Rome: École française.

Fuess, Albrecht (2001), "Rotting Ships and Razed Harbors: The Naval Policy of the Mamluks," *Mamluk Studies Review*, 5: 45–71.

Fusaro, Maria (2010), "Maritime History as Global History? The Methodological Challenges and a Future Research Agenda," in Maria Fusaro and Amélia Polónia (eds.), *Maritime History As Global History*, 267–82, Liverpool: Liverpool University Press.

Gardiner, Mark and Natascha Mehler (2007), "English and Hanseatic Trading and Fishing Sites in Medieval Iceland: Report on Initial Fieldwork," *Germania*, 85: 385–427.

Garipzanov, Ildar (2012), "Wandering Clerics and Mixed Rituals in the Early Christian North, *c*.1000–*c*.1150," *Journal of Ecclesiastical History*, 63: 1–17.

Gautier Dalché, Patrick (1995), *Carte marine et portulan au xiie siècle: le Liber de existencia riveriarum et forma maris nostri Mediterranei*, Rome: Ecole Française de Rome.

Gautier Dalché, Patrick (1996a), "Pour une histoire du regard géographique: Conception et usage de la carte au XVe siècle," *Micrologus*, 4: 77–103.

Gautier Dalché, Patrick (1996b), "L'usage des cartes marines aux XIVe et XVe siècles," in Enrico Menesto (ed.), *Spazi, tempi, misure e percorsi nell'Europa del Bassomedioevo: Atti del XXXII Convegno storico internazionale, Todi, 8-11 ottobre 1995*, 97–128, Spoleto: Fondazione CISAM.

Gautier Dalché, Patrick (1998), "Remarques sur les défauts supposés, et sur l'efficace certaine de l'image du monde au XIVe siècle," *La géographie au Moyen Âge: Espaces pensés, espaces vécus, espaces rêvés, Perspectives médiévales*, 24: 43–56.

Gautier Dalché, Patrick (2002), "Cartes marines, représentation du littoral et perception de l'espace au Moyen Âge: Un état de la question," in Jean-Marie Martin (ed.), "Zones côtières et plaines littorales dans le monde méditerranéen au Moyen Age," special issue of *Castrum*, 7: 9–33.

Gautier Dalché, Patrick (2009), *La Géographie de Ptolémée en Occident*, Turnhout: Brepols.

Gautier Dalché, Patrick (2017), "La carte marine au Moyen Age: outil technique, objet symbolique," in Christian Buchet and Michel Balard (eds.), *The Sea in History: The Medieval World / La mer dans l'histoire. Le Moyen Âge*, 101–14, Woodbridge: Boydell and Brewer.

Gelichi, Sauro (2018), "Aachen, Venice and Archaeology," in Mladen Ančić, Jonathan Shepard, and Trpimir Vedriš (eds.), *Imperial Spheres and the Adriatic*, 111–21, Abingdon: Routledge.

Gestsdóttir, Hildur, Guðrún Alda Gísladóttir, Lísabet Guðmundsdóttir, Howell M. Roberts, Mjöll Snæsdóttir, and Orri Vésteinsson (2017), "New Discoveries: Dysnes," *Archaeologia Islandica*, 12: 93–106.

Gillis, John R. (2012), *The Human Shore: Seacoasts in History*, Chicago: University of Chicago Press.

Gingras, Francis (2006), "Errances maritimes et explorations romanesques dans *Apollonius de Tyr* et *Floire et Blancheflor*," in Chantal Connochie-Bourgne (ed.), *Mondes marins du Moyen Age*, 168–85, Aix-en-Provence: Presses universitaires de Provence.

Glassé, Cyril (2001), *The New Encyclopaedia of Islam*, rev. edn., London: Stacey International.

Goitein, S.D. (1954a), "From the Mediterranean to India," *Speculum* 29: 181–97.

Goitein, S.D. (1954b), "Two Eyewitness Reports on an Expedition of the King of Kīsh (Qais) against Aden," *Bulletin of the School of Oriental and African Studies*, 16 (2): 247–57.

Goitein, S.D. (1966), "Letters and Documents of The India Trade in Medieval Times," in *Studies in Islamic History and Institutions*, 329–50, Leiden: Brill.

Goitein, S.D. (1967–93), *A Mediterranean Society, The Jewish Communities of the Arab World as Portrayed in the Documents of the Cairo Geniza*, 6 vols, Berkeley: University of California Press.

Goitein, S.D. and Mordechai A. Friedman (2008), *India Traders of the Middle Ages: Documents from the Cairo Geniza ('India Book')*, Leiden: E.J. Brill.

Golb, Norman and Omeljan Pritsak (1982), *Khazarian Hebrew Documents of the Tenth Century*, Ithaca, NY: Cornell University Press.

Goldberg, Jessica (2012), *Trade and Institutions in the Medieval Mediterranean: The Geniza Merchants and their Business World*, Cambridge: Cambridge University Press.

Goldie, Matthew Boyd and Sebastian Sobecki (2016), "Editors' Introduction. Our seas of islands," *Postmedieval: A Journal of Medieval Cultural Studies*, 7 (4): 471–83.

Granovetter, Mark (1983), "The Strength of Weak Ties," *Sociological Theory*, 1: 201–33.

Graziadei, Daniel, Britta Hartmann, Ian Kinane, Johannes Riquet, and Barney Samson (2017), "On Sensing Island Spaces and the Spatial Practice of Island-Making: Introducing Island Poetics, Part I," *Island Studies Journal*, 12: 239–52.

Grealy, Alicia, Kristina Douglass, James Haile, Chriselle Bruwer, Charlotte L. Gough, and Michael Bunce (2016), "Tropical Ancient DNA from Bulk Archaeological Fish Bone Reveals the Subsistence Practices of a Historic Coastal Community in Southwest Madagascar," *Journal of Archaeological Science*, 75: 82–8.

Green, Monica (2014), "Taking 'Pandemic' Seriously," *Medieval Globe*, 1: 27–62.

Green, Toby (2012), *The Rise of the Trans-Atlantic Slave Trade in Western Africa, 1300–1589*, Cambridge: Cambridge University Press.

Greif, Avner (2006), *Institutions and the Path to the Modern Economy*, Cambridge: Cambridge University Press.

Groom, Nigel (1981), *Frankincense and Myrrh*, London: Longman.

Gruszczyński, Jacek (2019), *Viking Silver, Hoards and Containers*, London: Routledge.

Gruszczyński, Jacek, Marek Jankowiak, and Jonathan Shepard, eds. (2021), *Viking-Age Trade: Silver, Slaves and Gotland*, Abingdon: Routledge.

Grydehøj, Adam, Otto Heim, and Huan Zhang (2017), "Islands of China and the Sinophone World," *Island Studies Journal*, 12: 3–6.

Guangqi, Sun (2000), "The Development of China's Navigation Technology and of the Maritime Silk Route," in Vadim Elisseeff (ed.), *The Silk Roads: Highways of Culture and Commerce*, 288–303, New York: Berghahn Books and UNESCO Publishing.

Guillot, Claude and Ludwik Kalus (2008), *Les monument funéraires et l'histoire du Sultanat de Pasai à Sumatra*, Paris: Association Archipel.

Guo, Li (2004), *Commerce, Culture, and Community in a Red Sea Port in the Thirteenth Century*, Leiden, Brill.

Guy, John (2017), "The Phanom Surin Shipwreck, a Pahlavi Inscription, and their Significance for the History of Early Lower Central Thailand," *Journal of the Siam Society*, 105: 179–96.

Guy, John (2019), "Shipwrecks in Late First Millennium Southeast Asia," in Angela Schottenhammer (ed.), *Early Global Interconnectivity Across the Indian Ocean World*, vol. 1, 121–63, Cham: Palgrave Macmillan.

Hägg, Inga (2016), "Silks at Birka," in Fedir Androshchuk, Jonathan Shepard, and Monica White (eds.), *Byzantium and the Viking World*, 281–304, Uppsala: Uppsala Universiteit.

Hall, Kenneth (2011), *A History of Early Southeast Asia*, Lanham, MD: Rowman & Littlefield.

Hamblin, William J. (1986), "The Fatimid Navy during the Early Crusades: 1099–1124," *American Neptune*, 46: 77–83.

Hamilton-Dyer, Sheila (2011), "Faunal Remains," in David Peacock and Lucy Blue (eds.), *Myos Hormos - Quseir al-Qadim: Roman and Islamic Ports on the Red Sea*, vol. 2, *Finds from the Excavations 1999–2003*, 245–88, Oxford: British Archaeological Reports.

Haour, Anne (2007), *Rulers, Warriors, Traders, Clerics: The Central Sahel and the North Sea 800–1500*, Oxford: Oxford University Press.

Haour, Anne, Anna Christie, and Shiura Jaufar (2016), "Tracking the Cowrie Shell: Excavations in the Maldives, 2016," *Nyame Akuma*, 85: 69–82.

Harland, Jennifer F. (2016), "Berst Ness Knowe of Skea: The Fish Remains," unpublished technical report for EASE Archaeology.

Harland, Jennifer F. (2019), "Dunbeath Broch (site code 60097): The Fish Remains," unpublished technical report for AOC Archaeology.

Harland, Jennifer F. and James H. Barrett (2012), "The Maritime Economy: Fish Bone," in James H. Barrett (ed.), *Being an Islander: Production and Identity at Quoygrew, Orkney, AD 900–1600*, 115–38, Cambridge: MacDonald Institute.

Harley, John B. and David Woodward, eds. (1987), *The History of Cartography*, vol. 1, *Cartography in Prehistoric, Ancient, and Medieval Europe and the Mediterranean*, Chicago: Chicago University Press.

Harley, John B. and David Woodward, eds. (1992), *The History of Cartography*, vol. 2.1, *Cartography in the Traditional Islamic and South Asian Societies*, Chicago: University of Chicago Press.

Harpster, Matthew (2019), "Sicily: A Frontier in the Centre of the Sea?," *Al-Masāq*, 31 (2): 158–70.

Harris, Oliver J.T., Hannah Cobb, Colleen E. Batey, Janet Montgomery, Julia Beaumont, Héléna Gray, Paul Murtagh, and Phil Richardson (2017), "Assembling Places and Persons: A Tenth-Century Viking Boat Burial from Swordle Bay on the Ardnamurchan Peninsula, Western Scotland," *Antiquity*, 91: 191–206.

Harvey, P. (2014), "Amber," in Ian Russell and Maurice Hurley (eds)., *Woodstown*, 285–7, Dublin: Four Courts.

Hassan, Naglaa Saad M. (2014), "The Sea," in John Andrew Morrow (ed.), *Islamic Images and Ideas: Essays on Sacred Symbolism*, 132–8. Jefferson, NC: McFarland.

Hassig, Ross (2006), *Mexico and the Spanish Conquest*, 2nd edn., Norman: Oklahoma University Press.

Hattendorf, John B. (2012), "Maritime History Today," *Perspectives on History*, February 1. Available online: https://www.historians.org/publications-and-directories/perspectives-on-history/february-2012/maritime-history-today (accessed October 20, 2020).

Hau'ofa, Epeli (2008), *We Are the Ocean: Selected Works*, Honolulu: University of Hawai'i Press.

Hayward, Philip (2012), "Aquapelagos and Aquapelagic Assemblages," *Shima: The International Journal of Research into Island Cultures*, 6 (1): 1–11.

Hegel, Georg Wilhelm Friedrich (1970), *Vorlesungen über die Philosophie der Geschichte*, ed. Eva Moldenhauer and Karl Markus Michel, Frankfurt: Suhrkamp.
Heim, Otto (2017), "Island Logic and the Decolonization of the Pacific," *Interventions*, 19 (7): 914–29.
Helms, Mary (1993), *Craft and the Kingly Ideal: Art, Trade and Power*, Austin: University of Texas Press.
Henderson, Julian (2016), *Ancient Glass*, Cambridge: Cambridge University Press.
Heng, Geraldine (2019), "An Ordinary Ship and Its Stories of Early Globalism," *Journal of Medieval Worlds*, 1: 11–54.
Hiatt, Alfred (2016), "From Pliny to Brexit: Spatial Representation of the British Isles," *Postmedieval: A Journal of Medieval Cultural Studies*, 7 (4): 511–25.
Hilberg, Volker and Sven Kalmring (2014), "Viking Age Hedeby and Its Relations with Iceland and the North Atlantic," in Davide Zori and Jesse Byock (eds.), *Viking Archaeology in Iceland*, 221–45, Turnhout: Brepols.
Hinkkanen, Merja-Liisa and David Kirby (2013), *The Baltic and the North Seas*, London: Routledge.
Hofmann, Catherine, Hélène Richard, and Emmanuelle Vagnon, eds. (2012), *L'âge d'or des cartes marines: Quand l'Europe découvrait le monde*, Paris: BnF/Seuil.
Hogendorn, Jan and Marion Johnson (1986), *The Shell Money of the Slave Trade*, Cambridge: Cambridge University Press.
Holm, Poul (1986), "The Slave Trade of Dublin," *Peritia*, 5: 317–45.
Holod, Renata and Tareq Kahlaoui (2019), "Guarding a Well-Ordered Space on a Mediterranean Island," in A. Asa Eger (ed.), *The Archaeology of Medieval Islamic Frontiers: From the Mediterranean to the Caspian Sea*, Louisville: University Press of Colorado.
Holt, Peter (1995), *Early Mamluk Diplomacy (1260–1290)*, Leiden: Brill.
Hoogervorst, T. and Nicole Boivin (2018), "Invisible Agents of Eastern Trade: Foregrounding Southeast Asian Agency in Pre-modern Globalisation," in N. Boivin and M. Franchetti (eds.), *Globalisation and the People Without History*, 205–31, Cambridge: Cambridge University Press.
Hope, Sebastian (2002), *Outcasts of the Islands: The Sea Gypsies of Southeast Asia*, Bangkok: Flamingo.
Horden, Peregrine and Nicholas Purcell (2000), *The Corrupting Sea: A Study of Mediterranean History*, Oxford: Blackwell.
Hornell, James (1942), "The Indian Chank in Folklore and Religion," *Folklore*, 53: 113–25.
Horton, Mark (1987), "The Swahili Corridor," *Scientific American*, 257: 86–93.
Horton, Mark (1994), "Swahili Architecture, Space and Social Structure," in Michael Parker Pearson and Colin Richards (eds.), *Architecture and Order*, 147–69, London: Routledge.
Horton, Mark (1996), *Shanga: The Archaeology of a Muslim Trading Community on the Coast of East Africa*, London: British Institute in Eastern Africa.
Horton, Mark and Catherine Clark (1985), *Survey of Zanzibar*, Zanzibar: Department of Archives, Museums and Antiquities.
Horton, Mark and John Middleton (2000), *The Swahili*, Oxford: Blackwell.
Horton, Mark and Nina Mudida (1993), "Exploitation of Marine Resources: Evidence for the Origin of the Swahili Communities of East Africa," in Thurstan Shaw, Paul Sinclair, Bassey Andah, and Alex Okpoko (eds.), *Archaeology of Africa: Food, Metals, and Towns*, 673–93, London: Routledge.

Hourani, George F. (1995), *Arab Seafaring in the Indian Ocean in Ancient and Early Medieval Tmes*, 2nd edn., ed. John Carswell, Princeton, NJ: Princeton University Press.

Howard, Robert E. (1936), "The Hyborian Age," *The Phantagraph*, February–August, October–November. Available online: http://www.gutenberg.org/files/42182/42182-h/42182-h.htm (accessed December 3, 2019).

Hreidarsdóttir, Elín (2014), "Beads from Hrísbrú and Their Wider Icelandic Context," in Davide Zori and Jesse Byock (eds.), *Viking Archaeology in Iceland*, 135–41, Turnhout: Brepols.

Huffman, Joseph (1998), *Family, Commerce and Religion in London and Cologne*, Cambridge: Cambridge University Press.

Hunt, Lucy-Anne (2015), "John of Ibelin's Audience Hall in Beirut," in Michael Featherstone, Jean-Michel Spieser, and Gülru Thnman, (eds.), *The Emperor's House: Palaces from Augustus to the Age of Absolutism*, 257–91, Boston: De Gruyter.

Inglis, Douglas (2014), "The Sea Stories and Stone Sails of Borobudur," in H. Van Tilburg, S. Tripati, V. Walker Vadillo, B. Fahy, and J. Kimura (eds.), *Proceedings of the 2014 Asia-Pacific Regional Conference on Underwater Cultural Heritage.The Mua Collection*. Available online: http://www.themua.org/collections/items/show/1637 (accessed October 19, 2020).

Ingrem, C. (2005), "The Sea: 1 Fish," in Niall Sharples (ed.), *A Norse Farmstead in the Outer Hebrides: Excavations at Mound 3, Bornais, South Uist*, 157–8, Oxford: Oxbow.

Insoll, Timothy (2003), *The Archaeology of Islam in Sub-Saharan Africa*, New York: Cambridge University Press.

Institut du Monde Arabe and MUCEM (2016), *Aventuriers des mers, VIIe-XVIIe siècle: De Sindbad à Marco Polo; Méditerranée-océan Indien*, Paris: Hazan.

Ivakin, Hlib, Nikita Khrapunov, and Werner Seibt, eds. (2015), *Byzantine and Rus' Seals* [*Vizantiis'ki ta davn'orus'ki pechatky*], Kiev: Sheremetievs' Museum.

Jacoby, David (2000), "Byzantine Trade with Egypt from the Mid-Tenth Century to the Fourth Crusade," *Thesaurismata*, 30: 25–77.

Jacoby, David (2019), "After the Fourth Crusade," in Jonathan Shepard (ed.), *The Cambridge History of the Byzantine Empire, c.500–1492*, rev. edn., 759–78, Cambridge: Cambridge University Press.

James-Raoul, Danièle (2006), "L'écriture de la tempête en mer dans la littérature de fiction, de pèlerinage et de voyage," in Chantal Connochie-Bourgne (ed.), *Mondes marins du Moyen Âge: Actes du 30ème colloque du CUER-MA, 3,4 et 5 mars 2005*, 217–29, Aix-en-Provence: Presses universitaires de Provence.

James-Raoul, Danièle and Claude Thomasset, eds. (2002), *Dans l'eau, sous l'eau. Le monde aquatique au Moyen Âge*, Paris: Presses de l'Université de Paris-Sorbonne.

Jašaeva, Tatjana (2010), "Pilgerandenken im byzantinischen Cherson," in Falko Daim and Jörg Drauschke (eds.), *Byzanz – das Romerreich im Mittlelalter*, vol. 2, 479–91, Mainz: RGZM.

Jaspert, Nikolas and Sebastian Kolditz (2018), "Entre mers—Outre-mer: An Introduction," in Nikolas Jaspert and Sebastian Kolditz (eds.), *Entre Mers—Outre-Mer: Spaces, Modes and Agents of Indo-Mediterranean Connectivity*, 7–30. Heidelberg: Heidelberg University Publishing.

Johns, Dilys A., Geoffrey J. Irwin, and Yun K. Sung (2014), "An Early Sophisticated East Polynesian Voyaging Canoe Discovered on New Zealand's Coast," *Proceedings of the National Academy of Sciences of the United States of America*, 111 (41): 14728–33.

Jolly, Margaret (2001), "On the Edge? Deserts, Oceans, Islands," *Contemporary Pacific*, 13 (2): 417–66.

Jones, Gwyn (1984), *A History of the Vikings*, 2nd edn., Oxford: Oxford University Press.

Jones, Gwyn (1986), *The Norse Atlantic Saga*, 2nd edn., Oxford: Oxford University Press.

Kalligas, Harris A. (2010), *Monemvasia: A Byzantine City State*, London: Routledge.

Kalus, Ludvik and Claude Guillot (2005), "Inscriptions islamiques en arabe de l'archipel des Maldives," *Archipel*, 70: 15–52.

Kammerer, Albert (1929–35), *La Mer Rouge, l'Abyssinie et l'Arabie depuis l'Antiquité. Essai d'histoire et de géographie historique*, 2 vols, Cairo: Institut français d'archéologie orientale du Caire and Société royale de géographie d'Égypte.

Kauz, Ralph, ed. (2010), *Aspects of the Maritime Silk Road*, Wiesbaden: Harrassowitz.

Kawai, Hayao (1995), *Dreams, Myths and Fairy Tales in Japan*, Einseideln: Daimon.

Kelly, J.E., Jr. (1979), "Non-Mediterranean Influences that Shaped the Atlantic in the Early Portulan Charts," *Imago Mundi*, 31: 18–35.

Khalilieh, Hassan S. (2010), "An Overview of the Slaves' Juridical Status at Sea in Romano-Byzantine and Islamic Laws," in Roxani Eleni Margariti, Adam Sabra, and Petra Sijpesteijn (eds.), *Histories of the Middle East: Middle Eastern Society, Economy and Law in Honor of A.L. Udovitch*, 73–100, Leiden: Brill.

King, D.A. (1991), "Maṭla'," in C.E. Bosworth, E. van Donzel, B. Lewis, P. Heinrichs, and Ch. Pellat (eds.), *Encyclopedia of Islam*, 2nd edn., vol. 6, 839–40, Leiden: Brill.

Kinoshita, Sharon (2006), *Medieval Boundaries: Rethinking Difference in Old French Literature*. Philadelphia: University of Pennsylvania Press.

Kinoshita, Sharon (2014), "Mediterranean Literature," in Peregrine Horden and Sharon Kinoshita (eds.), *A Companion to Mediterranean History*, 314–29, Oxford: Wiley-Blackwell.

Kirch, Patrick Vinton (2000), *On the Road of the Winds: An Archaeological History of the Pacific Islands Before European Contact*, Berkeley: University of California Press.

Kirkman, James (1964), *Men and Monuments on the East African Coast*, London: Lutterworth.

Kleppe, E. (2001), "Archaeological Investigations at Kizimkazi Dimbani," in Biancamaria Scarcia Amoretti (ed.), *Islam in East Africa: New Sources*, International Colloquium, Rome, December 2–4, 1999, 361–84, Rome: Herder.

Kloff, Dirk H.A. (1990) *Naukar, Rajput and Sepoy: The Ethnohistory of the Military Labour Market in Hindustan, 1450–1850*, Cambridge: Cambridge University Press.

Kowaleski, Maryanne (2010), "The Seasonality of Fishing in Medieval Britain," in Scott Bruce (ed.), *Ecologies and Economies in Medieval and Early Modern Europe: Studies in Environmental History for Richard C. Hoffman*, 113–45, Leiden: Brill.

Krahl, Regina, John Guy, J. Keith Wilson, and Julian Raby, eds. (2010), *Shipwrecked: Tang Treasures and Monsoon Winds*, Washington, DC: Arthur M. Sackler Gallery; Singapore: National Heritage Board of Singapore, and the Singapore Tourism Board.

Kramer, Philipp (1919), *Das Meer in der altfranzösischen Literatur*, Giessen: Christ and Herr.

Lai, Yu-chih (2014), "Historicity, Visuality and Patterns of Literati Transcendence: Picturing the Red Cliff," in Shane McCausland and Yin Hwang (eds.), *On Telling Images of China: Essays in Narrative Painting and Visual Culture*, 177–212, Hong Kong: Hong Kong University Press.

Lambert, Andrew, John Beeler, Barry Strauss, and J. Hattendorf (2010), "The Neglected Field of Naval History? A Forum," *Historically Speaking*, 11 (4): 9–19.

Lambourn, Elizabeth (2008), "India from Aden – Khutba and Muslim Urban Networks in Late Thirteenth-Century India," in Kenneth Hall (ed.), *Secondary Cities and Urban Networking in the Indian Ocean Realm, c. 1400–1800*, 55–97, Lanham, MD: Lexington Books.

Lambourn, Elizabeth (2016a), "Describing a Lost Camel – Clues for West Asian mercantile networks in South Asian maritime trade (Tenth–Twelfth centuries CE)," in Marie-Françoise Boussac, Jean-François Salles, and Jean-Baptiste Yon (eds.), *Harbours of the Indian Ocean: Proceedings of the Kolkata Colloquium 2011 (Median Project)*, 351–407, Delhi: Primus Books.

Lambourn, Elizabeth (2016b), "Towards a Connected History of Equine Cultures in South Asia - *bahrī* (Sea) Horses and 'Horsemania' in Thirteenth Century South India," *Medieval Globe*, 2 (1): 57–100.

Lambourn, Elizabeth (2018), *Abraham's Luggage: A Social Life of Things in the Medieval Indian Ocean World*, Cambridge: Cambridge University Press.

Lane, Paul J. and Colin P. Breen (2018), "The Eastern African Coastal Landscape," in Stephanie Wynne-Jones and Adria LaViolette (eds.), *The Swahili World*, 19–35, London: Routledge.

Lauri, Marco (2013), "Utopias in the Islamic Middle Ages: Ibn Tufayl and Ibn al-Nafis," *Uttopian Studies*, 24 (1): 23–40.

Lave, Jean (1991), "Situating Learning in Communities of Practice," *Perspectives on Socially Shared Cognition*, 2: 63–82.

Lavezzo, Kathy (2006), *Angels on the Edge of the World. Geography, Literature, and English Community, 1000–1534*, Ithaca, NY: Cornell University Press.

Lawrie, Margaret Elizabeth (1972), *Myths and Legends of the Torres Strait*, Brisbane: University of Queensland Press.

Leclercq-Marx, Jacqueline (2006), "L'idée d'un monde marin parallèle du monde terrestre. Émergence et développements," in Chantal Connochie-Bourgne (ed.), *Mondes marins du Moyen Age*, 259–71, Aix-en-Provence: Presses universitaires de Provence.

Leclercq-Marx, Jacqueline (2017), "Formes et figures de l'imaginaire marin dans le haut Moyen Âge et dans le Moyen Âge central," in "L'art roman et la mer," special issue of *Les cahiers de Saint-Michel de Cuxa*, 48: 9–22.

Leclercq-Marx, Jacqueline, ed. (1997), *La sirène dans la pensée et dans l'art de l'Antiquité et du Moyen Âge: Du mythe païen au symbole chrétien*, Brussels: Académie royale de Belgique. Available online: http://www.koregos.org/fr/jacqueline-leclercq-marx-la-sirene-dans-la-pensee-et-dans-l-art-de-l-antiquite-et-du-moyen-age/4389/#chapitre_4389 (accessed October 19, 2020).

Ledyard, Gari (1994), "Cartography in Korea," in John B. Harley and David Woodward (eds.), *The History of Cartography*, vol. 2–2, *Cartography in the Traditional East and South-East Asian Societies*, 235–345, Chicago: University of Chicago Press.

Le Goff, Jacques (1977), "L'Occident médiéval et l'océan Indien: un horizon onirique," in *Pour un autre Moyen Age: Temps, travail et culture en Occident: 18 essais*, 280–98, Paris: Gallimard.
Legrand, Emile (1897), *Description des îles de l'Archipel par Christophe Buondelmonti: Version grecque par un anonyme publiée d'après le manuscrit du Sérail, avec une traduction française et un commentaire*, Paris: E. Leroux.
Leont'ev, Aleksei N. and E.N. Nosov (2012), "Vostochnoevropeiskie puti soobshcheniia i torgovye sviazi v kontse VIII–X v." [Eastern European Routes and Trade Ties, End of the Eighth to Tenth Century], in Nikolai A. Makarov (ed.), *Rus' v IX–X vekakh* [Rus in the Ninth to Tenth Century], 382–401, Moscow: Drevnosti Severa.
Lerner, Michael (1985), *The Flame and the Lotus: Indian and Southeast Asian Art from the Kronos Collections*, New York: Metropolitan Museum of Art.
Lev, Yaacov (1984), "The Fatimid Navy, Byzantium, and the Mediterranean Sea, 996–1036," *Byzantion*, 54: 220–52.
Lewis, David (1994), *We, the Navigators: The Ancient Art of Landfinding in the Pacific*, 2nd edn., Honolulu: University of Hawaii Press.
Lewis, Martin W. (1999), "Dividing the Ocean Sea," *Geographical Review*, 89 (2): 188–214.
Leys, Simon (2003), *La mer dans la literature française*, Paris: Plon.
Linton, Jamie and Jessica Budds (2014), "The Hydrosocial Cycle: Defining and Mobilizing a Relational-Dialectical Approach to Water," *Geoforum*, 57: 170–80.
Llenín-Figueroa, Carmen Beatriz (2012), "Imagined Islands: A Caribbean Tidalectics," unpublished PhD diss., Duke University, Durham, NC, USA.
Lo, Jung-pang (1955), "The Emergence of China as a Sea Power during the Late Sung and Early Yuan Periods," *Far Eastern Quarterly*, 14 (4): 489–503.
Lo, Jung-pang (1969), "Maritime Commerce and its Relation to the Sung Navy," *Journal of the Economic and Social History of the Orient*, 12 (1): 57–100.
Lo, Jung-pang (2012), *China as a Sea Power, 1127–1368: A Preliminary Survey of the Maritime Expansion and Naval Exploits of the Chinese People During the Southern Song and Yuan Periods*, ed. and commented by Bruce A. Elleman, Singapore: National University of Singapore Press.
Lombard, Denys (1990), *Le carrefour javanais*, vol. 2, Paris: Éditions EHESS.
Long, Pamela O., David McGee, and Alan M. Stahl, eds. (2009), *The Book of Michael of Rhodes: A Fifteenth-Century Maritime Manuscript*, vol. 3, *Studies*, Cambridge, MA: MIT Press.
Lukin, Pavel (2014), *Novgorodskoe veche* [The Novgorodian Assembly], Moscow: Akademicheskii proekt.
Lunde, Paul (2013), "Sailing Times in Sulaymān al-Mahrī," in Anthony R. Constable and William Facey (eds.), *The Principles of Arab Navigation*, 75–82, London: Arabian Publishing.
Luo, Bin and Adam Grydehøj (2017), "Sacred Islands and Island Symbolism in Ancient and Imperial China: An Exercise in Decolonial Island Studies," *Island Studies Journal*, 12 (2): 25–44.
Mack, John (2011), *The Sea: A Cultural History*, London: Reaktion Books.
Mack, Merav (2018), "Genoa and the Crusades," in Carrie Beneš (ed.), *A Companion to Medieval Genoa*, 471–95, Leiden: Brill.
Maeda, Robert J. (1971) "The 'Water' Theme in Chinese Painting," *Artibus Asiae*, 33: 247–61.

Magdalino, Paul (2000), "Maritime Neighborhoods of Constantinople," *Dumbarton Oaks Papers*, 54: 209–26.
Magdalino, Paul (2007), "Isaac II, Saladin and Venice," in Jonathan Shepard (ed.), *The Expansion of Orthodox Europe*, 93–106, Farnham: Ashgate.
Magnavita, Sonja (2013), "Initial encounters," *Afriques*, 4. Available online: https://doi.org/10.4000/afriques.1145.
Mapping Our World: Terra Incognita to Australia (2013), [Exhibition Catalog], Canberra: National Library of Australia.
Margariti, Roxani Eleni (2007), *Aden and the Indian Ocean Trade: 150 Years in the Life of a Medieval Arabian Port*, Chapel Hill: University of North Carolina Press.
Margariti, Roxani Elani (2008), "Mercantile Networks, Port Cities, and 'Pirate' States: Conflict and Competition in the Indian Ocean World of Trade before the Sixteenth Century," *Journal of the Economic and Social History of the Orient*, 51: 543–77.
Margariti, Roxani Eleni (2015), "Wrecks and Texts: a Judeo-Arabic Case Study," in Deborah N. Carlson, Justin Leidwanger, and Sarah M. Kampbell (eds.), *Maritime Studies in the Wake of the Byzantine Shipwreck at Yassiada Turkey*, 189–201, College Station: Texas A&M University Press.
Marie de France (1990), *Lais de Marie de France*, ed. Karl Warnke, Lettres Gothiques, Paris: Livre de Poche.
Martinsson-Wallin, Helene and Susan J. Crockford (2001), "Early Settlement of Rapa Nui (Easter Island)," *Asian Perspectives*, 40 (1): 244–78.
Mauntel, Christopher (2018), "Linking Seas and Lands in Medieval Geographic Thinking during the Crusades and the Discovery of the Atlantic World," in Nikolas Jaspert and Sebastian Kolditz (eds.), *Entre mers—Outre-mer: Spaces, Modes and Agents of Indo-Mediterranean Connectivity*, 107–28, Heidelberg: Heidelberg University Publishing.
Mauntel, Christopher, Klaus Oschema, Jean-Charles Ducène, and Martin Hofmann (2018), "Mapping Continents, Inhabited Quarters and The Four Seas. Divisions of the World and the Ordering of Spaces in Latin-Christian, Arabic-Islamic and Chinese Cartography in the Twelfth to Sixteenth Centuries: A Critical Survey and Analysis," *Journal of Transcultural Medieval Studies*, 5 (2): 295–367.
Mayr-Harting, Henry (1992), "The Church of Magdeburg," in David Abulafia, Michael Franklin, and Miri Rubin (eds.), *Church and the City 1000–1500*, 129–50, Cambridge: Cambridge University Press.
McClanahan, T.R. and J.O. Omukoto (2011), "Comparison of Modern and Historical Fish Catches (AD750–1400) to Inform Goals for Marine Protected Areas and Sustainable Fisheries," *Conservation Biology*, 25 (5): 945–55.
McCormick, Michael (2001), *Origins of the European Economy*, Cambridge: Cambridge University Press.
McCormick, Michael (2011), *Charlemagne's Survey of the Holy Land*, Washington, DC: Dumbarton Oaks.
McCusker, Maeve and Anthony Soares (2011), *Islanded Identities: Constructions of Postcolonial Cultural Insularity*, Amsterdam: Rodopi.
McIntosh, Roderick and Susan McIntosh (1981), "The Inland Niger Delta before the Empire of Mali," *Journal of African History*, 22: 1–22.
McKillop, Heather (2005), *In Search of Maya Sea Traders*, College Station: Texas A&M.
Mehler, Natascha, Hans Christian Küchelmann, and Bart Holterman (2018), "The Export of Gyrfalcons from Iceland during the 16th Century: A Boundless Business

in a Proto-globalized World," in Karl-Heinz Gersmann and Oliver Grimm (eds.), *Raptor and Human – Falconry and Bird Symbolism throughout the Millennia on a Global Scale*, 995–1020, Kiel: Wachholtz Verlag-Murmann Publishers.

Mel'nikova, Elena (2001), *Skandinavskie runicheskie nadpisi* [Scandinavian Runic Inscriptions], rev. edn., Moscow: Vostochnaia literatura RAN.

Mentz, Steven (2009), "Toward a Blue Cultural Studies: The Sea, Maritime Culture, and Early Modern English Literature," *Literature Compass*, 6: 997–1013.

Mentz, Steven (2016), "The Bermuda Assemblage: Toward a Posthuman Globalization," *Postmedieval: A Journal of Medieval Cultural Studies*, 7 (4): 551–64.

Miller, James (2008), "Traditional Fishing Boats," in James R. Coull, Alexander Fenton, and Kenneth Veitch (eds.), *Scottish Life and Society: A Compendium of Scottish Ethnology, Boats, Fishing and the Sea*, 103–23, Edinburgh: John Donald.

Miller, Peter N., ed. (2013), *The Sea: Thalassography and Historiography*, Ann Arbor: University of Michigan Press.

Milner, Nicky and James Barrett (2012), "The Maritime Economy: Mollusc Shell," in James Barrett (ed.), *Being an Islander: Production and Identity at Quoygrew, Orkney, AD 900–1600*, 105–15, Cambridge: McDonald Institute for Archaeological Research.

Miquel, André (1967–88), *La géographie humaine du monde musulman jusqu'au milieu du XIe siècle*, Paris: Mouton.

Miran, Jonathan (2009), *Red Sea Citizens: Cosmopolitan Society and Cultural Change in Massawa*, Bloomington: Indiana University Press.

Moerman, D. Max (forthcoming), *Geographies of the Imagination: Buddhism and the Japanese World Map 1364–1865*, Cambridge, MA: Harvard University Asia Center.

Montgomery, James E. (2001), "Salvation at Sea? Seafaring in Early Arabic Poetry," in Gert Borg and Ed C.M. de Moor (eds.), *Representations of the Divine in Arabic Poetry*, 25–47, Amsterdam: Rodopoi.

Most, Ruth (2011), *"Dividing the Realm in Order to Govern": The Spatial Organisation of the Song State (960–1276 CE)*, Cambridge, MA: Harvard University Press.

Mostert, Michael (2020), "Linguistics of Contact in the Northern Seas," in Rolf Strootman, Floris van den Eijnde, and Roy van Wijk (eds.), *Empires of the Sea: Maritime Power Networks in World History*, 179–93, Leiden: Brill.

Msemwa, P.J. (1994), "An Ethnoarchaeological Study on Shellfish Collecting in a Complex Urban Setting," unpublished PhD diss., Brown University, USA.

Mudida, Nina (1996), "Subsistence at Shanga: The Faunal Record," in Mark Horton (ed.), *Shanga: The Archaeology of a Muslim Trading Community on the Coast of East Africa*, 378–93, London: British Institute in Eastern Africa.

Muir, Tom and James M. Irvine (2005), *George Marwick: Yesnaby's Master Storyteller*, Kirkwall: Orcadian.

Mukherjee, Rila (2014), "Escape from Terracentrism: Writing a Water History," *Indian Historical Review*, 41 (1): 87–101.

Murasheva, Veronika (forthcoming), "Rus, Routes and Sites," in Jonathan Shepard and Luke Treadwell (eds.), *Muslims on the Volga in the Viking Age: Diplomacy and Islam in the World of Ibn Fadlan*, London: I.B.Tauris.

Muthesius, Anna (1997), *Byzantine Silk Weaving*, Vienna: Fassbaender.

Nakamura, Hiroshi (1947), "Old Chinese World Maps Preserved by the Koreans," *Imago Mundi*, 4: 3–22.

Nakamura, Ryo (2011), "Multi-ethnic Coexistence in Kilwa Island, Tanzania," *Shima: The International Journal of Research into Island Cultures*, 5 (1): 44–68.

Nanda, Vivek and Alexander Johnson (2017), *Cosmology to Cartography: A Cultural Journey of Indian Maps*, New Delhi: National Museum, Kalakriti Archives.

Nedkvitne, Arnved (2014), *The German Hansa and Bergen 1100–1600*, Cologne: Böhlau Verlag GmbH & Cie.

Needham, Joseph ([1959] 1979), "Geography and Cartography," in *Science and Civilization in China*, vol. 3, *Mathematics and the Sciences of the Heaves and the Earth*, 497–590, Cambridge: Cambridge University Press.

Needham, Joseph, Wang Ling, and Lu Gwei-Djen (1971), *Science and Civilization in China*, vol. 4, *Physics and Physical Technology: Part III Civil Engineering and Nautics*, Cambridge: Cambridge University Press.

Needham, Stuart (2009), "Encompassing the Sea: 'Maritories' and Bronze Age Maritime Interactions," in Philip Clark (ed.), *Bronze Age Connections: Cultural Contact in Prehistoric Europe*, 12–37, Oxford: Oxbow.

Negri, Carolina and Giusi Tamburello, eds. (2009), *L'acqua non è mai la stessa. Le acque nella tradizione culturale dell'Asia. Atti del seminario, Lecce, 18 aprile 2007*, Milan: Leo Olschki Editore.

Nicholson, Rebecca A. (2007), "The Fish Remains," in John Hunter (ed.), *Investigations in Sanday, Orkney*, vol. 1, *Excavations at Pool, Sanday: A Multi-period Settlement from Neolithic to Late Norse Times*, 262–79, Kirkwall: Orcadian.

Nicolle, David (1989), "Shipping in Islamic Art: Seventh through Tenth Centuries A.D.," *American Neptune*, 49 (3): 168–97.

Noacco, Cristina (2006), "La surface métaphorique de la mer dans le *Livre de pensée* de Charles d'Orléans," in Chantal Connochie-Bourgne (ed.), *Mondes marins du Moyen Age*, 341–51, Aix-en-Provence: Presses universitaires de Provence.

Noonan, Thomas and Roman Kovalev (1997–8), "'Wine and Oil for All the Rus!'," *Acta Byzantina Fennica*, 9: 118–52.

Nosov, Evgenii N. (2012), "Novgorodskaia zemlia" [The Novgorodian Land], in Nikolai A. Makarov (ed.), *Rus' v IX–X vekakh*, 93–113, Moscow: Drevnosti Severa.

O'Doherty, Marianne (2011), "A Peripheral Matter? Oceans in the East in Late Medieval Thought: Report and Cartography," in Liz Mylod and Zsuzsanna Reed Papp (eds.), "Postcards from the Edge: European Peripheries in the Middle Ages," special issue of *Bulletin of International Medieval Research*, 16: 14–59.

O'Doherty, Marianne (2013), *The Indies and the Medieval West: Thought, Report, Imagination*, Turnhout: Brepols.

Ohler, Norbert (2010), *The Medieval Traveller*, trans. Caroline Hillier, rev. edn., Woodbridge: Boydell.

Oliver, Roland and Anthony Atmore (2001), *Medieval Africa, 1250–1800*, Cambridge: Cambridge University Press.

Orbell, Margaret (1991), *Hawaiki: A New Approach to Maori Tradition*, Christchurch: Canterbury University Press.

Orton, David, James Morris, Alison Locker, and James H. Barrett (2014), "Fish for the City: Meta-analysis of Archaeological Cod Remains and the Growth of London's Northern Trade," *Antiquity*, 88 (340): 516–30.

Östergren, Majvor (2009), "Spillings," in Ann-Marie Pettersson (ed.), *The Spillings Hoard*, 11–40, Visby: Gotlands Museum.

Owen, Olwyn and Magnar Dalland, (1999), *Scar: A Viking Boat Burial on Sanday, Orkney*, Phantassie: Tuckwell Press.

Paine, Lincoln (2013), *The Sea and Civilization: A Maritime History of the World*, New York: Alfred A. Knopf.

Palmer, Martin and Xiaomin Zhao (1997), *Essential Chinese Mythology*, London: Thorsons.

Park, Hyunhee (2012), *Mapping the Chinese and Islamic Worlds: Cross-Cultural Exchange in Pre-Modern Asia*, New York: Cambridge University Press.
Parrain, Camille (2012), "La haute mer: un espace aux frontières de la recherche géographique," *EchoGéo*, 19 (January/March). Available online: https://doi.org/10.4000/echogeo.12929.
Parry, John Horace (1981), *The Discovery of the Sea*, Berkeley: University of California Press.
Peacock, David and David Williams, eds. (2007), *Food for the Gods*, Oxford: Oxbow.
Peacock D. and L. Blue, eds. (2011), *Myos Hormos – Quseir al-Qadim: Roman and Islamic Ports on the Red Sea*, Oxford: British Archaeological Reports.
Pearson, Michael (2003), *The Indian Ocean: Seas in History*, London: Routledge.
Perdikaris, Sophia and Thomas Howatt McGovern (2008), "Codfish and Kings, Seals and Subsistence: Norse Marine Resource use in the North Atlantic," in Torben C. Rick and Jon M. Erlandson (eds.), *Human impacts on Ancient Marine Ecosystems: A Global Perspective*, 187–214, Berkeley: University of California Press.
Perdikaris, Sophia and Thomas Howatt McGovern (2009), "Viking Age Economics and the Origins of Commercial Cod Fisheries in the North Atlantic," in Louis Sicking and Darlene Abreu-Ferreira (eds.), *Beyond the Catch: Fisheries of the North Atlantic, the North Sea and the Baltic, 900–1850*, 61–90, Leiden: Brill.
Perry, W.J. (1921), "The Isles of the Blest," *Folklore*, 32: 150–80.
Peters, F.E. (1994), *Mecca: A Literary History of the Muslim Holy Land*, Princeton, NJ: Princeton University Press.
Phillips, Jonathan (2004), *The Fourth Crusade and the Sack of Constantinople*, London: Jonathan Cape.
Picard, Christophe (2015), *La mer des califes: Une histoire de la Méditerranée musulmane*, Paris: Seuil.
Picard, Christophe (2018), *Sea of the Caliphs: The Mediterranean in the Medieval Islamic World*, Cambridge, MA: Belknap Press of Harvard University Press.
Pillsbury, Joanne (1996), "The Thorny Oyster and the Origins of Empire: Implications of Recently Uncovered Spondylus Imagery from Chan Chan, Peru," *Latin American Antiquity*, 7 (4): 313–40.
Pillsbury, Joanne, Timophy Potts, and Kim N. Richter, eds. (2017), *Golden Kingdoms: Luxury Arts in the Ancient Americas*, Los Angeles: J. Paul Getty Trust.
Pinet, Simone (2011), *Archipelagoes: Insular Fictions from Chivalric Romance to the Novel*, Minneapolis: University of Minnesota Press.
Pinto, Karen C. (2013), "Passion and Conflict: Medieval Islamic Views of the West," in Keith D. Lilley (ed.), *Mapping Medieval Geographies: Geographical Encounters in the Latin West and Beyond, 300–1600*, 201–24, Cambridge: Cambridge University Press.
Pinto, Karen C. (2016), *Medieval Islamic Maps: An Exploration*, Chicago: University of Chicago Press.
Pirenne, Henri (1937), *Mahomet et Charlemagne*, Paris: Alcan.
de Planhol, Xavier (2000), *L'Islam et la mer: la mosquée et le matelot, viie-xxe siècle*, Paris: Librairie académique Perrin.
Pouwels, Randall (1984), "Oral Historiography and the Shirazi of the East African Coast," *History in Africa*, 11: 237–67.
Prange, Sebastian R. (2013), "The Contested Sea: Regimes of Maritime Violence in the Pre-Modern Indian Ocean," *Journal of Early Modern History*, 17: 9–33.
Prange, Sebastian R. (2018), *Monsoon Islam: Trade and Faith on the Medieval Malabar Coast*, Cambridge: Cambridge University Press.

Preiser-Kapeller, Johannes (2015), "Harbours and Maritime Networks as Complex Adaptive Systems," in Johannes Preiser-Kapeller and Falko Daim (eds.), *Harbours and Maritime Networks as Complex Adaptive Systems*, 1–24, Mainz: RGZM.

Prendergast, Mary E., Hélène Rouby, Paramita Punnwong, Robert Marchant, Alison Crowther, Nikos Kourampas, Ceri Shipton, Martin Walsh, Kurt Lambeck, and Nicole L. Boivin (2016), "Continental Island Formation and the Archaeology of Defaunation on Zanzibar, Eastern Africa," *PLOS One*, 11 (2): e0149565.

Price, Neil (forthcoming), "Vikings on the Volga?," in Jonathan Shepard and Luke Treadwell (eds.), *Muslims on the Volga in the Viking Age*, London: I.B.Tauris.

Prins, A.H.J. (1965), *Sailing from Lamu: A Study of Maritime Culture in Islamic East Africa*, Assen: Van Gorcum.

Ptak, Roderich (1987), "The Maldive and Laccadive Islands (liu-shan 溜 山) in Ming Records," *Journal of the American Oriental Society*, 107 (4): 675–94.

Ptak, Roderich (2007a), "Edward L. Dreyer: *Zheng He: China and the Oceans in the Early Ming Dynasty, 1405–14*," *Archipel*, 74: 256–60.

Ptak, Roderich (2007b), *Die Maritime Seidenstrasse: Küstenräume, Seefahrt und Handel in vorkolonialer Zeit*, Munich: C.H. Beck.

Pugh, Jonathan (2013), "Island Movements: Thinking with the Archipelago," *Island Studies Journal*, 8 (1): 9–24.

Pujades I Bataller, Ramon (2007), *Les Cartes Portolanes: La representació medieval d'una mar solcada*, Barcelona: Institut Cartogràfic de Catalunya.

Purcell, Nicholas (2005), "Colonization and Mediterranean History," in Henry Hurst and Sara Owen (eds.), *Ancient Colonizations: Analogy, Similarity and Difference*, London: Duckworth.

Purcell, Nicholas (2013), "Beach, Tide and Backwash: The Place of Maritime History," in Peter Miller (ed.), *The Sea: Thalassography and Historiography*, Ann Arbor: University of Michigan Press.

Qaisar, A. Jan (1987), "From Port to Port: Life on Indian Ships in the Sixteenth and Seventeenth Centuries," in Ashin Das Gupta and M.N. Pearson (eds.), *India and the Indian Ocean 1500–1800*, 331–49, Calcutta: Oxford University Press.

Questes Group (2018), *Le bathyscaphe d'Alexandre: L'homme et la mer au Moyen Âge*, Paris: éditions Vendémiaire.

Quintana Morales, Eréndira M. (2013), "Reconstructing Swahili Foodways: The Archaeology of Fishing and Fish Consumption in Coastal East Africa, AD 500–1500," unpublished PhD diss., University of Bristol, UK.

Quintana Morales, Eréndira M. and Mark Horton (2014), "Fishing and Fish Consumption in the Swahili Communities of East Africa, 700–1400 CE," *Internet Archaeology*, 37. Available online: https://doi.org/10.11141/ia.37.3.

Quintana Morales, Eréndira M. and Mary E. Prendergast (2018), "Animals and Their Uses in the Swahili World," in Stephanie Wynne-Jones and Adria LaViolette (eds.), *The Swahili World*, 335–49, London: Routledge.

Radimilahy, Marie de Chantal (1998), *Mahilaka: An Archaeological Investigation of an Early Town in Northwestern Madagascar*, Uppsala: Uppsala University.

Rainbird, Paul (2007), *The Archaeology of Islands*, Cambridge: Cambridge University Press.

Raj, Kapil (2016), "Rescuing Science from Civilization: On Joseph Needham's 'Asiatic Mode of (Knowledge) Production,'" in Arun Bala and Prasenjit Duara (eds.), *The Bright Dark Ages: Rethinking Needham's Grand Question*, 1–22, Leiden: E.J. Brill.

Ramaswamy, Sumathi (2004), *The Lost Land of Lemuria: Fabulous Geographies, Catastrophic Histories*, new edn., Berkeley: University of California Press.

Rao, Nalini (1991), "The Bodhisattva As Savior of Seamen," in S.R. Rao (ed.), *Recent Advance in Maritime Archaeology: Proceedings of the Second Indian Conference on Marine Archaeology of Indian Ocean Countries*, January 1990, 185–8, Goa: Society for Marine Archaeology, National Institute of Archaeology.

Rapoport, Yossef and Emily Savage-Smith (2018), *Lost Maps of the Caliphs: Drawing the World in Eleventh Century Cairo*, Chicago: University of Chicago Press.

Rapoport, Yossef and Emily Savage-Smith, eds. (2014), *An Eleventh Century Egyptian Guide to the Universe: The Book of Curiosities* [Kitāb ġarā'ib al-funūn wa mulaḥ al-'uyūn], Leiden: Brill.

Ray, Himanshu Prabha (1994), *The Winds of Change: Buddhism and the Maritime Links of Early South Asia*, Delhi: Oxford University Press.

Ray, Himanshu Prabha (2003), *The Archaeology of Seafaring in Ancient South Asia*, Cambridge: Cambridge University Press.

Reckin, Anna (2003), "Tidalectic Lectures: Kamau Brathwaite's Prose/Poetry as Sound-Space," *Anthurium*, 1 (1): 1–16.

Reddy, Srinivas G. (2021), "Seven Seas and an Ocean of Wisdom: An Indian Episteme for the Indian Ocean," in Himanshu Prabha Ray (ed.), *The Archaeology of Knowledge Traditions of the Indian Ocean World*, 19–37, Abingdon: Routledge.

Reid, Anthony (2007), "Muslims and Power in a Plural Asia," in Anthony Reid and Michael Gilsenan (eds.), *Islamic Legitimacy in a Plural Asia*, 1–14, London: Routledge.

Relaño, Francesco (2002), *The Shaping of Africa: Cosmographic Discourse and Cartographic Science in Late Medieval and Early Modern Europe*, Aldershot: Ashgate.

Remensnyder, Amy G. (2018), "Mary, Star of the Multi-Confessional Mediterranean: Ships, Shrines and Sailors," in Nikolas Jaspert, Christian A. Neumann, and Marco Di Branco (eds.), *Ein Meer Und Seine Heiligen: Hagiographie Im Mittelalterlichen Mediterraneum*, 299–32, Paderborn: Wilhelm Fink.

Richards, Colin (2008), "The Substance of Polynesian Voyaging," *World Archaeology*, 40 (2): 206–23.

Ridel, Elisabeth (2009), *Les Vikings et les mots*, Paris: Errance.

Riley-Smith, Jonathan (1997), *The First Crusaders, 1095–1131*, Cambridge: Cambridge University Press.

Rivers, P.J. (2012), "New Lamps for Old: Modern Nautical Terms for Ancient Marine Practices and the Navigation of the Zheng He Voyages," *Journal of the Malaysian Branch of the Royal Asiatic Society*, 85 (1): 85–98.

Roach, Andrew (2005), *The Devil's World*, Harlow: Longman.

Rodger, N.A.M. (1996), "The Naval Service of the Cinque Ports," *English Historical Review*, 111 (442): 636–51.

Ronan, Colin A. (1986), *The Shorter Science and Civilization in China: An Abridgement of Joseph Needham's Original Text*, vol. 3, *A Section of Volume IV, Part 1 and a Section of Volume IV, Part 3, or the Major Series*, Cambridge: Cambridge University Press.

Rosedahl, Else (1987), *The Vikings*, London: Allen Lane, the Penguin Press.

Rosiek, Jerry Lee, Jimmy Snyder, and Scott L. Pratt (2020), "The New Materialisms and Indigenous Theories of Non-Human Agency: Making the Case for Respectful Anti-Colonial Engagement," *Qualitative Inquiry*, 26 (3–4): 331–346.

Rubin, Jonathan (2018), *Learning in a Crusader City*, Cambridge: Cambridge University Press.

Rüdiger, Jan (2017), "Medieval Maritime Polities – Some Considerations," in Michel Balard (ed.), *The Sea in History: The Medieval World*, 34–44, Woodbridge: Boydell Press.

Russ, Hannah, Ian Armit, Jo McKenzie, and Andrew K.G. Jones (2012), "Deep-Sea Fishing in Iron Age Scotland? New Evidence from Broxmouth Hillfort, East Lothian," *Environmental Archaeology*, 17 (2): 177–84.

Rust, Martha (2008), *Imaginary Worlds in Medieval Books: Exploring the Manuscript Matrix*, Basingstoke: Palgrave Macmillan.

Sacks, David Harris (2014), "The Blessings of Exchange in the Making of the Early English Atlantic," in Francesca Trivellato, Leor Halevi, and Catia Antunes (eds.), *Religion and Trade: Cross-Cultural Exchanges in World History, 1000–1900*, 62–90, Oxford: Oxford University Press.

Sadhale, Nalini and Y.L. Nene (2005), "On Fish in Manasollasa (c. 1131 AD)," *Asian Agri-History*, 9 (3): 177–99.

Sahlins, Marshall (1985), *Islands of History*, Chicago: University of Chicago Press.

Sather, Clifford (1997), *The Bajau Laut*, Oxford: Oxford University Press.

Saussure, Léopold de ([1923] 1928), "Et l'invention de la boussole," in Gabriel Ferrand (ed.), *Instructions Nautiques et Routiers Arabes et Portugais des XVe et XVIe Siècles*, vol. 3, *Introduction a l'Astonomie Nautique Arabe*, 31–127, Paris: Librairie Orientaliste Paul Geuthner.

Sawyer, Peter (2013), *The Wealth of Anglo-Saxon England*, Oxford: Oxford University Press.

Scales, Len (2012), *The Shaping of German Identity*, Cambridge: Cambridge University Press.

Schmidl, Petra G. (1997–8), "Two Early Arabic Sources on the Magnetic Compass," *Journal of Arabic and Islamic Studies*, 1: 81–132.

Schröder Stefan (2012), "Wissenstransfer und Kartieren von Herrschaft? Zum Verhältnis von Wissen und Macht bei al-Idrisi und Marino Sanudo," in Ingrid Baumgärtner and Martina Stercken (eds.), *Herrschaft verorten. Politische Kartographie des Mittelalters und in der frühen Neuzeit*, 313–34, Zurich: Chronos.

Scott, Michael W. (2012), "The Matter of Makira: Colonialism, Competition, and the Production of Gendered Peoples in Contemporary Solomon Islands and Medieval Britain," *History and Anthropology*, 23 (1): 115–48.

Serels, Steven (2018), "Food Insecurity and Political Instability in the Southern Red Sea Region During the 'Little Ice Age,' 1650–1840," in Dominik Collet and Maximilian Schuh (eds.), *Famines During the 'Little Ice Age' (1300–1800): Socionatural Entanglements in Premodern Societies*, 115–29, Cham: Springer.

Shafiq, Suhanna (2011), "The Maritime Culture in the Kitāb 'Ajā'ib Al-Hind (The Book of the Marvels of India) by Buzurg Ibn Shahriyār (d.399/1009)," MPhil diss., University of Exeter, UK.

Shafiq, Suhanna (2013), *Seafarers of the Seven Seas: The Maritime Culture in the Kitāb 'Ajā'ib al-Hind (The Book of the Marvels of India) by Buzurg Ibn Shahriyār (d. 399/1009)*, Berlin: Klaus Schwarz Verlag.

Shapinsky, Peter D. (2014), *Lords of the Sea: Pirates, Violence and Commerce in Late Medieval Japan*, Ann Arbor: Center for Japanese Studies, University of Michigan.

Sharples, Niall (2005), "Resource Exploitation: The Shore. 1. Shellfish," in Niall Sharples (ed.), *A Norse Farmstead in the Outer Hebrides: Excavations at Mound 3, Bornais, South Uist*, 159–62, Oxford: Oxbow.

Shaw, Sarah (2012), "Crossing to the Farthest Shore: How Pāli Jātakas Launch the Buddhist Image of the Boat onto the Open Seas," *Journal of the Oxford Centre for Buddhist Studies*, 3: 128–56.

Shaw, Sarah (2013), "The Capsized Self: Sea Navigation, Shipwrecks and Escapes from drowning in Southern Buddhist Narrative and Art," in Carl Thompson (ed.), *Shipwreck in Art and Literature: Images and Interpretations from Antiquity to the Present Day*, 27–41, London: Routledge.

Shepard, Jonathan (2012), "Imperial Constantinople: Relics, Palaiologan Emperors, and the Resilience of the Exemplary Centre," in Jonathan Harris, Catherine Holmes, and Eugenia Russell (eds.), *Byzantines, Latins, and Turks in the Eastern Mediterranean World After 1150*, 61–92, Oxford: Oxford University Press.

Shepard, Jonathan (2015), "Communications Across the Bulgarian Lands," in Vasil Giuzelev and Georgi Nikolov (eds.), *South-Eastern Europe in the Second Half of 10th–The Beginning of the 11th Centuries*, 217–35, Sofia: Bulgarian Academy of Sciences.

Shepard, Jonathan (2016), "Back in Old Rus and the USSR," *English Historical Review*, 131: 384–405.

Shepard, Jonathan (2017), "Man-to-Man, Dog-Eat-Dog, Cults-in-Common: The Tangled Threads of Alexios' Dealings with the Franks," *Travaux et Mémoires*, 21(2): 749–88.

Shepard, Jonathan (2019), "Bolesław the Brave versus Byzantine Soft Power," in Stanisław Turlej, Michał Stachura, Bartosz Jan Kołoczek, and Adam Izdebski (eds.), *Byzantina et Slavica*, 349–66, Kraków: Historia Iagellonica.

Shepard, Jonathan (2021), "Why Gotland?," in Jacek Gruszczyński, Marek Jankowiak, and Jonathan Shepard (eds.), *Viking-Age Trade: Slaves, Trade and Gotland*, 1–12, London: Routledge.

Shepard, Jonathan (forthcoming), "Other Goings-On," in Jonathan Shepard and Luke Treadwell (eds.), *Muslims on the Volga in the Viking Age*, London: Bloomsbury.

Sheriff, Abdul (2010), *Dhow Cultures and the Indian Ocean: Cosmopolitanism, Commerce and Islam*, Oxford: Oxford University Press.

Siewers, Alfred K. (2009), *Strange Beauty: Ecocritical Approaches to Early Medieval Landscape*, Basingstoke: Palgrave Macmillan.

Silverstein, Adam (2007), "From Markets to Marvels," *Journal of Jewish Studies*, 58: 91–104.

Sinclair, P.J.J. (1982), "Chibuene – An Early Trading Site in Southern Mozambique," *Paideuma: Mitteilungen zur Kulturkunde* 28: 149–64.

Sindbæk, Søren (2007), "The Small World of the Vikings," *Norwegian Archaeological Review*, 40: 59–74.

Singaravélou, Pierre and Fabrice Argounès (2018), *Le Monde vu d'Asie: Une histoire cartographique*, Paris: Musée national des Arts Asiatiques-Guimet and Seuil.

Sivasundaram, Sujit (2010), "Sciences and the Global: On Methods, Questions, and Theory," *Isis: A Journal of the History of Science Society*, 101 (1): 146–58.

Smith, James L. (2016), "Brendan Meets Columbus: A More Commodious Islescape," *Postmedieval: A Journal of Medieval Cultural Studies*, 7 (4): 526–38.

Smith, James L. (2017), *Water in Medieval Intellectual Culture: Case-Studies from Twelfth-Century Monasticism*, Turnhout: Brepols.

Smith, James L. and Hetta Howes, eds. (2018), *New Approaches to Medieval Water Studies*, Open Library of Humanities. Available online: https://olh.openlibhums.org/collections/special/new-approaches-to-medieval-water-studies/ (accessed October 19, 2020).

Sobecki, Sebastian I. (2003), "From the *désert liquide* to the Sea of Romance: Benedeit's *Le Voyage de saint Brendan* and the Irish Immrama," *Neophilologus*, 87 (2): 193–207.

Sobecki, Sebastian I. (2008), *The Sea and Medieval English Literature*, Cambridge: D.S. Brewer.

Stahl, Alan (2019), "Where the Silk Road Met the Wool Trade," in Sophia Menache, Benjamin Z. Kedar, and Michel Balard (eds.), *Crusading and Trading Between East and West*, 351–64, London: Routledge.

Staley, Lynn (2016), "Fictions of the Island: Girdling the Sea," *Postmedieval: A Journal of Medieval Cultural Studies*, 7 (4): 539–50.

Staples, Eric (2013), "An Experiment in Arab Navigation: The *Jewel of Muscat* Passage," in Anthony R. Constable and William Facey (eds.), *The Principles of Arab Navigation*, 47–60, London: Arabian Publishing.

Star, Bastiaan, James H. Barrett, Agata T. Gondek, and Sanne Boessenkool (2018), "Ancient DNA Reveals the Chronology of Walrus Ivory Trade from Norse Greenland," *Proceedings of the Royal Society B*, 285: 20180978. Available online: https://doi.org/10.1098/rspb.2018.0978.

Star, Bastiaan, et al. (2017), "Ancient DNA Reveals the Arctic Origin of Viking Age Cod from Haithabu, Germany," *Proceedings of the National Academy of Sciences*, 114 (34): 9152–7. Available online: https://doi.org/10.1073/pnas.1710186114.

Stargardt, Janice (2014), "Indian Ocean Trade in the Ninth and Tenth Centuries," *South Asian Studies*, 30: 35–55.

Starr, Cindy (2016), "Annual Arctic Sea Ice Minimum 1979–2015, with graph," NASA Scientific Visualization Studio, March 10. Available online: https://svs.gsfc.nasa.gov/4435 (accessed October 9, 2020).

Steinberg, Philip E. (2001), *The Social Construction of the Ocean*, Cambridge: Cambridge University Press.

Steinberg, Philip E. and Kimberley Peters (2015), "Wet Ontologies, Fluid Spaces: Giving Depth to Volume through Oceanic Thinking," *Environment and Planning D: Society and Space*, 33: 247–64.

Storm, Mary (2013a), *Head and Heart: Valor and Self-Sacrifice in the Art of India*, London: Routledge.

Storm, Mary (2013b), "An Unusual Group of Hero Stones: Commemorating Self-Sacrifice at Mallam, Andhra Pradesh," *Ars Orientalis*, 44: 61–84.

Subbarayalu, Y. (2009), "A Note on the Navy of the Chola State," in Hermann Kulke, K. Kesavapany, and Vijay Sakhuja (eds.), *Nagapattinam to Suvarnadwipa: Reflections on the Chola Naval Expeditions to Southeast Asia*, 91–101, Singapore: ISEAS.

Szabo, Vicki E. (2008), *Monstrous Fishes and the Mead-Dark Sea: Whaling in the Medieval North Atlantic*, The Northern World, vol. 35, Leiden: Brill.

Tai, Emily Sohmer (2005), "Marking Water: Piracy and Property in the Pre-Modern West," paper presented at "Seascapes, Littoral Cultures, and Trans-Oceanic Exchanges," Library of Congress, Washington, DC, February 12–15, 2003. Available online: http://webdoc.sub.gwdg.de/ebook/p/2005/history_cooperative/www.historycooperative.org/proceedings/seascapes/tai.html (accessed October 19, 2020).

Talbert, Richard J.A. and Richard W. Unger, eds. (2008), *Cartography in Antiquity and the Middle Ages: Fresh Perspectives, New Methods*, Leiden: Brill.

Talbot, Cynthia (2001), *Precolonial India in Practice: Society, Region, and Identity in Medieval Andhra*, New York: Oxford University Press.

Tallack, Malachy (2016), *The Un-Discovered Islands: An Archipelago of Myths and Mysteries, Phantoms and Fakes*, London: Picador.

Taylor, Eva Germaine Rimington (1956), *The Haven–Finding Art: A History of Navigation from Odysseus to Captain Cook*, London: Hollis and Carter.

Thapar, Romila (2003), "Death and the Hero," in *Cultural Pasts: Essays in Early Indian History*, 680–95, Delhi: Oxford Paperbacks.

Thomas, Tim (2009), "Communities of Practice in the Archaeology of New Georgia, Rendova and Tetepare," in Peter J. Sheppard, Tim Thomas, and Glenn Summerhayes (eds.), *Lapita: Ancestors and Descendants*, 119–45, Dunedin: New Zealand Archaeological Association.

Thomas, R. (2011), "Fishing Activity," in David Peacock and Lucy Blue (eds.), *Myos Hormos – Quseir al-Qadim: Roman and Islamic Ports on the Red Sea*, vol. 2, *Finds from the Excavations 1999–2003*, 211–20, Oxford: British Archaeological Reports.

Tolias, George (2007), "Isolarii, Fifteenth to Seventeenth Centuries," in David Woodward (ed.), *The History of Cartography*, vol. 3, *Cartography in the European Renaissance*, 263–84, Chicago: Chicago University Press.

Toorawa, Shawkat (2012), "The Medieval Waqwaq Islands and the Mascarenes," in Shawkat Toorawa (ed.), *The Western Indian Ocean: Essays on Islands and Islanders*, 49–65, Port Louis: Hassam Toorawa Trust.

Traineau-Durozoy, Anne-Sophie (2017), "Jonas et le poisson," in "L'art roman et la mer," special issue of *Les cahiers de Saint-Michel de Cuxa*, 48: 115–27.

Tripati, Sila (2005), "Ships on Hero Stones from the West Coast of India," *International Journal of Nautical Archaeology*, 35 (1): 88–96.

Tsigonaki, Christina (2019), "A Border at the Sea: Defensive Works and Landscape-Mindscape Changes (Seventh-Eighth Centuries A.D.)," in Miguel Ontiveros, Catalina Mas Florit, and John F. Cherry (eds.), *Change and Resilience: The Occupation of Mediterranean Islands in Late Antiquity*, 163–92, Oxford: Oxbow.

Um, Nancy (2013), "Reflections on the Red Sea Style: Beyond the Surface of Coastal Architecture," *Northeast African Studies*, 12 (1): 243–72.

Vagnon, Emmanuelle (2013), *Cartographie et représentations occidentales de l'Orient méditerranéen (du milieu du XIIIe à la fin du XVe siècle)*, Terrarum Orbis 11, Turnhout: Brepols.

Vagnon, Emmanuelle and Éric Vallet (2017a), "L'océan Indien, invention d'un objet cartographique global," in Éric Vallet and Emanuelle Vagnon (eds.), *La fabrique de l'Océan Indien: Cartes d'orient et d'occident*, 285–314, Paris: Publications de la Sorbonne.

Vagnon, Emmanuelle and Éric Vallet, eds. (2017b), *La fabrique de l'océan Indien: Cartes d'Orient et d'Occident (Antiquité-XVIe siècle)*, Paris: Publications de la Sorbonne.

Vallet, Éric (2005), "Yemeni Oceanic Policy at the End of the Thirteenth Century," *Proceedings of the Seminar of Arabian Studies*, 36: 289–96.

Vallet, Éric (2010), *L'Arabie Marchande: État et Commerce Sous les Sultans Rasulides du Yémen (628–858/1229–1454)*, Paris: Publications de la Sorbonne.

Vallet, Éric (2017), "Les flottes islamiques de l'océan indien (VIIe-XVe siècles): une puissance navale au service du commerce," in Michel Balard (ed.), *The Sea in History: The Medieval World / La mer dans l'histoire. Le Moyen Âge*, 753–64, Woodbridge: Boydell Press.

Van Doorninck, Frederick (2009), "The Voyage," in George F. Bass et al. (eds.), *Serçe Limanı*, vol. 2, 3–6, College Station: Texas A&M University Press.

Van Neer, Wim and Anton Ervynck (2003), "Remains of Traded Fish in Archaeological Sites: Indicators of Status, or Bulk Food?," in Sharon Jones, Wim Van Neer, and Anton Ervynck (eds.), *Behaviour Behind Bones: The Zooarchaeology of Ritual, Religion, Status and Identity*, 203–14, Oxford: Oxbow Books.

Von Falkenhausen, Vera (2010), "Gli Amalfitani nell'impero bizantino," in Edward Farrugia (ed.), *Amalfi and Byzantium*, 17–44, Rome: Pontificio istituto orientale.

Vauchez, André (2006), "L'homme au péril de la mer dans les miracles médiévaux," in Jacques Jouanna, Jean Leclant, and Michel Zink (eds.), *L'homme face aux calamités naturelles dans l'Antiquité et au Moyen Âge*, 183–95, Paris: Académie des Inscriptions et Belles-Lettres.

Velázquez Castro, Adrián (2017), "Luxuries from the Sea: The Use of Shells in the Ancient Americas," in Joanne Pillsbury, Timophy Potts, and Kim N. Richter (eds.), *Golden Kingdoms: Luxury Arts in the Ancient Americas*, 91–8, Los Angeles: J. Paul Getty Trust.

Vérin, Pierre (1986), *The History of Civilization in North Madagascar*, Rotterdam: Balkema.

Vijayalekshmy, M. (2014), "Pirates, Shallows and Ship-Wrecks – On the Perils of Voyages in the Indian Ocean World in the Middle Ages," *Proceedings of the Indian History Congress*, 75: 982–8.

Villain-Gandossi, Christiane (2004a), "Au Moyen Âge, le domaine de la peur," in Alain Corbin and Hélène Richard (eds.), *La mer: Terreur et fascination*, 71–7, Paris: BnF/Seuil.

Villain-Gandossi, Christiane (2004b), "La perception des dangers de la mer au Moyen Age à travers les textes littéraires et l'iconographie," in Mickaël Augeron and Mathias Tranchant (eds.), *La violence et la mer dans l'espace atlantique (XIIe–XIXe s.)*, 439–56, Rennes: Presses Universitaires de Rennes.

Wade, Geoffrey (2013), "An Asian Commercial Ecumene, 900–1300 CE," in Fujita Kayoko, Momoki Shiro, and Anthony Reid (eds.), *Offshore Asia*, 76–111, Singapore: ISEAS Publishing.

Wade, Geoffrey (2015), "Chinese Engagement with the Indian Ocean," in Michael Pearson (ed.), *Trade, Circulation, and Flow in the Indian Ocean World*, 55–82, Basingstoke: Palgrave Macmillan.

Walcott, Derek (2007), "The Sea is History," in *Selcted Poems*, New York: Farrar, Straus and Giroux. Available online: https://poets.org/poem/sea-history (accessed October 9, 2020).

Walker Vadillo, Veronica (2016), "The Fluvial Cultural Landscape of Angkor," unpublished PhD diss., University of Oxford, UK.

Walker Vadillo, Veronica (2021), "Entangled Traditions: The Royal Barges of Angkor," in Himanshu Prabha Ray (ed.), *The Archaeology of Knowledge Traditions of the Indian Ocean World*, 194–210, Abingdon: Routledge.

Wallace, Patrick (2016), *Viking Dublin*, Sallins, County Kildare: Irish Academic Press.

Walsh, Kevin (2014), *The Archaeology of Mediterranean Landscapes*, Cambridge: Cambridge University Press.

Walsh, Martin T. (2007), "Island Subsistence: Hunting, Trapping and the Translocation of Wildlife in the Western Indian Ocean," *Azania*, 42 (1): 83–113.

Walz, Jonathan R. (2010), "Route to a Regional Past: An Archaeology of the Lower Pangani (Ruvu) Basin, Tanzania, 500–1900 CE," unpublished PhD thesis, University of Florida, USA.

Wang, Zhenping (2005), *Ambassadors from the Islands of Immortals: China-Japan Relations in the Han-Tang Period*, Honolulu: University of Hawai'i Press.

Ward, Robin (2009), *The World of the Medieval Shipmaster: Law, Business and the Sea c.1350–1450*, Woodbridge: Boydell Press.

Weiss, Richard S. (2009), *Recipes for Immortality: Healing, Religion, and Community in South India*, Oxford: Oxford University Press.

Wenger, Etienne (1998), *Communities of Practice: Learning, Meaning and Identity*, Cambridge, Cambridge University Press.

Westerdahl, Christer (1992), "The Maritime Cultural Landscape," *International Journal of Nautical Archaeology*, 21 (1): 5–14.

Westerdahl, Christer (2008), "Fish and Ships: Towards a Theory of Maritime Culture," *Sozialgeschichte der Schiffahrt*, 30: 191–230.

Westerdahl, Christer (2012), "The Ritual Landscape of the Seaboard in Historical Times: Island Chapels, Burial Sites and Stone Mazes–A Scandinavian Example. Part I: Chapels and Burial Sites," *Deutsches Shiffahrtsarchiv: Wissenschaftliches Jahrbuch Des Deutschen Shiffahartsmuseums*, 34: 259–370.

Westermann-Angerhausen, Hiltrud (2014), *Mittelalterliche Weihrauchfässer von 800 bis 1500*, Petersberg: Imhof Verlag.

Westropp, Thomas Johnson (1912), "Brasil and the Legendary Islands of the North Atlantic: Their History and Fable; A Contribution to the 'Atlantis' Problem," *Proceedings of the Royal Irish Academy: Section C; Archaeology, Celtic Studies, History, Linguistics, Literature*, 30: 223–60.

White, Monica (forthcoming), "Non-Elite Church Contacts between Byzantium and Rus in the Palaiologan Period," in Jonathan Shepard, Peter Frankopan, and Averil Cameron (eds.), *Byzantine Spheres*, Oxford: Oxford University Press.

Wigen, Kären (2007), "Introduction," in Kären Wigen, Renate Bridenthal, and Jerry H. Bentley (eds.), *Seascapes: Maritime Histories, Littoral Cultures, and Transoceanic Exchanges*, 1–18, Honolulu: University of Hawai'i Press.

Williams, Gavin (2015), "Viking Camps and the Means of Exchange in Britain and Ireland in the Ninth Century," in Howard Clarke and Ruth Johnson (eds.), *The Vikings in Ireland and Beyond*, 93–116, Dublin: Four Courts Press.

Williams, Joanna (1992), "The Churning of the Ocean of Milk— Myth, Image and Ecology," *India International Centre Quarterly*, 19 (1/2): 145–55.

Williamson, Andrew (1973), *Sohar and Omani Seafaring in the Indian Ocean*, Muscat: Petroleum Development (Oman).

Willson, Margaret (2016), *Seawomen of Iceland: Survival on the Edge*, Seattle: University of Washington Press.

Wilmshurst, Janet M., Terry L. Hunt, Carl P. Lipo, and Atholl J. Anderson (2011), "High-Precision Radiocarbon Data Shows Recent and Rapid Initial Colonization of East Polynesia," *Proceedings of the National Academy of Sciences*, 108 (5): 1815–20.

Wilson, T.H. and A.L. Omar (1997), "Archaeological Investigations at Pate," *Azania*, 32: 31–76.

Wincott Heckett, Elizabeth (2003), *Viking Age Headcoverings from Dublin*, Dublin: National Museum of Ireland.

Wink, Andre (1990–2004), *Al-Hind: The Making of the Indo-Islamic World*, 3 vols, Leiden: Brill.
Wolf, Mark J.P. (2012), *Building Imaginary Worlds: The Theory and History of Subcreation*, New York: Routledge.
Wolska, Wanda (1962), *La Topographie chrétienne de Cosmas Indicopleustès, Théologie et science au VIe siècle*, Paris: Presses universitaires de France.
Woods, Andrew R. (2021), "Viking Economies and the Great Army," in Jacek Gruszczyński, Marek Jankowiak, and Jonathan Shepard (eds.), *Viking-Age Trade*, 396–414, Abingdon: Routledge.
Woodward, David (1987), "Medieval Mappaemundi," in John B. Harley and David Woodward (eds.), *The History of Cartography*, vol. 1, *Cartography in Prehistoric, Ancient, and Medieval Europe and the Mediterranean*, 286–370, Chicago: Chicago University Press.
Wright, Christopher (2012), "Byzantine Authority and Latin Rule in the Gattilusio Lordships," in Jonathan Harris, Catherine Holmes, and Eugenia Russell (eds), *Byzantines, Latins and Turks in the Eastern Mediterranean After 1150*, 247–63, Oxford: Oxford University Press.
Wubs-Mrozewicz, Justyna (2009) "Fish, Stock and Barrel: Changes in the Stockfish Trade in Northern Europe, c. 1360–1560," in Louis Sicking and Darlene Abreu-Ferreira (eds.), *Beyond the Catch: Fisheries of the North Atlantic, the North Sea and the Baltic, 900–1850*, 187–208, Leiden: Brill.
Wynne-Jones, Stephanie and Jeffrey Fleisher (2016), "The Multiple Territories of Swahili Urban Landscapes," *World Archaeology*, 48 (3): 349–62.
Yeats, W.B. (1893), *The Celtic Twilight*, London: Lawrence and Bullen.
Yee, Cordell D.K. (1994), "Chinese Cartography among the Arts: Objectivity, Subjectivity, Representation," in John B. Harley and David Woodward (eds.), *The History of Cartography*, vol. 2–2, *Cartography in the Traditional East and South-East Asian Societies*, 128–69, Chicago: University of Chicago Press.
Yuan, Haiwang (2006), *The Magic Lotus Lantern and Other Tales from the Han Chinese*, Greenwood, CT: Greenwood.
Zakharov, S.N. (2012), "Beloozero," in Nikolai A. Makarov (ed.), *Rus' v IX–X vekakh*, 213–39, Moscow: Drevnosti Severa.
Zamora, Lois Parkinson and Wendy B. Faris, eds. (1995), *Magical Realism: Theory, History, Community*, Durham, NC: Duke University Press.
Zargar, Cyrus Ali (2014), "Water," in John Andrew Morrow (ed.), *Islamic Images and Ideas: Essays on Sacred Symbolism*, 112–23, Jefferson, NC: McFarland.
Zemon Davis, Natalie (1973), "The Rites of Violence: Religious Riot in Sixteenth-Century France," *Past and Present*, 59 (1): 51–91.
Zhao, Bing (2015), "Chinese-Style Ceramics in East Africa from the 9th to 16th Century," *Afriques*, 6. Available online: https://doi.org/10.4000/afriques.1836.

CONTRIBUTORS

Jennifer Harland is a zooarchaeologist working on the North Atlantic region, with a particular emphasis on fish consumption, fishing, and fish trade from the Viking Age to the later medieval period. Jennifer has held a number of postdoctoral positions, notably on the Leverhulme Trust project *The Medieval Origins of Commercial Sea Fishing* (McDonald Institute for Archaeological Research, University of Cambridge, UK) and at the University of York, UK. Since 2014 she has been a lecturer at the Archaeology Institute, University of the Highlands and Islands in Scotland, UK, and is currently a co-director of excavations at Skaill Farm, Orkney.

Sharon Kinoshita is Professor of Literature and Co-director at the Center for Mediterranean Studies, the University of California at Santa Cruz, USA. She is the author of *Medieval Boundaries: Rethinking Difference in Old French Literature* (2006) and has coauthored books on Chretien de Troyes, Marie de France, and most recently, *Can We Talk Mediterranean? Conversations on an Emerging Field in Medieval and Early Modern Studies* (2017). In 2016, she published a new translation of Marco Polo's *Description of the World*. She is currently working on a companion volume tentatively titled *Marco Polo and the Global Middle Ages*.

Elizabeth A. Lambourn is Professor of Material Histories at De Montfort University, UK. A historian of South Asia and the Indian Ocean world before 1500 CE she is committed to the interdisciplinary and cross-cultural study of medieval history and her work engages equally with texts and "things," and with texts as material "things." Elizabeth has published widely on the circulation of artifacts, animals, people, and ideas around the Indian Ocean area. Her most recent publication is the research monograph *Abraham's Luggage: A Social Life of Things in the Medieval Indian Ocean World* (2018).

Roxani E. Margariti is Associate Professor of Middle Eastern Studies in the Department of Middle Eastern and South Asian Studies at Emory University, USA. Her research interests include Middle Eastern social and economic history, maritime history and archaeology, material culture, and urban studies. She is the author of *Aden and the Indian Ocean Trade: 150 Years in the Life of a Medieval Arabian Port* (2007). In 2016 she was a Fellow of the American Academy in Berlin where she worked on her new project *Insular Crossroads: The Local, Regional and Global Story of the Red Sea's Dahlak Archipelago*.

Jonathan Shepard was University Lecturer in Russian History at the University of Cambridge, UK. With S. Franklin he coauthored *The Emergence of Rus* (1996) and coedited *Byzantine Diplomacy* (1992), and twelve of his studies appear in his *Emergent Elites and Byzantium* (2011). His edited volumes include *The Expansion of Orthodox Europe* (2007); *The Cambridge History of the Byzantine Empire* (rev. edn. 2019); with F. Androshchuk and M. White, *Byzantium and the Viking World* (2016); with M. Ančić and T. Vedriš, *Imperial Spheres and the Adriatic* (2018); and, with J. Gruszczyński and M. Jankowiak, *Viking-Age Trade: Silver, Slaves and Gotland* (2020).

James L. Smith is Government of Ireland Postdoctoral Fellow in the Department of Geography at Trinity College Dublin, Ireland, where he works on the project Deep Mapping the Spiritual Waterscape of Ireland's Lakes: The Case of Lough Derg, Donegal. His work explores intellectual history, cultural and spiritual geography, ecocriticism, digital humanities, environmental humanities, spatial humanities, and water history. His first monograph is *Water in Medieval Intellectual Culture: Case-Studies from Twelfth-Century Monasticism* (2018). James is the editor of *The Passenger: Medieval Texts and Transits* (2017), and coeditor with Dr. Hetta Howes of the Open Library of the Humanities collection "New Approaches to Medieval Water Studies."

Eric Staples is Assistant Professor at Zayed University in the United Arab Emirates. His areas of interest include shipbuilding, seafaring, and navigation. After a PhD on the maritime archaeology of Morocco's Atlantic coast, he has been actively involved in a variety of projects in the Indian Ocean, including the construction and sailing of the sewn-plank replica of a ninth-century dhow, the Jewel of Muscat, from Oman to Singapore in 2010. He is coeditor with Georg Olms Verlag of *Oman: A Maritime History* (2017) and author of numerous other articles and chapters. Eric was formerly Director of Maritime Heritage Projects for the Sultanate of Oman.

Emmanuelle Vagnon is a graduate of the Ecole Normale Supérieure in Paris and holds a PhD in Medieval History. Since 2013 she has been a Researcher with the Centre National de Recherche Scientifique (CNRS) in the Laboratoire de Médiévistique Occidentale in Paris, France. She was one of the curators and a catalog coeditor of the *L'âge d'or des cartes marines* exhibition, held at the Bibliothèque nationale de France in 2012. Most recently she coedited, with Eric Vallet, the first longue durée survey of the representation of the Indian Ocean through cartography, *La Fabrique de l'océan Indien: Cartes d'Orient et d'Occident (Antiquité–XVIe siècle)* (2017).

Stephanie Wynne-Jones is Senior Lecturer in the Department of Archaeology, University of York, UK. Stephanie specializes in the archaeology of East African coastal urbanism, material culture, and social practice. Stephanie has led a series of research projects in coastal Kenya, Tanzania, and Zanzibar, as well as working on inland caravan routes. Stephanie has held positions at the British Institute in Eastern Africa and University of Bristol and from 2015 to 2017 held a Pro Futura Scientia fellowship at the Swedish Collegium for Advanced Study, Uppsala. Her most recent publication is a jointly edited volume for the Routledge Worlds series entitled *The Swahili World* (2018).

INDEX

Aden attack 101–5, 109
'ajā'ib (wonders) 213, 215
Akhbār al-Sīn wa-l-Hind (Accounts of China and India) 146–7, 155 (see also al-Sirafi, Abu Zayd)
Alatiel 158
Alexander the Great 171
Alexios I Komnenos, Emperor 86
Amalfitans 86
amber 79–80
ambergris 69, 131
Anaweka voyaging canoe 22, 31, 202–3
Angkor Wat temple 12–13
Ao Guang 209
Aotearoa islands 202–6
Apollonius of Tyre 141
Arabian Gulf (see Gulf)
Ardnamurchan boat burial 63
astrolabe 43
Atlantic Ocean
   environmental navigation 31–2
   fish and fishing 49–50, 52–3, 58–62, 63, 65–7, 68, 70, 80
   islands 182, 216
   latitude sailing 40–1
   navigational instruments 44–5, 47
   navigational literature 35–8
Austronesian voyaging 19, 22, 31 (see also Polynesia)
Ayyubid galleys 112–14
Aydhab 85, 113, 114, 128, 155

beads 69, 76, 79, 80–1
Belitung wreck 51
Benincasa, Grazioso 182
Benjamin of Tudela 145
Bible stories 164, 165, 166, 168
al-Biruni, Abu'l-Rayhan 129, 175
Black Death 89
Black Sea 166
Blessed Isles 182, 208–8
Blue Humanities 198–9
boat (see ship and canoe)
Boccaccio, Giovanni (*Decameron, The*) 156–9
Book of Michael Rhodes, The 38
Borobodur 10
Brendan, St. 154, 168, 201
brokerage 135–6
Buddhism 10, 152, 187, 189, 210
building materials 136–8
Buondelmonti, Cristoforo 126
Buoninsegni, Domenico 182
burial sites 138–9

Cadamosto, Alvise de 43
Cairo Genizah 84, 85, 102, 104, 116, 137
Canary Islands 182
canoe
   Anaweka voyaging canoe 22, 31, 202–3
   Gulf and western India 107–8
   mash'iyya 105
   New Zealand settlement by 200–1

Carte Pisane 36, 178
cartography *see* maps
Catalan Atlas 180, 182, 217
Celtic myths 217
chanks 14, 130
Charlemagne 76
de Chatillon, Renaud 114
China
    art 184–5
    maps 187–9, 192–3
    myths 208–10
    navigational instruments 40, 44, 45, 47
    navigational literature 34, 35, 41
Chola campaigns 111–12
Ch'onhado 187
Christianity 24, 67, 80, 82, 86
    Crusades 86, 87, 114, 144–5, 155
    iconography 170–1
    pilgrimages 85–6
Churning of the Ocean of Milk 11–13
Cinque Ports 97
de Clari, Robert 144–5, 155–6
Clement, St. 152
Cligés (de Troyes) 145, 149–50
climate 53, 124
coastal sailing 145–6, 158
cogs 92
coins 77, 130
color of sea 166, 174
Columbus, Christopher 94, 218
commerce *see* trade
compasses 43–7, 171
Cordoba revolt 120
corsair (see pirate)
Cosmas Indicopleustes 173
cowrie shells 69, 132
Creation 165
Crete 120–1, 123, 126
cross-cultural trade 134–5
cross-staff 43
Crusades 86, 87, 114, 144–5, 155

Dandolo, Doge 87
death at sea 149
Decameron, The 156–9
De Naturis Rerum 44
Devisement du Monde (The Description of the World) 171
dharmic kingship 110

diet 55–8, 64–5
    shipboard 148–9
dirhams 77, 80
dragon spirit 209

Eight Immortals 208, 209
entre mers 216
environmental navigation 30–4
Eriugena, John Scotus 164
Evagatorioum (Wanderings) 160
exchange 74
ex-votos 170

Fabri, Felix 160
Fatimids 84, 85, 113
females
    Island of Women 202
    rulers 88
Ferrer, Jaume 92
fish and fishing 49–71, 80
    diet 55–8, 64–5
    dried and salted fish 66–7, 68, 81
    Fish Event Horizon 18–19, 61, 66
    herring 61–2, 63, 81
    islands 129–31
    line fishing 63
    nets 63
    pearl industry 69, 129, 130
    shellfish 64–5
    social organization 67–70
    taboo on eating fish 56, 58, 64
    technologies 54–5, 62–4
    trade 60, 65–7, 68–9
    wooden gorges 63
fleet (see navies)
Floire and Blancheflor 147
fog 153
fondaco 86, 87
food 55–8, 64–5
    shipboard 148–9
Fra Mauro map 181
Fulk Nerra, Count of Anjou 86

galley 96, 100, 102, 104, 112–15, 144–5, 148–9, 156, 157, 160
Gama, Vasco de 94
Gattilusio, Francesco 92
Genesis 165
Gerald of Wales 201

gift exchange 74
Gillis, John 18, 23, 24, 121–2
Gioia, Flavio 45
glass 76, 79, 80–1
Global Middle Ages 2, 124, 218
gold 85, 94
Gomes, Diogo 43
Gomito, Martuccio 159
Gostanza 159
Gotenjiku Zu map 187
grant documents 108
graves 138–9
Green Sea 166
Guanglun jiangli tu map 191
Guigemar 147–8
guilds 84
Gulf (Persian/Arabian)
    Hormuz 38, 189, 190
    Kish (Qays), attack on Aden 99–103, 107
    Ramisht of Siraf 101, 103
    Siraf 32, 55, 101, 126, 135
    zooarchaeological record 55

Hainei huayi-tu map 189
Hangzhou 35
al-Hariri, Abu Muhammad al-Qasim b.
    'Ali 133–4, 142, 171, 213 (see also *Maqāmāt*)
Hawaiki island 202–6
Henry the Navigator 29, 94
Herodotus 135
hero stones 105–9, 110, 127
herring 61–2, 63, 81
Hinduism 10, 11–14, 210
holy water 14
Homer 171
Hormuz 38, 189, 190
Horyu-ji temple map 187
Hourani, George 99, 100
Howard, Robert E. 211
Huangdi 208
Hyborian Age, The (Howard) 211
Hy Brasil 217
Hye ch'o 75

d'Ibelin, Jean 87–8
Ibn al-Mujawir, Yusuf ibn Yaq'ub 30, 102, 105, 109, 112–13, 114, 128, 136

Ibn Fadlan, Ahmad 77, 80
Ibn Jubayr, Abu'l-Husayn Muhammad 148, 149, 150–1, 155
Ibn Khurdadhbih, Abu'l-Qasim Ubaydallah 35
Ibn Majid, Ahmad 35, 38–9, 42–3
iconography 10, 12–14, 164, 165, 166, 168–71
al-Idrisi, Abu 'Abdallah Muhammad 107–8, 176–7
immram 154
incense 74, 84, 87
Indian Ocean
    color 166, 174
    conflicts 95–117
    environmental navigation 32–2
    fish and fishing 49–50, 51–2, 55–8, 130
    imaginary worlds 210, 212
    latitude sailing 41–2
    maps 174, 175–6, 193
    navigational instrument 45, 47
    navigational literature 35, 38
    networks 75, 82, 88–9
    shrines 138
Intan wreck 76
Irish myths 216–17
Isaac II Angelos 87
Isidore of Seville 173
Islam 24, 83–4, 88, 117
    environmental navigation 34
    imaginary worlds 212–15
    maps 174–5, 181
    navies 100
    navigational literature 34
    Swahili-speakers 75
    weights 80
islands 119–39
    Blessed 182, 208–9
    burial sites 138–9
    connectivity and isolation 122, 123–4
    Crete 118–19, 121, 124
    cross-cultural trade 134–5
    Dahlak 111, 126, 132
    depopulated 123
    economics 129–32
    as frontiers 122
    Hormuz 38, 189, 190
    imaginary 200–6, 217, 218
    Kish (Qays) 99–103, 107

Madagascar 19–20, 55
Maldives 66, 136
maps 125–6, 181, 182
materiality 136–8
Nicobar islands 133
Orkney islands 50, 58, 61, 78, 151–2
politics 126–9
prisons and places of exile 128
Shetland Islands 50, 58, 62, 78
shrines 137–9
silent trade 135
sugar islands 130
utopian 127
Íslendingasögur (Sagas of the Islanders) 147
isolario 182
ivory 79, 85

Jains 10, 110, 152
Japan
  maps 187
  mythology 209
John I, of Portugal 92–4
Joinville, Jean de 144, 148–9, 151, 153, 156
Jonah and the Whale 168

Kadamba hero stones 106, 107, 127
Kangnido 190–1
karīmī 89
khashaba 40
Kibu island 206
Kilwa Great Mosque 82–3
Kish, attack on Aden 101–5, 109
Kitāb 'ajā'ib al-hind (Book of the Wonders of India) 213
Kitāb gharā'ib al-funūn (Book of Curiosities) 175–6
Korean maps 187, 190–1
Kubilai Khan 190
Kumari kandam 211

landnám 147
landscape painting 184–6
Lapacino, Francesco 182
Las Siete Partidas 148
latitude sailing 39–43
Lemuria 210
limpets 65
linen 85

Little Ice Age 53, 124
littoral society 122
Luo Maodeng 193

Mabuiag island 206
Macrobius Ambrosius Theodosius 165
Madagascar 19, 22, 57
Madmun b. Hasan Japheth 103, 105, 116
Makira 201–2
Maldives 68, 138
Malta 123
Mānasollāsa (Delight of the Mind) 68–9
Mandelli, Giovanni 143
mangrove wood 137
Manuel I, Emperor 87
manuscript matrix 200
Mao K'un Map 41
Māori people 202–6
Mao Yuanyi 192
maps 125–6, 162–3, 165, 166, 172–8, 180–3, 183, 185–91, 192–3, 203
Maqāmāt (Assemblies) 133–4, 143, 171, 213
Marie de France 147–8, 151–2
mariner's astrolabe 43
mariner's compass 43–7, 171
maritories 129
Marriage to the Sea 87
Martellus, Henricus 182
marteloio 29
Martianus Capella 165
al-Mas'udi, Abu'l-Hasan 'Ali 35
mauru 203
mawsim 32
Ma Yuan 184–5
Medieval Climatic Anomaly (Warm Period) 53, 124
Mediterranean
  coastal sailing 145–6
  conflicts 99, 100–1, 112–15
  The Decameron 156–9
  iconography 164, 166
  maps 173–6, 190
  navigation 29, 36, 38, 47
  networks 74, 76–7, 84, 85, 87
  politics 126–7
mermaids 168
Michael VIII Palaiologos 89
Michael of Rhodes (Michalli da Ruodo) 29

mist 153
mollusc eating 65
Mongol maps 190–1
monsoons 32, 51, 74
mtepe 82
Muhammad, Prophet 138
al-Muqaddasi, Muhammad ibn Ahmad 35

natural navigation 30–4
natural philosophy 165
navies 96–7, 99–100, 105, 108–9, 111–15, 120–1
navigation 27–48
   environmental (natural) 30–4
   instruments 43–7, 171
   latitude sailing 39–43
   literature 34–9, 41, 178–80
   oral knowledge 38–9
Navigatio sancti Brendani 154
Naxos 123
Neckham, Alexander 44
new thalassology 163, 198–9
New Zealand 202–6
Nicholas, St. 86, 152, 170–1
Nicobar Islands 133
Nicon Repent 121
Norse myths 216

Orang Laut 84
Orkney Islands 78
   middens 58
   Orkneyinga Saga 153–4
   Scar boat burial 61
   Viking settlement 50
Orosius, Paul 173
Otohime, Princess 210
outre-mer 157, 216

Pacific Ocean 22–3
   Austronesian voyaging 19–20, 29
   environmental navigation 30–1
   islands 202–6
   Polynesia 20–1, 121, 200–1
paintings 171–2, 184–5
Paulin de Venise 178
pearls 69, 76, 129, 130–1, 142–3
Periplus Maris Erythraei 110
Persian Gulf (see Gulf)
Peter the Hermit 86

Petrarch, Francesco 143–4, 145–6, 151, 154–5
pilgrimages 85–6
pillar tombs 83
pirates 109, 111, 116, 143, 158–9
Pizzigano, Zuane 183
plague 89
poetry 38–9
Pole Star 41
Polo, Marco 90, 109, 110–11, 142–3
Polynesia 22–3, 123, 202–3
porcelain 76
portolan charts 36, 178–80
pottery 76
Psalter 166, 167, 168
Ptolemy (*Geography*) 173, 174, 182
Pytheas 40

al-Qalqashandi, Ahmad b. 'Ali 113
Qays island (see Kish)
al-Qibjaqi, Baylak 44
quadrants 43
Quseir al-Qadim (Myos Hormos) 58, 62, 64, 137

raiding 52, 76–7
Ramisht of Siraf 103
Rasulids 115, 117, 127, 130–1
Red Sea 57–8, 74, 85, 88–9, 112–15, 134, 136–7, 155, 166, 174
   Aydhab 83, 111, 112, 126, 153
   Ayyubid galleys in 110–13
   coral construction 134
   Crusaders in 112–13
   Dahlak islands 111, 126, 132
   Fatimid policy 83, 111
   fish processing 56
   Najjahids 132
   Quseir al-Qadim (Myos Hormos) 56
   representation of 164, 172
   sailing 153
relics 138
resonances 218
rhumb lines 46–7
rituals 13–14, 137–9
Romance of Eneas 152–3
Romance of Tristan 150
Rufolo, Landolfo 158–9
Rustichello of Pisa 142

saints
    Brendan 154, 168, 201
    Clement 152
    Nicholas 86, 152, 170–1
    Thomas 138
Salah al-din (also Saladin) 87, 114, 157
al-Saraqusti, Muhammad b. Yusuf al-Tamimi 143
Scar boat burial 63
sea birds, navigational aid 30
sea of peace 99, 101
sea snakes, navigational aid 30
sea turtles 203
Seebuch 38
Shanhaijing 187
shanka (chank) 14, 130
shellfish 64–5
shells 14, 69, 130, 131–2
Shetland Islands 78
    middens 58
    oared boats 62
    Viking settlement 50
Shi Huang-Ti 209
ship (see also canoe)
    Ardnamurchan boat burial 63
    Belitung wreck 51–2, 76
    design 28, 63–4, 82, 102, 104, 106–8, 112–13
    galley 96, 100, 102, 104, 112–15, 144–5, 148–9, 156, 157, 160
    Intan wreck 76
    Java Sea wreck 88
    jāshujiyā 100, 102
    mtepe 80
    Scar boat burial 61
    Serce Limani wreck 85
    shaffāra 100, 102
    shipwreck 10, 86, 150–4, 158–9, 170, 213
    Skuldelev 2 63
    timber reuse 137–8
shores *see* islands and shores
shrines 137–8
Silahara 106
silent trade 135
silk trade 81, 85
silverware 77, 81
al-Sirafi, Abu Zayd 127–8, 135 (see also *Akhbar al-Sīn wa-l-Hind*)

Sivacharyara, Kachiappa 211
skull towers 105
Skylitzae, Ioannis (John Skylitzes) 120, 171
slave trade 81, 90, 92, 94, 134, 160
spears 109
spices 84, 86
Spondylus shell 131–2
star-based navigation 39, 41–3, 45–6
stoneware 76
storms 150–4
sugar 94, 130
Suparaga 10
Swahili world
    Chibuene 62
    fish 67–8
    Islamization 80–2
    language 73
    maritime orientation 80, 118
    pillar tombs 87
    sources 17
    shellfish consumption 62–3
    zooarchaeological record 54–5

Tabepa 206
Tamil culture 211
Taoist myths 208
textiles 81, 85, 91, 90
thaghr 126
thalassography 163, 198–9
Theophanes 90
Thomas, St. 138
Tibet 14
tidalectic 200
tide tables 35
timber 137–8
Torello 157
trade 51, 60, 65–7. 68–9, 80, 81, 82, 84, 87, 91–2, 134–5
triskelion 79
de Troyes, Chrétien (*Cligés*) 145, 149–50
Tuki Tahua 203

'udwa 126
Ug of Kiba 206
Urashimotaro 210

Vesconte, Pietro 177–8
Vikings

boat burials 63
fish and fishing 60
latitude sailing 40–1
raids and settlement 52
wayfinding 31–2
de Villehardouin, Geoffrey 144, 145
Virgin Mary 170
Vishnu 11, 14
Voyage of Saint Brendan 154

walrus ivory 79
Wang Ao 184
Waq-waq (islands) 181–2, 214
warfare 97, 99
Wasobiowe 209
wayfinding 30–4
weights 80
Western Sea 188
windrose 47

winds 32, 51, 74, 94
wine trade 81
women
    Island of 202
    rulers 88
wood 137–8
wool 81

Xavier, Francis 129
Xu Fu 209

Yellow Emperor Huangdi 208
Yersinia pestis 89
Yu ji tu map 189

Zheng He 41, 191–3
Zhou Qufei 189
Zhufan zhi 189
Zinevra 157